T0355263

TORNADO GOD

Tornado God

AMERICAN RELIGION AND VIOLENT WEATHER

Peter J. Thuesen

OXFORD
UNIVERSITY PRESS

Oxford University Press is a department of the University of Oxford. It furthers
the University's objective of excellence in research, scholarship, and education
by publishing worldwide. Oxford is a registered trade mark of Oxford University
Press in the UK and certain other countries.

Published in the United States of America by Oxford University Press
198 Madison Avenue, New York, NY 10016, United States of America.

Library of Congress Cataloging-in-Publication Data
Names: Thuesen, Peter Johannes, 1971– author.
Title: Tornado God : American religion and violent weather / Peter J. Thuesen.
Description: New York, NY, United States of America : Oxford University Press, 2020. |
Includes bibliographical references and index.
Identifiers: LCCN 2019047318 (print) | LCCN 2019047319 (ebook) |
ISBN 9780190680282 (hardback) | ISBN 9780190680305 (epub) | ISBN 9780190680312 (online)
Subjects: LCSH: Disasters—Religious aspects—Christianity. | Tornadoes—
Religious aspects—Christianity. | Tornadoes—United States.
Classification: LCC BT162.T67 T48 2020 (print) |
LCC BT162.T67 (ebook) | DDC 231.7—dc23
LC record available at https://lccn.loc.gov/2019047318
LC ebook record available at https://lccn.loc.gov/2019047319

9 8 7 6 5 4 3 2 1

Printed by Sheridan Books, Inc., United States of America

For my sister,
Sarah Caroline Thuesen

and in memory of my brother-in-law,
Scott Russell Clarke
(March 4, 1967–November 1, 2015)

"Like a tree planted by the rivers of water."
—Psalm 1:3

Contents

Illustrations

Acknowledgments

I HAVE BEEN fascinated by the weather since childhood. One of my earliest memories is of being in my grandparents' house in Dike, Iowa, when the tornado siren went off at night and we had to take refuge in the basement. My father had stayed behind at my aunt and uncle's farmhouse out from town, and I wondered if he would get back safely. Though no tornado hit us that night, I still remember the frightening thought of a twister striking under the cover of darkness. I am sorry that my uncle, Neal Peter Thuesen, who had a farmer's vested interest in the weather, did not live to see this book. My dad left the farm as a young man but remained a weather watcher, an obsessive trait that I inherited. I am profoundly grateful to my parents, Mary and Ted Thuesen, for their abiding love and support. I also thank my father-in-law, Jack Kenyon, for his helpful input on this project, and my late mother-in-law, Janie Kenyon, for her earlier encouragement.

Colleagues at Indiana University–Purdue University Indianapolis (IUPUI) have been wonderfully supportive. A sabbatical leave in Spring 2016 approved by Nasser Paydar (then our executive vice chancellor, now IUPUI's chancellor) and Bill Blomquist (then dean of the School of Liberal Arts) came at a critical juncture. Rob Rebein, the current dean of Liberal Arts, lent me a book about the 2007 Greensburg tornado in his home state of Kansas. I pledge to him to avoid tired jokes about Kansans and *The Wizard of Oz*. Our former dean and my religious studies colleague, Tom Davis, helped me clarify my arguments over morning coffee. Philip

Goff, executive director of the Center for the Study of Religion and American Culture, shared my interest in Rudolf Otto and has promoted this endeavor from the beginning. Similarly, David Craig, chair of the Department of Religious Studies, was a constant cheerleader who helped with bibliography on the ethics of climate change. I thank my other colleagues in Religious Studies for offering suggestions through our faculty colloquium: Matthew Condon, Edward Curtis, Kelly Hayes, Andrea Jain, Joseph Tucker Edmonds, and Rachel Wheeler. I also acknowledge my emeriti colleagues Jan Shipps and Bill Jackson, who both share my love for Americana, and Ted Mullen, who offered bibliographical suggestions on storm gods of the ancient Near East. Similarly, I am grateful for the assistance and good humor of other Liberal Arts colleagues, past and present: Jon Eller, Art Farnsley, Amanda Friesen, Liz Goodfellow, Lisa Hoppes, Merle Illg, Joy Kramer, Edith Millikan, Lauren Schmidt, Mike Scott, Gen Shaker, Joy Sherrill, Brian Steensland, Thom Upton, Becky Vasko, Lauralee Wikkerink, Jeff Wilson, and Nate Wynne. At the IUPUI library, Teodora Durbin went the extra mile in tracking down missing microfilm. She and her colleagues also fulfilled my other interlibrary loan requests, even as I kept adding to the mountain of books I had already checked out from IU's own amazing collection.

Special thanks go to Lisa Sideris, the inaugural director of the Indiana University Consortium for the Study of Religion, Ethics, and Society, which awarded a grant for my research travel to Oklahoma. Lisa's own work on environmental ethics proved helpful for this project, as did her enthusiasm for tornadoes. At IU Bloomington, I also appreciated Winni Sullivan's ongoing interest in my progress, especially while we were both department chairs. Evan Haefeli, Joseph Blankholm, Courtney Bender, and the other members of the Religion in America Seminar at Columbia University provided a stimulating forum for an early proposal for the project in 2013. Mark Noll was a faithful supporter all along the way, as was Brooks Holifield. Ava Chamberlain and I exchanged e-mails about religion and the weather after lightning incinerated the "Touchdown Jesus" statue outside Cincinnati; I always enjoy her keen, wry insights. Sessions at the American Society of Church History in Atlanta (2016) and Washington (2018) gave me the chance to test out material for Chapters 3 and 4; I thank my fellow participants James Byrd, Kathleen Flake, Kathryn Gin Lum, David Holland, Philippa Koch, and Mark Noll. I also thank Howie Bluestein at the University of Oklahoma for graciously agreeing to an interview and for sharing his collection of personal photos. Others who helped with illustrations include Laura Duncan, Jen Gall, Jon Gard, Ian Graham, Marilyn Kennett, Patty Marcano, Ken Minkema, Nick Quigley, Daniel Smith, Ben Stas, David Stiver, and Nicole Wholean. Judith Kerman kindly granted me permission to quote her poem, "In Tornado Weather."

To John F. Wilson, my esteemed graduate mentor, I note with satisfaction that Chapter 4 brings me full circle to one of his own teachers, Reinhold Niebuhr. Another Niebuhr enthusiast, Wayne Boulton, moved to Indianapolis and befriended me midway through my work on this book. Terminal illness did not shake Wayne's Niebuhrian commitments. As Niebuhr himself once said in a sermon: "A genuine Christian faith must move between those who claim to know so much about the natural world that it ceases to point to any mystery beyond itself and those who claim to know so much about the mystery of the 'unseen' world that all reverence for its secret and hidden character is dissipated."

This is the third book I have completed under the editorship of Cynthia Read at Oxford University Press. I was but a lowly graduate student when I first met Cynthia, who appeared to me as a force of nature. Though I am now more comfortable in her presence, I remain in awe. The whirlwind of her energy and intellect has been a boon to the entire field of religious studies. I also salute the rest of the editorial and production team, including Drew Anderla, Prabhu Chinnasamy, Dorothy Bauhoff, Leslie Johnson, Cameron Donahue, and Salma Ismaiel. And heartfelt thanks to Sylvia Coates for preparing the index.

Finally, I thank closest family. Jane Kenyon has been in this for the long haul, patiently listening to my ruminations about tornadoes over the past decade and offering invariably wise advice. As a public health nurse, she is too busy to worry about the weather, but I thank her for loving me even though I do. Our children, Isaac, Joanna, and Margaret, likewise have endured much weather talk and are now lively debate partners on the religious issues explored in this book. All three are sensitive to life's mystery, whether expressed in literature, art, or music. I hope that the taste for mystery will always sustain them, even in hard times.

One person who has known hard times is my sister, Sarah. When her husband, Scott, fell ill and died from lymphoma, she suddenly confronted many of the same questions raised by a tornado. It seems only fitting, then, to dedicate this book to them.

The people of the United States are no longer strangers to that dreaded aerial monster, the Tornado. A single experience of this awful convulsion of the elements suffices to fasten the memory of its occurrence upon the mind with such a dreadful force that no effort can efface the remembrance of it. The destructive violence of this storm exceeds in its power, fierceness, and grandeur all other phenomena of the atmosphere.

—JOHN PARK FINLEY, *Tornadoes* (1887)

One does not kneel before a cyclone or the blind forces of nature, nor even before Omnipotence merely as such. But one does kneel before the wholly uncomprehended Mystery, revealed yet unrevealed, and one's soul is stilled by feeling the way of its working.

—RUDOLF OTTO, *The Idea of the Holy* (1917)

Introduction

THE MORNING NEWSPAPER had predicted "hot and heavy" weather, with a chance of a thunderstorm, on the afternoon of June 9, 1953, when Father Engelbert Devincq sat working in his second-floor office at Assumption College in Worcester, Massachusetts. Born in France, he had taken vows as an Assumptionist in Belgium in 1906 and was held prisoner by the Turks during World War I until papal intervention secured his freedom. Since 1922, he had enjoyed a quiet life as a professor of French at his order's college in Worcester, where he advised the drama and glee clubs and the student periodical.[1]

It was about 5:00 p.m., and outside Father Devincq's window, an approaching thunderstorm promised some temporary relief from the stifling heat. Half an hour earlier, and 25 miles to the west, the storm had produced a particularly menacing cloud that appeared to boil on its dark underside. As the cloud passed over the Quabbin Reservoir, the artificial lake that serves as greater Boston's water supply, it began to take the form of an enormous, revolving cylinder, as one account later described it. A few minutes later, the cylinder tightened into a funnel, and the funnel reached down until it made contact with the earth. The funnel cloud was now a tornado.[2]

A tornado is nature's most violent windstorm. In extreme cases, its winds can exceed 300 miles per hour, whereas the fiercest hurricanes rarely exceed 200 miles per hour.[3] The strongest rated tornado, an EF5, can rip whole buildings off their foundations, obliterating them in an instant and scouring the surrounding ground of dirt and vegetation, sand-blasting everything in its wake. Yet the most terrifying thing about a tornado is the unpredictable path of its fury. Despite vastly improved radar and warning systems, which now allow forecasters to anticipate tornado outbreaks hours, and even days, in advance, a tornado's precise track—why it obliterates one house but leaves a neighboring one untouched—defies prediction. The sight of a tornado, writhing in the sky like a snake coiled to strike, is both terrible and beautiful. Like apparitions from another world, tornadoes loom with a lifelike presence, often causing witnesses to feel pursued, as if by a malevolent spirit.

Tornadoes are also peculiarly American storms. Although they can form in other countries—a 1989 tornado killed 1,300 in Bangladesh, where poor housing conditions have often made twisters deadly[4]—strong tornadoes disproportionately afflict the United States because of its geography. In the vast Great Plains of North America, the dry line, where moist air from the Gulf of Mexico clashes with desert air from the west, provides the ideal environment for tornado formation. Especially during springtime, air currents of different speeds and directions generate wind shear and rotation. Combined with a powerful jet stream some six miles aloft, the ingredients are in place for supercell thunderstorms, the long-lived parent storms of the most violent tornadoes.[5] Yet the traditional Tornado Alley of the Great Plains is not the only tornado-prone region of the United States. Southern states, such as Alabama and Mississippi, and Midwestern states, such as Indiana and Illinois, also have a high incidence of twisters.[6] Because of their greater population density, these areas have seen some of the deadliest tornado outbreaks in US history. Cataclysmic tornadoes—Great Natchez (1840), St. Louis (1896), Palm Sunday (1920), Tri-State (1925), Tupelo-Gainesville (1936), Palm Sunday (1965), Super Outbreak (1974), and Super Outbreak (2011)—have indelibly imprinted the nation's landscape and psyche, repeatedly confronting Americans with the undomesticated power of nature and the haunting question of why sudden destruction or death befalls some persons and not others.

Despite tornadoes' ubiquity in American history, most people assume that such disasters will never happen to *them*. Tornadoes are comparatively rare in New England, moreover, so as the storm approached Worcester on that sultry June afternoon as Father Devincq sat working in his office, he likely did not realize what was happening until it was too late. By then, the tornado was at least an F4, according to later estimates based on the old Fujita scale. It was the most destructive tornado ever recorded in New England, and it slammed into Assumption College with the seeming force of a tactical nuclear weapon. In the college's brick main building, the floor and ceiling in Father Devincq's office gave way, burying him in an avalanche of mortar, leaving only one hand protruding from the rubble. Within seconds, the storm passed, leaving Assumption's campus in utter desolation. The college's dean, Father Louis Dion, himself bleeding heavily from lacerations to his head and elbow, spotted Father Devincq's hand and clasped it. Father Devincq, still clinging to life, squeezed his colleague's hand as Father Dion attempted to administer last rites. Today, at a rebuilt Assumption College, a stained glass "Tornado Window" commemorates the three members of the community—Father Devincq and two nuns, Sister Marie St. Jean de Dieu Martel and Sister Marie Ste. Hélène Simard— who died in the catastrophe.[7]

In its 84-minute path of destruction, the Worcester tornado took 94 lives, making it a watershed in the history of Massachusetts's second largest city. "Bodies were lying alongside the road," reported the *Boston Globe*. "They had been thrown from cars or hurled against buildings."[8] Thousands of people were injured and some 4,000 homes were destroyed. The casualty count was undoubtedly higher because the storm caught most people by surprise. Of 50 survivors interviewed for one government study, none received any official warning; 22 saw the tornado approaching,

FIGURE I.I. Sister Raymond Marie and Sister Mary Pascal salvaging books from the wreckage at Assumption College in Worcester, Massachusetts.
Photograph by Paul J. Maguire, *Boston Globe*, via Getty Images.

but only 14 recognized it for what it was. Indeed, despite the fact that the *Globe* and other newspapers had run front-page stories that morning on a devastating tornado that had killed more than 100 people in Michigan and Ohio the day before, the possibility of a tornado in Massachusetts simply did not enter the minds of most residents.[9]

In the storm's aftermath, the Commonwealth's citizens struggled to understand its causes and how its death toll might have been prevented. The *Globe* explained that a tornado should not be confused with a hurricane and quoted one expert claiming that a nationwide radar warning system could have reduced tornado fatalities that year by 98 percent. The Worcester disaster capped a deadly tornado season that left more than 500 dead, quadruple the average death toll of the previous five years.[10] The rash of twisters led many Massachusetts residents to call their representatives in Congress to ask if recent nuclear bomb testing in the Nevada desert had somehow agitated the atmosphere, which was now exacting its revenge. "Everywhere I had people ask me what the Government thought was the cause," said US Representative Edith Nourse Rogers, Republican from Lowell, in introducing a Congressional resolution demanding a federal investigation.[11]

In addition to spawning much consternation in Massachusetts, the 1953 tornado season also helped inaugurate the modern age of meteorological research. A few months before the Worcester disaster, Kansas climatologist Snowden Flora had published the twentieth century's first general-interest book on tornadoes. The volume, which Flora hastily revised the next year in light of Worcester, represented a significant advance in public education, given that between 1885 and 1938, the government actually banned the word *tornado* from forecasts, for fear of causing panic.[12] After 1953, several breakthroughs in meteorology, including the first Doppler-radar measurements of tornadoes, the pioneering work of Japanese immigrant Tetsuya Theodore (Ted) Fujita, and the advent of sophisticated computer modeling, led to dramatic improvements in warning times. Today, the federal government's Storm Prediction Center in Norman, Oklahoma, issues multiple daily Convective Outlooks that have often anticipated major tornado outbreaks with remarkable accuracy.[13] Yet even with all the recent advances, scientists concede that much about tornadoes remains mysterious. Howard Bluestein, a leading researcher at the University of Oklahoma, has put it best: tornadoes are "one of the last frontiers of atmospheric science."[14]

If tornadoes are still, in some sense, a scientific mystery, they also point to religious mysteries. Tornadoes, and weather generally, put us in touch with the origin of religions, which arose in part as humans struggled to account for the forces of nature. Tornadoes confront us with fundamental questions about the development of theism and its future prospects in a scientific age. We see this connection in the career of a young anthropologist, Anthony F. C. Wallace, whom the federal government commissioned to write a study of individual and community behavior in aftermath of the Worcester disaster.[15] Wallace's government report did not deal with religious questions, but 13 years later, he published a classic theoretical work, *Religion: An Anthropological View* (1966), in which he advanced a version of the evolutionary view of religion that had been current among anthropologists since the nineteenth century. He predicted that scientific advances would eventually make supernatural explanations of natural phenomena so implausible that religion itself would become extinct unless it could develop "nontheistic" theology and rituals.[16] Though Wallace recognized social value in ritual, he essentially echoed the Freudian and Marxist view that belief in God was an infantile projection—a personification of the forces of nature—that humanity would eventually outgrow.[17]

This perspective dated back to the Enlightenment, when figures such as Bernard le Bovier de Fontenelle (1657–1757), drawing on ancient Greek skeptics such as Democritus and Epicurus, argued that religious thought was a primitive form of science: an attempt to account for nature's power by attributing it to storm gods and other deities. "Men saw many things which they were not able to do—hurl lightning bolts, call forth the winds, stir up the waves of the sea," Fontenelle wrote, and they "imagined beings more powerful than they, who would be capable of producing these great effects."[18] The emergence of monotheism modified this archaic logic by casting violent weather in terms of the doctrine of providence, prompting Fontenelle's contemporary David Hume to scoff at the "vulgar" common people who attributed every natural calamity to God's will.[19]

Yet in their disdain for what they regarded as a moribund, unscientific worldview, Enlightenment critics and later theorists of religion underestimated the staying power of the Storm God. Weather disasters in the twenty-first century still stir up the same vortex of religious questions that has troubled humans for centuries. For monotheists, the most obvious is the issue of theodicy: Why does a loving God permit such evils? Enlightenment thinkers unwittingly exacerbated this problem because they assumed that the universe was governed by a benevolent, reasonable deity.[20] Tornadoes also raise age-old puzzles about the origins of the natural world and humans' place in it. In the Hebrew Bible, Yahweh thunders to Job out of the whirlwind: "Where were you when I laid the foundation of the earth? Tell me, if you have understanding" (Job 38:4). Far from settling such questions, modern science has only made them more acute. Is there divine purpose in the universe, or is nature blind and even random? And how does the discovery of quantum and chaotic uncertainties square with the predictable, divinely ordered Newtonian universe? For Americans, this whole nexus of religious questions comes together in the whirlwind.

The basic purpose of this book is to explore this fascinating and often unsettling connection between weather and religion, a relationship that appears in broader studies of comparative religion and the cultural history of weather but has never been the subject of an American-focused study in its own right.[21] Yet I also make a specific argument that has implications for both US history and the history of religion: in the tornado, Americans experience something that is at once culturally peculiar (the indigenous storm of the national imagination) and religiously primal (the sense of awe before an unpredictable and mysterious power). The tornado is therefore both American and transcendent, reflecting national identity even while exposing Americans to mysteries above and beyond themselves.

The culturally peculiar aspect of tornadoes is readily apparent. As "Nature's nation," to borrow a phrase from the historian Perry Miller, the United States was born in the encounter with the frontier and its weather.[22] Literary critic Camille Paglia has remarked that "foreign observers often fail to understand the vast drama of nature in America, where the political will is tested and defined against a catastrophic background of hurricanes, earthquakes, and raging wildfires." In this context, Paglia contends, the tornado looms as a uniquely "American sublime." It "comes and goes like a capricious god," dealing "staggering blows to human pride."[23] Judith Kerman's poem "In Tornado Weather" (1984) captures a similar sense of tornadoes as the habitual marauders of the American landscape. She recounts "driving with my foot to the floor" over a flat Midwestern highway and thinking of the wind: "one hundred miles to the west it has / sliced the top off a hospital / smashed two miles of Kalamazoo / nothing anyone will read tonight / is wild enough."[24]

The weather has consistently resisted Americans' efforts to subdue it, despite the hope of some of the earliest European colonists that they might conquer the elements just as they had expelled the land's indigenous inhabitants.[25] Occasionally, Native peoples even summoned the weather back in revenge. In 1966, an F5 tornado gouged a path through Topeka, the state capital of Kansas, killing 16 people and injuring more than 500. The storm passed right over Burnett's Mound, named for the Potawatomi chief Abram Burnett, or Nan-Wesh-Mah (1812–1870). According to local legend, the mound was the burial site of a group of Potawatomi killed long before by a tornado. During the burial ceremony, a medicine man reputedly asked the Great Spirit to protect the surrounding region forever from tornadoes—provided that the burying ground was never disturbed. But in 1960, the city of Topeka built a five-million-gallon water storage tank on the mound. Many Topeka residents wondered if the catastrophic 1966 tornado was the Great Spirit's or Chief Burnett's retribution.[26]

The indigenous spirits were not the only ones who used the weather for retribution. The earliest European colonists in the New World believed that their own god used storms to punish iniquity. That belief has never completely passed away, though fiery jeremiads echoing colonial preachers are comparatively infrequent today. More common, and a hallmark of the evangelical Protestantism that has so shaped American culture, is the tendency to see disasters through a broadly providential lens, especially in cases where individuals escape serious injury. People want to believe that tornadoes can be explained, that they make sense within some system of thought, whether an infallible Bible, or a theological creed, or the simple faith that everything happens for a reason.[27]

But something about tornadoes eludes rational explanation. Here we come to their transcendent quality—their larger-than-life presence that rises above anything narrowly American. What is it about tornadoes that keeps legions of storm-chasers returning to the Great Plains every spring in hopes of spotting one of these evasive storms? Paglia and others have described tornadoes as "sublime," and for certain Enlightenment thinkers, that term held the key to the special quality of all violent phenomena of nature. Derived from a Latin root meaning high or lofty, the sublime emerged as a concept in modern aesthetic philosophy in the work of Edmund Burke (1729–1797). Like the notion of the "beautiful," the sublime is hard to define. Burke associated it with things dangerous and terrifying, such as violent storms, which have a transcendent grandeur as long we are able to experience them without personal injury. "[I]t is impossible to look on any thing as trifling or contemptible that may be dangerous," Burke wrote. Consequently, when God is represented in scripture, "every thing terrible in nature is called up to heighten the awe and sublimity of the divine presence."[28]

Immanuel Kant (1724–1804) built on Burke's notion that the sublime is something threatening that we view from a safe vantage point: "thunderclouds piled up the vault of heaven, borne along with flashes and peals . . . hurricanes leaving desolation in their track, the boundless ocean rising with rebellious force." Kant defined what he called the "dynamically sublime" as that combination of fear and fascination that we experience when we realize we are dealing with forces beyond our physical ability to resist. Yet he drew a more moralistic conclusion than Burke, arguing that the sublimity of natural phenomena lay in their tendency to awaken within us "a power of resistance of quite another kind," a conviction that our highest moral principles are more transcendent and powerful than any purely physical forces. Unless the soul recognizes "the sublimity of its own vocation even over nature," he insisted, the fear of storms is little better than superstition. Kant thus contended that true contemplation of God could only occur when we rest confident in our own moral powers—not when we cower before divine wrath "in the tempest, the storm, the earthquake, and the like."[29]

It is tempting to agree with Kant that tornadoes are sublime in his sense. In an instant, they obliterate all that is impermanent and turn people sharply—the word "tornado" is related to the Latin *torno* (to turn round)—toward their own vocations as moral beings. Catastrophic tornadoes have repeatedly proven individuals' ability to turn themselves around: to unite with others, however temporarily, in the common goal of recovery. But as we will see, storms have also exposed Americans' chronic moral failings: indifference to racial and economic inequalities in disaster response, and, more recently, refusal to acknowledge human-induced climate change as a contributing factor in severe weather. Rather than summoning people to noble actions, violent storms have sometimes resulted only in political folly or stalemate.

What, then, is the tornado's deeper significance if it is not in leading people to the ethical sublime? A more helpful theorist than Kant is Rudolf Otto (1869–1937), who, like his intellectual forefather Friedrich Schleiermacher (1768–1834), conceived of religion not primarily in terms of ethics but in terms of feeling. (As Schleiermacher put it: "I do not think there is much to gain by using religion either against the unlawful actions it is supposed to hinder or on behalf of the moral actions it is supposed to produce. If this were all it could do to win respect, I should have nothing more to do with its case.")[30] Though Otto referred to the sublime (German: *das Erhabene*), he preferred his own concept of the "numinous," derived from the Latin *numen*, meaning divine presence or power. For Otto, the numinous was roughly equivalent to the holy, yet he coined the term to avoid the common association of the holy with something supremely good.[31] Goodness is a moral category, which inevitably entangles it in human standards of rationality. The numinous, by contrast, is nonrational or suprarational, meaning that it transcends any mundane standards of judgment.[32]

Put in terms of feeling, the numinous is something external, powerful, inexplicable, and inexorable that intrudes on ordinary life. It is dreadful and uncanny, an awe-inspiring mystery. Otto called this the *mysterium tremendum*, a fearsome or awesome mystery that is both daunting and fascinating at the same time.[33] He saw it in, among other examples, the biblical notion, found in both the Hebrew Bible and the New Testament, of the "wrath" of God, which he likened to "a hidden force of nature" or "stored-up electricity, discharging itself upon anyone who comes too near." He also identified it in God's speeches from the whirlwind in the Book of Job, which present what Otto calls a "dysteleology" (the opposite of teleology, or purposiveness) in showcasing animals, from the flightless ostrich to the lumbering Behemoth, that fly in the face of human standards of rational design. The "point of the whole passage," wrote Otto, is "an intrinsic value in the incomprehensible."[34] Indeed, Otto filled his classic study, *The Idea of the Holy* (1917), with such illustrations because of his firm conviction that the numinous could not be rationally defined but only felt

FIGURE I.2. Tornado near Dodge City, Kansas, on May 24, 2016.
Photograph by Howard B. Bluestein.

or evoked. The mystery underlying these phenomena, in his view, was the real object of worship. As Otto explained, "one does not kneel before a cyclone [*Wirbelsturm*, whirlwind] or the blind forces of nature . . . as such," but "one does kneel before the wholly uncomprehended Mystery."[35]

Because the numinous exists apart from our futile efforts to understand it, the ways in which it impinges upon ordinary life are profoundly unpredictable. Such is the case with religion in American history, which has perennially erupted with sudden, tornadic energy, from the whirlwind of the Great Awakening to the "rushing mighty wind" of the modern Pentecostal revival. Even in less dramatic contexts, religion inevitably takes on a life of its own, altering the course of culture, politics, and economics in unforeseen ways. Religion scholar Robert Orsi has written about the unpredictable, nonrational quality of the numinous in a provocative essay on Otto. "The 2 + 2 = 5 of holiness inserts a wedge of unpredictability into history and society, of the unforeseeable and unaccountable," Orsi notes.[36] The tornado is the perfect emblem of this unpredictability. As we will see, tornadoes helped inspire modern chaos theory, which showed that certain phenomena are inherently unpredictable because of their sensitivity to slight variations in initial conditions.

The sense of awe before an unpredictable, mysterious power is finally what I am identifying as the religiously primal aspect of tornadoes because such encounters with nature are as old as humanity itself. Otto went further in his claim for the numinous, insisting that it is not only primal but absolutely *sui generis* (of its own kind), irreducible to any nonreligious explanations.[37] Present-day scholars have deconstructed this claim, arguing that no religious experience, not even something as seemingly autonomous as the numinous, happens apart from human culture.[38] Even the apparently neutral idea of "religion," scholars have argued, is a cultural construct of modern thinkers who, unlike premodern people, distinguished it from the "secular" and separated it from other spheres of life (politics, economics, science).[39] These critiques are valid as far as they go. Yet the fact that people's *experiences* of the numinous, like religion itself, are conditioned by cultural factors does not disprove the involvement of some external thing, whether a god or a tornado or both, in causing the experience in the first place. As Orsi observes, Otto and those inspired by him wanted to account for "the really realness of religion" in a way that "called into question the absolute authority of naturalistic explanations."[40]

Recent scientific advances have only increased the sense that naturalistic explanations cannot capture the full complexity of a tornado. This is not to say that a tornado "proves" the existence of God—I am deeply skeptical of any such proofs— but simply that there are certain facets of the natural world (and our place in it) that will always remain a mystery. William Pollard (1911–1989), a nuclear physicist- turned-Episcopal priest whom we will meet later in these pages, recounted how his own reading of Otto helped him realize that science cannot decipher everything. For Pollard, the "non-conceptual numinous experience" so often experienced "in the midst of a storm" pointed to the limits of rational understanding.[41] Similarly, Otto himself, in a follow-up volume to *The Idea of the Holy*, charged that modern rationalism's "desire for explanation left no mystery, nothing that was wonderful or inexpressible, no profound riddle in the universe."[42] Time and again, Americans have tried to assimilate tornadoes into rational systems (whether theological or scientific), but like specters from a world beyond, they violently resist domestication, prostrating and confounding just as they did in the far distant past. "Descending suddenly, menacingly, and without reliable warning," writes journalist Mark Levine, "the tornado serves as a near-primal expression of the mysterious and fraught relationship between individuals and the skies above them."[43]

This book narrates that fraught relationship in five chapters whose titles are quotations from the King James Version (KJV) of the Bible, the translation that has most often furnished Americans with meaning and consolation in the wake of disaster.[44] (Most biblical quotations within the chapters are also from the King James, though in a few instances I use the New Revised Standard Version for the sake of clarity. In addition, I have followed the KJV's convention of using male pronouns for God since this is nearly universal in my sources.) The overall structure of the chapters is chronological, occasionally interrupted by vignettes, some of them from my research-related travels. As for the varieties of severe weather, the tornado looms largest here for reasons already explained, though I will also bring in other violent phenomena (lightning, hurricanes, blizzards, earthquakes, tsunamis) to the extent that they illuminate Americans' views of natural disasters.

Throughout the book, most of my primary sources are "public" and published: sermons and treatises by clergy and theologians, works by meteorologists or other scientists, and coverage of weather disasters in hundreds of daily newspapers and other periodicals. The religious perspectives of many ordinary people emerge in these newspaper accounts, and through their experiences I have tried to capture at least a glimmer of the awe and agony that only survivors can fully understand. Yet as an intellectual historian, I am first concerned with the professionals (clergy, theologians, scientists) who are paid to theorize about God or tornadoes.[45] Intellectual history takes inventory of the conceptual resources a society uses in approaching a problem. I examine how the resources available to Americans for thinking about violent weather have both endured and evolved over the centuries.

The story told here roughly parallels the geographic expansion of the American nation, beginning with the precolonial background and tracing the increasing encounters with severe weather as Americans pushed westward into the Mississippi Valley and beyond. The narrative ends in Oklahoma, ground zero of the most violent tornadoes on the planet, where an evangelical Protestant culture meets the frontiers of science and the fractious politics of climate change. At every step of the way, we will see how the tornado has taken Americans to the outer limits of their explanatory and predictive powers. Thus, even though meteorologists continue to make lifesaving advances in forecasting severe storms, the tornado remains a uniquely American totem—a symbol of Americans' quest for mastery, but the embodiment of primal, unconquerable Mystery.

Behold, a whirlwind of the Lord is gone forth in fury . . . it shall fall grievously upon the head of the wicked.

—JEREMIAH 23:19

Throughout the religious history of Israel, Yahweh shows himself a sky god and a storm god, creator and omnipotent, absolute sovereign and "Lord of Hosts."

—MIRCEA ELIADE, *Patterns in Comparative Religion* (1958)

1

"Whirlwind of the Lord"

THE ENDURING GOD(S) OF THE STORM

WHEN PIONEERS FROM the East Coast founded the town of Xenia, Ohio, in 1803, they named it after the Greek word for "hospitality." Xenia (population 25,000) is indeed a hospitable stop for travelers passing through the southwestern Ohio farm country east of Dayton. Yet five times since 1933, it has hosted visitors of a most unwelcome kind—tornadoes—that have made it well known in the annals of American meteorology. The worst tornado, part of the April 3, 1974, Super Outbreak, killed 34 of Xenia's residents and leveled much of the city. In the aftermath of the disaster, Xenia's name took on new meaning. Was the tornado a *theoxeny*, a visitation of a god in disguise?[1] Was it the latest malevolent apparition in what the native Shawnee Indians reputedly called the "place of the devil wind"?[2] Or was it purely a natural occurrence?

I wanted to see Xenia for myself, so I stopped there on the way from Indianapolis to North Carolina on an overcast morning in August 2015. Though the town is only 15 miles from the urban bustle of Dayton, it is surprisingly bucolic, nestled just north of the main east-west highway, US 35. A casual observer might never have suspected that nearly half of the town lay in ruins 41 years earlier. One of the few reminders is a simple granite slab next to city hall that lists the names of the 34 people who died.

Adjacent to city hall, the iconic 1902 courthouse, a Richardsonian Romanesque building with a 145-foot clock tower, still stands as the most monumental survivor of the storm. The late resident Helen Hooven Santmyer, author of the bestselling novel *". . . And Ladies of the Club,"* once recalled that on nearly every street there were chinks between roofs and chimneys where children running late for school knew that they could glimpse the clock.[3] After the tornado, the tower stood a bit taller than before, stark against the landscape of leveled buildings. Though the winds had shattered the clock's face, the tower was otherwise intact. It became "a symbol of communal endurance," according to journalist Polk Laffoon IV.[4]

As I walked around Courthouse Square, I discovered another monument that predated the tornado: a granite memorial to the Ten Commandments, erected by the Fraternal Order of Eagles as part of a nationwide campaign in the 1950s.[5] In the biblical diction of the King James Version, the inscription begins: "I AM the LORD thy God. Thou shalt have no other gods before me." The capital letters of "LORD" are a translator's convention—a pious substitution for the underlying Hebrew text, which is the unutterable sacred tetragrammaton, YHWH (Yahweh). What the monument, like most English-language Bibles, masks is that the God of Israel had a particular identity: it is Yahweh, not some nondenominational deity, whose worship is enjoined here. In the Bible, Yahweh competes with other gods for supremacy, and violent storms are one of his chief means of demonstrating his power. As I tried to imagine Xenia prostrate in the aftermath of the tornado, the Ten Commandments monument suddenly seemed slightly ominous underneath the cloudy skies. Was it Yahweh, as Hebrew storm god, who rode the clouds into Xenia on April 3, 1974?

THE WEATHER IN ANCIENT RELIGIONS

The attribution of storms to the gods is as old as humanity itself. Across the world's cultures, two types of weather-related deities—sky gods and storm gods—figure prominently in the myths of religious traditions. Scholar of religion Mircea Eliade contended that the "Supreme Beings of primitive races, as well as the Great Gods of the earliest civilizations of history, all display a connection" with "the sky, the air, and meteorological happenings."[6] The sky furnished a natural connection to the divine in that it is infinite and transcendent, wholly beyond human proportions. Storms, meanwhile, perfectly encapsulated what Peter C. Chemery has called "humankind's deeply rooted ambivalence toward the sacred" in that they are both life-sustaining (bringing rain) and life-destroying (bringing wind and lightning). Storms thus represented to ancient peoples both the benign and the chaotic aspects of the powers that control the world.[7]

Eliade noticed that in the evolution of certain religious traditions, sky gods eventually became remote, yielding their direct involvement in human affairs to storm gods or other meteorological beings.[8] The archetypal case comes from the world's oldest scripture in continuous use, the Rig Veda, a collection of Sanskrit hymns thought to have originated as long as 3,500 years ago. Here the primitive connection between religion and the weather is not just mythological but etymological: the name of the high god, Dyaus, literally means "sky" and is equivalent to the Greek *Zeus* (the head of the Olympian pantheon) and Latin *deus* (god).[9] Important as he was, the Sky Father Dyaus eventually took a back seat to his offspring, including the storm god Indra, who was both revered and feared in the Vedic stanzas. "Indra, who wields the thunderbolt in his hand, is the king of that which moves and that which rests. . . . He rules the people as their king." And again: "Even the sky and the earth bow low before him, and the mountains are terrified of his hot breath."[10]

In later Hinduism, as the Vedic religion of sacrifice gave way to devotional traditions, Indra himself was vanquished—fittingly, in another episode involving weather. In the Bhagavata Purana, the townspeople of Vrindavana were accustomed to offering sacrifices to Indra in hopes of receiving his life-giving rain ("his seminal discharge") rather than the wrath of his thunderbolt. But Lord Krishna revealed to them that Indra was powerless to affect their destinies, which were the inevitable fruit of their own actions (*karma*). Indra, enraged that the people had ceased to bring him sacrifices, sent "tremendously heavy showers full of hail-stones, accompanied by terrific stormy winds, out of season." The people appealed to Krishna in their distress, and though he was still but a boy, he lifted with one hand the hill Govardhana, creating an earthen umbrella to shelter both people and animals.[11]

Indra's stormy aspect and the heavenly preeminence of his father Dyaus were combined in Zeus, who functioned for the ancient Greeks as both a sky god and a storm god. In addition to reigning as the ultimate judge of both gods and humans, he was the "cloud gatherer," hurler of thunderbolts. He also sent rain, leading to the colloquial expression, "Zeus is raining." Because lightning was regarded as his direct epiphany, the Greeks typically set up a sanctuary to him wherever lightning struck.[12] As a deity of thunder and lightning, Zeus had rough equivalents in many other cultures. Among the pre-Columbian Inca, the storm god Illapa drew water from a celestial stream (the Milky Way) using pitchers that he left with his sister until he broke them with his thunder club.[13] The red-bearded Norse god Thor caused thunder by riding the sky in a chariot pulled by goats. He sent lightning by hurling his hammer, Mjölnir, which actually looks more like a double-edged axe. (Numerous archaeological discoveries have revealed that the Vikings—who could have included my distant Danish ancestors—wore amulets with Mjölnir and the Christian cross interchangeably.)[14] Among the Yoruba people of West Africa, the god Shango wielded a double-edged axe similar to Thor's. Shango's mastery over the thunderstorm led him to be conflated with a female saint, Barbara (patroness of people caught in storms), when the Atlantic slave trade brought West African traditions into contact with Catholicism. The twentieth-century folklorist Newbell Niles Puckett found instances of African Americans in Mississippi using axes to ward off thunderstorms.[15]

Alongside sky gods and storm gods, wind deities and spirits constituted a related class of meteorological beings. Like the wind itself, these deities were often mysterious and capricious, bringing either life or death, depending on which way the wind blew. Among the ancient Egyptians, Amun, whose name meant Hidden One, was the mysterious creator god whose presence was everywhere, invisible yet felt, like the wind.[16] In the Japanese Shinto religion, the *kami* (spirits or divinities) manifested totality and were therefore ambivalent, encompassing both good and evil. If people failed to pray to local *kami* of the wind, disaster could result. But a divine wind (*kamikaze*) could also bring deliverance, as in 1274 when a violent tempest destroyed many vessels of an invading Chinese and Korean force.[17] Indigenous wind spirits and deities also appeared in the traditions of many Native American tribes. Among the Shawnee of Ohio who were removed to Indian Territory in Oklahoma, tornadoes were equated with a female spirit known as Cyclone Person. She uprooted trees and lifted the roofs off houses by entangling them in the twisting locks of her long hair. Regarded as a friend of the Shawnees, she wreaked havoc on homes and businesses owned by whites but left Indian property untouched.[18]

STORM GODS IN BIBLICAL TRADITION

The Bible is no exception among the world's sacred texts in its frequent use of sky, storm, and wind imagery for God. As recent scholarship has shown, the cult of Yahweh was similar to other ancient Near Eastern traditions in which gods demonstrated their sovereignty through the weather. Indeed, some scholars have described Yahweh as a composite of two Syro-Palestinian (or Canaanite) deities: El, the sky god and patriarch of the pantheon, and Baal, the storm god and divine warrior. In texts dating from the mid-second millennium BCE from the Syrian city of Ugarit, El (which means "god") appears as the compassionate creator and arbiter of justice, whereas Baal (which means "lord") is the mighty Cloud Rider who brings both fertility and destruction.[19] In the early Iron Age (1200–1000 BCE), these traditions were so intermingled with Yahweh's cult that biblical scholar Mark S. Smith has concluded that "Israelite culture was largely 'Canaanite' in nature."[20] For example, Psalm 18 (quoted essentially verbatim in 2 Samuel 22) describes Yahweh simultaneously as the "Most High" (a frequent epithet of El) and in meteorological imagery associated with Baal: "The Lord [Yahweh] also thundered in the heavens, and the Most High uttered his voice. And he sent out his arrows, and scattered them; he flashed forth lightnings, and routed them."[21] Storm-god motifs associated with Baal—the Cloud Rider, who stirred up tempests or hurled lightning bolts from his chariot—are especially striking in a number of passages about Yahweh.[22] In Exodus 15:1–18 (the so-called Song of the Sea, considered one of the earliest literary units in the Bible), Yahweh is a divine warrior who piles up the water with the blast of his nostrils. In Habakkuk 3:2–15 (another ancient hymn), the mountains writhe as he sweeps by in a torrent; the lightning flashes as he treads the earth in his fury. In Psalm 77, the sea trembles at the sight of God; his thunder crashes in the whirlwind and his lightning lights up the world. Like Baal, Yahweh rides the clouds in Deuteronomy 33:26; Psalm 18:10; Psalm 68:4, 33; and Isaiah 19:1. Psalm 29 is even regarded by many scholars as a hymn to Baal in which the name Yahweh was simply substituted. Here Yahweh sits enthroned in the divine council of heavenly beings; he thunders over the water and flashes forth flames of fire. "The voice of the Lord causes the oaks to whirl, and strips the forest bare; and in his temple all say, 'Glory!' "[23]

The use of Baal myths in the cult of Yahweh was not simply a process of adaptation but also one of subordination, to prove that Yahweh was the most powerful storm god. As a number of biblical passages reveal, some Israelites were worshipping Baal, in violation of the "no other gods" injunction of the Ten Commandments. In the Bible, the rivalry between Baal and Yahweh reaches a meteorological climax when the prophet Elijah sets up a contest with the priests of Baal to see whose god will send lightning to kindle an animal sacrifice. The hapless priests of Baal cry in vain, "O Baal, answer us!" (1 Kings 18:26), before finally giving up. Elijah then douses the offering with water before calling on Yahweh to prove his supremacy. "Then the fire of the Lord fell and consumed the burnt offering, the wood, the stones, and the dust, and even licked up the water that was in the trench" (1 Kings 18:38). In the next chapter, however, as if to say that his power cannot be contained by meteorological phenomena, Yahweh shuns his typical stormy theophany. Though his manifestation to Elijah on Sinai (Horeb) at first resembles his appearance in lightning and thunder to Moses on the mountain (Exodus 19), this time the text repeatedly declares that Yahweh is not in the wind, earthquake, or fire—which are followed by "a sound of sheer silence" (1 Kings 19:12).[24]

This apparent polemic in 1 Kings 19 against the weather theophanies of Baal is an outlier in the Bible, which inevitably falls back on meteorology as an image of divine power. The reasons for this were partly geographic. While people in ancient Palestine likely knew nothing of tornadoes, much less the catastrophic ones that afflict the American Midwest, the region had its own indigenous storm-winds, including the sirocco, a hot, cyclonic wind that can reach hurricane force. This and other Mediterranean storms gave rise to the array of Hebrew words that underlie the Bible's many meteorological references.[25] The Bible's fixation on the weather was also theological. The fierceness of storms furnished a uniquely fitting metaphor for God's wrath against the unrighteous. Thus, the solemn cadences of the King James Version declare that God "shall take them away as with a whirlwind" (Psalm 58:9); he "will come with fire, and with his chariots like a whirlwind, to render his anger with fury" (Isaiah 66:15). Similarly, "a whirlwind of the Lord is gone forth in fury"; "it shall fall grievously upon the head of the wicked" (Jeremiah 23:19; cf. 30:23). And again: "I will even rend it with a stormy wind in my fury; and there shall be an overflowing shower in mine anger, and great hailstones in my fury to consume it" (Ezekiel 13:13). The unpredictability of weather also connoted the secret quality of the divine will, with storms serving as the instrument of God's inscrutable purposes. "The Lord hath his way in the whirlwind and in the storm, and the clouds are the dust of his feet" (Nahum 1:3).

Similar assertions appear in the later Abrahamic traditions. In Islam, the Quran says that God "shows you lightning, arousing fear and hope. . . . He sends forth the thunderbolts and strikes therewith whomsoever He will." Likewise, "God is He Who sends the winds," which cause the clouds to rise; God bestows the rain "upon whomsoever He will among His servants."[26] In the most recent of the Abrahamic faiths, the Bahá'í tradition, which emerged out of Shi'a Islam in the nineteenth century, the founder, Bahá'u'lláh, exhorted his followers to consider "how the wind, faithful to that which God hath ordained, bloweth upon all the regions of the earth, be they inhabited or desolate. Neither the sight of desolation, nor the evidences of prosperity, can either pain or please it. It bloweth in every direction, as bidden by its Creator."[27]

Yet in the monotheism that emerged from within the Abrahamic lineage, the seeming arbitrariness of the divine will posed a profound theological problem. If God alone was behind every instance of violent weather, this made him responsible even when righteous persons were injured or killed by storms. How could this square with divine justice and benevolence (qualities originally ascribed to the kindly patriarch, El, but later assimilated into standard Abrahamic definitions of God)? Polytheists could always appeal to a "good cop, bad cop" theism in which vengeful deities were balanced by compassionate ones. But for monotheists, all the world's suffering was on God.[28] And in the one place where the Bible confronts the problem head-on—the Book of Job—the answer is hauntingly inconclusive.

As an exploration of the problem of theodicy, or why the righteous suffer, Job has been called "the most sublime monument in literature."[29] The basic plot is straightforward. Job, a righteous man, is prostrated by a series of calamities that God (goaded by "the Satan," a Hebrew term meaning "adversary") visits upon him to test his faith. Marauders kill his oxen and donkeys; a fire consumes his sheep; thieves steal his camels; and, worst of all, a fierce wind demolishes his house, killing all of his children. Later, Job himself is afflicted with a loathsome skin disease. Amid these miseries, he must endure the philosophizing of his three friends, who in various ways all insist that suffering is caused by sin and that God does not punish persons without cause. Job continues to maintain his innocence and challenges God to hear his case.

"Then the Lord answered Job out of the whirlwind": So begins Yahweh's response to Job. God's appearance in "the whirlwind" (Hebrew, *ha se'ara*, sometimes translated as "tempest") is an emblem of what some scholars regard as the theme of the whole discourse, namely, that God's power cannot be domesticated, controlled, or understood.[30] The divine speech begins ominously for Job: "Gird up your loins like a man. . . . Where were you when I laid the foundation of the earth? Tell me, if you have understanding." God then extols his own control of the cosmos, contrasting this with Job's impotence. God surveys an array of natural phenomena, quickly falling back on the weather as a means of humbling Job: "Who has cut a channel for the torrents of rain, and a way for the thunderbolt? . . . Can you send forth lightnings, so that they may go and say to you, 'Here we are'?"[31] God continues this relentless line of attack in a second speech. "Have you an arm like God, and can you thunder with a voice like his?" After God discourses at length on the enigmatic Leviathan and Behemoth, two creatures who symbolize undomesticated divine power, Job finally relents. "I know that you can do all things, and that no purpose of yours can be thwarted. . . . Therefore I have uttered what I did not understand, things too wonderful for me, which I did not know."[32]

In an epilogue to the book, God rewards Job's contrition by restoring his fortunes, but the ambiguity of the tale remains, confounding scholarly interpreters. Some read it as ultimately hopeful, an affirmation of God's parental delight in his creation and an invitation to humans to participate in the created order, despite its many mysteries.[33] Others see a tragic sublime, an abasement of humans' rage for order and a realization of the danger and chaos inherent in creation.[34] The common denominator in both perspectives is the recognition that God never really solves the question of suffering. Whether one revels in it or recoils from it, the whirlwind remains a mystery. Job's words in the first chapter might well serve as a concluding doxology to divine inscrutability: "the Lord gave, and the Lord has taken away; blessed be the name of the Lord."[35]

Yet the story of Job is not the only material in the Bible relevant to theodicy. The cameo appearance by "the Satan" in the Book of Job hints at another biblical strategy for dealing with the problem: apocalypticism.[36] The term "apocalypse" derives from the Greek *apokalypsis*, meaning "revelation" or "disclosure." It has come to denote a particular genre of literature, typified in Hebrew scripture by Daniel and in the New Testament by Revelation, in which a vision of the End Time is revealed. A hallmark of apocalyptic literature is the notion that suffering in the present world is caused by the forces of evil—Satan and his minions—who are arrayed against God. (In the Book of Job, "the Satan" is simply a member of the divine council who remains subservient to God; in later Jewish and Christian apocalypticism, Satan evolves into a cosmic figure, God's archenemy.) A cataclysmic battle between God and the forces of evil is soon coming. God will ultimately prevail and set up his kingdom once and for all, but not before the outbreak of many tribulations, which will serve as harbingers of the End.[37]

Winds and storms loom large as signs of the End in apocalyptic visions. Daniel 7 begins with a vision of "the four winds of heaven stirring up the great sea," a possible echo of the creation account in Genesis 1:2, when a wind from God moves over the face of the waters. This time, however, rather than subduing the chaos, the four winds create it. Then, in a clear parallel to Baal as Cloud Rider, Daniel's vision reveals "one like a son of man coming with the clouds of heaven."[38] Christians later interpreted this as a foreshadowing of Jesus' coming to do battle against the forces of evil. Jesus himself quotes the verse in the Gospels (Matthew 26:64, Mark 14:62), one indication of his own apocalyptic perspective.[39] Later in the New Testament, the four winds return in the Book of Revelation, where John has a vision of four angels restraining the winds that will unleash fury on the earth (7:1). The angels must wait until God's elect are marked with a seal on their foreheads. After this interlude, the End Time tribulations resume, with weather again figuring prominently. An angel hurls a censer filled with fire upon the earth, causing thunder and lightning (8:5); another sends down hail and fire mixed with blood (8:7). Many more tribulations follow, until the final battle occurs and Satan and his forces are defeated.

XENIA, APRIL 3, 1974

To Americans captivated by the biblical drama of End Time tribulations, the year 1974 seemed eerily parallel. The hard-fought war in Vietnam, which had killed 58,000 Americans and wounded 300,000, was ending in bitter defeat. A stock market crash drained the Dow Jones Industrial Average of 45 percent of its value. Inflation, exacerbated by the Organization of Petroleum Exporting Countries (OPEC) oil embargo, topped out above 12 percent, and economic deprivation caused crime rates to soar. On March 1, a grand jury indicted the Watergate Seven and named President Nixon an unindicted co-conspirator. Nixon's approval rating sank to 27 percent, the lowest rating so far in his presidency. All of this upheaval spawned an industry of End

Time speculation among evangelical Protestant writers. John F. Walvoord, president of Dallas Theological Seminary, published *Armageddon, Oil, and the Middle East Crisis*, which sold 750,000 copies in English and in 12 foreign-language editions. Walter K. Price, in *The Coming Antichrist*, predicted that thousands of responsible leaders in government, industry, education, and other fields would soon be raptured by Jesus when he returned to reclaim his own. "With these leaders taken to meet the Lord in the air," he wrote, the structure of society "will be so weakened that it will reduce the United States to an impotent and prostrated nation." Meanwhile, Thomas S. McCall and Zola Levitt, in *The Coming Russian Invasion of Israel*, prophesied that the United States was in imminent danger of annihilation, either as a direct ally of Antichrist or as a "helpless casualty of global thermonuclear effects."[40]

On April 3, 1974, however, a gathering storm of another kind overshadowed any geopolitical threats. A dangerous mix of meteorological ingredients combined over the nation's midsection to produce the deadliest outbreak of tornadoes in US history up to that time. (The Tri-State Tornado of 1925 produced the most fatalities from what was believed to be a single storm.) With the first twister beginning over an Illinois cornfield around 2:30 p.m., over the next 22 hours, 148 tornadoes would kill at least 315 people and injure some 6,000. Seven of the tornadoes were F5, the strongest category, with estimated winds over 260 miles per hour. This single-day total of F5 storms has never been surpassed. Ten states were declared federal disaster areas, with property damage totaling at least $600 million (over $3 billon in today's dollars).[41]

The April 3, 1974, "Super Outbreak," as it came to be known, did not happen without warning. That morning, meteorologists at the National Severe Storms Forecast Center (then located in Kansas City) eyed the convergence of factors nervously. When the *Xenia Daily Gazette* hit newsstands in early afternoon, the paper's front-page forecast noted that the National Weather Service (NWS) had issued a severe storm watch until 3:00 p.m. At 2:35 p.m., the NWS extended the watch, and by 4:00, ominous clouds were gathering to the west of town. At 4:10, a local radio station received a teletype advisory that a tornado might be on the way. The station immediately interrupted its programming and urged listeners to take cover. By the time the tornado touched down in Xenia's Windsor Park subdivision at 4:33 p.m., it was an F5, a storm capable of "incredible phenomena," according to the old Fujita scale.[42]

What happened next would be forever seared in the memory of eyewitnesses. Among them was 16-year-old Bruce Boyd, who, as the monstrous tornado approached his neighborhood, grabbed the family's home movie camera and filmed it for nearly three minutes before he heeded his mother's pleas to come inside. Another resident made an audio recording, preserved today on the internet, that captures the whine

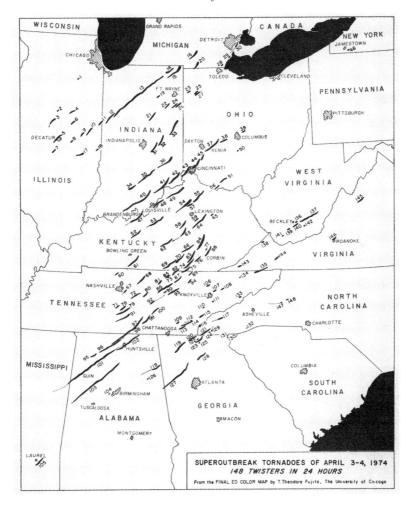

FIGURE 1.1. Map of the April 3–4, 1974, Super Outbreak, designed by University of Chicago meteorologist Tetsuya Theodore (Ted) Fujita.
National Weather Service.

of a train whistle as the roar of the wind and the sound of flying debris build to an unnerving crescendo.[43] Because the storm came up so quickly, residents scarcely had time to dive for cover—mostly in bathtubs or other above-ground enclosures, since many houses in the hardest-hit subdivisions lacked basements. Catherine Wilson, then nine years old, recalled that her mother grabbed her and her younger sister and lay down on top of them in the bathtub seconds before the tornado hit. "It sounded like a jet plane. It was a like a deep sigh, but with the wind and all the glass breaking in all the windows." She remembers her mother's screams: "Lord, make this stop, keep us safe!" Moments later, after it passed, the house's roof was gone and they looked up to see the sky.[44] Other residents were not so lucky. One woman climbed out of her bathtub to grab a radio but was decapitated as the funnel passed. A switchman for the Penn Central Railroad fled the flimsy tower that was his post only to be killed while making his way home on foot. (The tower survived.) A woman followed her husband's urging to drive from their home, which lacked a basement, to his office, which had one. She died when the basement windows exploded and a two-by-four struck her in the back of the head. Such individual tragedies haunted the survivors, among whom "the main subject of discussion was death—the way the storm picked off people as arbitrarily as buildings," according to the tornado's principal chronicler, Polk Laffoon IV.[45]

Equally striking in survivors' accounts is the sense of sublime terror and indescribability as they came face to face with the storm. Local journalists Rich Heiland and Randy Blackaby, trying to photograph the storm, stepped out of their car to find themselves looking "almost straight up at the funnel, swirling with dead birds and debris as it neared St. Brigid Church, which it ripped and killed like a demon that had waited 2,000 years for a victory." Jackie Hupman, one of a dozen people who took shelter in a beer cooler in the Hofbrau Haus, recalled that "it was like your hair was standing up on your body, and your ears felt like they were going to blow up." LaVersa Motes remembered that the "sound was indescribable—the rushing winds, glass crashing, roofs of buildings smashing down, cars picked up and thrown against others like matchbox toys."[46] Such feelings of encounter with an inexpressible power were shared by survivors of the other catastrophic tornadoes that struck that day across 13 states. "It is an unforgettable sight, caused by an incomprehensible force, a furious buzzsaw that gouges, chops, chews and spews its way across earth," noted Richard Des Ruisseaux of Louisville, Kentucky, where an F4 tornado killed three people, injured more than 200, and destroyed 900 homes. In Limestone County, Alabama, two massive tornadoes (at least one of them an F5), plowed through within less than an hour, killing 50 persons. Bob Dunnavant was among a group of people forced to take shelter in a shallow highway ditch. "There were about 30 of us . . . all competing with the grass for a connection to the dirt," he told the *Huntsville Times*. "It was like something out of the Old Testament, a pillar of clouds, black, majestic and ominous, moving across the farmlands."[47] After poring over Dunnavant's and similar accounts from Limestone County, journalist Mark Levine, in his lyrical book *F5* (2007), wrote of the "visionary quality of a tornado sighting—part natural phenomenon, part spiritual emanation," which he compared to Ezekiel 1:4: "And I looked, and behold, a whirlwind came out of the north, a great cloud, and a fire infolding itself, and a brightness was about it, and out of the midst thereof as the color of amber, out of the midst of the fire."[48]

Back in Xenia, the otherworldly specter of the tornado itself quickly gave way to visions of this-worldly horror. In the first 12 hours after the storm, Greene Memorial

Hospital treated 436 people, many of them seriously injured. A temporary morgue set up in the Old Soldiers and Sailors Orphan Home held victims who died of unspeakable trauma: a boy with a brick lodged in his head, a woman with a triangular trench from her mouth through her skull. A convoy of heavy equipment made the slow trip from nearby Wright-Patterson Air Force Base along State Road 235, which "looked more like the supply route to a combat zone," according to Laffoon.[49] Officials cordoned off the city, leaving residents who were Dayton commuters to park their cars as far as five miles away and walk into town, not knowing whether they would find their loved ones or their homes intact. As late as 1:00 a.m., distraught parents were still walking anxiously through town looking for their children. "Downtown," wrote reporter Delores Fisher, "sirens screamed from an endless success[ion] of ambulances, police cruisers, fire trucks, flasher-equipped private cars, utility vehicles, tree service trucks, dump trucks, bulldozers, cranes, and emergency light rigs."[50]

By sunrise the next day, the full extent of the devastation became clear. The *Xenia Daily Gazette*, which managed to publish an edition that day thanks to the printing press of its sister paper, the *Middletown Journal*, carried a large aerial photo showing

FIGURE 1.2. Aerial view of Xenia storm damage in the Arrowhead/Windsor Park neighborhood. Unknown photographer from Wright-Patterson Air Force Base, via NOAA.

the path of pulverized homes that the tornado had gouged out in its march through town. "In many instances it was almost impossible to determine houses ever existed," the *Gazette* reported.[51] In addition to wrecking some 1,200 homes (nearly half of those in the town), the storm also inflicted huge losses on educational, civic, and religious institutions. Xenia High School and five other schools were in ruins. Two nearby historically black colleges, Wilberforce and Central State, sustained extensive damage, with the latter nearly 80 percent destroyed. Nine churches, normally beacons of hope amid everyday adversities, were blown away. They included the largest of Xenia's congregations, St. Brigid's Parish, which had been a landmark for 123 years; even churches felt the wrath of what seemed like a divine judgment on the land.[52]

DAY OF WRATH: DIVINE JUDGMENT IN CHRISTIANITY

Xenia's desolated churches were the institutional embodiment of a Christian-dominated culture that interpreted calamities through a biblical lens. As we have already seen, ancient Christians appropriated storm-god imagery from Hebrew scripture in conceiving of Christ as the Son of Man riding on the clouds of heaven. A related idea was the "day of the Lord," which in the prophetic tradition in the Hebrew Bible came to mean the terrifying day when God would come to judge.[53] "For the Lord of hosts has a day against all that is proud and lofty... against every high tower, and against every fortified wall," declared the prophet Isaiah. He imagined Yahweh's judgment as coming with almost tornadic intensity and urged listeners to take cover: "Enter the caves of the rocks and the holes of the ground, from the terror of the Lord, and from the glory of his majesty, when he rises to terrify the earth." The divine appearance would be accompanied by great destruction: "See, the day of the Lord comes, cruel, with wrath and fierce anger, to make the earth a desolation, and to destroy its sinners from it."[54] Similar passages reverberate in other Hebrew prophets. So Joel: "Truly the day of the Lord is great; terrible indeed—who can endure it?" And Zephaniah: "The great day of the Lord is near"; it will be "a day of wrath" and "a day of ruin and devastation."[55]

Early Christians adopted this Jewish apocalyptic notion of the implacable divine wrath on the day of the Lord, but with a twist. Now Jesus appeared in the Apocalypse as the divine avenger, the one who "will tread the wine press of the fury of the wrath of God the Almighty [*pantocrator*]" (Revelation 19:15). The Book of Revelation also introduced a paradox. Jesus is the new Passover Lamb who was slain for the sins of the world, thus bearing the brunt of God's wrath.[56] Yet at the same time he is the instrument of God's wrath in the Apocalypse, prompting people of all classes of society to cry out to the mountains: "Fall on us and hide us from the face of the one seated on the throne and from the wrath of the Lamb; for the great day of their wrath has come, and who is able to stand?"[57] This desperate plea occurs in the Book of Revelation immediately before the passage about the angels holding back the four winds of the earth (Revelation 7:1), which became a recurring motif in the apocalyptic imagination of premodern European Christians. Medieval manuscript illuminations, mosaics, and stained-glass windows depicted the angels restraining the winds, sometimes juxtaposed with Byzantine-style images of the returning Christ as *pantocrator*, the almighty judge of the world.[58]

It is little wonder that medieval Christians associated the four winds with the apocalypse, for in premodern Europe, death and economic ruin were always just one severe storm away. Meteorological calamities were especially widespread in the early fourteenth century, when the Medieval Warm Period (which climatologists date from around 800 to 1300) began to give way to the Little Ice Age.[59] In 1315, at least three months of continuous rain across Europe destroyed wheat crops and caused seed to rot in the ground. The following year was scarcely better: in Saxony alone, some 450 villages, along with their people and livestock, were washed away in a flood. Violent storms and flooding in coastal areas were accompanied by extraordinarily long, hard freezes inland, further disrupting agriculture. The result was the Great Famine of 1315–22, which killed millions. Not surprisingly, when the Black Death began ravaging the population just 25 years later, many Europeans believed that the End Time had truly arrived.[60]

The precariousness of life in the Middle Ages gave rise to an elaborate tradition of popular devotions designed to stave off divine or satanic wrath, especially of the meteorological variety. Many of these rituals assumed that violent weather was the direct result of God's anger over human sin. An eleventh-century manuscript from Freising in Bavaria directed readers to insert the following petitions into their litanies: "From harmful storms, deliver us Lord. From the ravages of hail, deliver us Lord. From the provocation of your lightning, deliver us Lord. From the flails of your vengeance, deliver us Lord."[61] Similarly, a post-Communion collect in the Sarum missal (the variant of the Roman Rite used in England) beseeched the Lord to "hear the prayers of Thy people; and, by virtue of this Sacrament, let a calm change of weather bring to us the message of Thy peace: and do Thou, Who scourgest us for our offences, spare those who confess their sins."[62] Other rituals assumed that storms were often the work of the devil or those who did his bidding, including witches. The fifteenth-century anti-witchcraft manual *Malleus Maleficarum* (Hammer of Witches) directed this regimen to be performed at the outbreak of a hailstorm: throw three hailstones into a fire while invoking the Holy Trinity; then say the Lord's Prayer and the Hail Mary twice or three times, together with the opening of the Gospel of John

("In the beginning was the Word"); finally, repeat John 1:14 ("The Word was made flesh") three times, followed by the thrice repetition of "By the words of this Gospel may this tempest be dispersed." The manual assured readers that if the tempest was due to witchcraft, it would immediately cease.[63]

Prayers were not the only charms used against satanic assaults of violent weather. When storms broke out in Canterbury, England, some townspeople ran to the cathedral for holy water to sprinkle in their houses as protection against lightning. Also popular in England against lightning and thunder were *agnus dei* amulets, small wax cakes, made out of melted paschal candles and blessed by the pope, bearing the image of the Lamb of God. Another common protection against death or destruction by lightning was the ringing of church bells during a storm. Though such measures were sometimes ineffectual—an *agnus dei* did not keep St. Albans Abbey from being struck by lightning in the thirteenth century—the mere possibility that they might work perpetuated such practices among both laypeople and clergy.[64]

Fear of divine or satanic wrath also sustained the cult of the saints, which looked to holy men and women as more approachable helpers than God himself. Especially sought after was the intercession of the Auxiliary Saints, also known as the Fourteen Holy Helpers, three of whom—Barbara, Christopher, and Erasmus (Elmo)—were patrons of travelers and others caught in severe storms. Barbara's meteorological connection is especially vivid. Her father, enraged at her becoming a Christian, nearly killed her before he himself was struck by lightning and died. She thus became the patroness of those in danger of sudden death, particularly by lightning.[65] So popular were the Holy Helpers in the pre-Reformation West that they gained their own liturgical rite, the Office of the Auxiliary Saints, which included a prayer extolling their "special privileges before all others, that all who in their need invoke their help, shall obtain the salutary fulfillment of their prayer."[66] The office was eventually abolished in the wake of the Council of Trent when the Church became nervous that laypeople were forgetting the distinction, insisted upon in the Tridentine Catechism, between direct petitions (addressed to God alone) and requests for prayer (addressed to saints).[67]

Among the pre-Tridentine laypersons who apparently forgot this distinction was the young Martin Luther, who, as a law student in the summer of 1505, was caught in a violent thunderstorm on his way back to the university in Erfurt. Suddenly knocked to the ground by a lightning strike nearby, he spontaneously prayed, not to one of the Holy Helpers, but to another patroness of people in distress in storms: "Help me, St. Anne; I will become a monk." Luther's vow to St. Anne shows up only secondhand in the *Table Talk* 34 years later, causing some interpreters to doubt whether his turn toward a religious vocation was quite so spontaneous.[68] The incident nevertheless makes sense in the late medieval context. So does Luther's conviction that storms and other disasters were signs either from God or the devil, with the difference not always being obvious.[69] Luther's father, Hans, played on this uncertainty when, still bitter over his son's decision to become a monk and a priest, he needled Luther during the sumptuous feast celebrating his first Mass: What if an evil spirit had been behind the thunderstorm? Hans asked. Years later, after Martin Luther's death, his opponent Johannes Nas offered a different theory, that the thunderstorm was proof of God's anger at Luther himself.[70]

EARLY PROTESTANTS AND PROVIDENCE

In the years following his 1517 protest against the Catholic Church's sale of indulgences, Luther grew ever more skeptical about the mediating role of the saints and the legends associated with their cults. Preaching on St. Anne's feast day in 1527, he acknowledged that he could not find a word about her in scripture. (Anne, reputedly the mother of the Blessed Virgin Mary, is first mentioned in the apocryphal Gospel of James from the second century.) His judgment was harsher a few years later: "If you invoke Anne, you will soon be helping the devil."[71] Luther feared that the devil blinded people from accepting God's wisdom and supremacy in all of creation. While the credulity that led people to seek the help of dubious saints was bad enough, excessive inquisitiveness or caviling at the ways of God was equally dangerous. "If you were to search out everything about a kernel of wheat in the field," Luther wrote, "you would be so amazed that you would die. God's works are not like our works."[72]

Luther's trust in God's mysterious sovereignty over all things may explain why he never developed a full-fledged doctrine of providence.[73] But in the thought of the second-generation reformer John Calvin, providence gradually took on a much more prominent role. In the original edition of his *Institutes of the Christian Religion* (1536), Calvin discussed the doctrine only briefly, as part of his explication of the first sentence of the Apostles' Creed ("I believe in God the Father Almighty, Creator of heaven and earth").[74] By the final edition of the *Institutes* in 1559, however, the doctrine occupied two entire chapters.[75] The intervening years had brought to Calvin's Geneva a flood of Protestant refugees who, like himself, were fleeing persecution and the constant threat of religious warfare.[76] In this perilous context, Calvin railed against anything that would shake Christians' confidence that a wise God was in control. He thus attacked two mediating structures that might weaken people's direct reliance on God. The first was the cult of the saints, which he regarded as a violation of the Apostle Paul's proclamation that there is "one mediator between God and humankind, Christ Jesus" (1 Timothy 2:5). To Calvin it was "detestable" that

5:45). For a Puritan providentalist such as Charnock, this verse simply indicated that the just and the unjust experienced the provisioning benefits of God's general providence, whereas a just person would surely be more particularly blessed in the end. "A good man shall have what he needs, not always what he thinks he needs," Charnock added.[28] But Charnock's explanation still begged the question of whether some measure of contingency—some small degree of indifference as to where the raindrops fell—might be possible under God's larger providential control.

Christian theologians as far back as the medieval scholastics were sensitive to this issue, though one of the key figures, Thomas Aquinas (c. 1225–1274), was less concerned about understanding contingencies in the natural world than about preserving the contingency of freely willing human beings. Aquinas, like most theologians, believed that humans could not be held responsible for their sins unless they had some control over their actions. While God is the "universal cause" of all things, he allows secondary causes, including humans themselves, to operate contingently. That is, humans' actions are contingent, or freely chosen, within their own limited sphere, even though the contingency itself is part of God's plan. As Aquinas put it, "God's immediate Providence over all things does not exclude secondary causes from executing its ordered policy."[29] Aquinas further explained that since divine goodness is the end, or goal, of all things, the universe must encompass "every shade of reality," including contingencies and even evils. Regarding the latter, Aquinas insisted that one quality of divine providence was "to allow defects in some particular things so that the complete good of the universe" could be made manifest. Thus, "there would be no life for the lion were there no animals for its prey, and no patience of martyrs were there no persecution by tyrants."[30] Second causes, in other words, could be implicated in evil, even though God as First Cause was only good.

One of the first Protestant writers to apply the logic of secondary causation to the weather was the early English Puritan William Fulke (c. 1537–1589), who published a treatise on meteorology in 1563 that was reprinted at least five times over the next century. Fulke catalogued a variety of meteorological phenomena, all "very wonderfull & straunge to beholde." Identifying their causes could be "moste harde & difficulte" and required a careful balance. To say that weather events were directed by God did not mean that they lacked natural, or secondary, causes. But at the same time, to say that weather events had natural causes did not mean that they happened by chance, apart from God. Fulke assured his readers that though he had endeavored to explain meteorological events "by naturall reason," he also believed that "not so much as on[e] sparrow falleth to the grounde" without divine providence.[31]

By the time Calvinists in England formulated the Westminster Confession (1647), it was a truism of Reformed scholasticism that God normally works mediately (not *im*mediately), through second causes.[32] The confession noted that though people would "prostrate [themselves] before a statue of Barbara" or other saint "as if Christ were insufficient or too severe."[77] The second was the sophistry of skeptics who would lessen God's involvement in the world, either by overestimating the role of intermediary causes (the error of latter-day Stoics) or by positing God's withdrawal from earthly affairs after the world's creation (the error of latter-day Epicureans).[78]

Calvin's own view of providence resembled that of Augustine and Aquinas in that he insisted on God's continual upholding of the creation at every moment. Calvin buttressed this claim, as he was wont to do, with proofs from scripture, including Psalm 104:29 ("when you take away their breath, they die"), John 5:17 ("My Father is still working, and I also am working"), and Hebrews 1:3 ("he sustains all things by his powerful word"). Genesis 1:6 convinced Calvin, moreover, that the earth is suspended between waters and that it is only God's ever-restraining hand that keeps the waters from rushing forth and inundating the world, as happened in Noah's time. At all times, in fact, God holds back the chaos (which Calvin believed had infected nature as a consequence of the Fall) just as a man bridles a horse. The "bridle of divine providence" even curbs the devil, who engages in evil only as God directs. (Calvin found proof of this in Job 1:6.)[79]

Calvin's belief that "nothing takes place by chance" extended naturally to his view of the weather. It is certain, he declared, "that not one drop of rain falls without God's sure command"; likewise, "no wind ever arises or increases except by God's express command." Once again he found proofs in scripture, including Psalm 104:3 ("you make the clouds your chariot, you ride on the wings of the wind") and Amos 4:9 (he "scourged the people with burning winds").[80] To be sure, he admitted, there is a measure of natural regularity in the world: spring follows winter, summer follows spring, and so on. But the fact that each year's seasons are different in intensity proves that God's special providence is ever determining all events. Even occurrences that seem completely fortuitous only appear that way to us. If a branch breaking off from a tree kills a passing traveler, this cannot be random, as Exodus 21:13 suggests in speaking of an "act of God." Indeed, Calvin concluded that Basil the Great was correct when he insisted that "fortune" and "chance" are pagan terms.[81]

Calvin nevertheless understood why so many people persisted in thinking that bad things happen by chance. Humans often fail to appreciate God's working in the world, either because the divine wisdom is hidden from our limited view or because divine action is always mixed up with the schemes of the devil. Even the Bible speaks of a seemingly blind "fate" (for example, in Ecclesiastes 2:14), recognizing that the human intellect is incapable of comprehending the divine orchestration of all events.[82] Calvin thus resolutely refused to call providence an empirical doctrine, as Susan Schreiner has pointed out. Purely empirical observation might just as easily lead us to the conclusion that a loving God is not in control, given the fact that the wicked often prosper while the righteous suffer. A benevolent providence can only be learned by revelation or by theological inference. Calvin based the latter on the presumed unchangeability of God's nature: just as God was in the beginning the wise Creator, he never ceases to create and uphold the creation. He "cannot forget his office," as Calvin put it.[83] Those biblical passages that speak of God's "repentance" (e.g., Genesis 6:6, where he "repents" of having created humankind) are merely an accommodation to our limited understanding and do not indicate a change of mind on God's part.[84] If God were truly changeable—if his will were truly arbitrary, like that of a human tyrant—humans would be without hope. Similarly, if the world were actually governed by blind chance, life would be intolerably frightening because of the many dangers that constantly threaten. We need not look beyond our own bodies to realize the perils we face: "Since our body is the receptacle of a thousand diseases . . . a man cannot go about unburdened by many forms of his own destruction."[85] To say that fatal illnesses or other calamities strike at random is to abandon all hope of divine justice and mercy. As Schreiner has explained, Calvin "did not fear evil in itself so much as an evil that was irrational, uncontrolled, and without purpose. Consequently, he thought it better for God to decree the 'evils' that beset us than to make human beings the victims of a blind fortune or chance under the control of no divine power."[86]

Calvin thus banished the specter of chaos, which for him was the specter of atheism. In comparison with some earlier scholastics such as Aquinas, moreover, he tried to keep God closely tethered to secondary causes, lest these become an occasion for outright denial of divine involvement in the world.[87] Yet in allowing for no contingency, Calvin paid the price that all hard providentialists have had to pay: he greatly exacerbated the problem of theodicy. Calvin's Protestant zeal to cut out the intermediaries (saints, natural processes, the human will) between an all-determining God and the individual bequeathed to his descendants a heavy apologetic burden. Its weight would be felt after every storm-wind or other "natural" disaster.

EXPLAINING XENIA: THE THEOLOGICAL AFTERMATH

In the wake of the April 3, 1974, Super Outbreak, Xenia and other hard-hit communities were sucked into the vortex of theodicy and the broader question of whether there is purpose or chaos in the universe. As in centuries past, many observers saw the sure hand of providence, though some were less reticent than Calvin had been about claiming to know the exact reasons behind God's actions. "Nothing happens in this world that is not foreseen, permitted or willed by God, and all will be to our benefit if we but do His Holy Will," a Massachusetts man wrote to the *Xenia Daily Gazette*. "Let us therefore repeat the words of holy Job: 'The Lord giveth, the Lord taketh away; blessed be the Lord.' "[88] A woman from nearby Fairborn, Ohio, claimed that girls from her town were not allowed to date boys from Xenia because it was a latter-day Sodom and Gomorrah—as God's punishment in the tornado proved.[89] Likewise, a member of the local Nazarene church saw in the tornado an angry God working through Satan: "The devil is the power of air. I believe God let it happen. The Bible says that in the last days God will pour his wrath down upon man unless he changes his ways and repents. What we've seen is nothing to what's going to happen—not necessarily a tornado, but we're living in our last days. Things are going to get worse, not better."[90]

Such opinions drew a sharp rebuttal from Jack Jordan, editor of the *Xenia Daily Gazette*, who wrote that he resented "the near-glee which some people, mostly religious fanatics afar, seek to attach to our experience. My God is a merciful God, a compassionate God who does not express such wrath; and, most certainly, I don't recognize some of these self-appointed 'prophets' who interpret 'meanings' to the April 3 tornado. They're not smarter than you or I; I don't give them the time of day."[91] Similarly, when the *Gazette* asked local clergy what they were going to say in

FIGURE 1.3. Funeral procession for a tornado victim winds through a devastated section of Xenia on April 8, 1974.
Bettmann Archive via Getty Images.

their Easter sermons (the tornado had occurred four days before Palm Sunday, the start of the Christian Holy Week leading up to Easter), to a man they accentuated the positive. Some recounted narrow escapes by people in their congregations. Howard Rickey of First Church of the Nazarene said that it was a miracle that his staff was able to get their 145 daycare children to the basement before the tornado hit the building. "Had they been upstairs," he concluded, "it would have been the greatest tragedy of the storm." Raymond Pope of Faith Community United Methodist declared that "pessimists will be cast out after the first hymn" at his church's Easter service because the tornado proved the power of the Resurrection: "I've seen the hand of God not in the tornado but in the people after the storm went by. Now people love God on a person to person basis." James Hart of Christ Episcopal Church noted the miracle that there were no fatalities among his parishioners: "That is what my people are saying. 'Thank God no one died.'" He said his Easter message would be a celebration that both his church and the town had passed from death into life. Robert Von Holle of St. Brigid Catholic Church spoke of narrowly making it to the basement of the parish house before the upper part of the building blew into the church. "Christ rose to glory after losing everything," he explained. "We will be talking about faith for the future." Jack Jordan of the *Gazette* echoed the clergy's sentiments about providential survivals: "The tornado had its miracles. . . . Two hours earlier and it could have smashed into a crowded Xenia High School plus all the other schools that were destroyed. . . . Those are miracles. And only my God makes miracles."[92]

The doctrine of providence was therefore a kind of theological Rorschach test, capable of being interpreted in either sunny or stormy ways. But black-and-white interpretations were impossible for some people, for whom the enormity of loss produced only relentlessly unanswerable questions. Polk Laffoon tells the poignant story of Ricky Fallis, whose fiancée Diane Hall was killed in the storm. When rescuers found her body buried under a giant refrigerator at the local A&W restaurant, Fallis sat down beside her body and refused to leave. For days after her funeral, he spent hours at her graveside. He visited her parents, repeatedly asking them, "Why Diane? Why couldn't it have been me instead of Diane? I'm lonely every day. I'll never love another girl as much as Diane."[93] Similarly, Mark Levine tells of two residents of Limestone County, Alabama, who experienced Job-like losses when the Super Outbreak visited that place. Walter McGlockin was a lineman for the local electric company who was called in to work when the storm began assaulting the area. He was consequently not at home when the tornado leveled the house, killing his wife and two of their four children. When Levine interviewed McGlockin three decades later, he was still paying regular visits to the cemetery where his wife and children were buried. Though he had remarried and found joy again, he confessed that the theological mystery of his loss still haunted him. "The Bible tells you that you're not supposed to question God, but I have surely wondered why God let it happen," he said. "My wife was a good person. And those two little ones, my boy and my girl, they were too young to be accountable. So why would the good Lord take them away?" Like Fallis, McGlockin also admitted to having survivor's guilt: "If I hadn't been called into work, I would have been right here. . . . If it had been me instead of my wife, she could have done a better job raising the children than I did. I tried my best, I did. But she was their mother." Annias Green, a labor organizer and pastor of Macedonia Primitive Baptist Church, was at home with his wife and three sons when the tornado hit. His wife and one son were killed. He found a strange solace in the Book of Job's non-answer to the theodicy problem: "I had to learn to depend on the Lord. I couldn't try to make sense of it on my own. I would have lost my mind. I studied Job, and I saw what he had endured. I didn't seek explanations. It can't be explained."[94]

If the tornadoes of 1974 haunted some of their victims with a dreadful un-knowability (a key trait of Rudolf Otto's numinous), they also revealed glimpses, however fleeting, of the ethical sublime theorized by Kant—the sense of moral self-determination even in the face of nature's inexorable forces.[95] Reflecting in the *Gazette* a week after the Xenia disaster, Jordan said that "the whole story will never be told—the countless heroes, the many unknown acts of sacrifice." The "economics alone may force us to forget the former petty squabbles within our ranks." He argued that Xenia had an unexpected opportunity to rebuild the community in ways that improved life for all its citizens. "Our limits, in a sense, are what we make of them," he wrote. "We also will determine how sincere our verbiage of the past week has been about pulling together." A letter-writer to the *Gazette* echoed these sentiments, calling on his fellow citizens to "break the 'normal' syndrome" and get past their differences of "Methodists and Baptists and Catholics and so on."[96] Indeed, examples of ecumenical cooperation—what one researcher called the "post-disaster utopia"[97]—were not hard to find in towns laid low by the Super Outbreak. In the Ohio River town of Brandenburg, Kentucky, clergy normally forbidden from officiating with each other (Catholic, Baptist, Methodist, and Nazarene) presided at a mass funeral for 16 victims. In Louisville, 14 congregations (including Catholics, Protestants, the Salvation Army, and Bahá'ís) forged such an unexpected bond while working together on tornado relief that they later decided to establish a permanent cooperative ministry.[98]

In Xenia, a particularly notable example of moral action was set by the Mennonite Disaster Service (MDS), founded in 1950, which dispatches Anabaptist volunteers to catastrophes nationwide. Noted Laffoon: "Mennonites are present in almost any disaster setting, and inevitably, they are the most cherished volunteers there. They seek no publicity and work tirelessly until their job is done." MDS workers, many of them carpenters, focused their efforts in Xenia on uninsured and underinsured persons, as well as the elderly and others unable to help themselves.[99] Yet even as the Mennonites brought hope, other visitors brought trouble. Swindlers, especially people posing as contractors or consultants, arrived in Xenia almost as soon as the storm passed. "A lot of them are just going to come in and start a construction business on the spot, and they don't even know how to nail two 2-by-4's together," said Joel Stronberg, director of Ohio State Legal Services.[100]

Xenia also found itself in the middle of national and local political tensions. Six days after the tornado, an embattled President Nixon paid a surprise visit, commenting that it was the worst devastation he had ever seen among the various disasters he had witnessed. Though crowds generally greeted him with polite applause, there were a few boos, and the Secret Service had to stop a woman who confronted him with shouts of "Impeach Nixon, impeach him!" Nixon tried to defuse the situation with humor: "I talked to one youngster and he asked about rebuilding his school. I asked him if he really wanted it rebuilt and he said no," the president said, laughing. "He's an exception, though. His parents would want him back in school." Ironically, the issue of rebuilding schools turned into something of a minefield for Ohio governor

FIGURE 1.4. Dennis and Mary Ann Louderback with their daughter Mindy at the foundation slab of their demolished home in Xenia, Ohio. The sign reads, "We're OK. Leave slab."
Dayton Daily News, via Cox Media Group.

John Gilligan, a Democrat, after Nixon pledged federal disaster aid to rebuild the historically black colleges Wilberforce and Central State. When Gilligan suggested in a public forum that it might make more sense to merge Central State with nearby Wright State, he was shouted down by both black and white leaders. He later said that he had been wrong.[101]

Nixon's visit highlighted the moral choices that are inevitably involved in both disaster response and prevention. Where a society chooses to spend its money can be just as consequential as any "act of God" presumed to be out of human hands. Officials at the National Oceanic and Atmospheric Administration recognized as much when they cited the case of Xenia in a call for federal funds to improve tornado warning systems. A report by the agency estimated that 1,000 schoolchildren might have been killed in Xenia if the tornado had struck during school hours. Other communities might not be so lucky, which meant that better tornado warnings and local preparedness should be top priority.[102] Scientists also called for redoubled research on tornadogenesis, or why tornadoes form. In an interview with the *New York Times*, Stanley Barnes of the National Severe Storms Laboratory in Norman, Oklahoma, acknowledged that though meteorologists understood the "big picture" of what causes tornadoes, the details remained mysterious. Concluded the *Times*, "No storm is more violent, none so little understood."[103]

POSTSCRIPT: XENIA TO CARRBORO, AUGUST 11, 2015

On the morning I visited Xenia, I discovered in front of the Greene County Historical Society a state historical marker commemorating the tornado. The sign noted the 34 lives lost and recounted how the "mile-wide tornado entered in the southwest quadrant of the city and did not leave the ground until it had demolished hundreds of homes, schools, and commercial buildings." The inscription concluded: "This marker stands directly in the path taken by the tornado and serves to remind us that 'Xenia Lives.'"

Tornadoes scar the American landscape but also hallow the ground they touch, much like the spots struck by lightning in ancient Greece. The Greeks believed that lightning, as Zeus's divine form, marked a spot as *abaton*, inviolable or inaccessible, forever given over to *Zeus Kataibates* ("he who comes down").[104] I thought of storm gods during the last leg of my 465-mile drive from Xenia to see my sister and her family in Carrboro, North Carolina. All that day, bad weather had been threatening, and by the time I reached Greensboro on Interstate 40, the bottom fell out of the sky. For the next hour, the worst of the storm appeared to follow me on the highway. The rain was so hard that my car's windshield wipers could barely keep up, and several times lightning struck unnervingly close. Traffic slowed, but not enough for the dangerous conditions. Though I could hardly see the cars in front of me, I was afraid to pull off the road. It seemed safer to keep moving ahead, however blindly.

Wherever we turn in life, Calvin wrote, things "openly menace, and seem to threaten immediate death."[105] This was especially true for people in the ancient world, who would have feared the wrath of Zeus (or Indra or Baal or Yahweh) in a thunderstorm such as I encountered. Modern meteorology has at least allowed us to see many storms coming. Since the Super Outbreak of 1974, the implementation of a nationwide network of NEXRAD, or Next-Generation Doppler Radar, has dramatically improved warning times. Radar loop images are also constantly archived on the internet, which means that amateur meteorologists can reconstruct the path of any storm. The radar archive for the Raleigh-Durham NEXRAD loop on August 11, 2015, reveals that the most intense part of the storm really did follow me as I made my way to Carrboro late that afternoon. But why does lightning strike one place and not another? Why does a tornado kill one person while leaving others—even in the same household—unscathed? These terrible questions are still as haunting today as they were in ancient times. In the next chapter, we will pick up the story of religion and violent weather in colonial America, where Christian explorers and settlers began in earnest to apply theology to the Whirlwind.

For he hath given me certain knowledge of the things that are, namely, to know how the world was made, and the operation of the elements. The beginning, ending, and midst of the times . . . the violence of winds, and the reasonings of men.

—WISDOM OF SOLOMON 7:17–18, 20

[S]o long as there is any vice at all in the universe, it will very much puzzle you anthropomorphites, how to account for it.

—DAVID HUME, *Dialogues Concerning Natural Religion*

(published posthumously, 1779)

2

"The Violence of Winds, and the Reasonings of Men"

STORMS AND PROVIDENCE IN COLONIAL AMERICA

COTTON MATHER KNEW he was special. His very name combined the surnames of New England's most illustrious Puritan families. The first of nine children of Increase Mather and Maria Cotton, he could read Latin and Greek before he entered Harvard College at age 11, the youngest student ever admitted. After completing bachelor's and master's degrees, he became co-pastor with his father of Boston's Second (North) Church, a pulpit that secured the son's status as a rising star of New England's errand into the wilderness.[1] Mather's chosenness even received supernatural confirmation when, according to his diary, an angel visited him in his study and prophesied his great works for the church of Christ.[2]

Only Cotton Mather, then, could have been so oddly singled out by a thunderstorm that arose in Boston on September 12, 1694. As he prayed aloud in his congregation before commencing his Wednesday lecture, he had a premonition: "Lay aside what you had prepared for this Auditory, speak to them on the Voice of the Glorious God in the Thunder, [and] you shall not want Assistances." Obeying this inner voice, he abandoned his notes and began to extemporize on Psalm 29:3: "The voice of the Lord is upon the waters: the God of glory thundereth." After discoursing for several minutes amid loud thunderclaps, he stated his thesis: "In the Thunder there

FIGURE 2.1. *Cotton Mather.* Engraving by Peter Pelham, 1728, the year of Mather's death. Metropolitan Museum of Art, bequest of Charles Allen Munn, 1924.

is the Voice of the Glorious God." "There is—" he continued, when a messenger interrupted him with the news that his own house had been struck by lightning. No one was hurt, but the house was badly damaged. Mather did not miss a beat. He explained to his parishioners that he would proceed with his lecture in order to model a godly unconcern for the things of this life. "I would hope that this unhappy Accident will be made Happy, at least by procuring yet more of Edge to that Attention which the Voice of God is to have with you."[3]

Mather anonymously published the text of his lecture in London in 1695, along with a companion sermon preached the following Sunday, under the title *Brontologia Sacra* (brontology is the branch of meteorology devoted to thunder). He later reprinted the lecture, attributing it to "one among us," in his *Magnalia Christi*

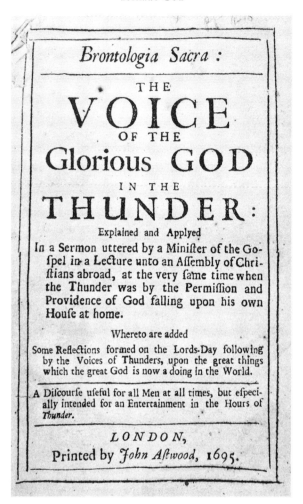

Brontologia Sacra :

THE

VOICE

OF THE

Glorious GOD

IN THE

THUNDER:

Explained and Applyed

In a Sermon uttered by a Minister of the Go-
fpel in a Lecture unto an Affembly of Chri-
ftians abroad, at the very fame time when
the Thunder was by the Permiffion and
Providence of God falling upon his own
Houfe at home.

Whereto are added

Some Reflections formed on the Lords-Day following
by the Voices of Thunders, upon the great things
which the great God is now a doing in the World.

A Difcourfe ufeful for all Men at all times, but efpeci-
ally intended for an Entertainment in the Hours of
Thunder.

LONDON,

Printed by *John Aftwood,* 1695.

FIGURE 2.2. Title page of Cotton Mather's anonymous *Brontologia Sacra* (London, 1695). Courtesy of the John Carter Brown Library.

Americana (1702).[4] But no doubt everyone in Boston knew who the author was. He expounded therein what amounted to the standard Puritan interpretation— the brontotheology—of violent weather. Though the lightning strike had been an "Accident," it nevertheless came from God. That is, though "Thunder is a Natural production" of the "Common Laws of Matter and Motion," God is still the Author and First Mover of those laws. Mather reiterated the point in the second sermon. Though there are "Natural Causes for Thunders," they are still "under the Conduct of God, the High Thunderer," for if even the hairs of our heads are numbered (Matthew 10:30), surely no thunderbolt falls without God's will. Should we therefore be afraid of a God who rains fire without warning? Not if we are in covenant with him. "As long as the Almighty Thunderer is our Own God, we need not fear that he will do us any Hurt by any of His Works," for he "will make All things work together for our Good" (Romans 8:28).[5] In the *Magnalia*, Mather added that New England had been afflicted by the "Mischiefs" done by thunderstorms more than most any place in the world. "If Things that are smitten by Lightning were to be esteemed Sacred," he noted, "this were a Sacred Countrey."[6] Yet according to Mather's own logic, the frequency of violent weather in the New World was no cause for concern for the elect followers of Christ.

Mather's *Brontologia* exemplified a recurring tension in early American theological reflections on violent weather. How could storms be acts of God but also natural events attributable to secondary causes? Deists could solve this problem by turning God into a Watchmaker, the cosmic designer who established the intricate machinery of natural laws and then let them run on their own, producing storms and other natural phenomena. But Mather was no deist. Instead, like many of his contemporaries, he took biblical assurances such as Matthew 10:30 quite literally to mean that God was actively involved in events both big and small. To deny God's hand in the lightning that struck his house was to flirt with atheism. At the same time, to deny that lightning had any "accidental" qualities entailed its own problems. For one, it ignored the apparently arbitrary aspects of nature—the meandering of rivers, the billowing of clouds, the drifting of snow. Another difficulty in attributing all weather events directly to God was that it seemed to complicate the scientific study of nature's laws. If God controlled everything, then surely he reserved the right to break his own laws at will. This threatened the reliability of any scientific theory.

On a broader level, Mather's *Brontologia* was representative of the earliest American attempts to theorize the doctrine of providence. Though the idea of divine causation in the world is thoroughly scriptural, the Bible nowhere defines providence as an abstract doctrine. In fact, apart from two occurrences in the Apocrypha (Wisdom 14:3, 17:2), the English noun *providence* appears only once in the King James Version, in Acts 24:2, and not in reference to God but to the foresight (Greek: *pronoia*) of the Roman procurator Antonius Felix. The earliest Europeans in America were nevertheless inheritors of an ancient tradition of reflection, dating to the Stoic philosophers of the fourth century BCE, on what the Latin church called *providentia*: God's providing for, or foreseeing of, all events.[7] Catholic and Protestant scholastics fleshed this out in considerable detail, and Puritan clergy such as Mather were fluent in this scholasticism. Yet in early America, which lacked the Old World's well-developed academic infrastructure, theological debates over providence were never far removed from popular religion. Intellectuals like Mather typically expounded doctrine not in the university lecture hall, but from the pulpit. They shared with their parishioners a common currency of biblical imagery, folk beliefs, and the language of an emerging Enlightenment, which they drew on selectively to explain what they observed in the world. These traditions all contributed to the providential assumptions held by clergy and laypeople alike.

The other key ingredient was the weather. Few things in life better captured the difficulties of an all-encompassing providence than the capriciousness of lightning, hail, blizzards, whirlwinds, and other meteorological phenomena. Though Americans during the colonial period were still devising a vocabulary to talk about indigenous storms—the word *tornado* rarely appears until the nineteenth century—the weather played a considerable role in debates about providence. These colonial debates set the parameters of American understandings of providence for the next 200 years. Only in the mid-twentieth century would some thinkers stray significantly outside of those boundaries. Even in the twenty-first century, many Americans still think about life's storms (meteorological and otherwise) in terms similar to those used by the fraternity of colonial clergy. "The violence of winds, and the reasonings of men": the phrase from the King James Apocrypha still resonates, even if the language is archaically patriarchal. The connection between weather and theological reasoning remains inseparable, driven as it is by the seemingly endless need to explain.

WORLDS OF WONDER

All of the earliest Europeans in America inhabited worlds of wonder. As Alexandra Walsham has observed, providential beliefs cut across the invisible iron curtain between Catholics and Protestants, as both scrutinized natural phenomena for moral messages. A lightning strike, a disastrous flood, a withering drought: all were presumed to be warnings or omens that the devout dared not ignore. Moreover, as we have seen, people assumed that prayers, fasts, or other formulae could sometimes avert meteorological disaster. Popular rituals related to the weather did not die with the Reformation, but often persisted in changed forms or contexts.[8] Nevertheless, in one critical respect, providence became a starker doctrine among Protestants. Whereas in a Catholic universe the saints functioned as mediators and buffers between the individual and an all-determining God, Protestantism cut out the intermediaries. When confronted with mortal danger, Catholics could call on a host of helpers as well as a sacramental system in which masses and pilgrimages or other acts of penance were thought to have a kind of automatic efficacy. Protestants faced God alone.

Catholics relied on holy helpers in their earliest forays into the New World. In February 1493, Christopher Columbus was sailing home aboard the *Niña* after his first voyage to America when he spotted lightning to the northeast. He lowered the sails and went under bare poles most of the night, hoping the storm would pass.

But the next day, the winds increased and the "sea became terrible," as Bartolomé de las Casas wrote in his abstract of Columbus's diary. That night, amid raging winds, Columbus lost contact with the *Pinta*, his signal lights proving futile. After daybreak, with the wind growing worse, he ordered that lots be drawn for a pilgrimage to the most important Marian shrine in Castile, Our Lady of Guadalupe in Extremadura. He directed the crew to count out as many chickpeas as there were men on the ship and mark one of the peas with a cross. The lot fell to Columbus himself, who vowed to make the pilgrimage if they survived the storm. Later, all the men vowed that as soon as they reached the first land, they would go in procession in shirtsleeves to offer prayers at the nearest church dedicated to the Virgin. To these pledges, Columbus added anguished reflections in his diary about whether the storm was due to his "small faith and loss of confidence in Divine Providence." Ultimately, the *Niña* reached safety at Santa Maria Island in the Azores, where the men kept their vow to pray at the local Marian shrine. A month later, after the *Niña* and the *Pinta* both made it back to Spain on the same day via separate routes, Columbus traveled to Extremadura to fulfill his own vow.[9]

Another Catholic example, and one of the earliest involving a tornado, comes from the Jesuit mission at Sault St. Louis (Kahnawake), Quebec, in 1683. On a midnight in August, "all the monsters of hell" were unleashed against the mission in the form of a "whirlwind" [*tourbillon de vent*], which destroyed the chapel. Yet the "statue of the Blessed Virgin, which was at an elevation of eleven feet, was simply overturned."[10] Even more miraculously, Father Claude Chauchetière and two other Jesuits who were in the chapel at the time survived without life-threatening injuries. Comparing notes, they discovered that each of them had gone to pray earlier that evening at the nearby tomb of Catherine (Kateri) Tekakwitha, a Mohawk convert to Christianity whose exemplary life had made her a revered figure. This was actually the second meteorological miracle attributed to Tekakwitha's influence. Three years earlier, the oak tree next to the chapel had been struck by lightning but the chapel was left unscathed. Chauchetière credited both deliverances to Tekakwitha, whom he believed to have been a saint. Few formal canonizations took place in the seventeenth and eighteenth centuries, and Tekakwitha's cause fell into obscurity until modern times.[11] She was finally canonized by Pope Benedict XVI in 2012.

Most Protestants—especially the Calvinists of New England, who had so vehemently repudiated the cult of the saints—recognized no mediator save Christ himself, the "one mediator between God and men" (1 Timothy 2:5). Zealous Protestants also stripped away or diminished the sacramental system, which had continually reinfused Catholics with grace when their faith in providence flagged, as in the case of Columbus. The phenomena of nature conveyed God's mercy or judgment directly,

FIGURE 2.3. *Kateri Tekakwitha*, by the Jesuit missionary Claude Chauchetière, circa 1696. St. Francis Xavier Mission, Kahnawake, Québec.

apart from human intercessors. Thus in 1643, when a possible tornado "lifted up" the meetinghouse at Newbury, Massachusetts, while worshippers were inside, Bay Colony governor John Winthrop noted in his journal that "through God's great mercy it did not hurt [anyone], but only killed one Indian with the fall of a tree."[12] Winthrop recorded numerous weather-related providences in his journal, beginning with the 1630 passage to the New World, when a fast was kept aboard the *Arbella* to solicit God's help amid "continual storms and rain." A month later, a "very great tempest" battered the ship, and though "the sea raged and tossed us exceedingly; yet, through God's mercy, we were very comfortable, and few or none sick, but had op-portunity to keep the Sabbath, and Mr. [George] Phillips preached twice that day."[13]

In the subsequent history of the colony, Winthrop described meteorological events (or individuals' deliverances therefrom) with repeated superlatives: "special," "wonderful," "miraculous," "great," and "good" providences.[14] Puritans typically took for granted that the more pious a person or society, the less harm they would suffer from violent weather. But the relationship did not always hold. In December 1638, the day after a general fast, "so great a tempest of wind and snow . . . as had not been since our time" killed at least 11 people and did extensive damage. This awful providence led "some of our ministers to stir us up to seek the Lord better, because he seemed to discountenance the means of reconciliation." On the advice of the elders, the General Court then agreed to call another fast day "and to seek further into the causes" of the Lord's "displeasure."[15] Such was the potential terror of providence for Protestants, for whom no fast or other penitential ritual, no sacrament or priestly absolution, was thought automatically capable of reconciling the faithful to the Almighty, whose intentions sometimes remained hidden.[16]

Yet the absoluteness of the Puritan doctrine of providence was, in its own strange way, a comfort because it banished the specter of randomness. Everything was part of a plan, even if that plan was not fully understood. Among the Puritan clergy, the lodestar of this absolutist providentialism was the passage cited earlier by Cotton Mather, Matthew 10:30 ("the very hairs of your head are all numbered") along with the preceding verse attesting that not a sparrow shall fall apart from the Father's will.[17] For the English Puritan Richard Sibbes (1577–1635), the passage proved that "God's providence extends to every particular thing."[18] Likewise, the later English Puritan Stephen Charnock (1628–1680) declared that God "numbers the very hairs of our heads, [so] that not one falls without his Will."[19] In America, Increase Mather regarded the verses as conclusive evidence that "there is nothing comes to pass in the Earth, but what was first determined by a wise decree in Heaven."[20] He invoked the text again amid a massive snowstorm, declaring to his congregation that "there is not a Flake of snow that falls on the Ground without the hand of God."[21] His fellow Boston minister Samuel Willard (1640–1707), who served the last six years of his life as acting president of Harvard, also directed his parishioners to the passage, arguing that it showed that God was not only the universal creator but also the particular cause of all things, great and small.[22]

For the Puritan ministers, the idea that God controlled every snowflake, every raindrop, was not a mere intellectual postulate but the basis for a providence-centered spirituality. A classic exponent was the English Puritan John Flavel (1630–1691). Like John Calvin, Flavel cautioned against excessive prying into the "secrets" of providence, a sin to which "Holy Job" fell prey.[23] But Flavel proceeded to pry into those very secrets in his *Divine Conduct: or, the Mysterie of Providence* (1678), which he billed as a method of "improving" (by which Puritans meant applying the lessons of) providences in one's own life. In his manual, reprinted at least eight times before 1800, Flavel counseled readers that since the providences in their lives were "more in number than the hairs of your heads," anything that happened might have moral significance.[24] In occurrences both dramatic and mundane, one could discern mercies or judgments from God. Christians had an obligation to understand these messages, not only for the improvement of their own conduct but to render God due praise for his blessings and corrections. Flavel even recommended a retrospective cataloguing of events, advising his readers to "search backward" though their lives for God's many interventions. Sometimes an incident's significance would become evident only upon repeated meditation. He cited as proof 1 Kings 18:43–45, where the prophet Elijah commands his servant to look to the sky for rain; when the servant sees nothing, Elijah tells him to look seven more times, whereupon he finally discerns a cloud rising out of the sea. "So you may look upon some Providences once and again, and see little or nothing in them," but eventually "you shall see its increasing glory, like that increasing cloud." Repeated examination would also make clear the "seasonableness" of many providences, or how they often came just in the nick of time, when all hope seemed to be lost.[25]

A timely extrication from danger was not hard to see as heaven-sent, though misfortunes too could fit into a providential scheme. Historian Keith Thomas has noted the "self-confirming" quality of providence, in which hardships could alternatively be interpreted as punishments of the wicked or tests of the godly. "There was no way in which the theory once accepted could be faulted," Thomas wrote.[26] The elasticity of providence rested on the assumption that all things happened for a logical reason. Flavel contended, for example, that afflictions are invariably caused by sin, as proved by Numbers 32:23 ("be sure your sin will find you out"). He explained that one common sin is security, or growing too comfortable before God. Such conduct is liable to bring some "rouzing, startling Providence" to shake a person's overconfidence. He conceded that God does not chastise "every sin with a rod," but this was his "usual way." "If we would carefully search out the seeds and principles of those miseries under which we or ours do groan," he insisted, "we should find them to be our own turnings aside from the Lord."[27]

THE WEATHER AND SECOND CAUSES

A problem still nagged, however, in any explanation of providence. Was there no contingency in the world—events that could fall out one way or another, apart from any moral reason or divine plan? Few things illustrated the difficulty more aptly than the weather. If isolated rain showers fell on adjacent farms on successive afternoons, was there any reason one farm received water on the first day and the other farm on the second? Or more to the point, if a pious man's crops withered in a drought but a wicked man's enjoyed plentiful rain, might this indicate that some events lack a moral purpose? One could always argue that the Lord was testing the pious man, but even the Bible seemed to suggest that this was not always the case, for God "maketh his sun to rise on the evil and on the good, and sendeth rain on the just and on the unjust," as Jesus taught in the Sermon on the Mount (Matthew

all things "come to pass immutably and infallibly" according to God's foreknowledge and decree, he nevertheless "ordereth them to fall out, according to the nature
of second causes." That said, the confession added that though God usually works
through the "means" of second causes, he is "free to work without, above, and against
them, at his pleasure." The document also stated unequivocally that God "doth uphold, direct, dispose, and govern all creatures, actions, and things, from the greatest
even to the least," and cited the go-to passage, Matthew 10:29–30.[33] The notion of
a God constantly intervening in creation loomed especially large in the 1650s after
the Puritan Oliver Cromwell overthrew the British monarchy and ruled England as
Lord Protector. Cromwell was inclined to see everything, from the weather to his
own military victories, as God's special favor. "When Cromwell's ships went forth
on God's behalf," writes historian Blair Worden, "the strength and the direction of
the wind, however unexceptionable, were divinely ordained."[34]

The Restoration in 1660 brought a swift backlash against the perceived excesses
of Puritan providentialism.[35] Anglican priest John Spencer (1630–1693), a scholar
of Hebrew at Cambridge, criticized the "rashness" of those who interpreted every
strange event as a supernatural prodigy or omen. A proper understanding of
second causes would banish superstition like "the shadows of the twilight before
the approaching beams of knowledg[e]" or like a man who leads a horse past something that startles it. Similarly, Thomas Sprat (1635–1713), the Anglican bishop of
Rochester, declared it "a disgrace to the Reason, and honor of mankind" that every
Puritan could claim the power to interpret special providences "though he be never
so ignorant of the very common Works of Nature, that lye under his Feet."[36] Such
latitudinarian sentiments would eventually surface on the other side of the Atlantic
as clergy like Boston's Benjamin Colman (1673–1747) and even Cotton Mather
spoke increasingly of the regularity of natural laws.[37]

But at what point did the "machinery of second causes," to quote historian Perry
Miller, risk becoming mere machinery? Second causes softened the hard edges of
providence in allowing not only for natural laws but also for a measure of contingency in the effects produced by those laws. Yet if those contingencies were nothing
more than pure, random chance, this raised the specter that no wise Superintendent
directed the machinery of second causes, a possibility that post-Restoration Puritans
found profoundly troubling. Thus, in England, Stephen Charnock, writing in the
1680s, cautioned that God "never left second causes to straggle and operate in a
Vagabond way."[38] In America, Samuel Willard, writing not long after, warned that
though "there is a Contingency in things with respect to Second Causes," it is blas-
phemy to say that anything is "meerly Casual" in reference to God. Willard feared
that the devil was tempting people to deny providential assumptions once taken

for granted: "If he can bring us to Dispute against Providence, he knows that our Religion doth soon come to an End."[39]

By the early eighteenth century, laments among American clergy about the alleged atheism lurking behind second causes had become a veritable chorus.[40] "When Stormy Winds happen," complained Increase Mather, "men are apt to impute it to Second Causes only, to the Disposition of the Air, the Season of the Year, of the Influence of the Constellations in Heaven, but we should look higher than the Stars when such things come to pass."[41] Cotton Mather adopted the same line when a fierce gale struck Massachusetts Bay in February 1723, producing floods in several towns. "Stop not at Second Causes," he urged his parishioners. "Let the Faith of the Operation of God, lun [lown or calm] the Storm." Mather did not shrink from the conclusion that just as God had the power to calm the storm, he also produced its destructive effects, for the Lord said "I make peace, and create evil" (Isaiah 45:7).[42] Mather died in 1728, and Jonathan Edwards (1703–1758) soon eclipsed him as New England's greatest theologian. Edwards echoed Mather's points in a fast-day sermon. The God who is angry with us for our sins "has all second causes in his hands," Edwards warned. "Let it be considered what God says; . . . 'I make peace, I create evil.'" Preaching on another fast day a few years later, Edwards charged that people "are not wont to look at the hand of God in things that happen, neither do they realize any such thing as a providence. They look no further than second causes."[43]

Given the clergy's constant admonitions not to stop at second causes, it is no wonder that laypeople expressed the same concern. Sarah Osborn (1714–1796), a devout evangelical who led revival meetings in her home in Newport, Rhode Island, testified in her diary of her trust in God's foreknowledge, power, and sovereignty "while some others' eyes are upon second causes." A few years later, after a "terrible tempest," she prayed: "O God, let not sinners remain secure, taking no notice of the signs of thy coming or ascribing them all to natural causes till thou come on them as a thief in the night, unlooked for."[44] Another evangelical diarist, Esther Edwards Burr (1732–1758), daughter of Jonathan Edwards, confessed related worries during a severe cold snap in Newark, New Jersey. Though the "present thretnings of heaven" ought to have turned people's thoughts to God, "the love of even Gods own Children waxes Cold," she lamented, noting that "my fingers are so numb that I cant write any more." Later that year, amid a "very hard Thunder," she bewailed her own "unfruitfulness" and prayed that people would not forget the Lord. "There is something very solemn in the sound of Thunder," she observed, adding that the description of it in the "37 chapter of Job is extreamly Natureal, and striking." "I don't think it is half so elegantly painted by any [other] poet."[45]

SINNERS IN THE HANDS OF AN ANGRY (STORM) GOD

Osborn and Burr's fear that New Englanders would reap the whirlwind for neglecting God illustrates another enduring theme of early American readings of violent weather: divine judgment. The indigenous climate undoubtedly heightened the sense that God was expressing his wrath meteorologically. The earliest European observers commented on the extremes of American weather—colder winters, hotter summers, and a wider variety of dramatic *meteors* (the term, dating back to Aristotle, for any sublunar, or atmospheric, phenomena).[46] To be sure, dramatic weather was not unknown in the Old World, though the terminology to describe it remained fluid throughout the colonial period. William Fulke, for example, explained how "a whyrlewynde" (a tornado) would suck up "bothe men and beastes" and then "neglygently letteth them fall from a great heyght." John Goad (1616–1689), an English Catholic and another early writer on meteorology, noted that storms, be they "Ordinary or Prodigious," are "known amongst us by the names of Spouts, Huracans, Tornados, Travados, &c."[47] But the greater severity of storms of the New World left early observers both fascinated and aghast. After satisfying the urge to describe these phenomena, sometimes in quasi-scientific detail, Americans inevitably fell back on the timeworn religious explanation that the storms were the product of human sin and God's (or Satan's) wrath.

The descriptive urge was on full display in Increase Mather's *Essay for the Recording of Illustrious Providences* (1684), which included a vivid account of a destructive tornado (a "Whirl-wind") at Cambridge, Massachusetts, in 1680. Drawing on two eyewitness reports, Mather noted the "great rushing noise of the Wind," which drowned out the sound of large trees crashing. As the funnel moved upon the ground, it was "filled with Stones, Bushes, Boughs, and other things that it had taken up from the Earth, so that the top and the sides of the Cloud seemed like a green Wood." John Robbins, "a Servant Man," was "suddenly slain," with "many Bones broken by the violence" of the wind.[48] Mather refrained from theological commentary, but as he was preparing his *Essay*, he invoked the same incident in a sermon, this time making clear that God's wrath was the cause. "Hath not the Lord been marching through the Land in Indignation?" he asked his parishioners. "Was it not so two years ago . . . when one that stood in the way of that Whirlewind of the Lord, was dashed to death in a moment?" God conveys either his mercy or his judgment through prodigies in the world, Mather argued, but lately the judgments seemed to come more frequently. Do not forget, he warned, that God has infinite power to execute his wrath: "He that by a word's speaking, made the World, is able by the breath of his Mouth to annihilate any Creature."[49]

Two decades later, advancing age had not tempered the 64-year-old Mather's zeal for meteorological jeremiad when news arrived of an unusually severe extratropical cyclone in England. Subsequently known as the Great Storm of 1703, it spawned consternation on both sides of the Atlantic. High winds toppled some 2,000 chimneys and church spires. The bishop of Bath and Wells was crushed in bed with his wife when their chimney fell through the ceiling. In London, damage was said to rival that caused by the Great Fire of 1666. Some 120 people died on land, but thousands more died at sea.[50] Mather seized upon the event for a sermon at Boston's Second Church. Taking as his text Psalm 148:8 ("stormy wind fulfilling his word"), he stated a familiar doctrine: "There is a Providence of the God of Heaven, in whatsoever Storms fall upon Men on the Earth." This time, though, he was more explicit about the reason for storms, which he identified as part of the curse that the first man's disobedience brought upon the world. "If Adam had not Sinned," Mather declared, there would have been "no hurtful storms known on the earth." Though sometimes tempests reveal God's mercy, as when a hailstorm killed many Canaanites who were fighting Israel, storms "for the most part" come for correction and judgment. Scripture often expresses God's anger in meteorological terms. Thus, Jeremiah 23:19: "A whirlwind of the Lord is gone forth in fury"; and Ezekiel 13:13: "I will even rend it with a stormy wind in my fury." The Bible attests, moreover, that "Stormy Winds do not come of themselves" but only as God directs them (Psalm 107:25: "He commandeth, and raiseth the stormy wind"). Mather concluded on an ominous note: "God can soon do to Boston, as He has done to London." When people are complacent, "sudden destruction cometh upon them" (1 Thessalonians 5:3). "Therefore beware of Security, which brings unexpected Storms."[51]

Mather was hardly alone in reading violent storms as tokens of divine judgment. In February 1717, back-to-back blizzards dumped up to six feet of snow in parts of New England. Drifts as high as 25 feet buried houses. Countless livestock perished, and the deer population was reduced by an estimated 90 percent. In the middle of the second storm, Eliphalet Adams (1677–1753) held forth from the pulpit of First Church, New London, Connecticut. He took as his text Nahum 1:3: "The Lord hath his way in the whirlwind and in the storm, and the clouds are the dust of his feet." This is true in both the metaphorical and the literal sense, Adams averred, for storms do not merely symbolize God's wrath but are divinely directed instruments of it. "With what Pomp and Majesty doth the Lord Come forth of his place to Execute Judgment on a Sinful People!" he declared. Adams then described how a tornado (a "Whirlwind") is produced by "the meeting of two Opposite winds which prevent Each others passage and are therefore Necessarily both of them carried Sideways in a circular motion." The storm makes "dreadful havock while it lasts," and its immense force and suddenness are aptly expressed by Jeremiah 30:23 ("Behold, the whirlwind

of the Lord goeth forth with fury"). Though wind, hail, rain, and snow all have natural causes, the Lord has his way in them: "they rage within the bounds of his permission only and they are hushed again at his bidding." The sole apparent proof to
the contrary, 1 Kings 19:11 ("the Lord was not in the wind"), refers only to the fact
that God did not speak to the prophet Elijah "by any Distinct Voice in that Wind,
as he did afterwards." But God is still the "Author, Causer, and Producer thereof."[52]

Eighteen years later, when lightning struck the New London meetinghouse,
killing one man and wounding a number of others, Adams again defended the prop-
osition that storms are a divine judgment, though this time he was more sensitive
to the charge that this made God seem arbitrary or harsh. For proof otherwise, he
pointed to his chosen text, Psalm 65:5 ("By terrible things in righteousness wilt thou
answer us, O God of our salvation"). God does indeed manifest himself in terrible
things, he explained, but instead of questioning his righteousness we should stand in
awe. While all people are sinners and deserve punishment, the Lord does not always
"observe a Mathematical proportion, in ordering out an equal Degree of Sorrow to
an equal Degree of Sin: That is reserved to the great & final Judgment." As for why
the lightning struck Adams's own church, he chided those who would "[c]ensure us
as greater Sinners than Ordinary," for as Matthew 7:1 warns, "judge not, that ye be
not judged."[53]

It was a common Puritan refrain, though one not always heeded: judge not—
especially not God. Jonathan Edwards had cautioned his flock on this point a few
years earlier. "It is not a thing a little provoking to the Most High, to have his justice called into question. They that sow the wind shall reap the whirlwind." Those
who think they know better than God are liable to be struck down suddenly. It is
no coincidence, Edwards claimed, that lightning typically strikes high things such
as towers and spires, for this "may signify that heaven is an enemy to all proud persons." Yet death need not befall a person by stroke of lightning but may happen in
thousands of unforeseen ways: "the least wrong turn of the foot, a slip of the hand, a
little mistake." That sudden deaths do not result in every case proves God's constant
government of the universe.[54]

Some laypeople absorbed this stark message a bit too well. In Newport, Rhode
Island, Sarah Osborn's friend Susanna Anthony (1726–1791) confessed in her diary
that "my fear and dread of thunder is so great, that I find no rest." She became convinced that Satan was stoking her fears in order to shake her confidence in God's providential care for her soul. Only after she struggled with this anxiety for years—"*God
be merciful to me a sinner*, was my prayer"—did lightning lose its power to terrify
her.[55] Meanwhile, the Quaker diarist Ann Cooper Whitall (1716–1797) expressed a
different kind of worry: that violent weather was not scaring people enough. When
a severe windstorm nearly blew down her home in New Jersey ("such a storm I never

FIGURE 2.4. *Jonathan Edwards*, by Joseph Badger, circa 1750, when Edwards was around 47.
Yale University Art Gallery, bequest of Eugene Phelps Edwards.

saw"), she lamented: "Oh, is it not enough to make every one tremble when we don't know but every minute will be the last? But as soon as it is over, then to laugh and mischief again! Oh, oh, what will make the world to leave wickedness!"[56]

Apart from concern for moral reformation, what seemed to unite most colonial observers, both laity and clergy, was the opinion that the Lord was at work in every storm. Anthony professed her belief that "my God gave each clap of thunder its commission." Eliphalet Adams assured his congregation that "even when Storms and tempests are raised by Satan . . . they are still under God's Ordering and Government. And no more Damage shall be done thereby than he is pleased to permit." Esther Burr testified to the Almighty's power after a violent tornado ("the most Tirrable Whirlwind that was ever known this side of the West Indies") hit West Orange, New Jersey. She and her husband, the Rev. Aaron Burr, Sr., president of the College of New Jersey (Princeton University), rode out to see the damage. "Twas truly an awfull sight, a Number of Houses torn to pieces, a vast many dammaged . . . not a Tree lef standing," she wrote in her diary. Yet through God's "aboundent Mercy" not one life was lost. "Mr. Burr was so affected with it that he concluded to preach somthing to the purpose and accordingly yesterday he preached all day from those words in the first of Nahum the 3rd verse." It was the same verse that Adams and other preachers cited as evidence of divine sovereignty: "The Lord hath his way in the whirlwind and in the storm."[57]

Even secular newspapers were unabashed in the conviction that storms brought divine judgments mixed with occasional mercies. A striking example is the coverage of the tornado outbreak that occurred in New England in August 1787 as the nation's founders were meeting in the Constitutional Convention in Philadelphia. The most dramatic of the twisters hit Wethersfield, Connecticut, on August 15. "Too much gratitude cannot be expressed by the inhabitants to that Being, who has his way in the whirlwind and the storm, that it passed a line where the least possible damage should be sustained," declared the *Connecticut Courant*, echoing Nahum 1:3.[58] Similarly, when another tornado took the roof off a home in Oakham, Massachusetts, but left the family inside only cut and bruised, a writer to the *Worcester Magazine* opined: "Is not a tribute of praise, for continual preserving mercy, due to him who has not only his way in the great deep, but also in the mighty winds?"[59] But the storms were anything but a mercy to other residents. The Wethersfield tornado, a "black column" of "undescribable horrour," took direct aim at the home of Wait Robbins, whose wife fled the house with their baby in her arms only to be hurled backward by the force of the winds. The infant survived but the mother and two other children were mortally wounded. The *Courant* concluded its report by reflecting on divine wrath: "The man of seriousness will consider that the voice of such providences is the voice of God, awfully denouncing his anger, and calling to consideration." Likewise the *Worcester Magazine* observed: "Who can stand the fury of him, who holds the winds in his fist?"[60] In succeeding issues, as more reports from the outbreak came in, the magazine continued to marvel at the storm's fury: "Where its force was collected within the smallest compass, its violence was almost incredible." The atmosphere was "tortured and convulsed, in a manner which defies description."[61] The magazine's editors also reflected further on the meaning of the storm, oddly blending the language of the Enlightenment, which cast the wrathful God of scripture as superstitious, with a tacit embrace of the notion that storms are divine punishment for sin. "It is a useful superstition which ascribes these events immediately to the displeasure of the Deity, if it produces a reformation in the manners of mankind," the editors wrote. "Indeed, however we may be touched with pity for the affliction of our brethren, we cannot but perceive how much it proceeds from their own misconduct."[62] The magazine did not specify of what misconduct the victims had been guilty.

The assumption that God sent his winds to punish iniquity was still evident in the last decade of the eighteenth century when an apparent squall line killed some 30 people, many of them on pleasure boats, in Philadelphia and New York on Sunday, July 1, 1792. An anonymous poem on a broadside attributed the deaths to divine anger over Sabbath-breaking. "A warning great and solemn call / To keep God's Sabbaths one and all," declared the poem, which added regarding the victims, "Not scarce had time one word to say, / Or to their God for mercy pray." Seven years later, when a tornado hit Bozrah, Connecticut, another anonymous writer used the occasion to polemicize against all who would exclude an angry God from the picture. Though some scientific "discoveries have lately been made in the doctrine of Winds," the writer noted, people should beware of hasty appeals to natural causes that discounted "Him who is the only and great first Cause." "Are there any among us," the writer asked, "who are so bewitched with the stupid Philosophy of modern days, as to deny the Being of a *GOD!*" The late "desolations," far from being a "thing of chance," were the "scourges of Heaven sent to instruct and reform Mankind." The "reflecting man" must acknowledge that such admonitions "command profound and reverential awe."[63]

BIBLICAL TEMPLATES

The ubiquitous talk of divine judgment tempered with mercies reflected the way in which colonial Americans used religion (in this case, the biblical ethic of retributive justice) to understand the weather. But Americans also used the weather to understand religion. Particularly in times of heightened religious fervor, they drew on a storehouse of meteorological imagery from scripture to describe the feeling of all-consuming divine power (what Rudolf Otto dubbed "numinous" experience).[64] Laypeople were conversant in this imagery not only because of their own devotional Bible-reading, but also because meteorological tropes loomed so large in the clergy's rhetorical arsenal.

Weather imagery is especially prominent in the context of Protestant revivalism. The Great Awakening of the 1730s and 1740s was part of a century-long series of revivals in which laypeople were seized with religious ecstasy or overcome with the feeling that the End was nigh. People often cast these experiences in terms of two weather-related templates—two winds from the New Testament. In the story of Pentecost, the spirit of God comes suddenly as the sound of a "rushing mighty wind" (Acts 2:2), overwhelming the apostles gathered at Jerusalem with the ecstatic ability to speak in tongues. Later, as the End Time scenario unfolds in the Apocalypse, God's wrath is briefly kept at bay when four angels hold back "the four winds of the earth" (Revelation 7:1). The empowering wind of Pentecost and the destroying wind of the Apocalypse alternated with each other in the colonial religious imagination, reinforcing the primal connection between weather and the experience of the divine.

Acts 2:2 reverberates in a number of accounts of revivalistic ecstasy. Observers of an awakening at Portsmouth, New Hampshire, in 1741 said that the divine presence "came down . . . like a mighty rushing Wind," touching people "young & old, Rich and poor, White & black." Missionary David Brainerd (1718–1747) recorded in his diary the day in 1745 when, as he was preaching to the Indians, "the power of God seemed to descend upon the assembly 'like a rushing mighty wind,' and with an astonishing energy bore down all before it." In the 1760s, Jacob Johnson (1713–1797) described a resurgence of religion on Long Island, where the Holy Spirit came down "as a mighty rushing wind, almost as glorious as on the day of pentecost." Another account from the same revival attested that the Holy Ghost "came down as a mighty rushing Wind; sometimes almost as sudden as a Flashing of Lightning." The evangelical Anglican Devereux Jarratt (1733–1801) recounted that at a meeting in his Virginia parish in 1776, "the power of the Lord came down on the Assembly, like a rushing, mighty wind."[65]

But even as the wind of Pentecost awakened listeners to the power of the Spirit, the four winds of the Apocalypse also threatened to destroy the unregenerate. Increase Mather declared to his congregation in 1684 that "four Winds of Heaven are striving upon the great Sea" and that there would soon be "Overturnings, Overturnings, Overturnings" as God unleashed "the most fearful and amazing Vials of wrath" upon New England's enemies.[66] A half century later, in 1735, Jonathan Edwards invoked the same passage to warn his listeners that God might be about to unleash the four winds of his wrath against New England itself because of the "dying of vital religion." Similarly, at the height of the Great Awakening, Edwards warned that "the four winds are going to be let loose upon this part of the earth" and that listeners should take care, lest they be caught without the seal of God on their foreheads.[67] In his most famous sermon, "Sinners in the Hands of an Angry God," Jonathan Edwards mixed wind imagery ("The sovereign pleasure of God for the present stays his rough wind") with the metaphor of an arrow to convey the righteousness of God's affliction of sinners: "The bow of God's wrath is bent, and the arrow made ready on the string, and Justice bends the arrow at your heart." Now was the last opportunity to turn from wickedness and take advantage of God's mercy. At any moment, his apocalyptic wrath could "rush forth with inconceivable fury."[68]

As ways of thinking and talking about conversion, pentecostal and apocalyptic winds became part of a Protestant religious vernacular that would endure long past the colonial period.[69] Both images stressed God's sudden intervention in the lives of individuals, an idea that would only be reinforced every time a natural disaster occurred. Douglas Winiarski has shown that colonists flocked to the churches in droves after an earthquake struck New England on October 29, 1727. In Haverhill, Massachusetts, where church admissions earlier in the 1720s had hovered around 10 persons per year, an astounding 202 people joined the parish in the 12 months after the quake. Cotton Mather commented approvingly on the upsurge in piety across the colony, noting that nobody slept in the pews anymore: "'Tis a Congregation of *Hearers*, that I am this Time speaking to."[70] Like a tornado, the earthquake made the winds of apocalypse seem not just metaphorical but frighteningly real, and the spike in church attendance was the tangible pentecost that followed.

Important as pentecostal and apocalyptic winds were to the rhythms of colonial piety, however, they were only a small part of the cornucopia of biblical-meteorological imagery from which individuals drew. New Englanders in particular were a literate, proof-texting people, as the laity's conversion narratives and the clergy's sermons reveal.[71] Quotations of scripture from the pulpit were especially influential in creating a richly biblical idiom, resonant in the cadences of King James English. We have already seen some of the recurring verses. Increase Mather's two-part sermon on the Great Storm of 1703, printed on 58 small (duodecimo) pages, refers to at least 120 different passages of scripture, many of them meteorological, including the following: "stormy wind fulfilling his word" (Psalm 148:8); "a mighty tempest in the sea" (Jonah 1:4); "a great wind from the wilderness" (Job 1:18); "his way in the whirlwind and in the storm" (Nahum 1:3); "fly upon the wings of the wind" (Psalm 18:10); "with storm and tempest" (Isaiah 29:6); "whirlwind of the Lord" (Jeremiah 23:19); "a tempest of hail and a destroying storm" (Isaiah 28:2); "the great rain of his strength" (Job 37:6); "stayeth his rough wind" (Isaiah 27:8); "very tempestuous round about him" (Psalm 50:3); and "tossed with tempest" (Isaiah 54:11).[72]

Hymns were another conduit not only of biblical-meteorological imagery, but also of a broadly providential theology. The most important source of early American hymnody was the English Nonconformist Isaac Watts (1674–1748). As Stephen Marini has noted, Watts devised a "new poetics of worship" with his metered paraphrases of psalms and other religious verse designed to be set to hymn tunes.[73] Several hymns in his most popular collections center on starkly meteorological notions of divine power. In a paraphrase of Psalm 148, in his first compilation, *Horae Lyricae* (1706), Watts drew on the biblical figure of Yahweh as Cloud Rider who commands the elements:

Winds, ye shall bear his Name aloud
Thro' the Ethereal Blue,
For when his Chariot is a Cloud,
He makes his Wheels of you.

Thunder and Hail, and Fires and Storms,
The Troops of his Command,
Appear in all your dreadful Forms,
And speak his awful Hand.[74]

In his next collection, *Hymns and Spiritual Songs* (1707), published in 47 American
editions before 1800, "God the Thunderer!—Or, The Last Judgment and Hell"
again depicts the Almighty as the Cloud Rider whose "Nostrils breathe out fiery
Streams" and whose "Thunder roars along." A footnote added that Watts composed
the text during a sudden thunderstorm. Finally, in his most popular compilation,
Psalms of David, Imitated (1719), which received 99 American editions before 1800,
paraphrases of Psalms 29 and 135 portray divine theophanies in blazing lightning
and roaring thunder. The second hymn adds: "He pours the Rain, he brings the
Wind, / And Tempest from his airy Store."[75]

By the latter half of the eighteenth century, American hymnody was moving beyond its Calvinist roots in Watts as the upstart Methodists took the frontier by
storm. Chief among Methodist hymn writers was the English divine Charles Wesley
(1707–1788), who founded the movement with his brother John (1703–1791). One
of Charles's most memorable hymns, "Jesu, Lover of my Soul," first published in
1740, opens with storm imagery. Though John included the hymn in the movement's
early anthologies, he deleted it from later collections, judging it "too sentimental."
But that did not prevent it from remaining the second-most reprinted number in
American hymnals until 1960. The opening stanza reads:

Jesu, Lover of my Soul,
Let me to Thy Bosom fly,
While the nearer Waters roll,
While the Tempest still is high:
Hide me, O my Saviour, hide,
Till the Storm of Life is past:
Safe into the Haven guide;
O receive my Soul at last.[76]

In counterpoint to Watts's emphasis on God as the almighty Thunderer who
causes the storm, here God (incarnate in Jesus) provides shelter from the storm.
The counterpoint has biblical warrant. It occurs, for example, in Psalm 46, which
proclaims that "God is our refuge and strength" (v. 1) even while crediting him for
the "desolations he hath made in the earth" (v. 8).

This scriptural dichotomy between God's destroying and preserving providence is on vivid display in the experiences of Sarah Osborn, whom we met earlier. As Catherine Brekus has pointed out, Osborn followed John Flavel's advice to keep a record of providences, both judgments and mercies, as evidence of God's involvement in every detail of her life. Throughout her journal, she describes events as happening according to an "all-wise providence." In one particularly memorable instance of divine preservation, a severe storm ("the most terrible wind that I ever knew") awakened her one morning at her home in Newport. Fearing that the roof of her house would be ripped off, she prayed earnestly to God to "abate the violence of the storm and to have compassion on the poor souls in distress" on the nearby harbor. After pleading with God for a while, she suddenly sensed the sufficiency of Christ to calm the storm. "It was only for him to say, 'Peace, be still,' and the winds and the seas would immediately obey him," she later explained, recalling Mark 4:39. Finally emerging from the garret where she had taken shelter, she went downstairs and peered outside: "The sea looked as calm and pleasant to me as if there had been no storm at all."[77] For Osborn, the incident illustrated the overarching goodness of divine providence.

But God the preserver was also God the destroyer, which meant he sometimes dealt sudden reversals in order to awaken his people from spiritual lethargy. Osborn recounted one such "awful dispensation" in the death of her pastor Jonathan Helyer at age 26, after he had served in Newport for barely a year. She prayed to God to "bring me nearer to thy blessed self by this great turn in the wheel of thy providence."[78] The notion of providence as a wheel, based on Ezekiel 1, had been elaborated by Calvin and by later Calvinist commentators such as Matthew Henry (1662–1714) and Jonathan Edwards. Edwards compared Ezekiel's wheels, "exceeding high and terrible," to the whirling wind, constantly returning to where it had started. So it is with the life of man, Edwards explained: "He is from the earth, and gradually rises, and then gradually falls, and returns to the earth again. Dust we are and unto dust we return." So also it is with the whole creation: "In the beginning of this revolution, all things come from God, and are formed out of a chaos; and in the end, all things shall return into a chaos again, and shall return to God."[79] In the eyes of exegetes such as Edwards, therefore, Ezekiel's vision was a fearsome yet sublime revelation of God's all-encompassing providence. Not coincidentally, the passage also combined several of the meteorological elements we have already seen: the whirlwind (v. 4), lightning (v. 14), the four directions (v. 17), and thunder (v. 24).[80] With respect to the whirlwind, Edwards noted that such was a "usual symbol of the divine presence."[81] It was, in other words, a template—and one of enduring power.

PROTESTANT WINDS

Thus far we have seen the weather as a template of mostly *individual* experiences, whether the rushing mighty wind of religious ecstasy, the apocalyptic winds of judgment on sinners, or the calming voice of the Savior in stilling the storm. But the weather was also a template of religious nationalism, a way of claiming divine sanction for British America in the face of its enemies. The precedent for this meteorological jingoism was set in old England in the so-called Protestant Winds of 1588 and 1688. The fact that the two events were separated by exactly a century abetted the belief that God had a glorious plan for the English people. In 1588, Spain's King Philip II, a devout Catholic, dispatched an armada of 130 ships and some 25,000 men to England with the goal of overthrowing Elizabeth I. Met by the Royal Navy, the Spanish Armada was forced to return to Spain via the North Sea and the North Atlantic, where severe weather destroyed up to half of the ships and killed many of the men. The triumphant English monarchy regarded the intervening gale as a divine vindication of Protestantism, and struck a commemorative medal with the inscription, "God blew and they were scattered." In 1688, English Protestantism again seemed under threat, this time by the accession to the throne of James II, a Catholic. Leading Protestants called on Prince William of Orange, the king's son-in-law and nephew, to mount an invasion force from the Dutch Republic. When this even bigger armada of nearly 500 ships, 40,000 men, and 5,000 horses set sail for England, fierce winds at first turned back the fleet. But on the next try, favorable winds propelled the invaders while keeping the Royal Navy at bay. After William successfully landed his troops, he reportedly quipped to his chaplain, Gilbert Burnet, a noted latitudinarian and later bishop of Salisbury, "Well, Doctor, what do you think of predestination now?" Partisans would hail William's overthrow of James II as the "Glorious Revolution," an event God had aided by the second Protestant Wind.[82]

Protestant colonists in America long cherished the memories of 1588 and 1688. After the Glorious Revolution, many became convinced that Britain and her dominions were the vanguard of an international Protestantism that would, with God's help, vanquish the papal menace.[83] Colonial clergy like Jonathan Edwards avidly followed the thwarting of successive Jacobite plots to reinstall a Catholic king on the British throne. Another colonial minister, Elisha Williams (1694–1755), the former rector of Yale College, penned an anonymous tract, *The Essential Rights and Liberties of Protestants* (1744), which drew on Lockean ideas of religious toleration and paid homage to William of Orange as "the late great Deliverer . . . of the British Nation from Popery and Slavery."[84]

By 1745, the colonists were so emboldened that they hatched a plan to capture the French fortress at Louisbourg (on Cape Breton Island), which posed a threat to the British colony of Nova Scotia. Led by William Pepperrell, the colonial force of 4,300 men laid siege to Louisbourg in May 1745, suffering heavy casualties when they attempted an assault on the fortress. The capture of a French resupply frigate buoyed the cause, and on June 16, just before Pepperrell was to mount another assault, the French surrendered. Recalling 1588 and 1688, the colonists pointed to the weather as a decisive factor in this latest victory against the papal Antichrist. As Jonathan Edwards explained to a correspondent in Scotland, "our army had almost a constant series of fair good weather" during the siege, which baffled the French, who were used to "almost perpetual rains and fogs" that time of year. Indeed, according to Edwards, the French were so surprised by this climatological anomaly that some of them concluded that "God was turned an Englishman."[85]

But from the colonists' perspective, the most spectacular meteorological intervention was yet to come. In October 1746, France sent a fleet of 64 ships and 11,000 men to retake Louisbourg. Known as the Duc d'Anville Expedition (after its commander), it was the largest military force to set sail for the New World until the American Revolution, and word of its coming struck fear in the colonists. In his sermon for a fast day called by the Massachusetts governor to implore God for victory, Boston minister Thomas Prince prayed: "Deliver us from our enemy! Send Thy tempest, Lord, upon the waters to the eastward! . . . Sink their proud frigates beneath the power of Thy winds!" Scarcely had he finished his prayer when the sky suddenly darkened and a violent wind ensued, causing the bell in the steeple to strike twice. With tears of joy streaming down his face, Prince exclaimed: "We hear Thy voice, O Lord! . . . Thy bell tolls for the death of our enemies." A week later, news arrived that a storm had dispersed the French fleet and disease had killed many of the men. Even d'Anville himself was dead of an apparent stroke.[86]

Apparently not recounted in full until much later, the story of Prince's prayer has the distinct whiff of legend, especially as it was later enshrined in a famous poem by Henry Wadsworth Longfellow.[87] The military victory was real, however, and in its long afterglow New England's clergy took to their pulpits to thank the Protestant Storm God for once again sending his winds. At Boston's First Church, on New Year's Day, 1747, Thomas Foxcroft recounted how the French armada, bent on revenge for the loss of Louisbourg, had come "breathing Slaughter and Ruin." But God "blast[ed] their Undertaking" by "repeated Storms, scattering, breaking, or disabling their Ships." "Here was the Finger of God!" he marveled. "We stood still, and saw his Salvation . . . Well may we set up our Eben-Ezer, and say as Samuel on a like Occasion, Hitherto hath the Lord helped us." Sixteen years later, once the conclusion of the Seven Years' War effectively ended the French military threat in North America, colonists were still exulting in 1746 as a providential turning point. At South Church in Portsmouth, New Hampshire, Samuel Haven recalled that when the Duc d'Anville and his troops were "within a few days of executing their bloody design," God "blew with his wind . . . and sent his destroying angel, who slew thousands of them." The deliverance was so remarkable that "even our popish enemies were obliged to confess the finger of God in it." As late as 1798, despite France's aid to America in the Revolutionary War, the memory of 1746 lingered. At South Church in Andover, Massachusetts, Jonathan French extolled the "hand of providence, which commands the winds and the seas," for coming to the aid of his Protestant plantations. "Never did that religion, for which this country was settled, appear more important, nor prayer more prevalent, than on this occasion," he declared. "What cannot a people do, when the Lord is on their side?"[88]

Such co-opting of providence for American Protestant nationalism did not go completely unchallenged.[89] In the midst of the nationalistic fervor of the 1740s, an intriguing minority voice emerged from the pages of the short-lived *American Magazine and Historical Chronicle*, published in Boston between 1743 and 1746. Though its editor is not known for certain, evidence strongly points to Jeremiah (Jeremy) Gridley (1702–1767), a lawyer and founding member of Boston's West Church who had opposed the idea that the Great Awakening revivals were a providential work of God.[90]

In May 1744, the *American Magazine* reprinted a revised version of an anonymous article, "Of Superstitious Fears, and their Causes natural and accidental," that had first appeared in the *Weekly Rehearsal*, which Gridley had previously edited. Throughout the ages, noted the writer (likely Gridley), "the Causes of Thunder and Lightning were unknown to the World; as they are to most People in it to this Day." We now realize the immense complexity of natural causes and how the earth itself is but "a Mustard-Seed to the visible World," to say nothing of the invisible one. We should not therefore "measure the Work of God by our scanty Capacities" or resort too quickly to supernatural explanations for "what may be very easily accounted for by our Ignorance of natural Ones."[91]

Two months later, the magazine carried a more pointed article that seemed to anticipate the jingoism of 1745–1746. Individuals are too quick to claim the favor of heaven in all their undertakings, the writer charged, which results in the absurdity of everyone having his own God "fashioned according to his own Temper." In this sense, "[p]olytheism does yet remain in the Christian World." Even worse, people hypocritically claim that when a disaster befalls those who differ from them, it is a divine judgment, whereas when it befalls themselves, it merely proves the biblical adage that the Lord chastens those he loves (Hebrews 12:6). Jesus warns against such hypocrisy ("judge not, that ye be not judged," Matthew 7:1) and also makes clear that the rain falls on the just and the unjust (Matthew 5:45). History shows that Christians do not always enjoy God's special favor. "Mahometanism [occupies] much more of the Globe than Christianity possesses." And within Christianity itself, "Papists are more numerous than the Protestants are, and have greater and better Countries." That there is a gracious providence presiding over the world is "undeniable," but how it works, and from what particular motives, "none but the Author of it can tell." The writer then ended on a jingoistic note of his own: "The Turks make God the Author of every Thing that they do, and of every Evil that others suffer from them." Unfortunately, this same error is common among American Christians: "Whoever applies the Judgment of God to others, has this Turkish Spirit in him."[92]

Bracing as this protest was, it was not enough to prevent the "Turkish Spirit" from creeping into the *American Magazine* itself. In August 1746, a few months after the Battle of Culloden in which Britain defeated a Catholic army in the failed Jacobite uprising led by Charles Edward Stuart ("Bonnie Prince Charlie"), the magazine reprinted selections from *Britain's Remembrancer* (1746) by the Whig propagandist James Burgh, an ardent anti-Catholic. Invoking the Protestant Winds of 1588 and 1688, Burgh listed a series of military engagements in which the weather had favored Britain. Are these deliverances not "[a]rguments for a Providence sufficient to silence Infidelity itself?" he asked. God may not care what "particular Sect or Subdivision" of Protestantism a person follows, but the difference between "the Popish & Protestant Religion is the same that is between Darkness and Light; between incredible Absurdities and certain Truth; between diabolical Cruelty and heavenly Benevolence; between Satan and Jesus Christ."[93]

ACTS OF GOD OR ACTS OF NATURE?

The *American Magazine*'s apparent ambivalence about providence foreshadowed fierce debates over the doctrine in the 1750s. The spark was the invention of lightning rods by Benjamin Franklin (1706–1790), who in 1751 published his conclusion that iron spikes on the roofs of buildings could save property by conducting electricity harmlessly to the ground. Lightning and electricity were the focus of intense inquiry in the transatlantic Enlightenment. Colonial clergy like Jonathan Edwards had approached the subject with a combination of scientific fascination and pious resignation. As a young tutor at Yale, Edwards recorded on his wish list of books the *Physico-Mechanical Experiments* of Francis Hauksbee (1660?–1713), inventor of the first continuous generator of static electricity. Soon thereafter, in another notebook, Edwards described the properties of lightning and thunder.[94] But in many other places in his writings, Edwards invoked "God's artillery" of lightning and thunder as perfect types of divine wrath. He also counseled a sort of Christian fatalism in regard to death by lightning. Preaching at a meeting of children in 1740, he explained that

FIGURE 2.5. Benjamin Franklin holding a book, "Electric Expts," with lightning striking a village in the background. Engraving by James McArdell, 1761, after a painting by Benjamin Wilson. Library of Congress.

"you need not be afraid of thunder, which is commonly very terrifying to children." (Edwards himself as a boy had been particularly scared of thunder.) "Thunder and lightning can never do them any hurt that love Christ, for if they are taken out of the world by it, yet it only carries them from this world to heaven, into the glorious presence of Christ."[95]

A similar line had been adopted by the Presbyterian revivalist Gilbert Tennent (1703–1764), famous for his divisive screed against opponents of the Great Awakening, *The Danger of an Unconverted Ministry* (1740). In July 1745, Tennent was working in his upstairs study during a thunderstorm when lightning struck the house. As he recounted, the bolt was "so violent as to tear my shoes to Pieces, twist one of my Buckles, and melt a little of two Corners of the other." He turned the incident into a sermon with a title from Ecclesiastes 9:2 ("all things come alike to all"). Upbraiding critics who had mocked him as a singular object of divine wrath, he maintained that this world is but a series of trials for the faithful, who will be vindicated in the end. Even if he had been killed by the lightning, he added, it would have been for him "the best Day" ever because it would have brought him into the presence of the Savior. He thus urged upon his listeners a mixture of holy fear and quiet confidence: "But tho' our Hearts should be fill'd with a solemn Awe of God's Majesty while we hear his Voice thundering in the Heavens, yet let the Friends of God beware of a slavish Dread of God's Judgments . . . and let them sweetly resign themselves by Faith into their Father's Hands."[96]

It was perhaps inevitable that Franklin's lightning rods would ignite a firestorm over whether it was proper to redirect thunderbolts from heaven. Ironically, Franklin himself had been on the side of the reactionaries in an earlier debate over providence in the 1720s. At issue then was whether people should tempt fate by submitting to the still-experimental practice of smallpox inoculation. While Cotton Mather had courageously advocated inoculation, Franklin, as a 16-year-old printer's apprentice, had contributed anonymous satires of Mather to the *New-England Courant*, the leading voice of the anti-inoculation faction. (Mather even survived an assassination attempt when someone lobbed a primitive grenade into his house with a note attached: "Cotton Mather, You Dog, Dam you; I'l inoculate you with this.") Franklin later lost his four-year-old son Francis to smallpox, noting in his autobiography how bitterly he regretted not having the boy inoculated.[97] Lightning rods therefore seemed to Franklin a providential way to inoculate people against needless harm from the heavens.

In 1755, however, the cause of lightning rods suffered a setback from an unanticipated source: an earthquake. A little after 4:00 a.m. on November 18, a powerful temblor roused people across coastal New England and sent them panic-stricken into the streets. "Never was such a Scene of Distress in New-England before," reported one observer, who described crying children, lowing livestock, and streets blocked by toppled chimneys and other debris.[98] In the aftermath, the clergy took to their pulpits to preach on divine wrath and urge societal repentance and reform. But at South Church in Boston, Thomas Prince singled out the presumptuous use of Franklin's "points of iron" as a possible reason for God's anger in the earthquake. "In Boston are more [lightning rods] erected than any where else in New England; and Boston seems to be more dreadfully shaken. O! there is no getting out of the mighty Hand of God!" Prince's accusation drew a swift rebuttal from John Winthrop (1714–1779), professor of natural philosophy at Harvard and great-great-grandson of the Bay Colony's first governor. Speaking in the chapel at Harvard, Winthrop declared himself "surprised and concerned" at Prince's comments, which he feared might discourage the use of lightning rods as a means of protection from the many "mischievous and sorrowful accidents, which we have so often seen to follow upon thunderstorms." Yet were lightning strikes merely "accidents"? Winthrop conceded that they might "justly be regarded as the tokens of an incensed Deity," though he hastened to add that lightning in general revealed God's benevolence, for it was nature's way of freeing itself of "a certain unwholesome sultriness."[99]

Traditionalists would have nothing of it. James Cogswell (1720–1807), pastor of First Church, Canterbury, Connecticut, denounced as "very stupid" those who would deny God's vengeance in both lightning and earthquakes. Such people are like an overfed ox "who wantons in the fat Pastures, till the fatal Ax approaches; and thinks nothing of Slaughter till the Moment he is sacrificed." At First Church, Boston, Thomas Foxcroft told his hearers that lightning and earthquakes were the "very legible Signatures" of God's righteous anger. "It would be Atheism to ascribe these events to meer Casualty or Chance," he warned. As proof of divine involvement, he pointed to the catastrophic earthquake that had devastated Lisbon, Portugal, in November 1755, killing between 50,000 and 100,000 people. Speaking in the familiar code of Protestant anti-Catholicism, he attributed the Lisbon disaster to the Lord's fury over that city's worship of "idols." Though Boston's escape from similar destruction revealed God's mercy, the New England quake put residents on notice that they should not be at ease in Zion.[100]

Winthrop was undeterred in what he regarded as a dispassionate search for scientific truth. Though he acknowledged in a letter to Ezra Stiles (later president of Yale College) that earthquakes and other "terrifying phenomena" must have a "grand moral purpose," his primary interest was in understanding the natural laws governing such events.[101] This was a challenging task, he conceded in an article in the *Philosophical Transactions* of the Royal Society. The subject was a tornado that hit near Worcester, Massachusetts, in 1759. Winthrop's description from eyewitness accounts and surveys of damage patterns is one of the most detailed from the colonial period, and it reveals him caught between providentialism and scientific empiricism. Fourteen people were inside David Lynde's public house when the building was "suddenly plucked off from the sills" and "taken up into the air," where, by the violent circular motion of the winds, "it was immediately hurled into ten thousand pieces, and scattered to great distances." It was an extraordinary divine providence, according to Winthrop, that only one person (Lynde's "negro man") lost his life. Winthrop admitted to being baffled by the tornado's natural operation: "It appears to me so difficult to assign a cause adequate to these effects, to shew by what means a small body of air could be put into a circular motion, so excessively rapid as this must have been, that I dare not venture any conjectures about it." He concluded by appealing to the "learned gentlemen" of the Royal Society for their own theories.[102]

As Winthrop was taking tentative steps toward an empirical explanation of meteorological phenomena, a truly radical empiricism was emerging in the work of Scottish philosopher David Hume (1711–1776). Hume penned his principal works on religion during the 1750s. It was a time of tremendous intellectual ferment in Europe, when a number of major figures were revisiting issues raised by the seventeenth-century Continental rationalists Descartes, Spinoza, and Leibniz. The Lisbon earthquake was a major catalyst of the debate because it posed such an intractable problem of theodicy, or why God permits evil. Hume did not write about Lisbon, but he was intensely interested in the related question of whether nature reveals divine purpose. More fundamentally, he was drawn to the problem of the origin of religion, which turned his attention to weather events and whether they are acts of God.[103]

The fullest statement of Hume's critique published in his lifetime is his *Natural History of Religion* (1757). There he argued that the earliest form of religion was not monotheism, as many people then believed, but polytheism, which originated as humans struggled to explain the contradictions at work in the world. "Storms and tempests ruin what is nourished by the sun," he wrote. "Sickness and pestilence may depopulate a kingdom, amidst the most profuse plenty." To primitive societies, the best explanation of this "constant combat of opposite powers" was anthropomorphic: multiple gods who were warring against humanity or each other. Even worse, in Hume's judgment, was that humans conceived of these gods in their own image, which led to the "absurdity" of representing them as "jealous and revengeful, capricious and partial," or like "a wicked and foolish man, in every respect but his superior power and authority."[104]

Monotheism, in Hume's view, was merely an outgrowth of this primitive anthropomorphism. In societies ruled by an absolute monarch, people naturally projected supremacy onto one of the gods. This god, through the doctrine of providence, then became the cause of disparate effects in the world: "The excessive drought of this season: The cold and rains of another. These [the monotheist] ascribes to the immediate operation of providence: And such events, as, with good reasoners, are the chief difficulties in admitting a supreme intelligence, are with him the sole arguments for it." When more "refined" theists (Hume was here referring to deists) dared to deny particular providence and argue instead that the world operates according to "fixed general laws" instituted by God, critics were apt to accuse them of "the grossest infidelity." But as Lord Bacon quipped, "A little philosophy makes men atheists: A great deal reconciles them to religion." Further reflection usually convinced people that the argument from design, based on the intricacy and regularity of natural laws, was the best proof of a supreme intelligence. Meanwhile, the "vulgar" common people continued to see God in "convulsions of nature, disorders, prodigies"; these "impress mankind with the strongest sentiments of religion; the cases of events seeming then the most unknown and unaccountable."[105]

For Hume, even the more "refined" monotheism of the deists presented insurmountable empirical problems. Can we really infer from the design of the world the existence of a supremely moral creator? How *do* we account for deadly violent weather? In his posthumously published *Dialogues Concerning Natural Religion* (1779), begun in the 1750s as he was working on his *Natural History of Religion*, Hume put his own doubts in the mouth of one of his fictional characters, Philo: "The winds are requisite to convey the vapours along the surface of the globe, and to assist men in navigation: But how oft, rising up to tempests and hurricanes, do they become pernicious? Rains are necessary to nourish all the plants and animals of the earth: But how often are they defective? how often excessive?" Rather than indicating benevolent design, the world too often betrayed mere chaos: "Look round this universe. . . . The whole presents nothing but the idea of a blind nature, impregnated by a great vivifying principle, and pouring forth from her lap, without discernment or parental care, her maimed and abortive children."[106]

It was a devastating critique—and one that would prove highly influential. Hume's naturalistic view of religion as a projection arising from human ignorance and fear would be echoed in the unabashed atheism of Feuerbach, Marx, and Freud.[107] But in his own time, what was Hume's impact in America? Benjamin Franklin exchanged friendly correspondence with him, and Hume in turn called Franklin America's "first great man of letters." Jonathan Edwards also revealed an acquaintance with Hume's work, telling a Scottish correspondent that he was glad to have the "opportunity to read such corrupt books" by "men of considerable genius." (Edwards, who died in early 1758, almost certainly never saw Hume's *Natural History*.) Outside of elite figures like Franklin and Edwards, it is hard to find eighteenth-century Americans who read Hume at all, much less agreed with him openly in print.[108] Hume's critics were more vocal, though some of them, such as Yale president Timothy Dwight (1752–1817), may have known Hume's work chiefly secondhand. Hume is the great bugbear of Dwight's *Nature and Danger of Infidel Philosophy* (1798), in which he dismissed as "repugnant to Common sense" Hume's opinion that "there are no solid arguments to prove the existence of God" and that "it is unreasonable to believe God to be wise and good." (Dwight also accused Hume, who never married, of condoning adultery. The charge seems to have been based solely on Hume's passing observation that adultery was tolerated in the France of his time.) Yet even Dwight seems unwittingly to have conceded part of Hume's critique of theism when he admitted that no two philosophers, "either ancient or modern, agree in their constructions of

Providence." Mere observation of nature cannot reveal the providential ends of creation, which "are a labyrinth without a clue." Christians must rely on the scriptures, Dwight insisted.[109]

In appealing to the Bible as the key to God's plan, Dwight harked back to the biblicism of his New England forebears, including his grandfather Jonathan Edwards. It was a reminder that traditional providentialism was alive and well at the end of the eighteenth century, despite the emergence of radical naturalism in Hume. Between these two poles were the ongoing attempts, as exemplified by figures such as Harvard's Winthrop, to reconcile providential and naturalistic views.[110] The freethinker and revolutionary pamphleteer Thomas Paine (1737–1809) made light of the resulting theological pluralism when he quipped in his *Age of Reason* (1794–1795) that "christian mythology has five deities—there is God the Father, God the Son, God the Holy Ghost, the God Providence, and the Goddess Nature."[111]

Paine's barb took aim at the blurring that often occurred between providence and nature, and the fact that Americans' use of the concepts frequently lacked theological precision. The best-known example of this fuzziness is the "act of God" defense, which became established in English common law by the eighteenth century. The legal doctrine arose as a way to absolve individuals from responsibility for damage or injury arising from natural disaster. As one modern legal dictionary put it, an act of God includes "all natural phenomena that are exceptional, inevitable, and irresistible, the effects of which could not be prevented or avoided by the exercise of due care or foresight."[112] What constitutes "due care or foresight" has been a point of contention in tort law. In a region prone to violent weather, for example, can certain types of storm damage be anticipated and prevented?[113] The phrase "act of God" also gives rise to a philosophical problem. When jurists invoke it, do they mean what they say, or do they really mean an act of nature? Logic would suggest that already by the eighteenth century, "act of God" had become unmoored from any theological meaning. Otherwise, judging a weather disaster an act of God could make an individual in an odd way liable for injury or damage since storms were traditionally regarded as divine punishments for sin. But the "act of God" doctrine depended in no way on the notion of divine retributive justice or even on the existence of God.[114]

The phrase "act of God" persists as a ghostly reminder of the debates over providence and weather in the Age of Reason. The ambiguities that haunted people then still haunt us today. As historian Jan Golinski has put it, we "still live in the house of enlightenment, after all, and we can still hear the wind and rain rattling at its windows."[115] In the endless quest to explain the storms that afflict us, the theological options available in the eighteenth century—act of God, act of nature, or some combination of the two—continue to find defenders in our own time. The two poles, if not the muddled middle, draw on scriptural precedents, according to Increase

Mather's sermon on the Great Storm of 1703. Lamentations 3:37 encapsulates Mather's providentialism: "Who is he that saith, and it cometh to pass, when the Lord commandeth it not?" But evidence of what Mather called the "atheism" of denying God's hand in natural events (in this case plague) can be found in 1 Samuel 6:9: "Then we shall know that it is not his hand that smote us; it was a chance that happened to us."[116] Little could Mather have imagined how much starker these options would appear to Americans facing the apocalyptic storms of the next century.

Fire, and hail; snow, and vapours; stormy wind fulfilling his word.

—PSALM 148:8

The wind, the storm, the phenomena of eclipses, the appearance of meteors—all these were divine spectacles to the thought of an ignorant and trembling race.

—HENRY WARD BEECHER, "Conceptions of God" (1882)

3

"Stormy Wind Fulfilling His Word"

METEOROLOGY AND THEOLOGY IN THE NINETEENTH CENTURY

WHEN THE MORMONS completed their temple at Nauvoo, Illinois, in May 1845, it was the largest building north of St. Louis and west of Cincinnati. Built on a bluff overlooking a bend in the Mississippi River, the edifice was 165 feet tall at the tower, a landmark visible from the far side of the river in Iowa. The outside walls were made of limestone blocks, some of them weighing up to 4,000 pounds, and the eaves were covered with 6,500 pounds of lead. Yet just as the temple was coming into use for celestial marriages and other rites, the embattled Latter-day Saints were abandoning Nauvoo to escape the mob violence that had killed their prophet, Joseph Smith, Jr., the year before. Hoping to raise money for their epic trek westward, Mormon leaders decided in September 1845 to sell or lease the building. Several Catholic dioceses expressed interest, including Cincinnati and its bishop, John Baptist Purcell. Various deals fell through, especially after a fire set by arsonists gutted the interior in 1848. By the spring of 1850, however, the situation was looking more hopeful for Nauvoo's remaining residents. Though the Latter-day Saints by then had migrated to the Salt Lake Valley, the town had experienced a rebirth when the Icarians, a utopian community led by the French socialist Étienne Cabet, acquired the temple for $2,000 to use as their headquarters. Soon after their arrival, the 280 French immigrants made plans to refit the temple with meeting halls and a refectory capable of holding a thousand people.[1]

Stonemasons were at work on the temple restoration at 3:00 p.m. on May 27, 1850, when they heard a distant rumble of thunder. One of the men, Icarian Emile Vallet, stepped outside and, seeing only an "insignificant cloud," reported that there was no danger. But unbeknownst to Vallet and his colleagues, a violent tornado—"the most terrible experienced in the country for many years," according to Pierre Bourg, secretary of the Icarian Association—was bearing down on the temple. "Suddenly," Vallet recalled, "a furious wind began to blow." Four of the masons fled the building, while Vallet and six others took refuge in the tool room on the south side. "Hardly had we taken our position than the tornado began to tear small rocks from the top of the walls and flew in every direction," he recounted. Realizing that they might be stoned to death, the men were paralyzed with fear. Before they could decide whether to stay or flee, one of the workers noticed that the north wall was shuddering. "A wall sixty feet high was coming on us, having only forty feet to expand," Vallet continued. "We fled to the southwest corner, deafened with terror. I for one heard nothing. The fall of that wall was heard three miles away in the country. We looked at one another. All alive, but as white as sheets." As the dust settled, they discovered that the north wall had stopped just short of their feet. Concluded Vallet: "If there is a Providence it was on our side."[2]

Vallet's agnostic "if" regarding providence echoed another account, published in a local newspaper and signed "Icaria," that the seven masons escaped injury by "a sort of miracle."[3] The noncommittal language was not surprising, given the rationalism of the Icarian movement under Cabet. In *Le vrai Christianisme suivant Jésus-Christ* (1846), published three years before his arrival in Nauvoo, he had declared that in Jesus' kingdom, "it will no longer be ignorance and error that will reign but Science, the true Science."[4] For Cabet, Jesus was a social revolutionary whose system was communism. The Christian gospel was not about supernatural deliverance in the next life but about enlightenment, liberty, and equality in this life. Though Cabet occasionally borrowed the supernatural imagery of the New Testament, his Christianity was deistic and this-worldly: "If you have Faith, you will appease the tempest and you will walk on the waves. And then you will emerge from the Shadows to pass into the Light."[5] When Cabet lectured on Christianity on Sundays in Nauvoo, Vallet recalled, he left out "the miraculous and supernatural part," in keeping with the agnosticism professed by the majority of the community.[6]

The contrast between the Icarians and the Latter-day Saints is striking. Both were fired with millennial zeal, but Joseph Smith inhabited a supernatural world of visions and omens in which God used violent weather to warn and to punish. Smith the Prophet had admonished the Saints' opponents in the meteorological idiom of

FIGURE 3.1. Ruins of the Nauvoo Temple. Engraving by Frederick Piercy, in *Route from Liverpool to Great Salt Lake Valley* (1855).

the Old Testament: "Let the unbelieving hold their lips, for the day of wrath shall come upon them as a whirlwind."[7] Likewise, at the dedication of the Kirtland, Ohio, Temple in 1836, he had prayed that God would send a tempest against the Saints' enemies, "that all their works may be brought to naught, and swept away by the hail."[8] Even in Nauvoo, when the tempest of persecution was threatening to destroy the Saints' own utopia, Smith had remained defiant in the certainty that they would be vindicated in the hereafter: "What can earthquakes, wars, and tornadoes do? Nothing. All your losses will be made up to you in the resurrection, provided you continue faithful. By the vision of the Almighty I have seen it."[9]

Smith's expectation of direct divine involvement in violent weather—that it would harm the heathen but only temporarily set back the Saints—typified the fervent apocalypticism of early Mormons and many evangelical Protestants in the nineteenth century. The Latter-day Saints' newspaper at Nauvoo, *Times and Seasons*, carried on ongoing feature, "Signs of the Times," chronicling natural disasters and other supposed portents of the Second Coming. "The age is big with events, *events* are big with meaning, but the whole world seems to be in a state of lethargy," the editors wrote in an 1841 installment. They ridiculed the "unbelieving world" for assuming that disasters were purely natural in origin, as if the "howling tempest" and "furious tornado" prove simply that "the wind has blown a little *harder* than usual." "We are ready to acknowledge," the editors declared, "that we are credulous enough to believe they portend coming events, and will take rank in the signs of the Son of Man."[10] Thirteen years later, after fire and tempest had destroyed the Nauvoo Temple, prompting thinly veiled schadenfreude in the secular press ("A fatality seems to attend the temple at Nauvoo," suggested one account),[11] President Brigham Young professed his unswerving belief in providence. "We have never yet had the privilege of completing and enjoying" a temple, he told the gathered Saints on the square in Salt Lake City. "Perhaps we may in this place, but if, in the providence of God, we should not, it is all the same. It is for us to do those things which the Lord requires at our hands, and leave the result with Him."[12]

The Nauvoo Temple thus symbolized a convergence of worldviews, like air masses colliding over the prairie to produce a thunderstorm, in the intellectual weather of the nineteenth century.[13] On the one hand there was the scientism espoused by the Icarians and by an emerging guild of professional scientists, including meteorologists. Theirs was an orderly millennium in which scientific progress would banish old superstitions and reveal the true workings of the cosmos. This universe did not necessarily exclude God or even miracles. Indeed, as we will see, the mid-nineteenth century was the heyday of a "doxological science" that posited a divine order behind all things. On the other hand was the apocalypticism professed by the Mormons and a host of others. Theirs was a world in which God spoke not primarily through the orderliness of nature but through its disorder—earthquake, fire, lightning, and tempest. "God's wrath is on the wheel of nature," noted *Times and Seasons*, bespeaking the traditional assumption that natural events have moral meanings.[14]

Common to both worldviews was an intellectual hubris about humans' ability to know God's purposes. As the nation's frontier expanded, this hubris would come under increasing assaults from the tornado, testing the explanatory power of both scientism and apocalypticism. Each proved remarkably durable, though in the era's religious debates we also find hints of alternatives, including the possibility that genuine indeterminacy was part of God's plan or that natural events were simply amoral. All the while, the tornado was emerging in the national consciousness as an indigenous American storm and as a powerful nexus of questions both meteorological and theological.

TORNADOES IN THE ANTEBELLUM REPUBLIC

At the turn of the nineteenth century, despite the clergy's frequent commentary on storms in general during the colonial period, few Americans were familiar with tornadoes. But between 1810 and 1840, two things brought tornadoes into wider public consciousness. The first was the westward expansion of the young republic into the Mississippi Valley, where there was a significantly higher incidence of violent tornadoes than on the Atlantic seaboard.[15] The two deadliest tornadoes of the nineteenth century—the Great Natchez Tornado of 1840 and the St. Louis Tornado of 1896—occurred in Mississippi Valley states that became part of the new nation after 1810: Mississippi (1817), Illinois (1818), and Missouri (1821). Population in these three states increased by an average of more than 500 percent between 1810 and 1840, thanks to a rapidly expanding system of roads, canals, and by the end of the period, railroads. The second factor was a greatly improved communications network. Expansion of the national postal service significantly reduced the amount of time needed for news to travel between eastern cities and points west. Likewise, newspapers, mostly delivered by mail, burgeoned in the early republic as technological innovations such as the steam-powered cylinder press enabled the first truly mass production of print.[16]

Amid this flood of periodicals, accounts of tornadoes, even from the less tornado-prone East Coast, multiplied steadily every decade between the turn of the nineteenth century and 1840.[17] Though the casualties from these storms were typically limited in number, the destruction made a vivid impression on the correspondents, who often described it in religious terms, frequently invoking the notion of providence. "Dreadful Calamity at Charleston," announced a September 1811 report from Charleston, South Carolina, about a tornado that "passed through the city with the rapidity of lightning, and in an instant involved in destruction and death both the habitation and the inhabitant." The "dreadful visitation," according to the *Charleston Courier*, was "preceded by a momentary deceitful calm, and was attended by a steady rumbling noise, resembling that of a carriage rattling over a pavement." The newspaper clearly regarded it as providential that fewer than 20 people died, with several of the dead being persons of lesser status: a "free mulatto man," three "mulatto children," and a "negro man belonging to Mr. Dener." "We have also heard of two or three other negroes killed, but did not learn to whom they belonged." Among the "many instances of divine protection . . . the following was peculiarly interesting": A pregnant woman was resting on a bed with her sister in an upstairs bedroom of a house when the storm approached. "The noise so alarmed a negro girl in waiting that she sought for refuge under the bed on which her mistress was lying." Though the tornado sent the upstairs bedroom crashing to the first floor below, "the ladies, we are happy to state, escaped without any injury." The "negro girl beneath the bed was crushed to pieces."[18]

The theme of a benevolent providence reappeared in an account of a "tremendous tornado" that hit Ross County, Ohio, near Chillicothe, in June 1814. "Its aspect on approaching was appalling and terrible in the extreme," like the "fiery curling volumes of smoke which issue from the crater of a volcano." The "hurricane" (a term then still used interchangeably with "tornado") left "awful desolations" in its wake, with "scarce one tree in a thousand" still standing, but God protected area residents: "Through the good Providence of him who 'rideth on the wings of the wind,' no human creature has been hurt, as far as yet known." Likewise, in "a fact truly remarkable," the local meetinghouse was untouched, "tho' situated in the very midst of the tempest's course."[19]

Two months later, in August 1814, Americans extolled another providential deliverance when a tornado descended upon Washington, D.C., as British troops burned the capital during the War of 1812. One British soldier said that the storm "produced the most appalling effect" he had ever seen, blowing down houses and burying some of his comrades. As the stunned enemy units regrouped on Capitol Hill, the British rear admiral George Cockburn is said to have exclaimed to a passerby, "Great God, Madam! Is this the kind of storm to which you are accustomed in this infernal country?" "No, Sir," she replied, "this is a special interposition of Providence to drive our enemies from the city." Cockburn shot back: "Not so, Madam. It is rather to aid your enemies in the destruction of your city."[20]

Other tornado accounts from the early republic spoke only of providential punishment or described the destruction in terms of awe-inspiring sublimity. A report of an 1821 New Hampshire tornado, reprinted in the *Christian Register*, described various horrors—a child snatched from bed and hurled to its death, a man's brains dashed against a stone—and noted: "We stood but awfully impressed with the thought that the place was one where the hand of Omnipotence had been put down in seeming anger, to teach man his impotence, in a manner that should be understood and remembered."[21] An account of an 1833 tornado in Springfield, Ohio, described an apparition that recalled Jacob's ladder: "The base of the column varied from five to eighty rods, and it gradually arose into the heaven in the form of a pyramid.... For twenty-five miles (and how much farther we cannot imagine) dwelling houses have been levelled with the earth, and the inhabitants killed or wounded." The tornado brought for many a terrible reversal of fortunes: "The bitterness of want will be felt by many who have heretofore lived in the enjoyment of plenty."[22] The Quaker journal *Friend* picked up the story of a twister near Petersburg, Virginia, in 1834 that wreaked havoc on several local plantations, killing and maiming both slaves and overseers. "The destruction of human life and of property of every kind is truly appalling.... The scene is represented, by those who had an opportunity of witnessing it, as one of surpassing and inexpressible grandeur and sublimity. Every thing, within its range, was laid prostrate."[23]

Perhaps the most publicized tornado prior to 1840, undoubtedly because it struck just outside New York City, was the storm (variously termed a "tornado," a "spout," and a "hurricane") that hit New Brunswick and Piscataway, New Jersey, in June 1835, killing five people and destroying 150 buildings. For weeks afterward, the ruins drew not only curious onlookers but also professors from Princeton, Yale, the University of Pennsylvania, and the Franklin Institute in Philadelphia who were eager to unlock tornadoes' secrets.[24] In describing the destruction, both the secular and religious press drew on a rich biblical vocabulary. The *New Brunswick Times* alluded to Isaiah 14:23 ("I will sweep it with the besom [archaic term for broom] of destruction, saith the Lord of hosts") and also to the idea from Ephesians 2:2 that Satan is the prince of the power of the air: "No pen, (or at least it would require a more able one than ours) can do justice to the passage of the Tornado through our town. It would seem as if the Spirits of the Air had gathered in the pride of their might, and in their wrath would sweep the besom of destruction over our devoted people, leaving naught but death and desolation to mark their track."[25] Similarly, the *Protestant Vindicator*, an anti-Catholic newspaper edited by the Scotsman William Craig Brownlee, pastor of the Collegiate Dutch Reformed Church in New York City, mixed scriptural metaphors, turning the empowering wind of Pentecost (Acts 2:2) into an instrument of destruction while also quoting from Psalm 107: "Of all the exhibitions of Omnipotence, probably none is more impressive than the thunder storm when accompanied with a 'mighty rushing wind.' Never does man more deeply realize his utter helplessness and puny insignificance." The Lord "commandeth and raiseth a stormy wind" and the people "reel to and fro, and are at their wit's end"; yet they "cry unto the Lord in their trouble, and he bringeth them out of their distresses."[26]

Though many Americans took such providentialism for granted, there were skeptical voices as well. A week after the New Brunswick tornado, the *Temple of Reason*, a radical newspaper published in Philadelphia by Russel Canfield, weighed in with an editorial on "Particular Providence." The article ridiculed storm survivors who credited the Almighty with saving them from destruction. Such believers were blind to the obvious fact that "the laws of nature have no respect to persons." Tornadoes and other natural disasters destroy "without the least regard to age or sex, to virtue or vice." If the destinies of humans are ruled by special providences, "why do we often witness the exact reverse of what we might rationally expect?" It is high time, the newspaper concluded, "that men should take common sense by the hand, and renounce these puerile remnants of an idle superstition."[27]

APOCALYPSE AT NATCHEZ

The New Brunswick tornado paled in comparison with the storm that would become known as the Great Natchez Tornado of May 7, 1840. Causing at least 317 fatalities (48 in Natchez itself), it was the deadliest tornado of the nineteenth century and the second deadliest single storm in US history.[28] In reality, the death toll was probably much higher, given reports that "hundreds of negroes"—slaves on nearby plantations—also died, but such deaths often went uncounted in the antebellum South. Besides killing an untold number, the storm leveled much of Natchez, a busy port city and the economic center of Mississippi. The tornado ranks as America's first tornadic apocalypse—or at least the first to be chronicled after print emerged as the nation's earliest mass medium.

The newspaper accounts paint a chilling picture. As guests in the city's hotels were seated at lunch, dark clouds gathered to the southwest, accompanied by an almost constant rumble of thunder. About 2:00 p.m., the sky became so dark that people suddenly needed candles at their dinner tables. Rain fell in "tremendous cataracts," obscuring the massive funnel bearing down on the city. "In another moment the tornado in all its wrath was upon us," reported the *Natchez Free Trader*. "The strongest buildings shook as if tossed with an earthquake; the air was black with whirling eddies of housewalls, roofs, chimneys, huge timbers torn from distant ruins, all shot through the air as if thrown from a mighty catapult." The violent winds smashed at least 60 flatboats and their crews into the churning whitecaps of the Mississippi River. In less than five minutes, the twister obliterated hundreds of houses and destroyed many landmark buildings, including several churches. It was, concluded the *Free Trader*, "such an awful scene of ruin as perhaps never before met the eye of man."[29]

Among the guests in town that day was 60-year-old Timothy Flint, a Congregational minister and well-known author of such works as *A Condensed Geography and History of the Western States* (1828). As the winds gathered, Flint hastily finished lunch and retreated to watch the storm from the hotel reading room. "I saw a terrific looking black cloud," he wrote, "as though a well defined belt of black broad cloth, seeming a mile and a half wide, shooting up the river with fearful velocity." A few seconds later, as he ran for the door with his son James at his side, the windows blew in. "I felt the pillars reel, seized one of them, and expected the next moment to have all my maladies effectually cured." Only the arching of two beams saved the two men from being crushed in the pile of rubble. Flint, bleeding from a nail that shot through his hat and grazed his temple, called for his son, who responded that he was alive. Within half an hour, someone freed them from the wreckage. "Many bodies were dug from our house," Flint recalled, "and the whole spectacle was one of sickening horror."[30]

In accounts of the aftermath, two types of reactions predominate: testaments to the sheer indescribability of the destruction, and awed reflections on the unrestrained power of God. The "sublime spectacle," wrote the *New Orleans Bulletin*, "is beyond the power of language to convey." So too the *Christian Watchman*: "The scene beggared all description."[31] The *Natchez Courier* likewise wrote that the desolation "beggars description" and (in the same article) that "we cannot even attempt a description." Editors at the *New Yorker*, reprising the *Courier*'s account, tellingly omitted the following: "'Twas the voice of the Almighty that spoke, and prudence should dictate reverence rather than execration."[32] The *Christian Secretary* sounded a similar note: "The very elements seem to conspire against us. Amid it all, let our conduct be prudent, and our language reverential." The *Vicksburg Sentinel* printed a poem by Mrs. V. E. Howard that began, "Lament— lament, for there hath been an awful stroke of fate; / Lament—lament, for God hath made a city desolate."[33] And the evangelical-leaning *Episcopal Recorder* spoke in apocalyptic terms not normally associated with genteel Anglicanism: "The Lord seems to have been speaking to our country, and rebuking our sins of late in the most solemn manner." The tornado reminds us, the article continued, "that there is a God above, the Inspector of human conduct, who loveth righteousness and hateth iniquity! How well it would be if the people would take warning, and flee from the wrath to come."[34]

Of all the religious interpretations of the event, the most expansive appeared in *Times and Seasons*, the Mormon organ at Nauvoo, 750 miles upstream on the Mississippi from Natchez. In its May 1840 issue, the paper reprinted two accounts from the *Natchez Free Trader* and offered an extended commentary, replete with biblical citations. "Behold a whirlwind of the Lord is gone forth in fury. . . . It shall fall grievously upon the head of the wicked," wrote editors Don Carlos Smith and Ebenezer Robinson, quoting Jeremiah 23:19. This, they argued, was one of several prophecies specifically fulfilled by the Natchez disaster. Another was Micah 5:14 ("And I will pluck up thy groves out of the midst of thee: so will I destroy thy cities"), which was confirmed in the destruction of Natchez's chinaberry groves (as reported by the *Free Trader*). Indeed, all signs pointed to Christ's imminent return: "The Son of man is about to make his second advent into the world, to reign a thousand years: in which time satan is to be bound. See Rev. 20:1, 2." Prior to that day, there will be many calamities: "men's hearts failing them for fear" (Luke 21:26), "blood, and fire, and pillars of smoke" (Joel 2:30), the wicked burned like stubble (Malachi 4:1), and the Lord "revealed from heaven in flaming fire" (2 Thessalonians 1:8). "Now we would ask the candid observer," concluded the paper, "are not these things beginning to take place? Is not the earth perplexed? Has not the whirlwinds [*sic*] desolated cities? Has not the destructive element of fire, travelled with unexampled fury, through our flourishing and delightful cities?"[35]

FROM METEOROLOGY TO THEOLOGY

During the middle decades of the century (1840s–1860s), the weather emerged as a site of theological ferment to a heretofore unrecognized extent. Scholarly debates have focused on the Civil War's role in either weakening or strengthening the doctrine of God's providential ordering of human affairs.[36] The publication of Charles Darwin's *Origin of Species* (1859) also raised new doubts about traditional teleological views of the universe.[37] Yet before either of these developments, meteorology was influencing religious discussions in ways that bore the unmistakable imprint of the westward-expanding American nation.

Sometimes this influence was simply quirky. Five years after the Natchez disaster, Andover Seminary professor Moses Stuart, the most celebrated evangelical biblical scholar of his day, published a new commentary on the Book of Revelation in which he identified the "four winds of the earth" (Revelation 7:1) with the "frequent changing and shifting of the wind in violent tornados." "It would seem that the same angels had raised the tornado (implied in the preceding chapter), who are now to restrain it," he wrote. "To this tornado, also, we must attribute the fearful commotion described in the preceding context," namely, the earthquake, mighty wind, and shifting mountain of verses 12–14.[38] Stuart, who was well known for his grammatical and philological exactness, likely did not know that tornadoes were a rarity in the Mediterranean region where the Book of Revelation was written. Though many Americans in the 1840s were aware of the Natchez calamity, the first book on tornadoes would not be published until 1887, so Stuart could have had little knowledge of their meteorological characteristics.[39]

The Natchez tornado lent new urgency to the scientific investigation, and it was scientists who brought meteorology to bear on religion in a more sustained way. The key crossover figure was James Pollard Espy (1785–1860). One of America's first professional meteorologists, Espy acquired the nickname "Storm King" after publishing a pioneering scientific treatise, *The Philosophy of Storms*, in 1841. He also had a strong interest in theology, owing in part to his strict Presbyterian upbringing. As Espy's friend Moncure Conway, a Methodist turned freethinker, would write, the Presbyterian Church of Espy's childhood "had not in those days adopted the compliant system now in vogue, which aspires to carry the Westminster Confession on one shoulder, and the spirit of science of the age on the other." According to Conway, the young Espy learned the New Testament "by rote" but also developed a skeptical, empirical temperament after reading John 14:13 ("whatsoever ye shall ask in my name, that I will do") and praying, "O God, give me a dollar!"—only to have his prayer go unanswered.[40] Empirical investigation became Espy's lifelong passion. He was among the scientists who flocked to tornado-stricken New Brunswick in

1835. By this point he was developing his thermal theory of storms. He posited that the atmosphere functions like a giant steam engine, producing updrafts that pump warm, humid air into the cold air above like pistons. He called this process "caloric rarefaction"; today it is called convection and is one of the foundational principles of modern severe storm meteorology.[41]

Espy was right about convection, but he also helped give rise to the understandable though mistaken idea that the destruction caused by tornadoes is entirely due to unequal air pressure—that buildings explode because a tornado suddenly reduces the pressure outside. Espy believed, moreover, that a tornado produced *no* whirling motion at the earth's surface, and thought that damage patterns at Natchez amply confirmed his theory. In his *Philosophy of Storms* he cited the testimony of Natchez resident Henry Tooley, a physician and Methodist minister, who listed numerous buildings that apparently had exploded from an imbalance of pressure. In a journal article, Espy reprinted a letter from Natchez resident and engineering professor Caleb Forshey, who wrote that *The Philosophy of Storms* could not have received "sublimer or more triumphant" vindication from the evidence at Natchez.[42] Newspapers quickly latched onto Espy's apparent discovery and advised readers that, if caught at home during a tornado, they should open windows to equalize the air pressure.[43] (Meteorologists now regard this as a dangerous myth. A tornado's violent winds will destroy a house before any drop in air pressure can have a significant effect; a person opening windows risks being killed by flying debris.)[44]

Not everyone bought Espy's theory of tornadoes. He bitterly disputed with fellow meteorologist William Redfield, first president of the American Association for the Advancement of Science, who insisted (correctly) that tornadic winds do rotate.[45] Espy's advocacy of rainmaking by lighting huge fires to generate convective updrafts also drew ridicule from fellow scientists.[46] Meanwhile, at least one religious periodical expressed doubts about the ultimate value of Espy's research. "However philosophically Mr. Espy and other scientific gentlemen may account for storms," opined the Latter-day Saints *Times and Seasons*, "yet the finger of God is made manifest and in them is fulfilled the saying of the prophets, 'there shall be terrible tempests and whirlwinds, that shall cause the children of men to fear.'"[47]

Mounting attacks on his work, as well as the death of his wife in 1850, left Espy so despondent that he abandoned his meteorological research. He found solace in the subject that had engaged him since childhood: religion. When he died in 1860, he was at work on a theological treatise, *The Human Will*, which was published posthumously by Conway, who by then was editor of the newly revived Transcendentalist periodical *The Dial*. In it, Espy repudiated the doctrine of eternal punishment that was part of the Calvinist bedrock of his birth, and embraced a Universalist-like doctrine of remedial punishment, or the idea that God inflicts pain only for the purpose of gently reforming the sinner. To Espy, this notion banished "all superstitious dread of almighty vengeance." Though he did not put it this way, Espy's God became in effect a correcting Father who, before inflicting a spanking, says, "This will hurt me more than it hurts you." Nature itself was, in Espy's words, a "great system of education"; "we are constantly reminded by some pain or inconvenience, every time we deviate from the path of rectitude or virtue." Even tornadoes were part of a harmonious whole designed by God for human remediation. Looking back on his life, Espy waxed rhapsodic about how he had been "enabled to unfold mysteries in meteorology which had been hidden from every previous examiner." "The curtain of the great theatre of the atmosphere was drawn up," he recounted, "and I was admitted behind the scenes, into the very council chamber of the Creator, when not only the *modus operandi* in producing storms, but the final causes of many most beautiful contrivances, were laid open to my delighted view." Echoing a sentence in his *Philosophy of Storms* about the "uniformity and regularity" of storms, he declared that God had designed both the physical and moral worlds to be a "perfect uniformity" of causes and effects. Without such regularity, humans would ever remain in darkness about the workings of the world, but the predictability of nature's causes and effects allowed humans to learn from their mistakes.[48] Espy did not hesitate to conclude that God arranged specific causes and effects for the moral betterment of individuals. "If it is better for me to suffer some pain hereafter for the sake of further improvement," he wrote in his Last Will and Testament, "I doubt not that an infinitely good and wise Father has so arranged it that I shall so suffer."[49]

WEATHER AND PROVIDENCE IN THE 1850S

While Espy's confidence in divine beneficence belied the seemingly random destruction he had witnessed as a pioneering tornado scientist, the optimism of his sunset years reflected a vogue in the 1850s for what Theodore Dwight Bozeman has called "doxological science." Its cardinal assumptions were design, benevolence, and order, and its high priest was the Anglican divine William Paley, whose *Natural Theology* (1802) went through 15 American editions before the mid-1840s. Paley's argument that the intricacies of the natural world revealed an intelligent, benevolent Designer became the reigning orthodoxy in antebellum Protestant seminaries. Numerous theologians and scientific popularizers built on his work, including the Congregational minister and geologist Edward Hitchcock, president of Amherst College, who, in *Religion of Geology and Its Connected Sciences* (1851), contended that the development of living organisms from inorganic matter proved God's creative intervention in the world.[50] Writing five years before Darwin's *Origin of Species*, Hitchcock asserted that God always acts according to fixed laws, even when working miracles, such that "in the same circumstances we may expect the same miracle." (The creation of humankind, in his view, was just such an example of a special divine interposition.) To suppose that God ever acts "without the guidance of a settled principle," Hitchcock insisted, "is to impute to him a want of wisdom and character, which we should be slow to charge upon an eminent man." Hitchcock was supremely confident that as scientists uncovered more and more of the laws of nature, they would find them in perfect harmony with religion. Christians, instead of fearing that science and revelation were in conflict, "would find that they sustain and illustrate each other, and that the heart of piety might be warmed at the shrine of nature, as well as at the cross."[51]

In explaining human origins as simultaneously the product of divine intervention and fixed laws, Hitchcock was walking a fine line that would become increasingly difficult to negotiate after Darwin.[52] Moreover, the looming debate over human origins was not the only front on which cracks were appearing in traditional views of divine providence. A now-forgotten address at Andover Seminary in 1854 by George Ide Chace (1808–1885), a geologist and chemist from Brown University, caused a considerable uproar and again turned the weather into a battleground over God's involvement in the world. A pious Baptist and reputedly austere instructor, Chace was interested in moral philosophy and was, in the recollection of James B. Angell (who eventually became president of the University of Michigan), "one of the few men who could talk well while conducting an experiment."[53] Chace's reputation earned him the invitation to speak at Andover, which had been founded in 1808 as an orthodox Congregational bastion after the Unitarians (and religious liberalism) gained control at Harvard.

On one level, Chace's argument in *The Relation of Divine Providence to Physical Laws* was nothing new. Like the seventeenth-century Anglican divines who ridiculed the Puritans for discerning God's hand in every thunderbolt, he decried the human "egoism" that would interpret weather and other natural events as either blessings or curses from God. History had amply proven the comic absurdity of such claims. He cited the case of England's Glorious Revolution of 1688: the first invasion attempt by the Protestant William of Orange was thwarted by a violent storm, which the Catholic James II interpreted as a divine intervention; when the weather cooperated with William on his second attempt, it was "the Protestants' turn to claim the favor of Heaven." Even the "narrowest and most humble" occurrences of everyday life became opportunities for some people to claim God's involvement. Such reasoning, in Chace's opinion, was little better than paganism because it falsely assumed that every event has a moral purpose—that people suffer or prosper according to their just deserts. (This was Espy's view, though he saw divine punishment as corrective rather than punitive.) Chace maintained that reason and even the scriptures—the

FIGURE 3.2. *George Ide Chace.* Undated oil painting by James Sullivan Lincoln (1811–1888). Courtesy of the Office of the Curator, Brown University.

Book of Job, as well as Jesus' own statement that God "sendeth rain on the just and on the unjust" (Matthew 5:45)—ought to discredit any Christian arrogance about divine messages in creation.[54]

Chace's purpose was far more than simply to poke fun at popular providentialism. He also raised doubts about the extent of God's control over natural events; the weather for him got to the crux of the matter. He appealed to the distinction, long debated by theologians but rarely put in terms accessible to laypeople, between foreknowledge and foreordination. God knows all events in advance, Chace believed, but this does not mean that "every thing was alike provided for and intended by Him" or that it was "the direct object of contrivance and purpose." Whereas Puritan ministers assumed that violent weather events such as lightning strikes were tokens of either God's or Satan's wrath, modern science had revealed lightning to "obey the ordinary law of material attraction," thus explaining its frequent descent on church steeples. Chace was confident that with further scientific research, other mysteries would be dispelled as well. "When the science of meteorology shall have been as fully developed as that of astronomy—when the cycles of atmospheric changes shall have been as accurately determined as the revolutions of the planets, the winds and the weather will cease to be regarded as subjects for the Divine interposition."[55]

Many Christians assumed that all events—even destructive storms—must be attributed to divine involvement; otherwise the world would appear frighteningly chaotic. But for Chace the world was *more* terrifying if everything, even bad things, could be attributed directly to God. It would "annihilate the distinction between good and evil, and render the Divine character a sphinx-like enigma, dark and difficult, beyond all hope of solution." The obvious solution was that only *good* things were directly attributable to divine providence. Other things were foreseen but not "desired or necessary consequences" of God's overarching plan for creation. Chace admitted that it was not always easy to distinguish things God specifically intended from things that arose "from the action of general causes, without being specifically ordered." But he felt that such discrimination was unnecessary. All that mattered was guarding against, on the one hand, too limited a view of providence that denied God's loving care over creation, and on the other, too robust a view that extended God's control to everything, including obvious evils as well as matters of little consequence. Chace felt that Jesus' words in Matthew 10:30 ("the very hairs of your head are all numbered") could not be taken literally. "I do not suppose that any one will seriously contend for an interpretation that shall make the number of hairs on the head of a disciple of Christ, the subject of a Divine decree."[56] Many things in life are simply part of the natural order. "Time and chance happen to all men," he wrote, alluding to Ecclesiastes 9:11. "The laws of physical nature ride over and through individual interests." To believe otherwise was to ignore the plain facts of physical science. "In your zeal for the interests of Christian truth, do not exalt the Scriptures at the expense of the reason."[57]

Chace concluded his treatise on a radical note that anticipated a theological movement that only emerged 150 years later: Open Theism, which posits that there are self-imposed limits on divine omnipotence. "The truth is," he wrote, "we are utterly unable to say a priori, what is, and what is not possible—what God can do, and what He cannot do." Part of the difficulty is that we cannot know exactly how other forces may impinge on God's designs. "On what intuition or revelation do we rest the postulate, that every thing which He desires and makes provision for, will certainly come to pass—no matter what the character of the agents upon which its accomplishment is made dependent?"[58]

We do not know how the crowd at Andover reacted to Chace's long discourse on that August day in 1854, but judging from the ensuing tempest in the press, the theological community was taken aback to hear such words from a devout Baptist. The *Christian Watchman and Reflector*, a Boston-based Baptist newspaper edited by the Rev. J. W. Olmstead, summed up the gravity of the situation: "When a Christian scholar, addressing the students of a theological seminary, attempts to disprove an opinion so nearly universal, his arguments deserve attention." How could Chace be sure that God's moral purposes do not lie behind natural phenomena? "Is our ability to discern God's purpose in any given case, a just reason for denying that he has a purpose?" Chace was treading on dangerous ground in saying that God does not concern himself with little things. What about the atom? (Though modern atomic physics was still in the future, the theory of atoms had been around since classical times.) "If it is not beneath the dignity of God to create an atom," the *Watchman* concluded, "we see no ground to doubt his care over it."[59]

A testy Chace replied to the *Watchman* that he never intended to cast doubt on "a general, all-embracing providence, including the little as well as the great." His only intention was to discredit overzealous notions of God's *special* providence. He expressed surprise that the *Watchman* had so misrepresented his position. "I can only account for it, from the habit of hasty reading and superficial thinking . . . which unfortunately is too characteristic of the times."[60] The *Watchman* fired back, noting acidly that perhaps it should withhold further comment, lest it be accused again of "hasty reading and superficial thinking." The newspaper nevertheless went on to say that Chace's special providence was not special at all because it excluded little things as well as evils from God's actual control, relegating both to God's mere foreknowledge. Chace had thereby emptied providence of "everything that makes it precious to the Christian heart," namely, the assurance that God leaves nothing to chance.[61]

The commotion quickly spread to other religious newspapers. The Unitarian *Monthly Religious Magazine* commended Chace for discrediting the persistent assumption that God uses the weather to punish individuals. On such a view, God seemed almost to be "associated only with calamites and horrors, as if his providence slept always except in tornadoes, conflagrations, thunder-storms, and shipwrecks." But the magazine echoed the *Watchman*'s warning that just because we cannot know God's purposes behind natural events, we dare not conclude that there is no purpose at all. Similarly, the Baptist *Christian Review* decried Chace's "chilling" view of providence as scarcely different from the deists' Watchmaker God, who set the world in motion only to let it run thereafter on its own. The *Review* added that Christians should not assume that violent weather is always an act of divine vengeance. When a man dies from a lightning strike, it may be a blessing in disguise sent by a benevolent Father who "would remove him to a better world" to spare him the "distress of an agonizing death." Meanwhile, the *Universalist Quarterly and General Review*, though questioning Chace's "ultra Arminianism" (an apparent reference to his closing argument that God's actions may partly depend on the actions of other agents), chuckled at the thought of Chace's airing such unorthodox views before the "Andover fraternity."[62]

The most extended response came from a member of that fraternity, Andover president Edwards Amasa Park (1808–1900). Born the same year as Chace, Park was a staunch defender of Edwardseanism—he was named for Jonathan Edwards and was married to his great-granddaughter—at a time when the cultural tide was turning away from absolute predestinarianism.[63] Park recalled the case of the Duc d'Anville Expedition in 1746 (recounted in Chapter 2), when a violent storm averted an attack by a French fleet. To Park, this story illustrated God's providential care of his New England commonwealth. Though one need not believe that any particular gust of wind was a divine answer to prayer, the protection of Protestant New England surely was. "The peculiarity of the coincidence between the phenomenon [of the wind] and the whole scheme of divine government brings with it a self-evidencing light," Park wrote. He conceded that God's purposes were sometimes inscrutable, but this was no justification for doubting his involvement. "If the intentions of God be hidden from us, the very concealment implies that there are intentions. If the event be mysterious, the very mystery implies that there are purposes of God wrapped up in it." Finally, he castigated Chace for assuming that some things, such as the number of hairs on a person's head, could not be the subject of a divine decree. "Why not?" he asked. "When we compare our own insignificance with the great scheme of Jehovah, and our own ignorance with the objects of scientific interest in the finest filament of the minutest leaf, we find ourselves incompetent to decide that any phenomenon is too unimportant for the Deity to foreordain."[64]

Park's extension of divine government to all things reflected the same Reformed Protestant traditionalism espoused by his rival Charles Hodge (1797–1878) of Princeton Seminary. Though not involved in the controversy with Chace, Hodge in the 1850s was then defending what he regarded as the biblical doctrine of providence: that a personal God directs all events, even while permitting the operation of second causes. In an 1857 article, Hodge attacked several alternative views, including fatalism and mechanism, which either bound God to inexorable forces or banished him entirely, and pantheism, which, in Hodge's view, too readily equated God with the world itself. He also opposed any emphasis on contingency that would threaten God's foreknowledge or assume that "his power is limited by impossibilities." Against all of these errors, Hodge believed, the biblical idea of divine government offered assurance of a world devoid of randomness. "Who would not rather be governed by a Father than by a tornado?" Hodge declared. "Give us certainty—the secure conviction that a sparrow cannot fall, nor a sinner move a finger, but as God permits and ordains." Yes, things happen according to natural laws, but God still directs all events toward the fulfillment of his purposes. "The force of gravity accounts for a stone falling to earth, but not for its falling here instead of there," he said. "The power to walk accounts for a man's walking, but not for his walking east rather than west."[65]

Hodge reiterated this argument in his *Systematic Theology* (1871–1873), the largest such work published by an American up to that time.[66] The biblical doctrine of providence "excludes both necessity and chance from the universe, substituting for them the intelligent and universal control of an infinite, omnipresent God." Nothing in human life or the natural world falls outside of God's control: "He makes the winds his messengers, and the lightnings are his ministering spirits." Even events that seem fortuitous or inconsequential to us—he invoked again the sparrow and the "hairs of your head" of Matthew 10:29–30—are part of the Father's all-embracing care. Indeed, the doctrine of providence "is the foundation of all practical religion, and the denial of it practically atheism, for we are then without God in the world."

Hodge was quick to caution against identifying God so closely with the world and its laws so as to preclude the possibility of supernatural intervention in creation. Hodge associated this error with Schleiermacher, whom he had met while studying in Europe. For Hodge, Schleiermacher's pantheism (a label Schleiermacher himself rejected) differed from deism only in allowing for God's supernatural manifestation in Christ; otherwise, God operated according to regular laws. Hodge insisted that just because God is the author of nature's laws, he is not bound by them. "He can change, annihilate, or suspend them at pleasure. He can operate with them or without them." Though God normally acts within the boundaries of his own laws, those laws concern only the complex interaction of physical forces in the universe. God remains the agent behind the forces, guiding all events toward predetermined ends. While condensation and other physical processes are the proximate cause of clouds and precipitation, God still "sends rain when and where He pleases." It is therefore rational to pray for seasonal weather or for protection from storms since God controls the laws of nature "and causes them to produce whatever effects He sees fit."[67]

Charles Hodge's all-encompassing providence was in many ways a throwback to Calvin's contention that "not one drop of rain falls without God's sure command." (Calvin too had appealed to the sparrow and hairs of Matthew 10:29–30.)[68] The difference was Hodge's more modern, scientific idiom, which stemmed in part from his amateur interest in the physical sciences, especially meteorology. For years, he recorded the temperature, wind direction and speed, and other weather phenomena.[69] In his view, theology was similarly inductive; it relied primarily on the data of the Bible. As he famously remarked: "The Bible is to the theologian what nature is to the man of science. It is his store-house of facts." All the facts revealed in nature are "contained and authenticated in Scripture," he added. "All truth must be consistent. God cannot contradict himself." Just as he ruled out any contradiction or chaos in the divine, Hodge also dismissed any theology not founded on rock-hard empirical certainties. "Whole systems of theologies are founded upon intuitions, so called," he scoffed, "and if every man is at liberty to exalt his own intuitions . . . we should have as many theologies in the world as there are thinkers."[70] Yet in rejecting intuition in favor of an infallible Bible, Hodge was increasingly at odds with an ascendant theological liberalism that embraced more flexible views of both experience and scripture.

PROVIDENCE AND PROGRESS IN THE GILDED AGE

Hodge died in 1878 as the Civil War and Reconstruction eras were giving way to the Gilded Age, a time when American religion, in the words of historian James Turner, "waxed fat and prosperous."[71] Among old-line Protestants, nobody embodied the spirit of the age better than the famous Brooklyn preacher Henry Ward Beecher (1813–1887). Son of the redoubtable New England minister Lyman Beecher and brother of bestselling novelist Harriet Beecher Stowe, Beecher had moved away from his ancestral Calvinism, repudiating as "spiritual barbarism" the Westminster Confession's doctrine that God unconditionally elects certain persons for salvation. Beecher likewise dismissed Westminster's doctrine of humans' total depravity as "so gross and so undiscriminating" as to be utterly useless in a modern age that appreciated humanity's evolutionary potential.[72] Like earlier liberals such as the Unitarian William Ellery Channing, who rebelled against a God who would punish humans endlessly for their inbred sinfulness, Beecher embraced a kinder, gentler deity and a liberalizing evangelicalism characterized by an emphasis on intuition, experience, and education.[73]

On providence, Beecher backed away from the inherited tendency to define the doctrine, sounding instead a note of agnosticism: "What God can do and what God cannot do in the immensity of His being lies beyond the grasp of human thought."[74] But he insisted that God, like humans, has a personality and that his character is overwhelmingly loving. Like a mother caring for her children, God represents "the nobleness, the sweetness, and the delicacy of love." Governing the world through natural laws, God influences humans' moral behavior.[75] In his sermon "Divine Influence on the Human Soul," Beecher contended that in all ages, God had sent the "mighty rushing wind" of his Spirit to awaken humans' "already established powers and faculties."[76] Human nature was not debilitated, as the Westminster Confession taught. Rather, God taught humans as parents would teach children, by stimulating their own natural capacities.

Beecher's optimism about the educability of the human race inspired his reforming zeal in the antislavery and temperance crusades and brought him into contact with other reformers, including his fellow Congregational minister Josiah Bushnell Grinnell (1821–1891).[77] Both men, convinced of the manifest destiny of Christian civilization, served stints west of the Alleghenies: Beecher in Indianapolis, and Grinnell in Iowa. Beecher fairly quickly returned East to take up his most famous post at Brooklyn, but Grinnell put down roots in Iowa, founding the town and college that today bear his name. Established in 1854 on the highest ground between the Iowa and Des Moines rivers, the town of Grinnell was intended to be a city upon a hill, both literally and figuratively. When Iowa College (as it was then known) relocated there from Davenport a few years later, Josiah Grinnell hoped that the school would be an incubator of antislavery and temperance activism. Over the next two decades, a small but beautiful new college emerged, with two large brick and stone buildings, more than 300 elm trees, and a railroad stop on campus.[78]

Grinnell also sat in tornado country, and on June 17, 1882, amid a statewide outbreak of severe weather, two tornadoes converged on the town, one of them hitting the college directly. Edwards A. Park reputedly called it the greatest calamity "ever to befall any college in the whole history of education."[79] Whether or not this was true, the Grinnell Cyclone, as it came to be known, was a fearsome apparition. Striking at 8:44 p.m. (the time registered on a clock found in the rubble), it burst forth from a sky "illumined by a weird and ghastly glow, as if from the sulphurous fires of Tartarus." Witnesses looked on in horror as the approaching funnel carried

FIGURE 3.3. Stereo card view of damage from the Grinnell tornado on June 17, 1882. Photograph by D. H. Gross. Courtesy of the Drake Community Library Archives, Grinnell, Iowa.

away parts of houses, barns, and human bodies. Many of the college's students were out of town at a ball game, but two of those who stayed behind, B. H. Burgett and Burritt Chase, died from massive trauma. In addition to destroying the college's two buildings and all of its graceful elms, the tornado lifted a locomotive and flattened many nearby homes, killing at least 30 townspeople. Personal effects from Grinnell residents were discovered as far away as Wisconsin. After the storm, people rang church bells to signal the crisis, as was the custom in rural communities. One local resident later captured the moment in verse: "Who will tell the strange disaster? / Who has heart to breathe the story? / Hasten now, to every steeple, / Ring the bells and rouse the people."[80]

Almost immediately, college president George Magoun, a Congregational minister, began leading the recovery. Just nine days after the storm, the college held its commencement exercises as scheduled and laid the cornerstone for a new building. Magoun's baccalaureate sermon, which he had left in his office, was blown away by the tornado. He preached instead on the topic, "And God Was in the Whirlwind," based on Psalm 148:8: "Fire, and hail; snow, and vapours; stormy wind fulfilling his word." He argued that the storm was not an act of divine vengeance, like God's destruction of Sodom and Gomorrah, but rather a test of the college's faith, reminiscent of God's testing of Job. Josiah Grinnell expanded upon Magoun's assurances, declaring that God would not test the people beyond their capacities, for he "tempers the winds to the shorn lamb."[81]

Soon after commencement, Josiah Grinnell headed East to raise funds for rebuilding the college. In Chicago, the Board of Trade called a rare halt to business so that he could make his appeal. In New York, Grinnell addressed an evening meeting at Beecher's Plymouth Church. Beecher reminded the congregation of the town of Grinnell's support for temperance and noted that there "has not been any liquor sold there for twenty-eight years." To loud applause, Grinnell exhorted the crowd: "Let it be known on earth and in Heaven that Plymouth Church and its people have not forgotten those whom storms have desolated." Grinnell's appeals did not go unanswered. Though accounts of the sum he raised vary, within two years of the tornado, the college had built three new buildings. Better yet, the storm and subsequent fundraising campaign brought the institution unprecedented publicity. "That cyclone," Grinnell reputedly quipped, "was a real windfall."[82]

The Grinnell success story fit perfectly into the triumphant narrative of progress that was so characteristic of the era.[83] A few months after Josiah Grinnell's visit to Brooklyn, Beecher delivered a pair of sermons in which he reflected on humanity's progress in the theological realm. In earliest Old Testament times, when people were no better than "Sodomites" and "lower than the animals," they had to be kept in line by "a God of storms, who rides on the storm; thunder and lightning are the flash of his eye and

FIGURE 3.4. Henry Ward Beecher, in an undated photograph by Mathew Brady (1822–1896). Library of Congress.

the voice of his anger." Later in biblical history, conceptions of God evolved from this primitive form, which equated him purely with power, to higher forms in which natural phenomena were no longer necessary for inculcating morality. Thus the Lord revealed himself to Elijah not in the wind or earthquake or fire but in "a still small voice" (1 Kings 19:12). This religious evolution culminated in the New Testament, where Jesus teaches us to address God as "Our Father." "Here is where the storms end," Beecher declared. God no longer rules by force and fear but by hope and love.[84]

Beecher was not alone in thinking that humans were evolving beyond the need to cower in the face of storms. A striking echo of his evolutionary optimism came, paradoxically, in the response to a devastating tornado that hit Sauk Rapids, St. Cloud, and Rice, Minnesota, in 1886, killing 72 people. Newspaper accounts were filled with haunting details: a man impaled in the forehead, gasping for his last breath; a woman mangled beyond recognition, her young daughter begging officials for a last look at the body. At a Lutheran church wedding, 12 people perished, including the bridegroom and the pastor. Whole blocks of residences were demolished, though here and there, for no apparent reason, a house was spared.[85]

Yet even in the face of this indiscriminate destruction, Henry Martyn Simmons, pastor of the First Unitarian Society of Minneapolis and a writer on the religious value of evolutionary science, was sanguine as he took to his pulpit. Not long ago, Simmons reminded his listeners, another tornado had destroyed Kristofer Janson's Unitarian chapel, an event that the local Lutheran press interpreted as divine judgment on liberal religion. Now the Lutherans themselves were in mourning. This reversal of fortunes, along with other instances of seemingly random devastation, disproved any idea that the weather was an instrument of divine retribution. "The tornado itself corrects that theology," Simmons said. So did Jesus himself, who taught that God "sendeth rain on the just and on the unjust" (Matthew 5:45). "Plainly Providence is more impartial than ever pictured," Simmons added. He further argued that providence is good, pushing humans through "trials and terrors" to tame the world with scientific knowledge. He extolled recent advances in tornado prediction, which promised dramatic reductions in fatalities. Just as lightning led humankind to master electricity, he said, "today the tornado is forcing men to study its problems and strengthen themselves" against its seemingly inexorable power. Simmons pointed out that whereas God had rebuked Job, asking, "Canst thou send lightnings . . . ?" (Job 38:35), today's technologically advanced man could rightly answer, "I can." "Who knows that he may not yet enslave the tornado," Simmons concluded, "and the voice will yet speak out of the whirlwind to proclaim not the weakness but the power of man."[86]

Simmons's faith in technology coincided with the rise of government-sponsored meteorology. In 1870 the US Army Signal Service (later Signal Corps) had begun issuing daily weather maps for the nation. Twenty-three-year-old John Park Finley (1854–1943), a recent graduate of Michigan State, enlisted in the Signal Service in 1877 and soon developed an interest in tornadoes. Realizing the dearth of systematic data on the subject, he began compiling a list of all published reports of tornadoes since 1794. He also enlisted more than 2,000 volunteer "tornado reporters" who could send in observations from around the country.[87] Promoted to the rank of second lieutenant for his tornado research, Finley in 1887 published the first general-interest book on the subject, *Tornadoes: What They Are and How to Observe Them; with Practical Suggestions for the Protection of Life and Property*. The volume begins somberly, noting that the "populous region of the United States is forever doomed to the devastation of the tornado. As certain as that night follows day is the coming of the funnel-shaped cloud." Where tornadoes had once left few marks on the "tree-less and uninhabited prairie," the rapid settlement of the central United States had put many more people at risk from these "dreaded aerial monsters," with their "immensity of power almost beyond calculation." Yet Finley's awe before tornadic winds (which he incorrectly estimated could reach 1,000 miles per hour or more) was not greater than his confidence that Americans could rise above the paralysis of fear and learn to protect themselves from the elements. "There is no country on the face of the globe where meteorology can be studied with so much advantage, practically and scientifically, as in North America," he wrote. Elementary meteorology should be taught in every school and town, and every college and university should require an advanced course in the subject. The rapid advances in scientific understanding of severe storms, Finley believed, were making tornado prediction no longer a "mere possibility" but "an accomplished fact."[88]

Finley had many disciples. One of his tornado reporters, William Eddy, in an article on progress in tornado prediction, wrote that "the control or anticipation of any form of destructive action in Nature is a benefit that will live in the annals of the race for many a century."[89] Finley continued his crusade to educate the public by publishing an abridged volume in which he reiterated his advice to homeowners to construct a reinforced tornado "cave" for protection from storms. He dismissed as foolish his critics who had mocked the idea of "burrow[ing] in the ground at the sight of a dark cloud." Nothing short of an underground shelter could afford adequate protection from a tornado. He decried what he viewed as a persistent religious fatalism regarding violent weather. "If any man looks upon the tornado as some mysterious convulsion of nature that is ordained to visit the earth by a revengeful God, then all thought of material protection is at an end and he waits submissively in his tracks until the death-blow comes."[90]

Ironically, the government infrastructure that Finley hoped would help to protect people from tornadoes ultimately put the brakes on his research. Finley also came under fire from real estate speculators and local officials in tornado-prone regions who worried that he was scaring people away from the country's midsection. In 1885, the head of the Signal Service, General William Babcock Hazen, banned the use of the word *tornado* in government forecasts for fear of causing panic; he directed forecasters to refer to "dangerous local storms" or "violent local storms" instead. The ban would remain in effect until 1938.[91] In 1887, Hazen's successor, General Adolphus Greely, relieved Finley of his forecasting duties, decreeing that routine anticipation of tornadoes was impractical. So "infinitesimal" was the area affected by a tornado when compared to the larger region in which the severe weather occurred, according to Greely, that even if the Signal Service could "say with absolute certainty that a tornado would occur in any particular state or even county, it is believed that the harm done by such a prediction would eventually be greater than that which results from the tornado itself."[92]

It was the beginning of the end of the military's involvement in severe weather forecasting. In 1890, Congress voted to make the US Weather Bureau a civilian agency under the Department of Agriculture. Finley left the Bureau in 1892 and spent the rest of his long career as a private meteorologist. Drawing on the mountains of severe weather data he had accumulated over the years, he founded the National Storm Insurance Bureau in 1920, to assist underwriters with risk assessment. In his 1888 book, he had called for the development of tornado insurance as a product available to the general public. "From a business view, and as affecting the question of life and property," he wrote, "the tornado must be considered as one of nature's agencies for destruction, which must forever be fortified against."[93]

Finley's call for tornado insurance faced a test two years later when a tornado outbreak hit Illinois, Indiana, and Kentucky, including the city of Louisville, where 76 people died. The day after the disaster, the Louisville *Courier-Journal* predicted "prolonged litigation" between policyholders and insurance companies, especially in cases where a secondary factor such as fire destroyed buildings.[94] The 1890 outbreak shocked the nation with its carnage, especially the fate of some 44 children and their mothers, who were crushed during a dancing lesson in Louisville's Falls City Hall. Also widely reported was the death of the beloved rector of St. John's Episcopal Church, Stephen Barnwell, who was reading in the rectory with his son, Dudley, when falling debris killed them both. Rescuers who recovered the priest's body found his face "horribly expressive of the terrible agony which for an instant he must have suffered."[95] The 1890 disaster followed similarly deadly outbreaks in 1884 (in central Iowa and northern Illinois) and 1860 (in Alabama, Georgia, and the Carolinas).[96] The rural locations of these outbreaks—even the 1890 disaster was mostly a rural event—confirmed some Americans' complacent confidence that "cyclones" mainly afflicted farmland and prairie.

APOCALYPSE AGAIN: ST. LOUIS, 1896

But in May 1896, the unthinkable happened: a catastrophic tornado struck St. Louis, the nation's fourth-largest city.[97] A bustling Mississippi River port, the city had grown exponentially in the mid-nineteenth century from an influx of Irish and German immigrants. In 1894, the new Union Station became the world's largest railroad terminal. Thousands of visitors would soon arrive there for the Republican National Convention in June 1896. Though St. Louisans were used to thunderstorms, which occurred frequently during the city's hot, humid summers, many assumed that a tornado would never strike the heart of such a metropolis, especially one built amid river bluffs that reputedly could halt a twister's advance.[98]

The forecast on the front page of the *St. Louis Post-Dispatch* on May 27, 1896, announced "severe thunderstorms this afternoon and to-night." Storm clouds began gathering at noon, and by mid-afternoon, residents were eyeing the darkening sky with alarm. Signs creaked in the mounting winds, and streetcars waited longer at corners to allow more people to climb aboard. Witnesses later recounted seeing ball lightning that flashed blue, purple, and red. By 5:07 p.m., the barometric pressure dropped to a frightening 28.95 inches. Soon after, the tornado—a half mile wide, as estimated from damage patterns—began its deadly rampage.[99]

In 20 minutes, the Great Cyclone, as it came to be known, "sliced like a turbine" through the city, gouging out a snake-like, seven-mile path that roughly followed today's Interstate 44 and crossed the Mississippi near where the Gateway Arch now stands.[100] "The scene on the river at the moment the cyclone passed over it was awe-inspiring," reported the weekly science journal *Nature*. "The river tossed and boiled as though it was a whirlpool."[101] The upper span of the landmark Eads Bridge collapsed, sending huge granite blocks crashing to the railroad tracks below. The storm sank nearly 20 riverboats and blasted through the East St. Louis rail yards. The entire electric streetcar system was disabled, and telegraph poles came down like long rows of dominoes. All told, some 7,500 buildings were either destroyed or badly damaged.[102] The human cost was appalling: at least 255 dead (137 in St. Louis and 118 in East St. Louis) and 1,000 injured.[103] The storm also sparked numerous fires that delayed the rescue of the injured, sometimes until it was too late. Two-year-old Oliver Bene was burned alive as his mother, trapped under heavy fallen beams and unable to reach him, watched in horror. The city morgue quickly filled up with the bodies of those killed by debris or fire. "Several persons were found whose bodies had been transfixed by the sharp ends of huge timbers," read one account. The tornado's "merciless devastation beggars description and calls for the use of words which would have to be coined for the occasion."[104]

In its wake, the storm left a city of traumatized citizens bereft of the usual infrastructure of spiritual comfort. Some two dozen churches were either destroyed or badly damaged, including historic structures like Trinity German Evangelical Lutheran, the mother congregation of the Lutheran Church–Missouri Synod, and Saints Peter and Paul, the wealthiest German Catholic parish in the city. The remaining houses of worship had to accommodate some 200 funerals on Sunday, May 31. The *Post-Dispatch* described the mournful "mingling of life and death" at St. Patrick's, East St. Louis, as 130 Catholic children, many of them bandaged and limping, were confirmed by Bishop John Janssen while bells tolled for the dead across the city.[105]

The death knells did not forestall the development of a near-carnival atmosphere as thousands of sightseers—nearly 150,000 in the first week—poured forth from special "excursion trains" and jammed the city's already strained hotels. Here was "the rise of natural disaster as a form of mass entertainment," as historian Ted

FIGURE 3.5. Ruins of Mt. Calvary Episcopal Church, St. Louis, after the 1896 tornado. Photograph by Orison H. Shores. St. Louis Public Library.

Steinberg has put it.[106] Thanks to improvements in communications technology, the Great Cyclone dwarfed the Great Natchez Tornado of 1840 as a nationwide sensation. Constant news updates traveled via telegraph, and many newspapers covered the story for days. (The *New York Times* devoted its entire May 29 front page to the disaster.) And though papers were still printing only line drawings, photographs could be reproduced in magazines and books. *Harper's Weekly* ran six pages of illustrations (both photographs and drawings). Dozens of photographs of the damage also appeared in at least three instant books on the disaster, one of them in German. Even the average tourist could now chronicle the event in pictures. An advertisement in the *Post-Dispatch* for Erker Brothers Optical Company announced that "Views of the Ruins of the Tornado Can be taken by any one with one of Our Kodaks."[107]

With the nation's attention fixed on St. Louis, commentaries on the disaster ensued. Civic boosters quickly chimed in with a narrative of progress. "After the storm, the sunshine," declared the *Post-Dispatch* on June 3. "In a few weeks, the scars which Nature's violence inflicted upon the devoted city of St. Louis will be healed by man's recuperative industry." The newspaper continued in same vein the next day, noting that one week before, East St. Louis was "a dismantled charnel house, reeking with blood and tears" and filled with people "stunned and dazed by the transcendent evil which had befallen them." Now that city too was astir with the sound of the hammer. "The transformation has been marvelous." Even the Eads

FIGURE 3.6. Ruins of Trinity German Evangelical Lutheran Church, St. Louis, after the 1896
tornado.
Photograph by Edward W. Schumann. St. Louis Public Library.

Bridge connecting the two cities was soon cleared of wreckage, just in time for the
Republican Convention to go on as scheduled.[108]

But the boosterism failed to stifle a religious debate that reprised many of the
themes of the previous two centuries. On the one hand were religious liberals
who, convinced by science or theology or both, insisted on the essential benevolence of God and creation. On the other hand were traditionalists who embraced
more supernatural, even apocalyptic, explanations. Just four days after the disaster, the *Post-Dispatch* anticipated this clash of worldviews, noting that some
would see in the tornado the operation of an impersonal natural law, while
others would see the wrath of God. Still others "will tell you [that] anything

and everything under any circumstances is 'all for the best.' "[109] The paper titled its editorial "The Passing Show," implying an amused indifference toward the competing opinions.[110]

Such secular nonchalance may have been more culturally viable by 1896 than it was at Natchez in 1840. The liberal Protestant critics of traditionalism were certainly louder and more numerous. Liberal voices dominated the *Chicago Tribune*'s coverage of sermons by clergy in that city on the first Sunday after the disaster. At the nondenominational Peoples Church, Hiram W. Thomas, who had been defrocked by the Methodists for heresy, was quoted as saying that science had emancipated people from traditional moral interpretations of violent weather. "Such phenomena as storms, earthquakes, fires, and floods are to be explained by the laws of nature, not by the good or evil deeds of man," he said. Few people now "will say that the destroying cyclone came upon St. Louis because of its wickedness. If that were God's way of punishing man, few, if any, cities would escape." Years earlier, Thomas had told his flock that nature is a benevolent order and he cautioned against complaining about its forces: "If we come into a habit of thinking and living in harmony with this vast order, it puts a new face upon everything" and frees us from going through life "as [if] following a funeral train."[111]

Other Chicago clergy echoed Thomas's sunny message. At Trinity Congregational Church, Theodore Clifton extolled the natural order and argued that the earth was relatively quiet now compared to the "battles of the elements" in the planet's primeval history. A "cyclone sweeping over a few miles—a little after-swell following great cosmic storms that have subsided into cosmic calms—should not disturb man's faith," he argued. Similarly, Newell Dwight Hillis, pastor of the independent Central Church, reminded his listeners that the St. Louis Tornado was part of a larger series of storms that had finally broken a two-year drought in the Western states. "Nature's laboratory is large," he said. "What has been a great mercy to many has brought grief to the few." The suffering in St. Louis was staggering, but it was not a punishment for sin. The tornado would have happened there even if the region had been a wilderness. God's "providential dealings are natural, not arbitrary"; they happen "according to law and not according to caprice." Finally, H. A. Delano of the Belden Avenue Baptist Church exhorted his congregation not to sin by "blaming God foolishly" or by "doubting the divine mercy" that underlies all things.[112]

The liberal chorus in Chicago did not go unchallenged. The Louisville-based *Christian Observer*, the largest circulating Presbyterian weekly in the United States, decried the Chicago pastors' "blunt denial that God had any special lesson for us in the disaster." To attribute such events purely to the laws of nature was to "exclude God from the incident." It behooved Christians to "recognize the hand of God in everything" and to acknowledge that God uses agencies that "are beyond the power or control of any man." The Bible testified to God's unpredictable power: "The wind bloweth where it listeth, and thou hearest the sound thereof, but canst not tell whence it cometh, and whither it goeth" (John 3:8). The St. Louis Tornado was a reminder to all Americans to heed God and his commandments.[113] The Missouri Synod's *Lutheran Witness* likewise invoked John 3:8 and noted the coincidence, which the editors apparently did not regard as such, that the verse was part of the gospel reading appointed in the lectionary for May 31, the Sunday following the disaster. (Though the magazine did not mention it, the Sunday preceding the disaster was Pentecost, which also entailed a meteorological theme in the lectionary—the "rushing mighty wind" of Acts 2:2.)[114]

Another Missouri Synod publication, *Concordia Magazine*, was more explicit. Noting that thousands of prayers had "escaped the lips of scoffers" during the tornado, the periodical called the storm a reminder of humans' "feeble insignificance" before God and a foretaste of the travails of Judgment Day. Baptist minister L. T. Mear wrote to the *Galveston Daily News* that the St. Louis Tornado and other twisters spawned in Texas by the same system were warnings from the Lord in accordance with Psalm 46:8 ("Come, behold, the works of the Lord, what desolations he hath made in the earth"). God sent such calamities to "teach man that in his fallen condition he is a creature incapable of self-government." As society hurtled toward destruction, people would be made ready to accept Christ at his Second Coming. Mears pointed to Haggai 2:7: "The desire of all nations shall come, which is Christ" ("which is Christ" was his own addition).

Not all traditionalists attributed the St. Louis catastrophe to the immediate agency of God. At least one blamed Satan instead. Five months after the tornado, Presbyterian minister David Calhoun Marquis, a professor at McCormick Seminary who officiated at the wedding of celebrity preacher Billy Sunday, spoke in St. Louis at the reopening of Lafayette Park Presbyterian Church, which had been badly damaged by the storm. "You may be assured, my friends," he told the congregation, "that whenever destruction falls upon the church of God, the author is always the same. No matter by what name you call it, the devil is the prime mover of it." Marquis's claim prompted an unlikely rebuttal from the so-called "Weather Prophet" Irl R. Hicks, a Congregational minister in St. Louis and amateur meteorologist who had gained nationwide fame for predicting an outbreak of tornadoes in May 1896. (He had singled out May 27, the day of the St. Louis disaster, as particularly dangerous.) A former Methodist, Hicks had studied theology and meteorology at the Methodists' Andrew College in Trenton, Tennessee. Even before the St. Louis storm, he had acquired enough celebrity from his weather almanac and other publications that one newspaper described him as a "household name." Like James Pollard Espy,

Hicks saw storms as instruments of God's benevolent government. Regarding the claim of the devil's involvement, Hicks quipped that "Dr. Marquis seems much better acquainted with the gentleman than I am." "I really look upon the tornado as an agency for good," he continued. "It came by the will of the Lord, working through the laws of nature." While the storm itself was terrible, God uses such events to turn people toward higher things. The "tornado has done more to make the people of this city think upon the serious problems and duties of life than anything else that has happened in years."[115]

Hicks's positive estimate of the tornado's moral outcome mirrored other commentaries in the disaster's immediate aftermath. Preaching at Grace Methodist Episcopal Church in New York City on the Sunday after the tornado, Ezra Squier Tipple, later president of Drew Theological Seminary, recalled the Johnstown Flood of 1889, which killed more than 2,000 people when a Pennsylvania dam failed. Johnstown happened because of human negligence, he said, but "man has no control over the tornado." Why does God permit such calamities? God's purpose, Tipple argued, is to turn people's attention from "the minor details of life" and to increase "sympathy among men." Similarly, Congregational minister W. C. Miller, preaching at Decatur, Illinois, noted that the St. Louis disaster seemed worse than Johnstown, despite the much smaller death toll, because the tornado was completely beyond human control. Yet God uses such catastrophes to lift humans beyond their self-centered existence and remind them that "we are all brothers," with a duty to care for each other.[116] The secular *Philadelphia Inquirer* also cited the seven-year anniversary of Johnstown and observed that the St. Louis disaster, by contrast, had no human cause. Invoking Matthew 2:18, the paper noted that in hundreds of homes in St. Louis, "Rachel is weeping for her children and will not be comforted." Nevertheless, the tragedy would make St. Louis stronger, for "one touch of nature makes the whole world kin."[117]

The famous preacher T. De Witt Talmage, speaking at the First Presbyterian Church of Washington, D.C., sounded a variation on the same theme, arguing that adversity refines humans by increasing their reliance on God. Taking as his text Exodus 10:13 ("the Lord brought an east wind upon the land all that day, and all that night"), he pointed out that the east wind in scripture often serves a threatening or punishing function. These tribulations do not come at random but fulfill a divine purpose. "I suppose God lets the east wind blow just hard enough to drive us into the harbor of God's protection," he said. "The best thing that ever happens to us is trouble. That is a hard thing perhaps to say, but I repeat it, for God announces it again and again."[118]

Talmage's conclusion that humans should bless God for the east wind indirectly highlighted the peril of drawing moral lessons from tragedy. The argument that God brings violent weather to instruct humankind fails to explain to particular victims why *they* must suffer as part of some divine pedagogy. Theodicy that works on the societal level, in other words, may be of little comfort at the individual level, where scientism—the idea that weather happens according to impersonal natural laws—may be more appealing. By the time of the St. Louis disaster, scientific voices had certainly gained more popular currency. But the concern of the traditionalists and the apocalypticists was far from idle: If the stormy wind does not fulfill God's word, how *does* God work in the world? The tornadic apocalypses of the nineteenth century had brought Americans no closer to solving these riddles, even though commentators still felt the need to try.

In a quixotic coda to the story, a month after the St. Louis disaster, Henry A. Hazen, a US Weather Bureau meteorologist and distant cousin of the late William Babcock Hazen (who banned the word "tornado" in government forecasts) weighed in with a scientific solution to the tornado problem. Noting the increasing danger to life and limb in "the so-called cyclone belt" as the region became more densely populated, he speculated that tornadoes could be halted if cities installed on their western perimeters a network of dynamite that could be set off by trained spotters. If this was too expensive, cities could plant forests on their southwestern edges to "draw off the electricity that gives to the 'cyclone' its energy." Hazen's suggestion drew an immediate rebuke from the chief of the Weather Bureau, Willis L. Moore, who insisted that "the theories advanced are not held by scientific men generally" and did not represent the views of the agency.[119]

Hazen's dream of fortifying the nation's cities typified Americans' seemingly irrepressible frontier optimism. Grounded in the notion of human self-determination and reinforced by the Gilded Age cult of progress, this outlook assumed that no problem—not even a tornado—was too big for Americans to handle. But what if American optimism was built on too limited a vision of the frontier? Among scientists, the possibility would soon dawn that not all frontiers are humanly measurable, just as not all scientific discoveries diminish uncertainty.

That we henceforth be no more children, tossed to and fro, and carried about with every wind of doctrine, by the sleight of men.

—EPHESIANS 4:14

The sin of pride, to which the prophets of Israel were so sensitive, is more obvious in our day than in theirs. Yet there are fewer prophets to recognize and challenge it. If this age is essentially irreligious, the basic cause of our irreligion is our sense of self-sufficiency. The achievements of science and technics have beguiled us into a false complacency. We have forgotten the frailty of man.

—REINHOLD NIEBUHR, *Beyond Tragedy* (1937)

4

"Every Wind of Doctrine"

EXPLAINING THE WHIRLWIND, 1900–1965

"AWFUL CALAMITY TO Befall Pine Bluff Says a Crazy Negro Woman."[1] So screamed the headline of the local newspaper on May 18, 1903, in Pine Bluff, Arkansas, a river port and cotton center and the state's third largest city. Ellen Burnett Jefferson, a 22-year-old domestic laborer, had predicted that a tornado would wipe Pine Bluff off the map on May 29. As word of her prophecy spread, "blacks and superstitious white persons," according to the *Cincinnati Enquirer*, began exiting the town, some of them selling their property for almost nothing. Newspapers across the country seized upon the story. "Negroes at Pine Bluff in a Panic," announced the *Pittsburgh Daily Post* on its front page. "Prophecy Empties a Town of Negroes," said the *New York Times*, which claimed that 8,000 black residents had fled, an improbable count given that the 1900 census had put the total number of African Americans at 5,771, just over half of the city's population.[2]

At the center of the uproar was an unlikely figure, described by the local papers as a diminutive, dark-skinned woman with short, tightly curled hair. Little is known of her background. Though the press sometimes referred to her by her maiden name, Ellen Burnett, the *Arkansas Democrat* reported that she had married Arthur Jefferson after moving to Pine Bluff from Texas early in life. A later account added that she was a member of the Sanctified Church, the name often given to the up-start Holiness and Pentecostal denominations that challenged the older Baptist and Methodist churches for dominance among African Americans in the post-Reconstruction South.[3] Because the Sanctified Church placed little value on formal ministerial credentials, women who felt called to preach often found a place there to exercise their spiritual gifts.[4]

Jefferson knew that in prophesying Pine Bluff's destruction, she would suffer ridicule, for Jesus had taught that a prophet is without honor in her own country. But she could not ignore the vision she had received. She recounted it to a reporter from the *Democrat*, who noted that her recitation at times "reached the high sing-song tone so familiar among many negro preachers of the old school." She told how on May 9 she had entered a trance and beheld God seated on a great white throne. Beside him was a tall man, barefoot and clad in a white robe. God instructed the man to weigh the city. Placing the city on a great scale (an image reminiscent of Daniel 5:27), the man concluded that "sin and grace were on an equality." God then decreed that he would not permit the just to suffer with the unjust, and he admonished Jefferson: "Go and warn my people to leave the city, and not to stop under six miles from it, for I will destroy the city and all that are left therein." Five nights later, Jefferson had another vision in which she foresaw ominous storm clouds and God pinpointed the date of the city's annihilation, May 29.[5]

Jefferson's vision paralleled Jonah's experience of God's warning about the coming destruction of Nineveh. In Pine Bluff, residents were less concerned with biblical allusions than with the possibility that her prophecy might be accurate. The prophetess (as Jefferson came to be known) stoked the fears by "keep[ing] up a harangue at her home day and night," according to the *Pine Bluff Daily Graphic*. Amid the accelerating exodus from the town, white mill owners deprived of their black employees began to lean on local officials to take action. The *Daily Graphic* asked Isaac Fisher, the newly appointed African American principal of Branch Normal College (today the University of Arkansas at Pine Bluff), to issue a reassuring statement. The 26-year-old Fisher, a protégé of Booker T. Washington, hoped to build Branch Normal College into an Arkansas version of the Tuskegee Institute, an effort for which W. E. B. DuBois would later deride him as a "white folk's nigger."[6] The newspaper's request put Fisher in an awkward position. He began by professing his "profound respect for that deeply religious temperament which ignorance converts into superstition." Though it would be unwise of him to try to dissuade people from leaving town if they felt unsafe, he personally would remain. Surely in this advanced age, he reasoned, "when men have learned to read God's will through the teachings of science," the deity would not turn back the clock to the "days when direct revelation was the only power which would move doubting man."[7]

Fisher's statement did little to quell the rising panic as townspeople rushed to buy insurance coverage on their property or even sell their homes. He soon issued a more emphatic appeal, admitting that he had originally guarded his words for fear of "arousing the resentment of my own people." "I do not believe that in any way God has revealed Himself to any person in Pine Bluff," he wrote. "I humbly beg that my people will return to reason." Lamenting "the injury which will be done to the progress of the race after this nonsense has had its course," he denounced the flight from the city as "the very quintessence of superstition."[8] The *Daily Graphic* weighed in with its own editorial, noting that it was understandable that gullible blacks might be taken in by a false prophet, but whites should know better. "The days of prophesying are past," the paper declared, and "all the true prophesies are given in the Bible." As Jesus himself warned, "beware of false prophets, which come to you in sheep's clothing" (Matthew 7:15).[9] Meanwhile, Jefferson County Sheriff James Gould had arrested Ellen Jefferson on a charge of lunacy and convened a largely futile meeting in the black community to appeal for calm. On May 27, two days before the anticipated doomsday, he attempted to transfer her to Little Rock, either to the state insane asylum or the state penitentiary, but neither institution would accept her. The sheriff of Pulaski County finally agreed to take her until the storm had blown over. Now there was nothing to do but wait.[10]

Pine Bluff residents awoke to cloudy skies on May 29. The *Daily Arkansas Gazette* reported that Jefferson's own family members had remained in the city, "evidently not believing in the prophecy." When nothing had happened by late afternoon, the mood in the town lightened. About 8:00 p.m., as local weather observer Harvie Hudson later recounted, a dark bank of clouds formed, and soon "quick tongues of lightning were almost continuously darting across the sky." The flashes and thunder became "terrific," and the earth "seemed to tremble and the windows vibrated in the houses, as trees swayed and responded to the increasing power of the wind." Hudson recalled fearing that Jefferson had been right. But by 11:00 p.m., the wind died down and people realized that it had been just another springtime thunderstorm.[11]

"Pine Bluff Still on Map," proclaimed the *Daily Graphic* in its next edition. By that time, the Pulaski County jail had released Jefferson, who told a reporter that it was "the Lord's business" if Pine Bluff was out of danger. "I didn't want to make this prophecy," she added. "I tried to get out of it, but the Lord wouldn't let me. . . . I hope if another [storm] is to come He'll give the word to somebody else. I'll kick mighty hard before I'll take it, for it's caused me a lot of trouble. But then I had to do it."[12]

Reaction in the local press to Jefferson's failed prophecy was unabashedly racist. "The negroes have been taught a lesson they should never forget," opined the *Daily Graphic*, "but it's dollars to doughnuts that many of them would flee again if another

FIGURE 4.1. Front page of the *Arkansas Democrat* (Little Rock), May 30, 1903, with a photograph of Ellen Burnett Jefferson.
Arkansas Democrat via Library of Congress and Newspapers.com.

Ellen Burnett should predict a calamity." The *Arkansas Democrat* regarded the incident as proof of the "pitiable" superstition and essential inferiority of blacks: "The white race was evidently made to rule and the negro to serve, since they were not created capable of ruling for themselves." Even the national press could not pass up the opportunity for editorial comment. The August 1903 issue of *Current Literature* magazine, based in New York, carried an overview of the incident, "An Extreme Case of Negro Superstition," by the white Methodist minister William Pearson Whaley, whose later writings included *The Divinity within Us* (1907). Noting that "prophets frequently appear among the negroes," Whaley observed that none of Pine Bluff's "negroes could give an intelligent reason for believing the prophetess." "They were smitten with awe; and it was pitiable to see thousands of the poor creatures driven away from their homes by the dread that held them in its spell."[13]

The disdain for "negro superstition" bespoke more than simply the paternalism of white commentators. It also pointed to a significant cultural shift. Little more than two centuries earlier, Cotton Mather had matter-of-factly announced to his parishioners that God had directed him to lay aside his prepared sermon and preach instead on the voice of the Lord in the thunder. By Ellen Burnett Jefferson's day, many of the mainline clergy—Mather's descendants in the erstwhile establishment—took a dim view of direct communication with the deity, much less one who thundered from the heavens. Doomsday visions from God were definitely beyond the pale, the province of the lower classes, women, people of color, and the mentally unbalanced.[14] Weather calamities could be explained rationally, either through the rapidly advancing science of meteorology or by cheerful theodicies that took for granted societal progress and God's ultimate benevolence. As the Gilded Age gave way to the Progressive Era, many religious leaders were convinced that humans would soon outgrow the childhood of the race, no longer to be "carried about with every wind of doctrine," as the Apostle Paul had put it. The angry storm god would finally be banished, and scientific management would mitigate the weather's worst effects. Even religion itself would enter a new era of ecumenical reasonability.

But a strange thing happened. The more technically advanced the society became, the more calamitous were its meteorological disasters. Though humans had always been vulnerable to sudden blows from the weather, modern Americans had more complex infrastructure to lose. Americans' sense of security would likewise suffer as broadcast (and later digital) media revealed storm-wrought destruction to far greater audiences than those reached by the print-only media of the nineteenth century. On a deeper level, the weather disasters of the twentieth century also laid bare the lingering difficulties of accounting for deadly storms theologically. While the traumas of two world wars are usually credited with chastening the optimism of prevailing liberal theologies, the weather played an important role too, especially in pushing some thinkers beyond the assumptions of traditional theism toward revisionist models of God. By the latter half of the twentieth century, some theologians were rehabilitating the theme of the Book of Job—divine inscrutability—while drawing on the quantum revolution to stress a world of radical uncertainty. In this context, a frustrated prophet such as Ellen Burnett Jefferson appears less naïve than she did to her contemporaries. "The Lord selected me," Jefferson had explained, "and I just had to do what He said."[15] As the Apostle Paul had taught, the Lord's judgments are unsearchable and his ways past finding out.[16]

APOCALYPSE AT GALVESTON, 1900

Ellen Burnett Jefferson's prophecy of the wholesale destruction of an American city may have frightened her listeners all the more because such a thing had happened just three years before in her home state of Texas. The Great Galveston Hurricane of 1900 remains the most catastrophic storm in American history, killing more than 6,000 people and leaving the city a nightmarish wasteland of mangled bodies and twisted wreckage. Much has been written about the failure of local authorities to anticipate the danger in time for residents to evacuate. Isaac Cline, the US Weather Bureau's man in Galveston, had argued that hurricanes as a rule did not strike Texas but generally followed a parabolic track beginning near the equator, arcing toward the northwest, and then turning northeastward away from the Texas coast.[17] Another weather prophet, Andrew Jackson DeVoe, forecaster for the Chattanooga Medicine Company's *Ladies' Birthday Almanac* (issued annually in 15 million copies), had predicted that a great cyclone would form over the Gulf of Mexico on September 9 and move up the Atlantic seaboard. Though the hurricane made landfall on the evening of September 8 and subsequently moved inland over the country's midsection, DeVoe's prediction was close enough that the national media credited him with anticipating the storm.[18] Tragically, few in Galveston heeded the almanac or Cline's frantic efforts (later disputed) to warn residents that the hurricane was about to hit.[19]

When it slammed ashore, the hurricane was likely a strong Category 4, with a barometric pressure estimated at 27.50 inches. Sustained winds of 150 miles per hour "hurtled grown men across streets and knocked horses onto their sides as if they were targets in a shooting gallery," as Erik Larson put it in his bestselling book on the tragedy. A violent 15-foot storm surge inundated anything not toppled by the winds. If the hurricane had struck the coast at an oblique angle, some of the surge's depth and energy would have dissipated, but the storm hit at a nearly perfect 90-degree angle. The onrushing water and fierce winds capsized Cline's own house, tossing his family into the flood. He barely escaped drowning. His wife, Cora, was not so lucky. Searchers later found her body amid a tangle of debris.[20]

Daybreak on September 9 revealed the enormity of the disaster. Ida Smith Austin, teacher of a popular Bible class at First Presbyterian Church, recalled how "the sobbing waves and sighing winds, God's great funeral choir, said their sad requiem around the dead." Over the next few days, as makeshift morgues quickly filled, the odor of thousands of decomposing bodies became intolerable. Men were conscripted, and given all the whiskey they needed, to tie weights to bodies and load them onto barges for burial in the Gulf. But many of the corpses floated back to shore. The city soon resorted to burning the bodies, most of them still unidentified, on giant funeral pyres. Thomas Monagan, an insurance adjuster who volunteered to help run a relief train from Houston to Galveston, wrote years later of his horror at the burning of the bodies: "it seemed too awful in a civilized country."[21]

As news of the catastrophe reached the rest of the nation, clergy took to their pulpits to reflect on the perennial problem of theodicy, or how to square such a tragedy with a loving God. For some, the obvious answer was that Satan, not God, had caused the storm. B. C. Hartman, pastor of the Heidelberg Reformed Church in Philadelphia, noted that Jesus had rebuked a storm on the Sea of Galilee. If that storm had been from God, Hartman reasoned, then Jesus would have been working against God. Storms must therefore come from Satan, whom the Apostle Paul called the "prince of the power of the air" (Ephesians 2:2). Walter Lewis of the First Methodist Church of Atlanta, in a sermon entitled "The Prince of the Power of the Air," confessed that he could not "think God is even the efficient cause of the great disasters that have befallen the earth," for these bore the imprint of one who could only delight in woe. "Where, then, does God come into the scene?" Lewis asked. "In the use He make[s] of human misfortune and in the grace that repairs the desolation which has been wrought. 'All things are made to work together for good to them that love God' [Romans 8:28]."[22]

Other clergy pointed a finger not at satanic malevolence but at human negligence. At Monroe Avenue Methodist Church in Rochester, New York, F. D. Leete dismissed the traditional ascription of disasters to God's anger over human sin. Alluding to Matthew 5:45, he noted that meteorological "visitations fall upon the just as well as the unjust." Human carelessness or ignorance, rather than divine wrath, was more likely to blame, which meant that humans bore the responsibility to make amends through offerings of money and other assistance. "In the great trials of life we are one," Leete said. Cortland Myers, pastor of the Baptist Temple in Brooklyn, New York, was more direct: "The city of Galveston should have been fortified against the storm. The possibility [of disaster] was always there. It was understood by most men." Galveston had in fact been built on an unstable barrier island, making it particularly vulnerable to inundation from tropical storms.[23] Clayton Youker, pastor of Euclid Avenue Methodist Church in Oak Park, Illinois, decried the "foolishness of those who founded [Galveston] upon the sand." He also took issue with the idea of a divine hand in the weather. "God never sent that awful storm; natural conditions produced it." The resultant loss of life was largely a consequence of humans' own poor choices. "Much of so-called providence is human improvidence," he concluded. "An ounce of common sense is worth a pound of providential nonsense." Youker nevertheless insisted that Galvestonians deserved the financial assistance, not merely the prayers, of Christians everywhere. "It is a burlesque on prayer to ask God to do something which the petitioner should do himself," he declared. "Man is never so divine as when unselfishly serving his fellow."[24]

Common to these reactions was an optimistic theism, a holdover of nineteenth-century liberal Protestantism, that reflexively distanced God from anything other than the good. Galveston's failure to protect its residents—only after the hurricane did the city build a 10-mile-long, 17-foot-high seawall—was paradoxically comforting because it absolved God of culpability and offered reassurance that such tragedies were preventable. As a theodicy, this view embraced the culture's faith in technology and human self-determination, and the notion that society would learn from its mistakes.[25] Like the other clergy, Mary Augusta Safford, a Unitarian minister in Des Moines, Iowa, denied divine involvement in the hurricane, stressing instead the impartiality of nature. "We have learned that lightning is quite as apt to strike a church as a saloon," she told her parishioners. She emphasized the remedial quality of natural disasters: "If we are to hold fast our faith in the goodness of God, we must grasp the truth that pain and death, as well as joy and life, are meant to educate and bless humanity." Great calamities, she said, have spurred humans to "acquire that mastery over the forces of nature which makes them help instead of hinder human progress."[26]

Technology would indeed afford Americans greater mastery over their destinies in the face of hurricanes. Later in the century, the advent of radar and satellites would give people hours, even days, of warning for storms like the one that surprised Galveston. Altogether more elusive was the tornado, which could be invisibly embedded in a larger storm (including a hurricane) and could touch down and lift again before ever being detected by weather observers. Whereas a hurricane's cloud bands could extend over hundreds of miles, a tornado's pinpoint strikes were the epitome of arbitrariness. One researcher has estimated that even within an area under an official tornado watch, the odds of a tornado passing within a mile of a particular location are about one in a thousand.[27] The odds of a tornado hitting a particular house within that mile radius are of course even smaller. Death by tornado thus posed the problem of theodicy with uniquely American starkness: Why me? In singling out particular persons, the tornado seemed to confirm Americans' rugged individualism even while mocking the possibility of individual control. Every new tornado disaster produced stories of seemingly miraculous escape as well as unbelievable bad luck. In struggling to explain the latter, many clergy fell back on habitual theodicies. But each successive tornado increased the strain on conventional explanations.

THE "TORNADIC REIGN OF TERROR"

Three days after the doomsday that Ellen Burnett Jefferson had prophesied for Pine Bluff failed to materialize, a catastrophic tornado did strike—560 miles away in Gainesville, Georgia, on June 1, 1903. Back in Pine Bluff, the local newspaper carried the wire story on its front page, describing how the storm of "terrific force" came suddenly "out of a clear sky" and within two minutes had killed nearly 100 people. Many of the dead were women and children employed at two local cotton mills. At one, some 250 child laborers were working on the top floor of a five-story, wood-frame building when the structure collapsed.[28] The *Atlanta Constitution* quoted physician

Floyd W. McRae on the "ghastly" sight of the bodies of four girls whose "heads had been literally bisected to the chin" and had to be tied up to keep them from falling apart. The newspaper printed a statement from Hall County Commissioner W. B. Hawkins, who said that the disaster "is simply appalling, and Gainesville is stunned and bleeding at the foot of the storm king."[29]

In a self-congratulatory editorial, the *Constitution*, while noting that it would be unseemly to boast, reported that the Atlanta city council had proffered $1,000 in assistance to Gainesville before the town had even asked. "The grace of helpfulness lies in its promptness," the newspaper concluded, adding that there is "a heart in humanity" equal to any woe caused by "the storm-god."[30] The following Sunday, at Atlanta's Moore Memorial Presbyterian Church, Pastor A. R. Holderby, who had served as an army surgeon during the Civil War, spoke similarly of the need to help the victims, having just returned from volunteering his surgical skills in Gainesville. Holderby's sermon also highlighted the moral and theological ambiguities of the event. Tacitly acknowledging the role of social class, he observed that "hundreds of those poor mill people have lost their all" and "will need all they can get to relieve their sufferings and their deep poverty." God, he insisted, sympathizes with the "poor factory people" in their distress and would bring good out of the storm. And yet, why lowly Gainesville? If the tornado had struck proud Atlanta, continued Holderby, with its record of Sabbath desecration, intemperance, and gambling, "some people would not have wondered at such a judgment." Was it simply "blind chance" that Gainesville was so afflicted? Holderby, whose sermon text was Nahum 1:3 ("The Lord hath his way in the whirlwind and in the storm"), could not go there. "No storm or tempest can come save at His bidding and by His permission," he told his congregation. Perhaps God sent tornadoes to make humans "feel their own littleness." "No man can doubt God in the tornado or cyclone," he observed. "The fool may say that God is not in the storm, but he does not doubt it in his heart." Still, the question nagged: Why Gainesville? Holderby did not tackle it directly, professing faith only that God would use the tragedy for good.[31]

The Gainesville storm was but a prelude to what meteorologist Thomas Grazulis has dubbed the twentieth century's "tornadic reign of terror." Between 1908 and 1974, there were 16 years with at least 300 tornado deaths. A period of comparative quiet followed, lasting until 2011.[32] The century's first great spike in activity, the so-called Dixie Outbreak of 1908, killed 324 and injured more than 1,300 across the Deep South.[33] Many of the dead were African-American sharecroppers or tenant farmers, whose cabins, "noted for their flimsy, happy-go-lucky construction," were "converted by the wind into wholesale death traps," according to the *St. Louis Post-Dispatch*. Particularly hard hit was Amite City, Louisiana, where the storm struck while many residents were at home for their noontime meal. Nearly every building in town, save for the courthouse, was either fully or partially destroyed.[34]

Among those who perished at Amite City, none received more attention nationwide than Father Felix Rumpf, the local Catholic priest. Born Joseph Rumpf in Ottersweier, Baden, Germany, he received the name Felix when he took his vows as a Benedictine monk at St. Meinrad Abbey in Indiana in 1874. Ordained a priest in 1880, Father Felix was beloved for his cheerful, industrious personality. According to some accounts, he had just rung the noontime Angelus when the sudden wind caused the bell tower to collapse on him. More likely is the report of the New Orleans *Times-Democrat*, according to which, despite the fierce wind, the priest was walking from the rectory to the church to say his customary prayer of thanksgiving after his noon meal when the church's cupola fell, crushing him.[35] The most arresting detail was not the manner of his death, but that he had several weeks earlier had a dream that seemed to foretell the disaster. He had used it in a sermon to illustrate "man's utter dependence on God and his eternal mercy," the *Catholic Advance* of Wichita, Kansas, wrote. In the dream, he beheld a terrible tornado or earthquake that caused the trees and buildings of the town to fall all around him. As the townspeople shrieked in terror, Father Felix also screamed, causing someone to exclaim, "What, you, a priest, afraid?" Father Felix said that while it might surprise some people that a priest of the gospel should feel fear, he was afraid and "smote his breast three times and cried aloud to God for mercy and protection." To the *Catholic Advance*, the dream showed "Father Felix's sturdy faith and implicit confidence in Divine Providence." To the *Assumption Pioneer* of Napoleonville, Louisiana, the story proved that "nothing is impossible to God," who can reveal the future in dreams when he so chooses.[36]

The *Times-Democrat* did not mention the dream, the story of which apparently originated with the rival *Picayune*. But two days after the tornado, alongside an editorial calling on the people of New Orleans to assist the sufferers, the *Times-Democrat* offered a lengthy opinion, "Why Sermons So Seldom Count," arguing that modern science and rising education levels in the general population had diminished the once-unquestioned authority of the clergy's preaching. To be sure, said the newspaper, science had not touched the "ultimate realties" and had "answered one set of questions by asking another." Nevertheless, "Darwin and Huxley and Spencer" had introduced a new worldview in which "imperious law, guiding alike the atom and the star" had replaced "a stern deity, ruling by mere whim." Members of the "priestly caste," formerly "set apart from the mob by the mere ability to read and write," now faced a tougher audience and needed to abandon dry, dogmatic sermons in favor of a more artful, persuasive, and emotional oratory. "In religion, as in art," concluded the editorial, "Horace's canon holds good—'If you would have me weep, you yourself must first shed tears.'"[37]

Appearing so soon after the tornado, the editorial indirectly revealed the increasing competition the clergy faced from the mass media as the arbiters of religious meaning in the wake of disaster.[38] More importantly, the opinion illustrated the persistent tension between traditional theism (the "stern deity" questioned by the newspaper and supplicated by Father Felix in his dream) and modern conceptions of God which no longer took for granted divine involvement in the natural world. As we saw in Chapter 2, this tension was as old as the Enlightenment, but in the twentieth century the tornadic reign of terror brought it to the fore repeatedly, and to ever wider audiences. Though most Americans probably would have been hard-pressed to define the term "theodicy," they were nevertheless becoming aware of the theological questions posed by tornadoes.

Those questions were once again raised when an F4 tornado struck Omaha, Nebraska, on Easter Sunday, March 23, 1913, killing at least 94 people. Part of a two-day sequence of outbreaks in which more than 200 died, the tornado descended upon Omaha so suddenly that many people did not know what had hit them. Carving a path of destruction nearly a quarter of a mile wide, the storm was no respecter of persons, according to the *Omaha Daily Bee*, invading "the hovel and

FIGURE 4.2. Desolation at 35th and Cass Streets in Omaha after the Easter Tornado of 1913.
Bain News Service, George Grantham Bain Collection, Library of Congress.

the palace, the dwelling of the wage worker, and the mansion of his employer." The shocked survivors "in many cases lost their composure to such an extent that their stories are incoherent."[39] To the city's Christian majority, the storm's appearance on Easter was especially cruel, but Jews also felt singled out because many of the fatalities were in the Near North Side neighborhood, the center of both the Jewish and African-American communities.[40]

With Omaha still reeling, the postmortem theologizing began. Among conservative Protestants, two nationally prominent preachers seized the opportunity to give a shout-out to the "stern deity" of traditional providentialism. Charles Reign Scoville, perhaps the most celebrated Disciples of Christ evangelist of the era, told a large crowd at the municipal auditorium in Lincoln, Nebraska, that recent disasters were visitations of God's wrath to repay humans for their sins. "When God gets into the game," he declared, "something happens." He urged his listeners to get right with God by being "born again," a condition he said could not be described but only experienced.[41] Meanwhile, at Broadway Baptist Church in Ardmore, Oklahoma, visiting preacher J. Frank Norris (later known as the "Texas Tornado" for his fiery, fundamentalist oratory) told a packed house that "God uses the things of nature" to "execute his divine judgment." He cited as evidence not only the Omaha tornado but also the Dayton flood, which the same week had inundated Ohio's fifth-largest city with 20 feet of water, killing an estimated 360 people. In neither of these events, Norris said, was there any conflict between nature and God, whose handwriting was in all things. God had already determined everybody's time to die. "If it is predestined that I am not going to be killed by a cyclone," he said, "it is also predestined that I shall get in a storm cellar." He then returned to a familiar line of attack, heaping scorn on the lily-livered liberals who tried to explain away supernatural Bible stories such as Jonah's being swallowed by a whale. If the story were the other way around, with Jonah swallowing the whale, Norris said he would still believe it if the Bible said it. "I would rather a thousand times swallow the biggest whale that ever floated on the water than swallow [the liberals'] theology," he added.[42]

At least one liberal Protestant—the sort of mainliner whom Norris loved to hate—also cautioned against discounting the God of wrath. Howland Hanson, pastor of the First Baptist Church (Northern Baptist) of Des Moines, Iowa, conceded that the indiscriminate carnage produced by the tornado lent ammunition to the "cynicism" of those who would attribute the storm to blind fate. But God still exercised a power beyond human control or understanding. "As man's hand ruthlessly sweeps away the web of spider or nest of bird, so omnipotence sweeps away our homes, our handiwork," he said. "Humility is still needed as a virtue. . . . God has not been conquered. We have something to learn, something to fear. There is still a God of Tornado! We should seek to know his will."[43]

Other religious leaders blanched at any suggestion of a Tornado God. Hanson's ministerial colleague in Des Moines, William B. Gage of Highland Park Presbyterian Church, chalked up the Omaha disaster to a "freakish wind" and contrasted it with the Dayton catastrophe, which he blamed on human negligence in the building of the city in the flood plain of the Great Miami River. Back in Omaha, the Jewish relief committee also credited the tornado to the inexorable forces of nature, endorsing the opinion of the *Bee* (and of its Jewish editor, Victor Rosewater) that "no precautions of ours could have prevented the terrible visitation." The *Bee* had observed that "before the irresistible onslaught of nature's gigantic forces, human beings are but as atoms, and their most substantial houses prove to be but fragile shells." All we can do, the newspaper editorialized, "is to succor the injured, comfort the bereaved, house the homeless, and help to put the lamed ones again on their feet."[44] Similarly, T. J. Mackay, rector of All Saints Episcopal Church, exhorted his parishioners to "a tighter bond of fellowship" with their fellow citizens. As for the cause of the tornado, he decried the "foolish people who want to saddle everything onto the Lord." Ascribing the storm to God was as primitive as the idea that persons in heaven revel in the tortures of the damned in hell. If God were behind the tornado, Mackay asked, why did he send it on Easter Sunday, of all days? "God's will is not death or tornadoes," he said, "but our purification and education."[45]

Letters to the editor of the *Bee* echoed the debate among the religious leaders. Anthony Easterling, who said he was not "a church man," denounced the "flabby-spined, weak-brained men" who claimed that God would wantonly kill his own subjects in a tornado. Such ideas, Easterling predicted, would eventually yield to the light of science, going the way of hellfire, infant damnation, and other discredited doctrines. "Wake up, O wake up," he concluded. "The sun is high." An anonymous correspondent, writing apparently tongue-in-cheek, complained that enlightened critics of religion failed to understand "the morality of a supreme being who crushes (even by the operation of secondary causes) the life out of so many helpless human beings." Adolph Hult took issue with Easterling, saying that it was religion's skeptics who needed to wake up. Hult called on Omaha's citizens to reject the materialist philosophy of the present day, which eliminated God's hand in the storm. " 'The sun is high'—the sun of truth eternal proclaimed by the Christian church," Hult wrote. The lesson of the tornado was that Omahans should incline their hearts and minds upward to the eternal God. Even the work of disaster relief must not take priority over the most important "post-tornado occupation" of approaching God with all "seriousness, reverence, and submission."[46]

GOD'S "STRANGE POWER" IN THE WHIRLWIND

The tornadic reign of terror was soon joined by a storm of human origin: World War I. When the United States entered the Great War on April 6, 1917, American troops faced the existential horrors of trench warfare and chemical weapons on the Western Front. Many soldiers described the experience in quasi-religious terms, or what historian Jonathan Ebel has called the "combat numinous." It resembled Rudolf Otto's numinous in that it was nonrational and therefore defied description. It also entailed an almost ecstatic "creature-consciousness" (to use Otto's term), or a sense of nothingness before an overwhelming higher power.[47] One soldier, Louis Ranlett, recalled the shell-shocked faces of his comrades in the trenches. The men "had run into It—whatever It had been." Another soldier, James Norman Hall (later the co-author of *Mutiny on the Bounty*), said that in combat "I doubted my own identity, as one does at times when brought face to face with some experiences which cannot be compared with past experiences or even measured by them. I groped darkly, for some new truth which was flickering just beyond the border of consciousness."[48] On the battlefield, the men had encountered a power that was dreadful and irresistible, something that could not be equated simply with good or evil but that was profoundly mysterious and unsettling.

Americans on the home front were confronting the same inexorable, ambivalent power in the tornado. Seven weeks after the United States declared war on Germany, in an eight-day period tornado outbreaks killed some 383 people across multiple states. One of the hardest hit towns was Mattoon in central Illinois, where a probable F4 twister, half a mile wide, killed 53 people and destroyed nearly 500 homes on May 26, 1917.[49] As the local newspaper described it, the storm formed in early afternoon from "clouds of inky blackness" that turned "greenish yellow" just before the funnel descended. "With a roar the tornado struck, and the devastation wrought was more terrible than anything which the people of the city have ever before been called upon to witness." Hailstones of more than seven inches in diameter rained further destruction. Some terrified residents rushed to their cellars "only to be crushed to death by the brick and mortar which were piled therein" by the mighty wind. The storm imprinted on their minds an experience that would haunt survivors "throughout the remainder of their lives."[50]

As the daunting recovery began, Mattoon's clergy assumed their traditional role of explainers in the wake of disaster. Their sermon titles, announced in the newspaper, tell the tale: "Special Providences" (First Presbyterian); "Why Did the Tornado Come to Mattoon?" (Central Baptist); "Calamities, Why Permitted" (International Bible Students Association); "Comfort Ye, Comfort Ye My People" (Broadway Presbyterian); and "Gathering Up the Fragments" (First Christian). The local ministerial association took out an advertisement inviting the town's citizens into the churches. "Some of you have not been in a church for years," the ad noted, "but this is a good time to begin what you have been postponing for so long a time." The spirit of Christ binds all people together, rich and poor, in time of need: "Let the worship of God and the fellowship of saints be first in your minds. Then shall you forget what manner of clothes you wear."[51]

Clergy elsewhere in the country also attempted to wrest meaning from the storm. A particularly striking message came from A. H. Kennedy, interim rector at the Episcopal Church of the Good Shepherd in Ogden, Utah. Preaching the day after the Mattoon tornado on the feast of Pentecost, he invoked the "rushing mighty wind" of Acts 2:2. The wind, Kennedy said, is a peculiarly apt image for God's power because it is both commonplace (the air we breathe) and filled with "such dreadful possibilities, as the calamities of the last few days have revealed." So it is with God, who is ever with us, working below the surface of everyday events, and sometimes rushing forth in another Pentecost. "The cyclone is but God moving in the wind," Kennedy declared. It discloses to us God's "strange power" and his "strange work." Kennedy's sermon drew an angry reply from one townsperson, who asked how anyone could believe that God was responsible for such a deadly and destructive event. "I would rather believe that 'Kaiser Bill' was in that wind," wrote Aubrey Parker, referring to Kaiser Wilhelm II of Germany. But Kennedy had seemed uninterested in addressing questions of causation or theodicy, pointing instead to the wind as a metaphor for divine potency and unpredictability. "The wind bloweth where it listeth, and ye hear the sound thereof, but canst not tell whence it cometh or whither it goeth," he said in the sermon, appealing to John 3:8.[52]

Three years later, Pentecost symbolism gave way to Passiontide when a tornado outbreak on Palm Sunday, March 28, 1920, sowed terror across the Midwest and South.[53] In the twentieth century, Palm Sunday, a movable feast that always falls within the peak springtime tornado season, would prove a meteorologically fateful day, marked by major tornado outbreaks in 1920, 1936, 1965, and 1994. The 1920 event saw many deaths and injuries in greater Chicago. The storm came out of the southwest with "great suddenness" around 12:30 p.m., according to newspaper accounts. At the First Congregational Church in Elgin, Pastor J. W. Welch had just closed the morning service with the words, "Be prepared, for you know not when you will be called," when heavy rain and high winds commenced. Most parishioners sheltered in place within the building. Minutes later, they heard a "terrific roar," and the church's tower fell through the roof, killing two adults and one child. A similar scenario played out at First Baptist Church, where one person died. Outside the churches, other Passion dramas ensued. In the storm's aftermath in Melrose Park, photographers congregated around an elderly woman, her head wrapped in a bloody towel, who refused to leave the spot where her house once stood. She "rocked continuously to and fro, mumbling incoherent words," according to the *New-York Tribune*.[54]

Newspaper coverage of the Palm Sunday tornadoes had barely subsided when another outbreak April 19–21, 1920, killed 243 people in several Southern states.[55] By then, the public was becoming aware that tornadoes often came in "flocks," as James H. Scarr, head of the US Weather Bureau office in New York, put it. Harry C. Frankenfield, of the Weather Bureau's Washington headquarters, told a wire service that the "tornado menace is becoming more serious because of the rapid increase in population." He stopped short of calling for more explicit tornado warnings. (The word "tornado" had been banned from government forecasts since 1885.) "If we predicted tornadoes," he explained, "people in several states would quit work."[56]

Editorial writers, sensing the potential for public panic, tried to project nonchalance but probably succeeded only in calling more attention to the tornado threat. After the 1917 tornadoes, the *Citizen-Times* of Asheville, North Carolina, had noted that while Europe may have earthquakes and other disasters, the tornado is a peculiarly American institution that wreaks havoc on a truly American scale. Yet fortunately for citizens of the mountainous oasis of Asheville, "storms pass harmlessly over us." "So while our hearts go out in deepest sympathy to the stricken sections of the middle west," the newspaper explained, "we are not without a feeling of gratitude that our section has been, and is so signally favored." Even the *Daily Eagle* of Wichita, Kansas—smack in the middle of Tornado Alley—sought to reassure its readers that they had nothing to fear. The day after the 1920 Palm Sunday tornadoes, the newspaper claimed that a person's chances of being killed by a tornado were "far less" than the odds of being killed by lightning. "The individual in any given Kansas town," the paper added, "runs about the same risk of being killed by a tornado as he does of being taken up alive to heaven in a chariot of fire."[57]

The statistical unlikelihood of dying in a tornado only heightened the agony for towns where deaths occurred. Indeed, the unpredictable randomness of tornadic violence engendered a special American anxiety. Syndicated information columnist Frederic Haskin voiced this fear a few weeks after the 1920 outbreak. The tornado, he wrote, is "a marauder which gives no warning." This "truly American institution" remained the "mysterious devil of the weather" because it had eluded reliable prediction. While forecasters had been able to track the larger cyclonic storms from which tornadoes emerged, individual twisters descended too quickly to alert persons in their sights. "There is no weather phenomenon which gives such an impression of deadly power and malignant intent," he added, "and none which causes more terror."[58]

The tornado as American Marauder was frightening enough to give pause even to the sunniest of clergy. Dr. Frank Crane was known as the "Oracle of Optimism" for his "Four Minute Essays" and other syndicated columns. Ordained a Methodist minister, he later served a Congregational church before becoming a full-time writer. H. L. Mencken once mocked him for his "canned sagacity," but Crane boasted five million daily readers, who were drawn to his aphoristic and affirming style.[59] When Crane entitled a column "Why Tornadoes?" in the wake of the 1920 Palm Sunday outbreak, his followers paid attention. Not claiming to have easy answers, he fell back on the hauntingly enigmatic non-theodicy of the Book of Job. The problem of whether there is rational purpose in the universe, Crane began, is the "oldest question of the race." Why, moreover, is there so much seemingly senseless suffering in the world? Job's friends gave the "cheap and easy explanation" that he was afflicted because of his sins. But as the tornado reveals, events in the world are not just, and "nature is pitiless." Humankind "insists that the Creator is good, not because this is proved by events, but because it is contradicted by events," Crane explained. "Morality in man is his eternal protest." Man is moral only when he cries, as Job did, "Though he slay me, yet will I trust in him" (Job 13:15). The things of the natural world pale before the noble aspirations of the human soul, Crane wrote, ending on an optimistic note after all. "Not in the sun nor the sea, not in the laws of Nature nor the train of events, but in the Soul of Man, and there alone, is the Undying Fire."[60]

TRIAL BY TORNADO: THE 1925 TRI-STATE DISASTER

Frank Crane was not the only celebrity pondering the whirlwind in the 1920s. Another was the three-time presidential candidate and "Great Commoner" William Jennings Bryan, whom Crane had known when their careers overlapped in Omaha in the 1890s. The day of the 1920 Palm Sunday tornadoes, Bryan had been in Lincoln, Nebraska, railing against the God-denying thought of Darwin and Nietzsche, which, he charged, had been foisted upon America's youth by the universities. Every living thing, Bryan maintained, bears testimony to a living God. Divine purpose, not randomness, is the order of the universe. "Chance cannot fashion even a little flower," he said. A few years later, in his weekly syndicated "Bible Talk," Bryan turned his attention to the question of non-living nature—the wind— and whether it exhibits rational design. The movements of the air currents are a mystery to humans, he conceded, for "the wind bloweth where it listeth" (John 3:8). But nothing is a mystery to God, who can compel the winds to do his will, just as Jesus stilled the storm on the Sea of Galilee. "He can turn them loose and harness them again; He can set them in motion and He can also calm them," Bryan wrote.[61]

Bryan himself was destined to be associated with the wind in American popular culture. The 1960 motion picture *Inherit the Wind*, dramatizing the 1925 Scopes Trial, indelibly linked his name with that phrase (taken from Proverbs 11:29) and with a belligerent, know-nothing fundamentalism.[62] The trial, in which Bryan represented the prosecution seeking to convict John Scopes of teaching evolution in a public school, in violation of Tennessee state law, still looms large as a symbol of the cultural clash between science and religion. For many conservative Protestants, evolution came to represent the specter of a godless nature, pitiless (to borrow Crane's term) in its random variation and natural selection. But three days before Tennessee governor Austin Peay signed the statute that would precipitate the Scopes Trial, another watershed event occurred that for many middle Americans—Bryan's constituency—would raise the specter of a godless nature more immediately.

The event was the Tri-State Tornado (1925), which remains the deadliest tornado in American history, killing 695 people and injuring more than 2,000.[63] On one level, the storm simply offered an outsize example of recurring themes we have seen, including apocalypticism and its skeptics, and post-disaster ecumenism even amid persistent divisions of denomination, race, and class. But in the immense suffering that it inflicted, especially among children, the storm was also the most powerful image yet of an American crucifixion, imprinting the Midwestern landscape with the stigmata of the Tornado God, and leaving many of its survivors at a theological loss. The Tri-State Tornado represented the obverse of American exceptionalism—that instead of Nature's nation, blessed by God, the United States was the singular recipient of Nature's wrath.[64] Though other factors, including the First World War, had freighted the era's religious thought with a new pessimism, the Tri-State Tornado was a symbolic tipping point toward new ways of thinking about God, nature, and American chosenness.

There is no shortage of historical accounts of the disaster.[65] Nationwide newspaper coverage at the time painted a vivid picture. At 1:01 p.m. on Wednesday, March 18, the F5 storm touched down near Ellington, Missouri, in the Ozarks. For the next three and a half hours, it churned on a 219-mile path through southeastern Missouri, southern Illinois, and southwestern Indiana. At times it was nearly a mile wide with a forward speed varying from 56 miles per hour to an astonishing 73 miles per hour, more than twice that of the average tornado. It took merely seconds to obliterate some small towns, arriving with little warning. The weather forecast in one local newspaper the day before had noted innocuously, "rain probable tonight and Wednesday."[66]

When the storm crossed the Mississippi River at 2:23 p.m., eyewitnesses reported an almost biblical apparition of a pillar of cloud—a great wall of smoke preceded by white billows, water swept up from the river. The tornado then began its deadly progress across the region of southern Illinois known as Little Egypt, taking aim first

FIGURE 4.3. Man with his overturned piano after the Tri-State Tornado of 1925 destroyed his home in Princeton, Indiana.
Hulton Archive via Getty Images.

at the village of Gorham. Local resident Judith Cox was in a restaurant when the sky suddenly darkened. She opened the door to see the monstrous funnel approaching. "The air was full of everything, boards, branches of trees, garments, pans, stoves, all churning around together," she said. "I saw whole sides of houses rolling along near the ground." Fourteen-year-old Alice Summer was in school when the daylight vanished. The children rushed to the windows, angering the teacher, who ordered them back to their seats. Seconds later, the walls caved in. "I can't tell you what happened then," Alice recounted, amid tears. "I can't describe it. I can't bear to think about it."[67]

After killing 37 people at Gorham, the storm took aim at Murphysboro, Illinois (population 10,703), where 234 would die—the first time in American history that a single city would suffer more than 200 fatalities from a tornado.[68] "As chaff before it went hut and mansion, the old and the young, freightage on the winds to a port of no return," noted the Murphysboro *Daily Independent*. At the Longfellow Grade School, 450 students had just returned to their classrooms from recess. Principal Joe Fisher, hearing the gathering storm, glanced out his window and realized to his horror that the dark approaching cloud was a tornado. As the howling winds drew closer, the whole building began to shake. In a split-second decision, he ordered the students to evacuate. About half were clear of the building when it was "crushed like a shell and piled down within itself," according to the *Independent*. Many of the students fortunate enough to have made it outside survived, shielded by the remains of the building in which other students were buried by debris. After the funnel passed, some dazed children wandered home, only to discover that their houses were missing. One girl found only an open field—along with her decapitated grandmother, still sitting in her rocking chair.[69] Similar nightmares played out in De Soto, the next town in the storm's path, where Garrett Crews, then in eighth grade, watched from an upstairs classroom as the winds hurled a girl against the schoolyard fence. She was later found dead. Fifteen students were killed instantly and almost all the others were injured when the school building collapsed. Crews landed on top of the school's janitor, who managed to free himself and then the boy. Only later did Crews discover he was covered in blood from a laceration on the janitor's scalp.[70]

In the aftermath of the storm, devastating fires broke out, especially in Murphysboro. With the municipal water system down, firefighters were unable to douse the flames, resorting instead to dynamiting some buildings in a desperate effort to halt the firestorm. The few available physicians felt equally helpless in caring for the injured. In Murphysboro alone, some 463 people required amputations and other surgery, but anesthetics and tetanus antitoxin quickly ran out. One woman

FIGURE 4.4. The devastated Longfellow Grade School in Murphysboro, Illinois. From a 1925 postcard, via CardCow.com.

trapped in the rubble of her home had to have her leg amputated on the spot so rescuers could pull her to safety from the advancing fire.[71]

All along the 219 miles gouged by the tornado, survivors were stunned and be-reft amid a desolate landscape. It was "as if death had stalked through . . . with an enormous scythe," as one correspondent put it.[72] The day after the storm, the *Daily Independent* printed a one-page extra edition bearing only a list of the dead.[73] African-American victims appeared with "colored" appended to their names. As news of the catastrophe hit front pages across the nation and overseas, official condolences poured in. At the Vatican, the usually austere Pope Pius XI is said to have wept upon hearing of the hundreds of dead, among them Italian immigrants in Murphysboro's "Little Italy." The pope ordered special prayers to invoke God's mercy on the stricken regions.[74]

On Sunday, March 22, more than 1,000 people gathered for an ecumen-ical memorial service on Murphysboro's town square. Participating clergy represented eight denominations: Catholic, Lutheran, German Evangelical, Baptist, Presbyterian, Christian (Disciples), African Methodist Episcopal, and the two white Methodist bodies—North and South. A. F. Haynes of Centenary Methodist Church (South) admitted that the storm posed "a challenge to our faith." "If our faith means much," he added, "we will realize it now." William Boatman of First Lutheran Church urged listeners to accept the tornado as one of the inscrutable acts of God, which had brought residents to "a feeling of near-ness to the things of religion." John R. Goelz of St. Andrew's Catholic Church prayed for God's mercy on both the dead and the living. Earl G. Hamlet, Haynes's colleague from Centenary, implored the crowd not to think that the storm was a divine judgment, for "it was not God who hurt Murphysboro's babies." Victor P. Frohne of St. Peter's German Evangelical Church reminded the assembly of Romans 8:18 ("the sufferings of this present time are not worthy to be compared with the glory which shall be revealed") and concluded, "Some day we shall understand."[75]

Outside of the disaster zone, some clergy were less circumspect. Robert F. Hall of the Unity School of Practical Christianity in Des Moines, Iowa, offered a twist on the familiar theodicy attributing calamities to God's punishment of human sin. A New Thought movement combining Christian liberalism with ideas from Theosophy and other sources, the Unity School promoted education to help people realize their divine potential. Because Unity taught that God is absolutely good, Hall insisted that the tornado victims themselves, not God, were to blame for their suffering. These victims' sin, however, was not the usually cited profligate living but racism, as evident in the Ku Klux Klan activity prevalent in the region. "Hateful

FIGURE 4.5. Ecumenical memorial service on the town square in Murphysboro, Illinois, on March 22, 1925.
Courtesy of the Jackson County (Illinois) Historical Society.

thoughts invariably destroy the things that produce them," Hall said.[76] S. Edward Young at Bedford Presbyterian Church, Brooklyn, however, cited the perils of profligacy. The tornado, he said, ought to sober up people in their "mad rush for money and pleasure" and prompt them to ponder "the exceeding fragility of our tenure upon this earth." Editorial writers also weighed in. In Dayton, Ohio, where memories of the devastating flood were still raw, the *Daily News* wrote that the tornado was a reminder that humankind, for all its technical accomplishments, "stands naked in the presence of nature in her irate moods."[77]

Underneath such reactions lurked unexamined theological questions. Is nature a bearer of moral judgments? Does God act through nature, or is nature an impersonal agent? If God is in the tornado, then what kind of God does this imply? This last question ignited a fierce exchange in the town of Alexandria, Indiana (population 4,172). Five days after the storm, the *Alexandria Times-Tribune* editorialized that it had no patience for people who blamed the tornado on divine wrath. "If we thought for a moment that God was such a monster," the newspaper's editors wrote, "we would never again mention His name with reverence." This elicited a rebuke from a reader, who advised the editors to remember Nahum 1:3 ("The Lord hath his way in the whirlwind and in the storm"). The newspaper retorted that it would take "a most vivid imagination" to say that the "hundreds of babies" killed in the tornado were God's enemies. "We do not believe in that kind of a God," the editors declared, "and what's more, we never will."[78]

REINHOLD NIEBUHR AND THE WEATHER

Though such sniping over God's role in storms had by now become a fixture of post-disaster news coverage, few Americans had devoted sustained thought to the theological issues at stake. In the wake of the Tri-State Tornado, a 33-year-old Detroit pastor was at work on his first book, which not only would help win him a professorship at Union Seminary in New York, but would foreshadow his emergence as the century's most important thinker on the problem of God, nature, and evil. In *Does Civilization Need Religion?* (1927), Reinhold Niebuhr (1892–1971) anticipated some of his later critique of nineteenth-century religious liberalism, characterizing it as grounded in a naïve optimism that was true to the facts of neither nature nor history. He argued that modern urban-dwellers suffered from "an atrophy of the religious sense" because they had lost much of their premodern ancestors' reverence for nature's perennial benevolences, as well as fear of its cruel caprices. Modern people mistakenly assumed that nature reflected a moral order, whereas in reality the natural world was "morally indifferent." God bestowed love impartially, not in conformity with human standards of judgment. God "sendeth rain on the just and on the unjust," Niebuhr observed, citing Matthew 5:45.[79]

Niebuhr had learned to respect the weather during his boyhood in the Mississippi Valley, the region affected by the Tri-State Tornado. Born in Wright City, Missouri, he was three years old when his father, Gustav, became pastor of a church at St. Charles, Missouri, just across the Missouri River from St. Louis. The following year, the St. Louis Tornado of 1896 killed 255 people and leveled much of that city, a catastrophe that surely persisted in the family's collective memory. When Reinhold was 10, the family moved to central Illinois, where severe thunderstorms often rolled across the prairie. As he wrote in *Beyond Tragedy*, "I remember how wonderful was the experience of my boyhood when we ran to the barn, warned by ominous clouds of an approaching storm, and then heard the wind and the rain beating outside while safe and dry under the eaves of the haymow." To the adolescent Niebuhr, it evoked Psalm 91:10 ("There shall no evil befall thee"), which he had memorized in confirmation class. But as a parish pastor and later a professor, he came to realize that this verse expresses an "illusion" that often tempts people of faith—"that the child of God will be accorded special protection from the capricious forces of the natural world." "Any such faith," Niebuhr continued, "is bound to suffer disillusionment. Nor does it deserve moral respect."[80]

Not long after Niebuhr settled into his new professorship at Union Seminary, the capricious forces of the natural world took another cruel turn. The Plains States were stricken with a drought that would result in the Dust Bowl of the Depression era. In September 1930, the *Christian Century*, flagship magazine of liberal Protestantism, enlisted nine prominent churchmen to contribute to a forum, "Does Prayer Change the Weather?" Niebuhr had written frequently for the *Century* in the 1920s, and though he was not among the nine contributors, the forum mirrored his concerns. Only two of the nine—James M. Gray, president of Moody Bible Institute, and Mark A. Matthews, pastor of First Presbyterian, Seattle—upheld the traditional view of God's absolute sovereignty over the weather. The other opinions ranged from mild skepticism to outright disdain. "Of course prayer does not affect the weather," wrote Harry Emerson Fosdick, pastor of New York's Riverside Church and outspoken opponent of fundamentalism. "Evidently this still needs to be said in this benighted and uncivilized country." Samuel Harkness, pastor of the Community Church of Winnetka, Illinois, argued that if prayer affects the weather, "meteorology ceases to be a science and becomes an article of theology." Walter M. Horton of Oberlin Theological Seminary appeared to deny the literal truth of Christ's calming of the storm (Matthew 8, Mark 4, Luke 8), insisting that it "is only in pious legend that tempests are stilled at a word of command." W. P. Lemon of Andrew Presbyterian Church observed that destructive natural phenomena such as tornadoes, typhoons, and lightning "seem utterly regardless of humankind." For this reason, he added, prayer for favorable weather "would seem to be a piece of special pleading to an obsolete deity who made rain only for his favorites."[81]

Such assertions that nature is autonomous and impervious to prayer were a striking reversal from the colonial era, when Thomas Prince beseeched God to send a tempest against the Duc d'Anville Expedition. While most of the clergy who contributed to the *Century* forum seemed ready to divorce God from the weather, the magazine's readers were less eager to abandon a more traditional providentialism. Of 11 published letters responding to the forum, seven defended the power of prayer for rain, two denied it, and two wavered in between.[82] Underlying the debate was an unspoken and acutely American anxiety: Are the "laws of nature and of nature's God" still trustworthy? Or is chaos the only order of the universe?

Niebuhr took up these questions in the 1934 Ware Lecture to the American Unitarian Association. Modern culture, he argued, rejected the dualism and pessimism of medieval religion, which saw the world through a biblical lens of contending forces of good and evil. In place of this biblical mythology, the modern world substituted "a simple naturalistic monism and optimism" that identified change with progress and ascribed divine attributes to nature. Modern people thus "discovered in 'the laws of nature' the very guarantee of the meaningfulness of the universe which it is the business of religion to find." The problem, said Niebuhr, is that the laws of nature "are not laws at all, but projections of human ideals." The faith of modern culture is "a superficial religion which has discovered a meaningful world without having discovered the perils to meaning in death, sin, and catastrophe." The old biblical mythology, for all its inexactitude, at least recognized that "the world is not only a cosmos but a chaos." The Hebraic tradition does not flinch from this chaos, but simply accepts that the ultimate center of meaning transcends the world. Niebuhr later elaborated this point in *Beyond Tragedy*. "The meaning of life," he wrote, "lies rooted in a power too great and good to be overcome by the momentary anarchies of history or by the periodic suggestions of chaos and meaninglessness which arise from man's strange relationship to nature's blind and morally indifferent forces." This is what the Apostle Paul meant, Niebuhr added, when he wrote that "neither death, nor life, nor angels, nor principalities, nor powers," nor anything else in creation would be able to separate us from the love of God in Christ Jesus (Romans 8:38–39). "Every possible peril and evil is anticipated—and discounted," Niebuhr noted, "because it cannot destroy the faith."[83]

All the while, the perils mounted. In 1936, another Palm Sunday tornado outbreak slammed the South, this time in Tupelo, Mississippi, and the next day in Gainesville, Georgia (again), killing a total of 454 people. Among those who narrowly escaped injury in Tupelo was the one-year-old Elvis Presley. A newspaper in Mississippi reacted indignantly to a local minister's plan to preach on the subject, "Did God Send the Tornado?" The answer is no, the paper declared, and "no twisting of theological dogmas will convince thinking people" otherwise. "In nature the deer may starve because his antlers are caught between the forks of a tree. And nature is at times equally unkind to the human race."[84]

As if such real-life tornadoes were not frightening enough, the release of the film *The Wizard of Oz* on August 25, 1939, burned the image of a twister into the memory of millions of Americans. Producers created the movie's famous "cyclone" scene, in which Dorothy's house was lifted into the air by a tornado, using a large canvas stocking for the funnel. Dangled onto the stage by a crane, the stocking was rotated by a D.C. motor and fastened at its base to a car traveling on predetermined track. The effect was realistic enough to be unnerving, at least for a juvenile audience. Eight-year-old reviewer Hubbard Keavy remarked: "The tornado came whirling along and picked up the house Dorothy was in. That scared me."[85]

By this time, Reinhold Niebuhr was well on his way to becoming the nation's leading theologian. The 1940s saw him preoccupied not with disasters of the natural variety (what theologians call natural evils) but with a calamity of human origin (moral evil in theological parlance): the rise of Nazi fascism. In *The Nature and Destiny of Man* (1943), the first part of which he delivered in 1939 as the Gifford Lectures at the University of Edinburgh even while German planes were bombing a nearby naval base, Niebuhr wrestled with the paradox that humans are created in the image of God and yet are inclined toward sin. Endowed with reason and freedom, humankind is capable of greatness but also perpetually given to dangerous self-delusion. At the national level, human pride can prove catastrophic if left unchecked by prophetic judgment. This is what happened in Nazism, which had become "a daemonic form of national self-assertion."[86] Niebuhr returned from Scotland convinced that the United States must intervene on behalf of Britain in the war against Hitler. Rejecting the pacifism and isolationism of the *Christian Century* and its editor, Charles Clayton Morrison, Niebuhr founded a rival journal, *Christianity and Crisis*. The evil of going to war, he believed, was less than the evil of allowing the Nazis to triumph. As he put it, "ambiguous methods are required for the ambiguities of history."[87]

After the war, Niebuhr returned to thinking not only about the ambiguities of history but also the ambiguities of nature, and how they converge in the American experience. In "The Providence of God" (1952), delivered at Union Seminary, he brought together themes from his earlier writings in what is arguably the most brilliant sermon on the weather in the American literary canon. For his scriptural text, he returned to Matthew 5:45, a passage that the two most important colonial interpreters, Cotton Mather and Jonathan Edwards, completely ignored in their biblical commentaries.[88] Though the verse had received scattered mention in the nineteenth century (as we saw in the previous chapter), Niebuhr fully grasped its profound implications. This passage, he noted, is one that "we never quite take in" because it is "set squarely against most of our religion." It teaches the "very radical concept" that God is like "the impartial nature which you could accuse of not being moral at all, because the sun shines upon both the evil and the good, and the rain descends upon the just and the unjust." A "nonmoral nature," Niebuhr explained, is to Jesus the symbol of God's "transmoral mercy." This flies in the face of the typical American faith in special providence, which Niebuhr called the "real defect in our Puritan inheritance." The Puritans believed that "every rain and every drought was connected with the virtue and vice of their enterprise," a view manifested in later American culture's dangerous self-righteousness. Even a more general providentialism is wrong, Niebuhr insisted, if it assumes that life can be "correlated easily into simple moral meanings." We learn otherwise from the Bible, especially the Book of Job, which shows that God is not "a God of simple justice." "We cannot speak simply of a moral order which if defied, would destroy us," Niebuhr said. God's mercy transcends good and evil, like nature itself. Nature moves by its own laws, which frustrate our moral expectations. We therefore cannot look to nature for ultimate meaning. Humans occupy the realm of history, which is a "vast middle ground" between the realm of nature and the realm of grace. "Our Christian faith lives in the realm of grace," Niebuhr concluded. The lower realms of history and nature are "a threat, not only to the sense of the meaning of life, but finally to the morals of life."[89]

TORNADOES AND PROVIDENCE IN AN AGE OF UNCERTAINTY

In 1953, the year after Niebuhr's sermon at Union Seminary, history and nature intersected frighteningly—or so many people suspected. The Cold War had ignited into the Korean War, and at the Nevada Test Site that spring, the United States was exploding atomic weapons in Operation Upshot-Knothole, which culminated in the detonation of a 61-kiloton device, four times the yield of the bomb dropped on Hiroshima.[90] Five days later, on June 9, the worst tornado ever to hit New England devastated parts of Worcester, Massachusetts (see Introduction). Many people worried that the atomic tests were roiling the atmosphere, spawning tornadoes and other violent weather. The Worcester storm indeed capped a season of wild weather that included an earlier tornado outbreak that killed 144 people in Waco, Texas, and elsewhere. "Is it entirely beyond the bounds of possibility," asked the *Christian Century*, "that there could be some connection between these unprecedented changes in the normal weather pattern and the long continued series of atomic bomb explosions in Nevada?"[91]

Other developments also heightened the public's anxiety. During the 1950s, the Federal Civil Defense Administration, created by President Truman, attempted to implement a siren warning system to alert the nation of imminent nuclear attack. Many towns eventually used the same sirens to signal tornado warnings. For millions of Americans, the wail of a civil defense siren became an instantly recognizable and unnerving harbinger of doom.[92] Tornado preparedness gained additional attention with Snowden "Frosty" Flora's *Tornadoes of the United States*, published in 1953 and updated in 1954 in light of the Worcester disaster. Flora, for 44 years a meteorologist at the US Weather Bureau in Topeka, Kansas, painted an ominous picture from the book's first page, overestimating tornadic winds as approaching 500 miles per hour (more recent measurements have put the maximum closer to 300) and describing the "terrific roar" of a tornado as "resembling the noise of a thousand railway trains crossing trestles" (scientists are still uncertain of the sonic qualities of a tornado).[93] The 1950s also brought the advent of television in American homes, along with the new phenomenon of TV weathercasting. Television had considerably more dramatic potential than radio, though the earliest weathercasts were visually primitive compared to much later ones with digital graphics. In 1952, Oklahoma City's WKY (now KFOR) issued the first televised tornado bulletin. Two years later, the federal government opened the National Severe Storms Forecast Center in Kansas City to coordinate warnings nationwide.[94]

The climate of anxiety, fed by repeated warnings to prepare for meteorological or nuclear disaster, inevitably led some theologians back to the question of divine control over human affairs.[95] Between 1956 and 1960, a trio of important new works on providence appeared. Aimed at the educated general reader, all three books sooner or later touched on the weather as a classic locus of questions about divine sovereignty. The first to appear was Roger Hazelton's *God's Way with Man* (1956). Hazelton (1909–1988) was Abbot Professor of Christian Theology (the chair once held by Edwards Amasa Park) at Andover Newton Theological School, located just 40 miles from storm-ravaged Worcester. Not surprisingly for a scholar of Calvinist lineage—Hazelton was an ordained minister in the United Church of Christ—he began by lamenting the scant attention to providence in academic theology and by decrying the "crude" form the doctrine often assumed in popular religiosity. This neglect belied the inseparability of providence from theism, for "either we believe that God has actual, active power to direct our human steps or else we do not believe in God at all." "A do-nothing God is no God," he added. Part of the difficulty of providence stemmed from people's failure to acknowledge that the doctrine "has always had to presuppose the tragic." Belief in providence may actually be harder for Christians than for non-Christians because Christians "expect so much from God." Christians forget that a certain degree of "agnostic deference and stoical resolve" is necessary for weathering life's devastating reversals of fortune. A farmer's bumper crop may be ruined by drought; a once-happy marriage may wind up on the rocks of divorce. In "all things mortal we are menaced by hazard, nonfulfillment, and frustration." The twists of what humans call fate are the mystery that stands between themselves and God. Confronted by this uncertainty, we must allow ourselves to complain to God, insisted Hazelton, because doing so is amply attested in scripture, whether in psalms of lament or in prophetic cries of "How long?" Hazelton also appealed to Kierkegaard, who in *Repetition* (1843), urged: "Complain! The Lord is not afraid, He is well able to defend Himself. . . . Speak, lift up thy voice, speak aloud, God surely can speak louder, He possesses the thunder." Even if the thunder crushes a man, Kierkegaard continued, it is "more glorious than gossip and rumor about the righteousness of providence which are invented by human wisdom."[96]

Hazelton's meditation centered on the human response to life's uncertainties. The next work on providence turned a scientist's eye to the uncertainties themselves. In *Chance and Providence* (1958), William G. Pollard (1911–1989) applied his expertise not as a trained theologian but as a nuclear physicist. After working on the Manhattan Project during World War II, he founded the Oak Ridge Institute of Nuclear Studies (later, Oak Ridge Associated Universities) in 1946 as a way to link faculty experts to the Oak Ridge National Laboratory. Along the way, he became interested in existential questions. He later recalled how his exhilaration over the successful bombing of Hiroshima turned to "something approaching terror" after the second bomb devastated Nagasaki. From his research in physics, he realized that "there were many things which could not be explained by any universal law or scientific theory." Reared as an Episcopalian, he grew more active in church. Eventually, he began studying for the Episcopal ministry, and in 1951 he was ordained a deacon. Three years later, the "Atomic Deacon" (as he had been dubbed by *Time* magazine) was ordained a priest. It was in this dual career that he would make his most memorable contributions as a writer on science and religion.[97]

Pollard began *Chance and Providence* by suggesting that no doctrine of the Christian faith is "so remote from contemporary thought forms" as providence. "The farmer who believes rain to have been providentially provided for his crops finds his beliefs challenged by the meteorologist who explains it in terms of the physics of the atmosphere and the movement of the air masses," he wrote. The Enlightenment and scientific revolution introduced the idea, foundational to classical mechanics, that the universe unfolds according to fixed and predictable laws, which operate apart from the intervention of the Creator. This worldview had reached an apex in the work of French mathematician Pierre-Simon Laplace (1749–1827), who claimed that if he could know the exact position and velocity of every particle in the universe at a given moment in time, he could accurately predict the universe's state

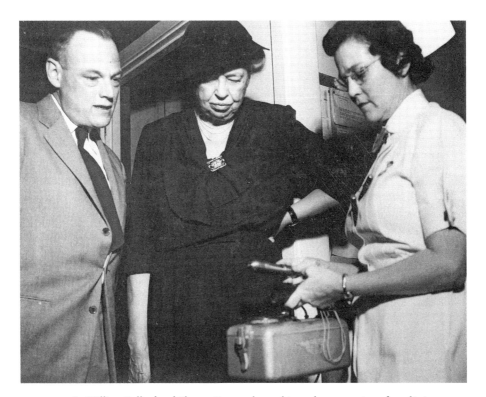

FIGURE 4.6. William Pollard and Eleanor Roosevelt watching a demonstration of a radiation counter at Oak Ridge, Tennessee, in 1955, the year after Pollard became an Episcopal priest. Photograph by Ed Westcott. National Archives.

at any desired time in the future. But classical mechanics failed at the subatomic level, Pollard explained. As Werner Heisenberg (1901–1976) demonstrated in his *Physical Principles of the Quantum Theory* (1930), the more accurately a subatomic particle's position is known, the less accurately can its momentum be calculated, and vice versa. This is the famous Heisenberg uncertainty principle, and it proved that Laplace's optimism was an illusion. Subatomic physics is at its core statistical; it must deal in probabilities rather than certainties. "Whether we like it or not," Pollard observed, we live in "a world in which indeterminacy, alternative, and chance are real aspects of the fundamental nature of things, and not merely the consequence of our inadequate and provisional understanding."[98]

But what has this to do with providence? Whereas classical mechanics had relegated God to the sidelines, enshrining him as the remote Lawgiver, quantum mechanics introduced a new wrinkle by revealing uncertainty or indeterminacy to be the underlying order of the universe. There are two sources of indeterminacy in history, argued Pollard: chance and accident. Chance is involved in all natural processes, down to the random behavior of an electron in an atom. Accident is when two or more happenings with no causal connection coincide in a way that alters the course of events. Accidents, of course, can easily be read as providential, while chance and providence seem contradictory. But it is a fallacy, Pollard insisted, that providence cannot include chance. In fact, chance and accident together constitute an impenetrable "curtain." We cannot raise the curtain "to establish objectively God's purposive activity," but neither can we get behind the curtain in order to deny God's working in the world. To claim that an event happened by "mere chance" says nothing of ultimate theological import, for chance is "the dead end in the path of causal explanation." Chance and accident are simply part and parcel of reality.[99]

Pollard found a uniquely compelling illustration of chance and accident in the weather. In the story of the Exodus, the storm god Yahweh causes a strong east wind to drive back the waters of the Red Sea, allowing the Israelites to cross on dry land. Later, the sea surges back, engulfing the Egyptians. For Pollard, the story symbolized the problem of a chance meteorological occurrence that is also accidental (in coinciding with the movement of the Egyptian army). From a biblical perspective, the episode is providential, yet to the detached scientific observer, it neither proves nor disproves divine involvement but simply the presence of chance and accident. Pollard also pointed to an example from American history, borrowed from Oscar Handlin's book, *Chance or Destiny*. During the American Revolution, a well-timed storm aided General Washington in defeating Lord Cornwallis at Yorktown. Was the fateful convergence of meteorological and military circumstances simply a contingency? That "is indeed the fundamental question which men down through the ages have posed to history," according to Pollard, and it brings us up against the impenetrable barrier of chance and accident. "Yet the very raising of the question," Pollard concluded, "implies the imperative we all feel for penetrating this barrier in some way."[100]

The third response to this imperative came in *The Providence of God* (1960) by the Methodist theologian Georgia Harkness (1891–1974). Born to a farming family in upstate New York, she graduated from Cornell and later Boston University, where she completed a Ph.D. in philosophy. After 15 years teaching at Elmira College in New York, she became the first woman to hold a full-time chair in theological studies at a Protestant seminary in the United States when she was appointed professor of applied theology at Garrett Biblical Institute (later, Garrett-Evangelical Theological Seminary) in Evanston, Illinois. By the time *The Providence of God* appeared, she had published 23 books and had taken a new position at the Pacific School of Religion in Berkeley, California.[101]

Harkness had extensive experience writing for popular audiences, and she commanded a more accessible and pastoral style than either Pollard or Hazelton. Her *Providence of God* also returned to the perennial challenge of theodicy: How can Christians reconcile suffering with a loving God? Much of the pain of the world— war, for example—is caused by human sin, but natural disasters such as tornadoes are harder to understand. These phenomena, by a "curious twist of legal language, invading the province of theology," are called "acts of God." Harkness maintained that a Christian must regard natural disasters as acts of God in an "ultimate sense," for if they are not, then something other than God controls the world. At the same time, "we cannot suppose that when the floods and the tornadoes come, God de-liberately sends them to smite their victims with the wrath of His displeasure." One must therefore distinguish between God's power and God's purpose. Tornadoes happen by the former but not necessarily by the latter. The indiscriminate destruc-tion dealt by a tornado clearly indicates that chance is involved, though Harkness explained that, unlike Pollard, she preferred to speak of "spontaneity or flexibility or simply the possibility of alternatives."[102]

An earlier work Harkness had written as a young professor at Elmira appeared friendlier to the language of chance as well as to the idea of limitations on divine control. In *The Recovery of Ideals* (1937), she argued that God is voluntarily "limited by inertia in things and chance in events." These mechanisms do not operate with any concern for values but can be unrelentingly cruel, like an element of "cosmic drag." It is as if nature is telling us "not to set too high a store by our cherished dreams" because there is an "element of fickleness" that seems, "like the rain, to fall on the just and the unjust, and like the lightning, to strike at random." God is limited not only by inertia and chance but also by human freedom (which wrongly exercised leads to sin) and the system of predictable natural laws (which, though benevolent as

FIGURE 4.7. Georgia Harkness, circa 1960, as a professor at the Pacific School of Religion. Courtesy of the Pacific School of Religion.

a whole, produces some outcomes that neither humans nor God may desire). Inertia and chance are so woven into the structure of human freedom and natural law that "it is futile to attempt to say where one begins and the other ends." The upshot is that "one must say frankly, without any hedging about to preserve a theoretical omnipotence, that there are actual limitations upon God's power." The Christian does not stop there, however, but instead insists that God suffers with his creation when disaster happens. The cross of Christ is the proof that God takes on the agonies of humanity. It is "the place where love and sorrow meet."[103]

While Hazelton, Pollard, and Harkness were reappraising providence for a broad readership, another scholar was reflecting on the doctrine's status within the specialized guild of theologians. Langdon Gilkey (1919–2004) had grown up in a religious household: his father was a Baptist minister and the first dean of the chapel at the University of Chicago; his mother was a former national president of the Young Women's Christian Association (YWCA). As an undergraduate at Harvard, Gilkey had fallen away from religion, writing his senior thesis on the atheistic naturalism of the philosopher George Santayana. But in his last semester, he heard Reinhold Niebuhr preach in the Harvard chapel. He was overwhelmed by the rapid-fire performance and muttered to a fellow philosophy student, "Who the hell was that?" Within two weeks, Gilkey had purchased and devoured three of Niebuhr's books.

"For the first time," he later recalled, "I regarded myself as a Christian." He went on to study with Niebuhr and Paul Tillich at Union Seminary. As a young theologian, he became fascinated by the relationship between science and religion and what the human experience of contingency meant for the doctrine of providence.[104]

In 1963, as he was preparing to leave a teaching post at Vanderbilt for a new appointment at the University of Chicago, Gilkey took stock of providence in Chicago's *Journal of Religion*. Modern thought, he observed, had effectively killed the doctrine. He did not mention Hazelton, Pollard, or Harkness, though they likely would have agreed with his characterization that in academic theology, at least, providence had become "a rootless, disembodied ghost, flitting from footnote to footnote." The question, for Gilkey, was why. One reason, in his judgment, was the Arminian and humanitarian thrust of modern theology, which assumed that both human sins and natural evils were directly counter to the will of a loving God.[105] (Arminianism rejected the absolute predestination of Calvinism, positing instead that humans freely choose their actions, which are foreknown but not determined by God.)[106] Another reason was modern empirical science, which presupposed a finite causality for natural phenomena. "A storm, a flood, an earthquake," Gilkey wrote, arise from purely material factors and nothing higher, according to this view. Consequently, in contemporary religious thought, any talk of God's rule in natural events has "an air of unreality to us." In eyeing natural disasters or other events that cause suffering, modern theologians end up taking the logically contorted position that God can somehow "bring good out of these evils he has not caused." The theologians thus find themselves mired in contradiction: in one breath, they repeat the Bible's "thunderous claims" about divine sovereignty; in the next, they accept the finite causalities of modern science. For Gilkey, this situation was untenable. He concluded by calling for a radical rethinking of how theologians speak of God's action in the world.[107]

Gilkey would eventually make good on his own call, publishing a pair of books that took as their titles the biblical image of God as Whirlwind: *Naming the Whirlwind* (1969) and *Reaping the Whirlwind* (1976).[108] Drawing in part on the philosopher Alfred North Whitehead (a focus of his doctoral dissertation), he maintained that God is not static but changing and becoming through interaction with the world. This idea of divine changeability is associated with the Whitehead-influenced Process Theology of John B. Cobb, Schubert M. Ogden, and others. Yet unlike the Process Theologians, Gilkey rejected panentheism (the idea that God is in all things and that the world and God are mutually dependent for their fulfillment) in favor of a revisionist theism in which God, in an act of divine self-limitation, allows himself to be influenced by the world.[109]

In speaking of God as self-limiting, Gilkey arrived at the same place that Harkness had earlier reached, though Gilkey's work was written in a far more forbidding style.[110]

Its challenges were not lost on academic reviewers. C. T. McIntire commented that *Reaping the Whirlwind* is "a formidable book which will definitely not serve as bed-time reading." Avery (later Cardinal) Dulles noted that nontheologians would lack the "leisure to follow all the ins and outs of Gilkey's laborious argument."[111] These criticisms indirectly highlighted two important truths. The first is that reconciling providence with modern scientific thought is no simple matter. Insofar as Gilkey was sucked into his own theological whirlwind, he only experienced the difficulties that all responsible theologians have faced in updating theism for the quantum age. Second, there is an enduring disconnect between theorizing the whirlwind and encountering it on the ground—that is, between high academic theology and the lived theology that arises *in extremis*. In the midst of real-life natural disasters, old (and sometimes conflicting) winds of doctrine still blow. The ultimate test of any explanation is the extent to which it helps people cope.

PALM SUNDAY 1965

Just two years after Gilkey declared providence all but dead in academic theology, a new crisis for lived theology occurred in the Palm Sunday tornado outbreak of April 11, 1965, which killed more than 250 people across six states.[112] Hardest hit was Indiana, where 137 deaths made it the worst tornado disaster in the state's history. The outbreak was also a landmark from a scientific perspective. In the week after the tornadoes, Gilkey's University of Chicago colleague, meteorologist Tetsuya Theodore (Ted) Fujita, flew 7,500 miles in a Cessna aircraft to conduct aerial surveys of the damage patterns. Comparing his photographs to film of radar echoes taken during the storm, he compiled detailed plots of the various tornadoes. He discovered that some tornadoes spawn multiple vortices (suction vortices or suction spots), which account for some of the bizarre randomness of storm damage. The outbreak also led to important government initiatives, including the SKYWARN storm spotter program and the NOAA weather radio system, as well as the use of "watch" and "warning" language (rather than the milder "forecast") in storm alerts.[113]

In all, more than 40 tornadoes hit that day, 21 of them killers. Of the latter, eight touched down in Indiana, which endured two lines of assault: one in the northern part of the state near South Bend and Elkhart, and the other in north-central Indiana from Crawfordsville and Kokomo to points east. Whole towns were practically obliterated. In Russiaville (population 1,064), near Kokomo, an F4 tornado damaged or destroyed more than 90 percent of the buildings.[114] At 7:26 p.m., evening services were underway at the Baptist and Friends congregations as the sky suddenly grew dark. Next door to the Friends meeting, a neighborhood boy, Gene Carter, had been watching television and heard a report that a tornado was in the area. He ran into the church and warned the people, who quickly took refuge in the basement. Seconds later, the walls shuddered, the roof was blown away, and the whole building collapsed, but everyone escaped without serious injury. Other residents were not so fortunate. Eight-year-old David Evans was outside when the storm hit, and though he tried to run for cover, he was killed by flying debris as the two houses on either side of him exploded.[115]

Meanwhile, 110 miles to the north in Elkhart County near Dunlap, Paul W. Huffman, reporter for the *Elkhart Truth*, was driving on US 33 when he spotted a tornado closing in from the southwest less than a mile ahead. Grabbing his camera, he shot a sequence of photos as the funnel divided into a double vortex. Huffman's "double tornado" photograph would eventually be enshrined in the Smithsonian as one of the most celebrated storm pictures of all time. The twin monsters appear as an otherworldly apparition, dwarfing a white frame house in the foreground. Utility poles standing beside the road look like two-barred crosses, somber witnesses to the imminent crucifixion. About a minute after the tornado split in two, it reorganized into a single funnel and roared into a nearby trailer park, killing 10 people.[116] Almost unbelievably, less than an hour later, a second F4 tornado blasted Dunlap, leveling most of the Sunnyside subdivision and killing or maiming more of the town's residents. In all, 48 people died in Elkhart County that day. In neighboring Lagrange County, the heart of Amish country, a local physician looked out his window as the churning storm passed by and saw what looked like a doll suspended in the air. To his horror, he realized it was a small child. The winds drove her body violently into the ground. Seventeen other county residents also perished. In addition, hundreds of badly injured people quickly overwhelmed the region's hospitals. When Elkhart General Hospital overflowed, two floors of a Goshen College dormitory became an emergency field hospital.[117]

In the aftermath of the outbreak, President Lyndon Johnson, with two hundred journalists in tow, visited several of the affected areas, including Sunnyside. As Johnson walked somberly through the wreckage, reporters heard him mutter simply, "Horrible! Horrible!" Religious reflections on the disaster ensued in the local press, with familiar disagreements resurfacing. After the *Kokomo Morning Times* editorialized that "no one believes God, the Merciful, is veng[e]ful," two readers took the newspaper to task, insisting that God is given not only to mercy but also to vengeance and consuming fire. Other interpreters betrayed ambivalence, if not outright contradiction, in seeming to explain the disaster in both naturalistic and religious terms. An unsigned editorial that appeared in newspapers in Rhode Island and Maryland on the same day asserted that "of course, we can account for tornadoes as natural phenomena," but "the supernatural cause is something else."

FIGURE 4.8. Paul Huffman's famous photograph of the double-vortex tornado in Elkhart County, Indiana, April 11, 1965.
Courtesy of the *Elkhart Truth*.

Why, asked the papers, did the outbreak occur on Palm Sunday, just as millions of Americans were hearing the story of Christ's Passion? "There is enough evil in the country to bring on divine wrath. Was it a visitation from heaven, a warning?" On Easter Sunday back in Russiaville, residents gathered at the Methodist church, the town's only house of worship still standing, as Pastor Wayne Baxter struggled to make sense of the tragedy. "Why did God send the tornado?" he asked. "God didn't send it. Sometimes He permits things. But He is not angry. Maybe we were too complacent, too self-satisfied in our luxuries."[118]

Perhaps the most widely circulated religious interpretation came a few months later. David Wagler, an Amish farmer in Ontario, Canada, self-published a book-length account, *The Mighty Whirlwind*, through the small printing business he ran out of this home. Orders for the volume soon totaled 12,000 copies. One of the chapters featured an imaginary dialogue in which two characters pondered why no Old Order Amish died in the tornadoes. "I can not explain it, other than that God has a purpose in everything that comes to pass," says the main character, clearly speaking for Wagler. But his interlocutor presses: "Would you say then it's

FIGURE 4.9. Paul Huffman holding the April 12, 1965, edition of the *Elkhart Truth* with his famous photograph on the front page.
Courtesy of the *Elkhart Truth*.

all a matter of chance?" "Definitely not!" the Wagler character replies. "When God created the world, He established certain laws of cause and effect, and they are still in force. . . . God can overrule all laws according to his purpose, but ordinarily He allows the laws of nature to take their course." The interlocutor pushes further: "Do you believe that God intervened in every case where no one was killed?" "Of course not!" Wagler replies. "We believe that a time is set for each person's life and when that comes, his life ends." God *can* intervene to save a righteous person, but it is not always his will to do so. "If no true Christian ever died a violent death," Wagler concludes, "some people might want to serve God for a selfish reason, just to avoid certain dangers. We should serve God because we love him."[119]

POSTSCRIPT: PALM SUNDAY 1965—50 YEARS ON

On a chilly April day in 2015, I stood in the bright sunshine with about 75 people in an empty lot in Dunlap's Sunnyside subdivision, which the storm had ravaged

FIGURE 4.10. President Lyndon Johnson amid the ruins of the First General Baptist Church, Sunnyside, Elkhart County, Indiana.
Goshen News via Elkhart County Historical Society.

exactly a half century earlier. We were gathered to remember Elkhart County's own Sunday of the Passion, when the tornado outbreak upended the lives of so many. Among those in the crowd was Elizabeth (Betty) Huffman, whose late husband, Paul, snapped the iconic photo of the double tornado. Another was Brenda Ford Elliott, who as a six-year-old was with her parents and four siblings at her grandparents' house that day when the weather turned ominous. Her mother wanted to stay with the grandparents, but her father insisted on driving home. It was a fateful decision: their Sunnyside house took a direct hit as the family was huddled in a bedroom. Elliott's father was on the bed, trying to shield her and her sister, Carolyn. But he lost his grip on Carolyn when a brick hit his head. Carolyn was sucked out of the house and was later found dead underneath a pickup truck. Two-year-old Steve was missing for a couple of days until the family discovered that he had been taken to the makeshift hospital at Goshen College. Thirteen-year-old Doug, who like his father had been struck in the head by a brick, suffered a traumatic brain injury and had to relearn to walk and talk. At the memorial gathering,

Elliott spoke of how the memories of the tornado and its aftermath had haunted her. "The mental and emotional scars—they never go away," she said. "My family still doesn't talk about it."[120]

The gathering was the brainchild of Debbie Forsythe Watters, who, like Elliott, was six years old at the time of the disaster and lost a sibling to the storm. The panicked words of her 10-year-old brother Stevie as he looked out of the family's picture window are seared in her memory: "Mom! There's a tornado coming here!" Seconds later, the twister hit, crushing Stevie under the debris. The family decided not to rebuild on the same lot at the corner of Cole Street and Amy Avenue in Dunlap but left the property vacant. Eventually the land was donated by the owner for use as a memorial. Since then, Watters has organized remembrances on the spot every five years. During the 2015 event, Watters helped read the names of the 48 Elkhart County residents who died. Attendees then released balloons to commemorate the victims.[121]

As the balloons drifted into the sky, I felt a lump in my throat—an intimation of that aching longing that lingers in all of us after a loved one has flown away, to a world beyond. I was struck by how that unassuming plot of land had been consecrated by the deaths that happened there, just as more famous American places like Gettysburg had become hallowed ground. Unlike the dead of Gettysburg, who could be construed as a blood sacrifice to redeem the nation, the casualties of Sunnyside and other natural disasters remain hard to explain.[122] The timeless enigma of natural disasters is evident in a granite marker left by the Forsythe family at the site of their former home. Splicing together three quotations (Ecclesiastes 3:1, Nahum 1:3, and a line from a gospel song by the African-American preacher Charles Albert Tindley), the inscription reads: "To every thing there is a season, and a time to every purpose under heaven. And the Lord hath his way in the whirlwind and in the storm, and the clouds are the dust of his feet. Someday we will understand it better by and by." The words exemplify what sociologist Robert Wuthnow has called the "inscrutability script," or one of the ways that Americans often talk about natural disasters. Such language makes it possible, Wuthnow says, "to believe God exists and is in charge of everything that happens without having to assume that God intervenes specifically and deliberately in particular events." In a 2007 poll, only about 17 percent of Americans agreed that God directly *causes* disasters. Emphasizing divine inscrutability relieves some of the burden of theodicy while acknowledging that the riddle remains unsolved. One of Wuthnow's interviewees put it succinctly, "I think God has a reason for everything. I just don't know what the reason is."[123]

The inscrutability script is as old as Job, who surrenders to the mysteries of the divine will: "Though he slay me, yet will I trust in him" (Job 13:15). Pastor Wayne Baxter quoted this verse on that melancholy Easter Sunday in Russiaville. "We must have the same spirit as Job," he said.[124] The responses to the 1965 tornadoes revealed that the available options for lived theodicy had changed fairly little in the millennia since Job was written. Job's pious resignation before a chasm of uncertainty remained preternaturally relevant in an era struggling to reconcile science and faith. The question was whether future scientific advances might lead to new winds of doctrine—and whether these too would be consumed by the intractable mysteries of the Whirlwind.

They are as stubble before the wind, and as chaff that the storm carrieth away.

—JOB 21:18

Almighty God, we bring our praise and worship before you. . . . You have made us, and not we ourselves. Help us to remember the limits of our power and our wisdom, but help us, too, to do our duty within the limits of our power and our wisdom.

—REINHOLD NIEBUHR, Prayer published posthumously in *Justice and Mercy* (1974)

5

"As Stubble Before the Wind"

DIVINE MYSTERY AND HUMAN RESPONSIBILITY

THE OMINOUS FORECASTS appeared several days in advance. On Wednesday, May 15, 2013, the Storm Prediction Center (SPC) issued a severe weather outlook anticipating "strong destabilization" and "favorable [wind] shear" for the following Sunday and Monday in the SPC's own backyard of central Oklahoma. The outlook added that Monday, May 20, "may be the day of highest tornado potential." At 1:00 a.m. Sunday, the forecast remained essentially the same, anticipating two waves of storms on Sunday and Monday, with both likely to bring "very large hail and tornadoes."[1]

The prophecies began to come true late Sunday afternoon when tornadoes erupted in central Oklahoma along the dry line, the boundary between moist air from the east and dry air from the west. These twisters, including a violent EF3 and EF4, left two people dead and dominated the entire front page of the *Oklahoman* newspaper on Monday.[2] By then, residents of metro Oklahoma City were already focused on the second wave, expected that afternoon. Local weathercasters discussed the threat on the morning news shows, and just after lunchtime, the National Weather Service (NWS) issued a tornado watch, prompting several television stations to switch to uninterrupted coverage.[3]

At Plaza Towers Elementary School in Moore, an Oklahoma City suburb, parents began arriving to pick up their children early, which often happened on stormy days. Like many schools in Oklahoma at that time, Plaza Towers had no basement or storm shelter. Most private homes in the state had no basements either. In colder-weather regions, building codes typically required houses to be constructed with the footing below the frost line, which meant that builders already had to excavate deep enough for a basement. But few contractors bothered to build basements amid the clay soil and high water table of central Oklahoma. For most of the children at Plaza Towers, therefore, it was not clear whether they would be safer at home or at school.[4]

At 2:12 p.m., the NWS issued a severe thunderstorm warning. Plaza Towers principal Amy Simpson was nervously monitoring the situation as she interviewed a candidate for a teaching position. Her secretary stuck her head in to inform her of the larger-than-usual crowd of parents lined up to sign out their children. Simpson wrapped up the interview and announced to the parents they could go back to the classrooms and find their children themselves. Then, at 2:40 p.m., sirens wailed as the NWS issued a tornado warning. Simpson immediately went to the intercom and ordered students and teachers to the interior hallways, where they knelt and covered their heads, as they had rehearsed many times.[5]

Sixteen minutes later, at 2:56 p.m., a tornado touched down a few miles west of Moore. The storm swiftly grew into a mile-wide monster, with its "debris ball" (the ring of debris picked up by the funnel) showing up as an unmistakable signature on the radar. Simpson, who had been walking the halls at Plaza Towers checking on students, returned to the front office as massive hailstones began pelting the building. Some students were still leaving with their parents, and Simpson handed the children hardcover textbooks to hold over their heads.[6]

Oklahoma-born journalist Holly Bailey paints a chilling picture of what happened next: "A mother and father rushed past Simpson with their kid. She paused, watching them as they raced out the front entrance and ran toward the parking lot. Silently she prayed they would be safe. But suddenly she saw them glance west and stop dead in their tracks. Their faces wrenched in fear, they grabbed their child and quickly ran back toward the school." Simpson knew at that moment that the tornado was about to hit. She seized the intercom microphone and issued a final warning: "It's here."[7]

In a corridor of the building, third-grade teacher Jennifer Doan, who was two months pregnant, was crouching next to three boys from her class, trying to shield them with her body. One was Nicolas McCabe, who was just a couple of weeks shy of his ninth birthday. As the boys sobbed in fear, Doan tried to comfort them, but soon their cries were drowned out by a loud rumbling and the shattering of glass as the windows inside the classrooms exploded. Then the walls caved in, burying Doan and the students in rubble. After the storm passed, Doan lay in complete darkness, pinned by debris and struggling to breathe. She had suffered a fractured sternum and spine, and a jagged piece of rebar had pierced her left hand. Eventually, rescuers pulled her and two of the boys to safety. But Nicolas was dead. He was one of seven children at Plaza Towers—six of them from Doan's own class—who perished that day.[8]

In all, the storm took 25 lives, injured more than 200, and caused $2 billion in damage, making it the costliest tornado in modern Oklahoma history. Incredibly, it was the fifth tornado to hit Moore in 15 years, giving the town the dubious distinction of being the "tornado alley of tornado alley." The worst in terms of casualties was the May 3, 1999, tornado, which killed 36 and injured more than 500. That storm was also meteorologically historic: its estimated wind speed of 301 miles per hour, based on researcher Joshua Wurman's measurement with mobile radar, was the fiercest ever clocked on the face of the earth.[9]

But the loss of the seven children at Plaza Towers made the 2013 tornado especially poignant. Sociologist Tony Walter has suggested that one reason people find the deaths of children so upsetting is that they symbolize modernity's faith in progress and the future. Traditional societies, by contrast, revere the elders because they represent the authority and wisdom of the past.[10] A child's death shakes the American civil religion of self-determination and unbounded possibility, a creed epitomized

FIGURE 5.1. President Barack Obama hugs Amy Simpson, principal of Plaza Towers Elementary School, beside the remains of the school on May 26, 2013.
White House photograph by Pete Souza.

by John Locke's observation that "in the beginning all the World was America."[11] The snuffing out of a life so full of promise strikes many people as the epitome of senselessness and injustice.

The geographical location of the 2013 tornado was significant. In Oklahoma, the evangelical culture of middle America meets the frontiers of meteorology, casting a unique light on questions both theological and ethical. The persistent theological issue concerns divine control: Is God behind everything that happens? Whether the answer is yes or no, the implications are potentially unsettling for people of faith. Then there is the question of God's very existence: Does nature's random violence suggest a godless universe? Even in churchgoing Oklahoma, this possibility is voiced more often than it once was. Ethically, the issues center on human control. How much responsibility do humans bear for deaths from tornadoes? What precautions (for example, requiring storm shelters and stricter building codes) should societies be obligated to take? In recent years, tornadoes have raised the troubling question of human complicity in climate change. Is global warming increasing the incidence or destructiveness of severe weather? In this chapter, we will travel to the front lines of these debates, beginning and ending in Oklahoma, while also tracing parallel discussions in other American places.

FIGURE 5.2. Aerial view of the damage in Moore from the 2013 tornado.
Photograph by Jocelyn Augustino, FEMA.

BIBLE BELT AND TORNADO ALLEY

Tornadoes have been a way of life in Oklahoma ever since the first Sooners staked their claims during the land rush of 1889, which opened the area to white settlement. (Sooners were so called because they entered the territory before the legally appointed time.)[12] The new settlers soon got more than they bargained for when they discovered the region's wild weather. Just seven years after Oklahoma became a territory, a multiple-vortex tornado struck the town of Chandler on March 30, 1897, and "all but wiped that thriving little city of 1,500 souls off the face of the earth," according to one newspaper account. About 10:00 a.m., as clouds gathered in the southwest and thunder rumbled, an elderly Kickapoo Indian tried to warn other residents of an approaching cyclone. Few people paid attention, least of all the rowdy group at Elmer's Saloon, whose roof would collapse in the storm. When the dust settled, one of the inebriated patrons is said to have crawled out from under the debris and exclaimed, "Elmer, whoinell started that fight?" Other townspeople were not so lucky: 16 died and many more were injured.[13]

Tornadoes, like Rudolf Otto's numinous, both frightened and attracted Oklahomans at the same time. Holly Bailey, who grew up in Oklahoma City and attended grade school in Moore, has noted that "it was as if it were somehow ingrained in the collective DNA of an entire region to love thunderstorms and want to be near them." Every stormy day brought an "odd mix of fear and anticipation." Long before the Weather Channel made meteorology a national pastime, she adds, "weather coverage had become a tense and obsessive form of reality TV in Oklahoma." Weathercasters became local superstars. In 2010, an Oklahoma City blog polled its readers on who was the most powerful person in the state: Gary England, meteorologist at KWTV since 1972, came in first; Jesus was second.[14]

The state's epic storms became a magnet for tornado chasers from around the world. The most remarkable of these was native Coloradan Tim Samaras, a self-taught engineer and meteorologist, who repeatedly took to the back roads of Oklahoma in his quest to place weather instrument probes in the path of twisters. Eleven days after the 2013 Moore storm, Samaras was killed trying to outrun a multiple-vortex, 2.6-mile-wide tornado (the largest ever measured) at El Reno, Oklahoma. Though Samaras's safety precautions were legendary, in the end they were not enough. The allure of tornadoes proved irresistible. As Samaras's biographer Brantley Hargrove writes, even the most "hardened researchers are reduced to monosyllabic expressions of awe" in the presence of these fearsome storms of the Great Plains.[15]

If tornado-chasing was a religion, notes Bailey, then "central Oklahoma was the holy land."[16] The region was indeed long considered the epicenter of tornado activity worldwide, the hub of the traditional Tornado Alley extending from Texas

FIGURE 5.3. The El Reno, Oklahoma, tornado, on May 31, 2013.
Photograph by Howard B. Bluestein.

to South Dakota. Because this imaginary corridor intersects in Oklahoma with another one—the Bible Belt—the religion of tornadoes is highly inflected by evangelical Protestantism. In a 2014 survey by the Pew Research Center, nearly half of
Oklahomans (47 percent) self-identified as evangelical Protestant, a proportion
comparable to that of Alabamians (49 percent). Some climatologists have in fact
identified Alabama as part of a second tornado alley, dubbed "Dixie Alley," that
includes a large swath of the Bible Belt. The nation's tornado hot spots, in other
words, are largely coterminous with evangelical strongholds.[17]

The intersection of the Bible Belt and Tornado Alley has brought three characteristics of evangelicalism to bear on American discourse about natural disasters.[18]
The first is biblicism, particularly the tendency to treat the Bible as a storehouse
of facts or proof texts that can be mined to settle any disputed question. Liberal
Protestant theologians such as Reinhold Niebuhr or Langdon Gilkey were untrou-
bled by any need to ground every assertion in empirical evidence from scripture,
preferring instead to draw on the Bible for illustrative and liturgical material. But
because evangelicals regard scripture as an infallible guide, they must reckon with
the numerous verses in which God controls the weather for his purposes. A second
feature is conversionism, or an emphasis on a dramatic, life-changing experience of Christ's saving grace. Whereas many mainline Protestants, like Catholics,

historically stressed gradual catechesis in the Christian faith, evangelical conversion is often a sudden affair—like a tornado. The stories of evangelical survivors of natural disasters frequently bear the hallmarks of conversion narratives. A third feature, less recognized because it is so hardwired into the culture, is providentialism, or the belief that all events are under God's control and everything ultimately happens for a reason. A 2011 poll by the Public Religion Research Institute and Religion News Service found that 84 percent of white evangelicals agreed that God is in control of everything that happens, compared to 55 percent of mainline Protestants and 52 percent of Catholics. More specifically, nearly 6 in 10 white evangelicals (59 percent) identified natural disasters as signs from God, compared to 34 percent of mainline Protestants and 31 percent of Catholics.[19]

Evangelical providentialism often goes unnoticed until it becomes judgmental and politicized. In 2005, after Hurricane Katrina devastated New Orleans and killed as many as 1,800 people across the Gulf coast, evangelical broadcaster and onetime presidential candidate Pat Robertson suggested that the storm was divine retribution for legalized abortion, while Texas televangelist John Hagee blamed it on God's anger over homosexuality. A fierce backlash ensued. Donald Wildmon, head of the American Family Association, which has lobbied against abortion and same-sex marriage, called Robertson's comments "most unfortunate," while evangelical writer Os Guinness deemed them "idiotic." A few years later, Republican presidential nominee John McCain rejected Hagee's endorsement after the preacher's Katrina statement resurfaced (along with other inflammatory opinions, including that God sent Hitler to help the Jews reach the Promised Land).[20]

The pushback against Robertson and Hagee did not prevent another evangelical from drawing a similar connection between homosexuality, divine wrath, and the weather. In 2009, the popular evangelical Calvinist author John Piper caused a stir when he commented on a tornado that damaged the Minneapolis Convention Center during the assembly of the Evangelical Lutheran Church in America that voted to permit the ordination of LGBT clergy in committed relationships. Piper called the storm, which also damaged the Central Lutheran Church across the street, a "gentle but firm warning to the ELCA and all of us: turn from the approval of sin." Conservative Lutherans echoed Piper's sentiments.[21]

When it comes to the fates of particular individuals in storms, however, evangelicals tend to be more circumspect. Here, the indiscriminate violence visited upon Moore and other places poses an acute existential problem. President Barack Obama put it well at a memorial service in Joplin, Missouri, after an EF5 tornado killed 158 people there in May 2011: "The question that weighs on us at a time like this is: Why? Why our town? Why our home? Why my son, or husband, or wife, or sister, or friend? Why? We do not have the capacity to answer."[22] Evidence suggests that most evangelicals would agree that Christians cannot know why one person dies and another lives, but they assume that God is involved nonetheless. And because they believe in divine involvement, evangelicals seek to relate stories of both death and survival in a way that edifies, as in classic conversion narratives.

The tales of survival are easier to explain providentially. On May 4, 2007, a 1.5-mile-wide, EF5 tornado destroyed 95 percent of Greensburg, Kansas, killing 11 people. Residents said it could have been far worse if not for a 20-minute warning that allowed them to take shelter.[23] Many survivors ultimately credited God with keeping them safe. Townspeople Eric and Fern Unruh collected some of their stories in a book published a few months after the disaster. The overriding theme is one of trust in divine power and protection. Typical was the case of Roger and Marsha Yost, who took cover along with eight other people under their basement stairs as the storm approached. "When our ears started popping and the house started going, we were audibly praying for God to protect us and keep us," Roger said. "God answered and He was there." The Unruhs' book does not address the question of why some people survived the storm and others did not, but it invokes scriptural evidence that God is in control: Nahum 1:3 ("The Lord hath his way in the whirlwind and in the storm"), Psalm 60:2 ("Thou hast made the earth to tremble"), and Psalm 148:8 ("stormy wind fulfilling his word").[24]

A similar account of divine deliverance appeared in the aftermath of an EF4 tornado that hit Union University, a Southern Baptist institution in Jackson, Tennessee, on February 5, 2008. Though the storm destroyed 18 dormitories on campus, no students were killed or suffered life-threatening injuries. The Jackson tornado was part of a larger "Super Tuesday Outbreak" (so called because it coincided with the Super Tuesday presidential primary) that killed 57 people across four states.[25] A week after the storm, Union president David Dockery published a column in the local newspaper thanking community members for their help in recovery efforts and acknowledging God's providential care. "We praise our creator for preserving and protecting each precious human life," he wrote. Likewise, Tim Ellsworth, the university's director of news and media relations, compiled a book of students' accounts of survival, citing the Puritan John Flavel's exhortation to record providences in one's life as an antidote to atheism. As for why God spared Union's students but not the victims elsewhere, Ellsworth noted that "we're not privy to the mind of God on such matters." "All we know for sure," he added, "is that God protected the lives of everyone on campus, and for that He deserves our praise and gratitude."[26]

The Moore tornado of 2013 also brought stories of survival, including that of Barbara Garcia, 74, who sheltered in her bathroom and escaped serious injury even as the tornado destroyed her house. Though grateful that she survived, she was heartbroken because she had lost her grip on her little dog, Bowser, and feared he was dead. As she described the dog to a television crew, someone noticed movement in the rubble. It was Bowser, covered in debris but unharmed. "I thought God just answered one prayer, 'let me be OK,'" Garcia told a reporter. "He answered both of them because this was my second prayer." Video of the interview quickly went viral, with some people questioning how Garcia could assume divine favor for a pet when so many human beings, including children, had died. The story caught the attention of syndicated columnist Connie Schultz, who noted that though claims of divine intervention during tragedies often made her wince, she felt no outrage toward Garcia. "She can praise God all she wants," Schultz wrote. Schultz then related the case of a woman who, as the Moore tornado was approaching, faced the agonizing dilemma of whether to stay in her house or flee. Opting for the latter, she grabbed her 19-month-old baby and sped away by car. The choice likely saved their lives since their house was demolished. CNN's Wolf Blitzer later asked the woman, Rebecca Vitsmun, "Do you thank the Lord for that split-second decision?" The woman smiled shyly and replied, "I, I, I'm actually an atheist." To Schultz, the two stories illustrated the intractable mysteries that haunt in the wake of disaster.[27]

In the face of these mysteries, evangelicals default to providence. Indeed, to interpret miraculous survivals as anything other than God-given would strike many religious people, not just evangelical Protestants, as ungrateful if not blasphemous. (Rebecca Vitsmun's hesitancy to admit her unbelief reveals the perceived stigma of atheism, though she was not alone: the 2014 Pew survey found that 4 percent of Oklahomans identified as atheists—more than the state's combined percentage of Jews, Muslims, Hindus, and Buddhists.) Finding the providential blessings in tragic deaths is more difficult, yet even in such instances, evangelicalism is resiliently optimistic. The case of Scott and Stacey McCabe, whose son Nicolas died at Plaza Towers, is particularly compelling. His parents told their story in a documentary film, *Where Was God?* (2015), produced by Steven Earp, pastor of Elevate Church in Moore. "I still question. I'm still angry," Scott confessed. "And Steve [Earp] pointed out to me . . . that even Jesus Christ asked why. So it's not wrong to ask why." But in the midst of death the McCabes found life when Scott converted to faith in Jesus. For Stacey, the blessing of Scott's conversion outweighed her tremendous grief over Nicolas. "We know that we're all going to see Nicolas," she said through tears. "And if that was the purpose of my son's death, for his daddy to be able to be with him for eternity, then it was worth it. It was worth every bit of it." "Yes," Scott agreed.[28]

In a companion book to the film, Earp expanded on this evangelical confidence in providence. Two months after the Moore tornado, he reported, his church had contacted 40,000 households in the affected zip codes and polled them on what they would ask God if granted just one question. Overwhelmingly, the top queries began with "Why?" Why did God allow the tornado? Why does God allow suffering?

Why does God allow evil? Earp responded that broadly speaking, natural disasters and other examples of brokenness in the world were due to the disobedience of the first humans in the Garden of Eden. As for why some people survive tornadoes and others do not, there are no simple answers, he said. Christians must trust in God's unchangeable goodness and his ability to bring hope and triumph out of tragedy. Earp added that to say that God merely "allows" bad things to happen is to risk losing sight of divine sovereignty. "It may not feel 'right' or even holy to suggest God is responsible in the face of disaster, but the Bible does not shrink away from the fact that God is sovereignly responsible," he explained. "We don't know the reason He didn't prevent this particular tragedy, but He is still God, He is still good, and we can still trust Him."[29]

Earp cited Oklahoma City pastor Sam Storms, who in a blog post after the Moore tornado insisted that "God is absolutely sovereign over all of nature." Storms, a onetime president of the Evangelical Theological Society, is a leading voice of evangelical Calvinism, which has produced some of the strongest contemporary affirmations of providence.[30] Another leading Calvinist, the late R. C. Sproul, memorably declared that if any part of creation lies outside of divine control, then God is not sovereign. "If there is one single molecule in this universe running around loose, totally free of God's sovereignty, then we have no guarantee that a single promise of God will ever be fulfilled," he wrote. As if to emphasize the point that even tornadoes contain no errant molecules, a reprint of Sproul's 1986 book on providence, *The Invisible Hand*, pictured a tornado on the cover. In that volume, Sproul channeled Calvin himself on the lack of randomness in the universe. "The doctrine of the providence of God leaves no room for fate, blind or otherwise," Sproul asserted. "With God there are no cases of chance events." Erwin W. Lutzer, former pastor of Moody Church in Chicago, echoed admonitions by colonial Puritans not to stop at secondary causes. "The secondary causes of a tornado are unstable atmospheric conditions combined with warm, moist air," he wrote. "Yet we can be sure that the ultimate cause of these events is God."[31]

Such evangelical avowals of divine control have from time to time provoked equally vigorous rebuttals from liberals. In 1994, an F4 tornado collapsed the roof of Goshen United Methodist Church in Piedmont, Alabama, during the Palm Sunday service, killing 20 worshippers. Among them was Hannah Clem, the four-year-old daughter of the church's pastor, Kelly Clem. Kelly's husband, Dale Clem, also a United Methodist pastor, recalled his numbness when the national media descended on Piedmont and reporters repeatedly asked him whether he believed God was behind the tragedy. He also remembered the sick feeling that came over him when he opened his mail one day and found an anonymous note attributing the tornado to God's anger over female clergy such as his wife.

"God does not like women pretending to preach the holy Word of God," the note warned. It added: "If you keep this message from Rev. Clem you will burn in hell." Dale Clem's agony—his Palm Sunday Passion experience—convinced him that "silence may be the only appropriate response" to the haunting question of God's role in disasters. Yet he was also adamant that God did not cause the tornado, which was "simply an act of wind." "This cause-and-effect way of looking at the world," he added, "oversimplifies the contradictions inherent in the world and in ourselves."[32]

After the 2013 Moore tornado, mainline Protestant as well as Catholic leaders distanced themselves from the idea of divine involvement in the storm. "I think the victims in this instance were victims of circumstance—they lived in a place where a tornado happened," said Justin Lindstrom, dean of St. Paul's Episcopal Cathedral in Oklahoma City. Another of the city's pastors, Bill Pruett of St. James the Greater Catholic Church, insisted that "the divine role is always a sustaining role." "God is never the one who causes suffering and disasters," he said. "Evil seems to be a function of a flawed universe. It is the shadow side of human choice. You can't blame God because of the choices people make, and you can't blame God because the laws of nature are what they are."[33]

OPEN THEISM: WHAT CAN GOD CONTROL?

Pruett's claim that God cannot be blamed for the laws of nature begs the deeper question of whether God is limited in certain ways—that is, whether classical theism's assumption of divine omnipotence fails to account for the possibility that nature might constrain even God himself. Such a complicated issue is rarely debated in the immediate aftermath of a disaster, when clergy gravitate toward more pastoral responses (for example, assurances that God will bring good out of tragedy). In the late 1990s, however, a lively debate arose among evangelical theologians and pastors over Open Theism, or the idea that God is limited in his knowledge of future events. Many of the leading revisionists were evangelicals of an Arminian bent, or those who opposed the absolute predestination of Calvinism. Arminians (including Methodists) traditionally taught that God foreknows but does not predetermine the free choices of his creatures on whether to accept or reject Christ, whereas Calvinists maintained that God not only foreknows but also predetermines who will be saved.[34] Open Theism went beyond Arminianism by positing that unless human choices are unknown even to God, they are not really free. The question of whether God must discover the free choices of his creatures is thorny enough, but perhaps an even more vexing problem concerns the apparent contingencies of the natural world. Is God bound by natural laws, and if so, is this a divinely accepted self-limitation (as we saw Georgia Harkness argue in the previous chapter) or a limitation inherent in God himself? Natural evils such as violent weather focus the problem especially clearly: Does God—*can* God—have anything to do with a tornado, or does a tornado represent an element of radical openness or contingency?

The debate over limitations in God dates back at least to the Middle Ages. In the eleventh century, Anselm pointed out that humans could do certain things—change, for example—that God, whom he believed to be bound by his own immutability, could not. Two centuries later, Aquinas argued that God is logically restricted by the law of noncontradiction and cannot decree that white is black or that up is down. Anselm and Aquinas still took for granted the axiom of traditional theism that God is all-powerful. That God cannot get around a logical contradiction did not mean, in their view, that his power is deficient but simply that certain things are inherently impossible.[35] By the early twentieth century, however, some Christian theologians were beginning to wonder if divine omnipotence was a straitjacket because it created an insurmountable problem of evil. If God had unlimited power, why did he not prevent needless suffering? Determined to preserve divine goodness even at the expense of omnipotence, these thinkers concluded that certain natural evils such as tornadoes are best explained by a limitation in God.

Among the initial proponents of this line of reasoning were the liberal theologians known as the Boston Personalists, so called because of their association with Boston University and their insistence that the intrinsic value of both humans and God lies in their personhood. A key early figure was Francis John McConnell (1871–1953), who after studying with the pioneering Personalist Borden Parker Bowne went on to serve as president of DePauw University and later as a Methodist bishop. In *Is God Limited?* (1924), McConnell wrote that "we may as well face the truth that we live in a grim universe," or a world characterized by "more pain that we can see any use for." This suggested to him that God is limited in certain respects, but he stopped short of conceiving of God as finite, preferring instead to emphasize the Christlike suffering that God willingly accepts in solidarity with humanity.[36]

The next-generation Personalist, Edgar Sheffield Brightman (1884–1953), also a student of Bowne, was more radical. In his view, the traditional doctrine of divine omnipotence was the product of wishful thinking. "It is not a question of the kind of God we would like to have," he wrote. "It is a question of the kind of God required by the facts." The facts revealed a world that the creator was still struggling to subdue and perfect. "We certainly cannot impute to man the blame for the slow and painful processes of life, or for the presence of earthquakes, cyclones, and disease germs in the world," Brightman insisted. Borrowing a metaphor from the secular Jewish philosopher Horace Meyer Kallen, Brightman proposed that a surd (the mathematical term for an irrational number) might lurk beneath the laws of nature. That is, certain phenomena such as tornadoes seemed dysteleological, or lacking in rational purpose. To claim, as Christians often did, that God had a positive purpose in sending tornadoes and other calamities was to "break down distinctions of good and evil or to build faith on our ignorance of what is good." Why, then, do tornadoes exist if the universe is governed by a benevolent God? Brightman concluded that there must be elements of the divine consciousness—he called it "the Given"—that God himself is forced to strive against. The Given consisted of not only the uncreated laws of reason but also whatever nonrational elements were the source of surd evil. Brightman admitted that to hold that there is something beyond reason in the reasonable God "is a hard saying, against which I have often rebelled." Yet he appealed to Rudolf Otto, who spoke of the nonrational aspect of the numinous. "God is not simply a happy, loving Father; he is the struggle and the mysterious pain at the heart of life," Brightman explained. "He is indeed love; but a suffering love that redeems through a Cross."[37]

Later Methodists backed away from Brightman's radicalism. His student, Georgia Harkness, expressed her unease with the notion of a nonrational "Given" in the divine nature against which God must contend. To her, evil was better explained by God's *voluntarily* limiting his control over the world. Similarly, the Methodist theologian and ecumenical leader Albert Outler (1908–1989) doubted that it was necessary to locate the surd in the divine being in order to exculpate God from rationally willed evil.[38] At the same time, at least two aspects of Brightman's revisionist theism would eventually resurface—this time in evangelical Open Theism. The first was a return to a more Personalist God whose nature was sometimes reactive and who occasionally changed his mind. The second was a recognition of the disorderly elements of the world and an emphasis on an unfinished creation still striving toward perfection. To Open Theists, these themes were not borderline heretical but thoroughly scriptural.

Indeed, it was the biblicism of Open Theists that opened their eyes to the themes of disorder, contingency, and change in the divine life. In the Bible, God changes his mind some 40 times, according to Terence Fretheim, a Lutheran biblical scholar friendly to the Openness perspective.[39] Fretheim's exegesis of Hebrew scripture buttressed the claims of the leading Open Theists: Minnesota pastor Gregory Boyd; theology professors William Hasker, Richard Rice, and John Sanders; and the Canadian theologian Clark Pinnock.[40] They reasoned that unless God must react to contingencies in humans and in nature, there could be no authentic freedom in the world. These contingencies sometimes cause God to change his mind, even as he remains changeless in his perfect love and reliability. Like Harkness, Open Theists rejected the concept that God is inherently limited or finite and maintained instead that he is self-limited. God delights in a universe that he does not completely control, but he also mourns with humans when they suffer from the universe's chaos.[41]

Open Theists insisted that the notion of God's self-limitation rescued them from one of the errors of Brightman's Personalism and also of the liberal Process Theology inspired by Alfred North Whitehead: the idea that God cannot be all-powerful, either because of limitations within himself (Brightman) or because of his interdependence with the world (the Process theologians).[42] In Open Theism, God remains omnipotent but relinquishes control or takes risks. Conventional theism, noted Pinnock, with its "obsession for control, makes God the author of evil and condemns itself to defending something untenable." To Open Theists, God exercises a general sovereignty in creating the world but fashions it in such a way that created beings, whether persons or things, have real freedom. Biblical texts mentioning God's control over natural phenomena, according to Sanders, should not be mistaken as proofs that God causes *everything* that happens in the world. Sanders faulted John Calvin for citing Jonah 1:4, where God sends a "great wind" against Jonah, as evidence that, as Calvin put it, "no wind ever arises or increases except by God's express command." Many bad things happen that are not part of a divine plan, Sanders contended. He recalled his own conversion to Christian faith after his brother died in an accident and how some people assured him that God had ordained his brother's death for that reason. Sanders could not convince himself that "God kills people and causes disasters in the hope that some may then repent and confess Christ." Some events, he argued, are simply "pointless evils." In allowing such things to occur, God is taking a genuine risk that humans will trust him less. But God's answer to suffering, Sanders concluded, is the cross of Christ.[43]

As a way of understanding nature's randomness, Open Theism struck its advocates as more believable than traditional providentialism for at least two reasons. One was its apparent consistency with modern science, which has shown that the world is, in Boyd's words, a "balance between openness and settledness." Everywhere we look, Boyd observed, we see both predictability and unpredictability: "We can predict in general terms when a tornado may form, and we're getting better at this, but we also now know that no amount of information will allow us to specify the exact time and place it will form, and still less how it will behave after it has formed."[44] Another reason for Open Theism's appeal, as already noted, was its congruence with themes from scripture. Fretheim argued this most extensively in his *Creation Untamed: The Bible, God, and Natural Disasters* (2010). In his view, the Augustinian explanation that all natural suffering is traceable to original sin is "much too anthropocentric." The preponderance of biblical evidence suggests instead that natural disasters are a byproduct of the world's continuing creation. It is no coincidence, according to Fretheim, that God appears to Job in a whirlwind, which is "a prime example of nature's disorderly elements." The book of Job shows that the world is "not a tightly woven system" and "does not run like a machine." Other scriptural passages corroborate this idea. Time and chance happen to all people (Ecclesiastes 9:11). The rain falls on the just and the unjust (Matthew 5:45).[45]

Yet such biblical warrants failed to convince some evangelicals that Open Theism was not a dangerously seductive heresy. In 2001, the Evangelical Theological Society in effect repudiated the movement, declaring by a vote of 253 to 66 that "the Bible clearly teaches that God has complete, accurate, and infallible foreknowledge of all events, past, present, and future." Pinnock and Sanders, whose views had been singled out for scrutiny, were allowed to remain in the society, despite Sanders's public complaint about the "evangelical Taliban."[46] Ironically, the common commitment of both Open Theists and their opponents to the evangelical shibboleth of biblical inerrancy (which all the society's members are required to affirm) only made the controversy more acrimonious because both sides believed they were on firm scriptural ground.[47] Presbyterian theologian John Frame, for example, took exception to Sanders's criticism of Calvin, accusing Sanders of ignoring numerous passages in the Psalms and other places where God seems to direct the weather.[48] The tacit assumption among many conservative Protestants—that an errorless, infallible Bible teaches just one clear-cut doctrine of providence—seemed to condemn evangelicals to a limbo of endless exegetical disputes.

The internal evangelical rift over divine control flared into a wider discussion in late 2004. The day after Christmas, an earthquake of an estimated 9.0 magnitude triggered a gigantic tsunami in the Indian Ocean, killing as many as 230,000 people in South and Southeast Asia and dwarfing the scope of natural disasters seen in the comparatively wealthy United States. Prominent evangelical theologian R. Albert Mohler, Jr., president of the Southern Baptist Theological Seminary, called on Christians to mobilize humanitarian efforts. Yet he also wrote that Christians must not hesitate to affirm divine involvement in such tragedies because the Bible teaches that "there is not one atom or molecule in the entire cosmos that is not under the sovereign rule of God." Mohler charged that liberal theologies, in establishing "a truce with the naturalistic worldview," sacrificed God's omnipotence to preserve his benevolence, thus denying the clear scriptural testimony that God is not only all-good but also all-powerful.[49]

Such Calvinist providentialism had already drawn a sharp response in the *Wall Street Journal* from Eastern Orthodox theologian David Bentley Hart, who denounced the "odious banalities" that evangelicals often repeated in claiming divine purpose amid disaster. The New Testament nowhere teaches that the suffering of the present world serves any purpose whatsoever, Hart insisted in a short book that grew out of his op-ed. Christians must await God's final triumph over the forces of darkness, but in the interim, "the cosmos as we know it is obviously a closed economy of life and death."[50] Similar ideas of an impersonal cosmos also surfaced when journalist Gary Stern interviewed non-Christian leaders after the tsunami. Hinduism scholar Vasudha Narayanan, the onetime president of the American Academy of Religion, emphasized the endless cycle of creation and destruction, adding that many Hindus thought of the tsunami as something that happened naturally. "No one is singled out in any way," she said. Similarly, Buddhist convert Kusala Bhikshu stressed the impartial quality of nature. "The world has no intention," he said. "It's not punishing anybody. It's simply in process." Instead of causing consternation, natural disasters confirmed the Buddhist truth of the inevitability of suffering. For both Hindus and Buddhists, moreover, the law of karma operated as an impersonal structure whose consequences in the world could never be fully known.[51]

A response closer to the Open Theist viewpoint came from Rabbi Harold Kushner, whom Stern also interviewed after the tsunami. "People would like to believe that somebody is in control of the world," he said. "My response is that if there is, he is not doing a very good job." In his bestselling book, *When Bad Things Happen to Good People* (1981), written after his 13-year-old son died of an incurable genetic disease, Kushner reached the same conclusion as Brightman that God cannot be perfectly benevolent and omnipotent at the same time. Kushner chose benevolence, arguing that while God cannot prevent suffering, he can help people endure it. "God is kind, fair, loving, and moral," he told Stern. "Nature is not."[52] The book of Genesis depicts God subduing the primeval chaos as his spirit hovers over the face of the waters. But much chaos still remained. "It is too difficult even for God to keep cruelty and chaos from claiming their innocent victims," Kushner wrote in *When Bad Things Happen*. "But could man, without God, do it better?" (Mohler, in the wake of the tsunami, criticized Kushner for popularizing the view that, as Mohler put it, "God is doing the best He can under the circumstances.") Kushner recalled God's speech from the whirlwind in Job, suggesting that one possible paraphrase of its message might be, "If you think that it is so easy to keep the world straight and true, to keep unfair things from happening to people, *you* try it." Kushner nevertheless held out hope that perhaps God was not finished creating order out of chaos. "It may yet come to pass," he wrote, that as "the world's evolution ticks toward the Great Sabbath which is the End of Days, the impact of random evil will be diminished."[53]

STORMS AND CLIMATE CHANGE: WHAT CAN HUMANS CONTROL?

Kushner weighed in again after Hurricane Sandy killed at least 230 people and left nearly $70 billion in damage along the US Atlantic seaboard in October 2012.

"Nature is value-free," he told the *Huffington Post*. "God's role is not to decide where the hurricane goes and how severe it is. God's role is to motivate people to help neighbors and improve methods to predict hurricanes. God is found not in the problem, but in the resilience."[54] His focus on human action pointed to the question of societal responsibility in the face of storms. How natural are natural disasters? Do humans bear some complicity—either through action or inaction—for magnifying weather catastrophes? In recent years, as scientists have dubbed the present age the Anthropocene (the geological epoch in which human activity is the dominant influence on the environment), policymakers and religious leaders have debated two ways in which society is complicit in meteorological disasters.[55] The first is in failing to prepare for, or respond adequately to, major storms, thereby compounding human suffering. The second is in actually altering the climate in ways that may increase the force or frequency of destructive weather.

The first problem was starkly evident after Hurricane Katrina in 2005. No event in modern US history seemed to disprove the pure "act of God" theory of natural disasters so convincingly. Though President George W. Bush called it a "blind and random" tragedy, Katrina was in fact a colossal failure of societal responsibility, especially toward the poor and racial minorities. As environmental historian Ted Steinberg showed in a devastating critique, the Bush administration had slashed funding for flood control even though the Federal Emergency Management Agency knew about the huge potential for loss of life. Katrina was nevertheless a "bipartisan disaster," according to Steinberg, in that both Republicans and Democrats were committed to a neoliberalism that favored developers and other corporate interests over protecting society's most vulnerable members. Steinberg excoriated the "blind faith in the market coupled with rampant deregulation" that led to unrestrained development up and down America's coastline. Whereas black residents of the Lower Ninth Ward in New Orleans waited in vain for months for disaster assistance, Congress approved $148 million to restock beaches in Florida and elsewhere that had lost sand to erosion in four hurricanes in 2004. Beach nourishment was just one example of government subsidies that, like federal flood insurance, usually came with few restrictions on where developers could build new hotels and condominiums. Steinberg concluded that the federal government had repeatedly bailed out coastal property owners "in classic neoliberal fashion, just like it did the savings and loan industry." Disaster relief, in other words, frequently goes to the haves rather than the have-nots.[56]

These racial and economic inequalities are sometimes overlooked in the aftermath of disasters, when responders cross boundaries of race and class in the cause of rebuilding. Historian James Hudnut-Beumler noticed this phenomenon among the faith-based groups, mostly white, that descended on the Gulf coast after Katrina.

While admiring their benevolence, Hudnut-Beumler could not shake the feeling that it was "some kind of Protestant penance for a societal and governmental failure."[57] Similarly, a half century earlier, psychoanalyst Martha Wolfenstein spoke of the "post-disaster Utopia," characterized by short-term acts of interracial and economic cooperation that inevitably tapered off once immediate needs were met.[58] Survivors were then left with the same old structural inequities—problems requiring legislative fixes and the societal will to enact them.

The second problem, the specter of wild weather made worse by anthropogenic climate change, has loomed in recent years every time a catastrophic storm occurs, but 2011 was particularly unnerving. That year worldwide economic damage from natural disasters hit a new high, toppling the previous record set in 2005.[59] For Americans, the most frightening statistic was 553, the year's total tornado deaths, exceeded only by the approximately 800 people killed in 1925, the year of the Tri-State Tornado. (In addition to the Joplin tornado, the 2011 storms included the Super Outbreak of April 25–28 in the Deep South, which surpassed the 1974 Super Outbreak as the most numerous spate of tornadoes in US history.)[60] The *Newsweek* cover of June 6, 2011, said it all: "Weather Panic," superimposed upon a silhouette of a tornado. "Even those who deny the existence of global climate change are having trouble dismissing the evidence of the last year," wrote the story's author Sharon Begley.[61] In actuality, the 2011 tornado season by itself likely indicated little or nothing about climate change. Meteorologist Howard Bluestein, one of the nation's foremost authorities on tornadoes, cited natural variability, explaining that intense tornado years often alternated with comparatively quiet periods. Similarly, Joshua Wurman, founding president of the Center for Severe Weather Research in Boulder, Colorado, noted that "any particular years you can't attribute to changes in global climate."[62]

Longer-term changes in weather patterns, however, were another matter. The 2011 tornadoes raised public awareness of the possibility that if humans were altering the climate, this could open a Pandora's box of local meteorological consequences. Within the scientific community, there was little doubt that anthropogenic climate change was real. As journalist Nathaniel Rich has written, the actual science of global warming is not complicated. The burning of fossil fuels has dramatically increased the carbon dioxide in the atmosphere. Because CO_2 is a greenhouse gas, the more carbon dioxide in the atmosphere, the warmer the planet. The seriousness of the problem was recognized as far back as 1979, when scientists from 50 nations at the first World Climate Conference in Geneva declared unanimously that curbing carbon emissions was "urgently necessary."[63] The evidence of climate change only mounted thereafter. By 2013, the United Nations Intergovernmental Panel on Climate Change (IPCC) reported that 1983–2012 was likely the warmest 30-year period of the last 1,400 years, an alteration that fell outside what could be explained purely by natural variation.[64]

The year 2013 also brought a scary milestone when average daily CO_2 levels reached 400 parts per million, a proportion not seen for three million years, before human evolution, when the earth's geological conditions were radically different due to volcanic activity and other factors.[65] A new IPCC report in October 2018 estimated that human activities had increased the earth's average surface temperature approximately 1 degree Celsius since the Industrial Revolution and that if the present rate of warming continued, the increase would likely reach 1.5 degrees between 2030 and 2052. The small numbers belie the huge changes they could bring: a rise of just 2 or 3 degrees probably would melt ice caps and raise sea levels enough to inundate many coastal areas.[66] And the rate of warming seems to be accelerating. In 2018, the *New York Times* reported that 17 of the 18 hottest years since modern record-keeping began had occurred since 2001.[67]

One likely consequence of a hotter planet is more destructive hurricanes. Higher air temperatures mean warmer ocean waters, which provide the principal fuel for tropical cyclones. Scientists have documented that the potential intensity of hurricane winds increases by about five miles per hour for every 1-degree-Fahrenheit increase of tropical sea surface temperature. In his 2005 book on hurricanes, Kerry Emanuel, a leading authority at the Massachusetts Institute of Technology, warned that anthropogenic warming of the atmosphere could lead to more intense, even if not more frequent, hurricanes. Skeptics cautioned that any uptick in average hurricane strength could have other possible explanations, including incomplete or inaccurate data about the intensity of past storms. But by 2018, accumulating evidence seemed to corroborate Emanuel's hypothesis.[68] Hurricane Michael intensified rapidly to just below Category 5 strength as it barreled into the Florida Panhandle on October 10, 2018. The previous year, Hurricane Maria's maximum sustained winds reached 175 miles per hour (Category 5) before the storm made landfall in Puerto Rico as a high-end Category 4, killing more than 3,000 people. Other storms brought record-breaking rainfalls and catastrophic flooding, likely owing in part to higher air temperatures (which hold more water vapor) and higher sea levels (which worsen storm surge). Hurricane Florence set a new record in September 2018 for the wettest tropical cyclone ever to hit the Carolinas, dumping more than 35 inches of rain in at least one place in North Carolina. The year before, Hurricane Harvey deluged Houston, a disaster made worse by both massive rainfall and higher sea levels, which pushed water from the bayous into the city. Astoundingly, Harvey was the third "500-year flood" to hit Houston in just three years.[69]

Could global warming also lead to more or stronger tornadoes? Here there was less scientific consensus. In 2013 Richard A. Muller, a physicist at the University of

California, Berkeley, argued in a *New York Times* op-ed that an apparent increase in tornadoes in recent decades was simply due to better reporting and documentation. He suggested that the number of intense tornadoes had actually declined. A group of six scientists rebutted Muller, noting that stricter government evaluation standards for tornado damage might have led to an underrating of recent tornadoes.[70] Significantly, neither Muller nor his critics denied the reality of climate change but simply disagreed about its effects on tornadic activity.

Subsequent research indicated that a more likely effect of climate change than an increase in the frequency or intensity of tornadoes might be an eastward shift of "Tornado Alley." A 2018 study by Victor Gensini of Northern Illinois University and Harold Brooks of the National Severe Storms Laboratory found that tornadoes were becoming less frequent in the Great Plains and more so east of the Mississippi. This was consistent with other research showing an eastward shift in the dry line, the explosive boundary between arid and humid air. The idea that the Great Plains were becoming more arid, and thus less tornado-prone, was "super consistent with climate change," said Gensini, though he cautioned that it was too early to confirm that the change was anthropogenic. He warned that more tornadoes in the Midwest and South would expose larger populations to economic losses and risk of injury or death. The Deep South already had the highest rate of fatalities from tornadoes, according to a study by Gensini's colleague Walker Ashley, who suggested that the higher density of mobile homes was a major reason.[71] The 2011 Super Outbreak, which killed more than 300 people in Alabama and neighboring states, showed the dire potential for loss of life in that region.

As scientists contemplated the meteorological consequences of a warmer globe, religious groups took increasingly public stands. As early as the 1990s, mainline Protestant denominations were voicing concern about anthropogenic climate change. A 1990 statement by the Presbyterian Church (USA) called the greenhouse effect "one of the most serious global environmental challenges" of our time and insisted that the United States must take the lead in reducing CO_2 emissions. Two years later, the United Methodist Church declared that human activity "now threatens the planet itself" and pointed to the "noticeable warming of the globe" caused by carbon dioxide from fossil fuels. In 1993, the Evangelical Lutheran Church in America decried "dangerous global warming, caused by the buildup of greenhouse gases, especially carbon dioxide."[72] In 2001, the United States Conference of Catholic Bishops noted the "broad consensus of modern science" that "human activity is beginning to alter the earth's atmospheric characteristics in serious, perhaps profound ways." Pope Francis pointed to that consensus in his encyclical *Laudato Si'* (2015), and cited "an increase of extreme weather events, even if a scientifically determinable cause cannot be assigned to each particular phenomenon."[73]

Some evangelical Protestants also sounded the alarm. Most notable was "Climate Change: An Evangelical Call to Action," issued by the Evangelical Climate Initiative in 2006. Signatories included the megachurch pastor Rick Warren, author of the bestselling *Purpose-Driven Life* (2002), as well as the presidents of 39 evangelical colleges. Calling human-induced climate change real, they urged immediate action by the United States to reduce CO_2 emissions. Failure to act would lead to rising sea levels and more extreme weather events, including torrential rains and floods. All of these impacts, the statement warned, would hit the poor the hardest.[74]

Other evangelicals turned the argument about the poor on its head, contending that regulation of CO_2 emissions, not climate change itself, would disproportionately burden the poor by phasing out cheaper fossil fuels.[75] One source of this counterargument was a group known as the Cornwall Alliance. Organized officially in 2007, it first came to prominence in the "Cornwall Declaration" of 2000, a statement spearheaded by E. Calvin Beisner, a theologian then at Knox Theological Seminary and a fellow of the pro-free market Acton Institute.[76] The declaration lamented the "tendency among some to oppose economic progress in the name of environmental stewardship" and insisted that humans should be regarded as "producers and stewards" of the environment rather than as "consumers and polluters." Signatories included a *Who's Who* of conservative evangelicals: Bill Bright, founder of Campus Crusade for Christ; Chuck Colson, founder of Prison Fellowship; James Dobson, founder of Focus on the Family; D. James Kennedy, founder of the Coral Ridge Presbyterian megachurch; and Donald Wildmon, founder of the American Family Association. Some Jewish and Catholic conservatives also signed, including David Novak, theologian and ethicist at the University of Toronto; Robert Sirico, founder of the Acton Institute; and Richard John Neuhaus, founder of the Institute on Religion and Public Life.[77]

In the wake of the Evangelical Climate Initiative's 2006 "Call to Action," the Cornwall Alliance produced another statement, "An Evangelical Declaration on Global Warming" (2009), which refuted anthropogenic climate change on the grounds of divine providence over creation. The document hailed God's "intelligent design" of the world and the "robust, resilient, self-regulating, and self-correcting" nature of earth's ecosystems. It denounced the notion that the planet's systems were "the fragile and unstable products of chance" or that they were "vulnerable to dangerous alteration."[78] This time the signers included not only evangelical theologians and pastors but also two prominent broadcast meteorologists and evangelical Christians: Neil Frank, former director of the National Hurricane Center and retired weather chief at KHOU-TV, Houston, and James Spann, the Birmingham, Alabama, weathercaster whose word Alabamians considered "the next best thing" to the Gospel, according to journalist Kim Cross. Frank had called global warming a "hoax," while Spann had charged that environmental activists were motivated by "billions of dollars of grant money."[79]

As trusted television personalities, Frank and Spann were a boon to the climate change denial movement.[80] But the most politically potent voice of climate change denial came from the senior senator from Oklahoma, Republican James (Jim) Inhofe. A former real estate developer and insurance executive, Inhofe served as mayor of Tulsa before being elected to the US House of Representatives in 1986. In 1994, when Democratic senator David Boren announced he would resign to become president of the University of Oklahoma, Inhofe was elected to fill his seat. After the Republicans gained control of the Senate in the 2002 midterm elections, Inhofe became chair of the Senate Committee on Environment and Public Works for the first of two stints in that role (2003–2007 and 2015–2017).

Inhofe quickly burnished his reputation as the Senate's most implacable foe of environmental regulation.[81] In repeated speeches from the Senate floor, he called anthropogenic global warming a "hoax" and criticized former Vice President Al Gore for whipping up fears with his 2006 documentary, *An Inconvenient Truth*. He also excoriated the press for abetting liberal activism. "The media endlessly hypes studies that purportedly show that global warming could increase mosquito populations, malaria, West Nile virus, heat waves and hurricanes, threaten the oceans, damage coral reefs, boost poison ivy growth, damage vineyards and global food crops, to name just a few of the global warming-linked calamities," he told the *Tulsa World*. He challenged the media to give up its addiction to "climate porn."[82] In 2007, when Senators Joseph Lieberman (Independent from Connecticut) and John Warner (Republican from Virginia) introduced America's Climate Security Act, a so-called "cap-and-trade" bill to reduce greenhouse gas emissions, Inhofe published an op-ed in the *Wall Street Journal* calling the bill the "largest tax increase in U.S. history" and claiming it would fall disproportionately on the poor. The bill died three days later after Democrats failed to overcome a Republican filibuster.[83]

Inhofe's opposition to environmentalism was partly economic—reflecting a deep suspicion of regulation, formed during his days as a real estate developer—but it was also rooted in religion. A longtime member of Tulsa's First Presbyterian Church, he has professed his abiding belief in God's providential care over creation.[84] He expounded his position in his book *The Greatest Hoax: How the Global Warming Conspiracy Threatens Your Future* (2012), wherein he testified to the influence of another Oklahoman, his friend Bill Bright, founder of Campus Crusade for Christ (now known as Cru). "Many times during my global warming fight," Inhofe recalled, he had turned in Bright's daily devotional book, *Promises*, to Day 36, which features "one of my favorite Bible verses, Genesis 8:22: 'As long as the earth remains there will be springtime and harvest, cold and heat, winter and summer, day and night.'" "This is what a lot of alarmists forget," Inhofe continued. "God is still up there, and He promised to maintain the seasons and that cold and heat would never cease as long as the earth remains." Genesis 8:22 thus cuts through "all the hysteria, all the fear, and all the phony science."[85]

Inhofe's confidence that God would not allow humans to mess up the climate inspired him to stage a much-ridiculed publicity stunt in February 2015. In the midst of an unusually severe winter in Washington, D.C., he smuggled a snowball onto the Senate floor. "In case we had forgotten, because we keep hearing that 2014 has been the warmest year on record," he declared, "I ask the chair, do you know what this is? It's a snowball, just from outside here. It's very, very cold out." He then tossed the snowball to the presiding officer. Late-night comedian Jon Stewart skewered the senator: "You think global warming is a hoax because in February you were able to collect one ball's worth of snow?"[86]

But Inhofe's religious zeal against environmental regulation was no laughing matter. In April 2015, he joined forces with another religious conservative, Oklahoma attorney general Scott Pruitt, to support a bill granting the state legislature oversight over any implementation of new Environmental Protection Agency (EPA)

FIGURE 5.4. Senator Jim Inhofe holding a snowball in the US Senate on February 26, 2015. Video capture via C-Span.

emissions standards issued under President Barack Obama's Climate Action Plan.[87] The bill passed, but Republican Governor Mary Fallin vetoed it, opting for the more direct way of resisting the EPA regulations by simply not filing a state-level plan for implementing them.[88] Pruitt, meanwhile, was becoming known for his multiple lawsuits against the EPA on behalf of Oklahoma utilities.[89]

The Inhofe-Pruitt alliance foreshadowed the much larger influence Oklahomans would wield on federal climate policy after the election of President Donald Trump in 2016. Four weeks after the election, Trump announced the nomination of Pruitt to head the EPA, the agency against which Pruitt had fought so strenuously. Conservative evangelicals immediately rallied to Pruitt's defense. The Cornwall Alliance supported him in an open letter to the president, and a group of leaders from Pruitt's own denomination, the Southern Baptist Convention, also sent their endorsement. Among the signers of the latter were the presidents of all six of the denomination's seminaries, including R. Albert Mohler, Jr., president of the Southern Baptist Theological Seminary at Louisville, of which Pruitt was a trustee. On the other side of the climate-change divide, a statement from the Evangelical Environmental Network urged the president to withdraw Pruitt's nomination. Signers included Ron Sider, founder of Evangelicals for Social Action, and Jim Wallis, founder of *Sojourners* magazine.[90]

The Senate confirmed Pruitt by a 52–46 vote in February 2017. In filling out his staff, he drew on key Inhofe veterans, including the senator's former chief of staff, Ryan Jackson, who became Pruitt's own chief of staff. Inhofe's former chief counsel, Andrew Wheeler, who had later served as chief counsel for the Committee on Environment and Public Works during Inhofe's chairmanship, was confirmed by the Senate as deputy EPA administrator. Pruitt also used his new platform to cast doubt on climate science. Though in his confirmation hearing he had said that climate change is not a hoax, three weeks after being sworn in at EPA, in an interview on CNBC, he denied that CO_2 is "a primary contributor" to global warming.[91] His true doubts soon became clear as he took steps to reverse or delay dozens of Obama-era environmental regulations.[92] Most significantly, he was at Trump's side on June 1, 2017, when the president announced his plan to withdraw the United States from the Paris climate accord, the historic pact, signed in December 2015 after nine years of negotiations, that represented the broadest-ever international commitment to reduce greenhouse gas emissions. Perversely, the Trump administration treated the Rose Garden announcement as a celebration, complete with a military band playing soft jazz.[93]

Pruitt's deregulatory crusade eventually hit a snag of his own making. In July 2018, he was forced to resign as EPA administrator amid a firestorm of ethics allegations, including traveling first class at government expense, installing a $43,000 soundproof booth in his office, using staff to secure special favors for his family, and leasing a D.C. townhouse at a bargain rate from a couple employed by a firm lobbying the EPA.[94] In his resignation letter to the president, he decried the "unrelenting attacks" on himself and his family and praised Trump as the Lord's instrument: "I believe you are serving as President today because of God's providence. I believe that same providence brought me into your service."[95]

Pruitt's departure did little to halt the war on regulation from within the EPA; Trump immediately installed Pruitt's deputy, Andrew Wheeler, as acting administrator. Early signs indicated that he would continue his predecessor's lack of attention to climate change. In October 2018, when the IPCC issued its dire warning that global warming might soon pass the 1.5-degree Celsius threshold, the Trump administration was silent. An EPA spokesperson later said that the agency would not endorse the report's findings.[96] In November 2018, Trump announced the nomination of Wheeler, who in addition to serving Inhofe had worked as a coal lobbyist, as the permanent head of the EPA, and he was confirmed by the Senate in February 2019.[97]

All the while, Trump had been following the playbook of tapping foes of federal agencies to run them. In 2017, the president nominated Barry Lee Myers, CEO of AccuWeather, the for-profit forecasting company, as administrator of the National Oceanic and Atmospheric Administration (NOAA), the parent agency of the National Weather Service. Myers had a long history of fighting to limit NOAA's ability to compete with AccuWeather's forecasting products. The most notorious attempt was a bill introduced in 2005 by Senator Rick Santorum, Republican from Pennsylvania, whose campaign Myers had supported, that would have limited direct NWS communication with the public except to issue severe weather alerts. (The bill died in committee.) As journalist Michael Lewis put it: "Pause for a moment to consider the audacity of that maneuver. A private company whose weather predictions were totally dependent on the billions of dollars spent by the U.S. taxpayer to gather the data necessary for those predictions . . . was, in effect, trying to force the U.S. taxpayer to pay all over again for what the National Weather Service might be able to tell him or her for free." Lewis's exposé also revealed that Myers had successfully lobbied to block the NWS's effort in the wake of the Joplin tornado to offer the public a new weather app to better disseminate severe storm warnings.[98]

AccuWeather's profit motive was again nakedly apparent, as Lewis discovered, when the company touted its spotting of a short-lived tornado in Moore, Oklahoma, in March 2015, that the National Weather Service had initially missed. AccuWeather later used the incident in an advertisement for its "Enterprise Solutions" forecasting product for corporate clients, noting that its subscribers received a warning of the Moore tornado 23 minutes before the NWS alerted the general public.[99] Such monetization of weather warnings for business clients paralleled AccuWeather's aggressive marketing of premium products designed for individuals using mobile devices. Three former NOAA administrators came out in opposition to Myers's nomination to lead the agency as a blatant conflict of interest. Critics also questioned his credentials, noting that only one other administrator in NOAA's four-decade history lacked a science degree (Myers majored in business at Pennsylvania State University and earned a law degree from Boston University).[100] Defenders countered that business acumen was exactly what NOAA needed, an opinion that Myers himself had expressed in a hearing before Congress in 2013 on America's forecasting infrastructure. "The weather industry has innovated in ways the government could not nor should be expected to do," he said.[101]

The notion that innovation is the province of the private sector, a cherished assumption of free-market conservatives, ignored the reality that much basic research in the sciences, which private companies rely on to develop new products, would never happen except under government auspices because it is not directly geared toward making a profit.[102] Myers's quest to put weather data behind a customer-only firewall also raised fundamental ethical questions. Should any private company own basic weather information? Ought weather forecasting not be a government activity, much like air traffic control? The Trump administration's apparent willingness to circumscribe NOAA, along with the parallel weakening of EPA, suggested not only a lack of understanding of these agencies' vital functions for public safety, but also a retreat from the idea of government-sponsored science as an enterprise for the common good.

WICKED PROBLEMS, POLITICAL AND THEOLOGICAL

The Trump administration's cavalier attitude toward the weather and climate was in some ways the outgrowth of long-standing American hubris toward the natural world. Just as Americans considered it their manifest destiny to overspread the continent, they also thought the forces of nature would present no obstacle to national ambitions. The American mind, as historian and conservationist Bernard DeVoto wrote in 1954, "went on believing that there must be some way of licking climate or that climate would adapt itself to men's desires."[103] Comedian Will Ferrell satirized this attitude in his imitation of President George W. Bush, imagining the president as saying: "Global warming, don't worry about it. . . . We just need to get nature to cooperate with us. We don't need to listen to nature. Nature needs to listen to us."[104] Bush, who backed out of the 1997 Kyoto Protocol signed (but not ratified) during the Clinton administration, eventually came around to stricter emissions standards and even expressed openness to a cap-and-trade system.[105] President Trump, who over the years had derided climate change as a "hoax," "a total hoax," "an expensive hoax," and "a total and very expensive hoax," seemed less likely to change. In an interview with Lesley Stahl on *60 Minutes* in October 2018, he said that he no longer believed climate change was a hoax, but he quickly hedged: "I don't know that it's man-made." He also said he did not want to "give trillions and trillions of dollars" or "lose millions and millions of jobs" through any policies to combat global warming. As journalist Robinson Meyer summarized Trump's perspective, "There's a sense of grievance: the idea that even if climate change *isn't* a hoax, its only role is to cost people money and harm American industry."[106]

As Trump nursed his sense of grievance, the planet continued to get hotter. A study by the Climate Impact Lab projected that cities across the United States would experience many more days of at least 90-degree highs by the end of the century. New York could see 20 more than it did on average between 1950 and 1970, while such days could increase by 37 in Washington and by 46 in Atlanta.[107] These projections assumed that the world's countries would curb greenhouse gas emissions roughly in line with the pledges made in the Paris accord. But a review by the journal *Nature* found that all major industrialized countries were failing to meet their benchmarks. One reason was a continuing global reliance on coal, especially in Asia, where some 1,200 new coal plants were either under construction or in the planning stages in late 2018.[108]

As if these trends were not worrisome enough, the 1,656-page National Climate Assessment, issued by 13 US federal agencies in November 2018, predicted that economic damage from climate change could by the year 2100 reduce the nation's gross domestic product by up to 10 percent—more than double the losses of the Great Recession of 2007–2009. The report also noted that though the precise effects of climate change on severe weather were still being analyzed, some extreme events had already become more frequent, intense, or widespread. The document cited a NOAA estimate that since 2015 the United States had experienced 44 weather or climate disasters that each caused a billion dollars or more in damages. The Trump administration quickly discounted the report, mandated by Congress every four years, since it was begun under President Obama. A statement from the White House dismissed it as "largely based on the most extreme scenario" of global warming and said that the next assessment would afford a chance for greater balance.[109]

The impasse between the Trumpist denial of a climate crisis and scientific warnings of looming catastrophe highlighted the intractability of climate change as a social issue. Ethicist Willis Jenkins has aptly called climate change the "wicked problem" of the Anthropocene because it defies any easy solution. Its difficulty consists in its sheer complexity, entangling science, politics, economics, ethics, and religion. An added complication lies in the irreversible imprint that humans have already made on the world. "There is no response that can dissolve the problem by reverting earth systems to a state in which humanity has insignificant influence," Jenkins explains. To manage the problem, societies must agree on climate objectives, which will require weighing multiple factors. How much CO_2 in the atmosphere is acceptable? Which social impacts of planetary warming are tolerable?[110] Then there are the challenges of commitment and enforcement. Is the Paris accord salvageable without US participation, or is a new instrument already needed? And what becomes of any global regulatory mechanism in an era of populist, anti-government nationalism?

Resistance to government "intrusion" has complicated not only climate policy but also local responses to severe weather, as the case of Oklahoma makes clear. In the wake of the 2013 tornado, several grieving parents from Plaza Towers Elementary helped mount a campaign to raise private money for storm shelters in Oklahoma schools. "Our children should be safe," said Scott McCabe. "We assumed they were."[111] But this grassroots effort soon spawned a contentious debate about whether shelters should be publicly funded, and if so, how the money should be secured. A group called Take Shelter Oklahoma launched a petition drive to let voters decide whether the state should fund the shelters with up to $500 million in bonds, which would be repaid with revenues from franchise taxes (charged to certain corporations for doing business in the state). With the petition drive already underway, Scott Pruitt, who was still Oklahoma's attorney general at the time, revised the language for the ballot, contending that it must clearly explain that franchise tax revenues flow to the state's general fund, which would see a loss if the bond measure were approved. Supporters of the petition accused Pruitt of sabotaging the effort and asked the Oklahoma Supreme Court to throw out his revisions.[112]

In April 2014, the court upheld Pruitt's revisions but granted Take Shelter Oklahoma 90 more days to seek the 155,000 signatures needed to put the initiative on the November ballot. The group declined the extension and opted to start a revised petition, this time calling for a bond issue to be repaid over 25 years from the general fund, rather than through franchise taxes. In the new attempt, the group enlisted civil rights icon Jesse Jackson, who visited the state in June 2014. "What happens to Oklahoma directly affects the rest of us," Jackson said, explaining his involvement. "We're all members of one family." But in the opinion of the *Oklahoman*, the state's largest daily newspaper, Jackson's visit proved only that the petition drive "reek[ed] with politics." "Why not bring in a nationally known figure associated with, say, meteorology, instead of a professional race-baiter?" the paper asked. The *Oklahoman* also alleged a political motivation on the part of the Democratic candidate for governor, State Representative Joe Dorman, who had filed a bill to enact the $500 million bond issue directly. His opponent, Republican incumbent Mary Fallin, favored a different bill that would allow voters to decide whether to allow individual school districts to increase their bonding debt limits to fund shelters.[113]

Ultimately, Dorman's effort and the Fallin-backed bill both failed, while the reincarnated petition drive fell nearly 100,000 signatures short.[114] (Fallin beat Dorman in the gubernatorial election, 55 to 41 percent.) The collapse of any state-wide initiative put the onus on local school districts, some of which were better equipped than others to protect their students. An investigation by the *Oklahoman* found that dozens of school districts still lacked certified storm shelters as of mid-2018. Terry Heustis, superintendent of the Westville Public Schools in Adair County, one of the state's poorest, told the newspaper that the lower tax base in rural communities such as his meant that they were unable to bond for as much money as bigger school districts. In comparatively affluent Moore, voters in 2015 approved a $209 million bond issue to build certified safe rooms in the schools that still lacked them. The rooms are capable of withstanding winds of up to 250 miles per hour.[115] Such protection was a feature of the new $12 million Plaza Towers Elementary, which the district finished rebuilding just 15 months after the tornado. The city of Moore also passed some of the nation's strictest residential building codes, requiring new homes to be able to withstand winds of up to 135 miles per hour.[116]

I visited the new Plaza Towers in April 2015. Nearby, new homes were still under construction, reinvigorating a neighborhood that had been virtually flattened less than two years earlier. The gleaming new school building testified to one community's moral resolve to protect its children, but a memorial erected at the front entrance also reminded me, as the father of three children myself, of the dreadful absence that must haunt every parent who has lost a child. Seven stone benches, each inscribed with the name of one of the dead children and images of his or her favorite things, now greet students as they arrive for school. The privately funded memorial also includes along the entryway stone slabs with silhouettes of each child, depicted as smiling and walking into school with backpacks and sports gear.[117]

The memorial turned my attention again to the theological questions that persist in the aftermath of disaster. How does one make sense of the violent deaths of seven children? From a pastoral perspective, of course, no answer seems wrong if it helps survivors cope. For the many Oklahomans who identify as evangelical Protestants, a deadly tornado cannot shake their faith in divine providence, even if God's purposes are not always clear. The *Oklahoman* expressed this prevailing view

FIGURE 5.5. Memorial benches at the rebuilt Plaza Towers Elementary School, 2015.
Photograph by the author.

in an editorial the day after the 2013 tornado: "Through death and destruction, in chaos and calamity, but also in recovery and redemption, God is in control."[118] Yet a few weeks later, the newspaper gave space to the opposite perspective by publishing a feature on Rebecca Vitsmun, the tornado survivor who had confessed her atheism to Wolf Blitzer on CNN. The awkward encounter had gone viral on the internet, prompting an outpouring of support from atheist groups in Oklahoma and elsewhere. "Natural disasters are a product of our environment, not supernatural forces," said Roy Speckhardt, executive director of the American Humanist Association, in a statement of solidarity.[119]

These opposing views—faith in the Tornado God versus the skepticism of "Tornado Atheists," as Vitsmun described herself[120]—remain as irreconcilable today as they were in the eighteenth century when colonial clergy railed against atheistic naturalism. It is a classic Enlightenment problem in that both sides assume a rationality (whether providential or scientific) that could explain the Whirlwind if fully understood. And it is a classic American problem in that each side assumes that the other can be persuaded in the free marketplace of religious ideas. Even dissenters from the dichotomy, such as Open Theists whose deity limits himself by the scientific outworking of the world, still put their faith in humans' ability to *know* the ways of God.

But what if the meaning of this argument is not to be found in the competing solutions but in the mystery the argument conceals? That is, what if the mystery of the Whirlwind is far deeper and more fundamental—both scientifically and theologically—than most Americans have realized? In the Conclusion, we will return to Oklahoma, where the frontiers of scientific investigation are oddly converging with primal religious uncertainties.

It is hardly necessary to say that in the religion of the future there will be no personifications of the primitive forces of nature, such as light, fire, frost, wind, storm, and earthquake.

—CHARLES W. ELIOT, *The Religion of the Future* (1909)

Under the same firmament on which the stars move as the symbols of invariable laws of nature, the clouds form, the rain pours, the winds change, apparently as symbols of the opposite principle. Amongst the phenomena of nature they are the most capriciously variable ones, the most fugitive, the most impossible to grasp; they escape every attempt of ours to catch them in the enclosure of law.

—HERMANN VON HELMHOLTZ, "Wirbelstürme und Gewitter" (1876)

Conclusion

THE PRIMAL WHIRLWIND

TWENTY MILES SOUTH of Oklahoma City, just below Moore, is the city of Norman, home to the University of Oklahoma (OU) and epicenter of severe weather research in the United States. The drive from Oklahoma City to Norman on Interstate 35 takes travelers right through the path of the 2013 tornado, which crossed the freeway in a stretch crowded with homes and businesses. The urban density seems almost to defy the deity, as if filling the landscape with dwellings might serve as a human shield to stay the divine wrath. On the day I made the trip under a vast, mostly cloudless sky, I had for a moment the eerie sensation of smallness, of how human civilization might look to a tornado, if the storm had eyes. Such intimations are fleeting: we quickly revert to our limited horizons and bounded logic, despite warnings from the gods about our presumption. Yahweh the Storm God admonished Job and the prophet Isaiah: "Who is this that darkeneth counsel by words without knowledge?" (Job 38:2); "For my thoughts are not your thoughts, neither are your ways my ways, saith the Lord" (Isaiah 55:8).

By the time I traveled to Norman, I had already spent several years immersed in the seemingly futile theological debates over the Whirlwind. If theologians were still divided over how to explain tornadoes, I wondered, were scientists doing any better? There is no better place than Norman to investigate this question. Its status as a weather hub dates back to the 1960s, when Edwin Kessler (1928–2017), a pioneer in the use of Doppler radar for tracking storms, established the National Severe Storms Laboratory (NSSL) in cooperation with OU. Eventually, OU's School of Meteorology grew to be the largest in the nation, attracting scientists from all over the world to study the atmospheric fireworks that come every spring to central Oklahoma.

One of the young scientists whom Kessler enticed to OU was Howard Bluestein, who regarded Oklahoma as another country when he arrived from Boston in 1976. Bluestein had just finished his Ph.D. at MIT, where Kessler, also an MIT graduate, had recently completed a sabbatical. Bluestein went on to become one of the world's leading authorities on severe convective storms, the kind that can spawn tornadoes. On the popular level, he gained fame for the Totable Tornado Observatory, nicknamed "TOTO" (in homage to Dorothy's dog in *The Wizard of Oz*), that he developed with NOAA scientists Al Bedard and Carl Ramzy. Though the 400-pound, barrel-like contraption proved too cumbersome and dangerous to deploy very successfully in the path of a tornado, it inspired a similar device, "Dorothy," in the 1996 movie *Twister*.[1]

My main purpose in Norman was to interview Bluestein, but first on the agenda was a tour of the National Weather Center (NWC), a joint facility of the federal government and OU. The initial proposal for such a center came in 1994 from OU provost Jeff Kimpel, a meteorologist and later the director of NSSL. Senator David Boren had just resigned from Congress to become president of OU, and his Washington connections would help secure $33 million in federal appropriations for the project. Opened in 2006 at a final cost of $69 million, the NWC is a gleaming 250,000-square-foot, five-story complex housing 550 federal and university employees and students. OU's School of Meteorology, located on the top floor, includes a student laboratory with 250 feet of southwest-facing windows—a prime location for observing the thunderstorms that regularly rise up from the prairie. When the weather turns dangerous, the building's ground-level auditorium, with 19-inch reinforced concrete walls, doubles as a storm shelter. Besides housing numerous NOAA-related entities, the NWC has been a magnet for private meteorological firms wishing to locate adjacent to the federal hub of severe storm research. David L. Boren Boulevard, where the center is located, has become something of an Embassy Row of weather agencies. On the day I visited, the tour guide said that atmospheric scientists are so numerous in Norman that if

FIGURE C.1. The National Weather Center at the University of Oklahoma, Norman, 2015.
Photograph by the author.

you go to the local Walmart, "there's a good chance you're going to bump into a meteorologist."

From the standpoint of the safety of Americans, the most important agency housed in the NWC is NOAA's Storm Prediction Center (SPC), which is responsible for issuing all severe weather alerts for the nation. Every watch or warning for tornadoes or severe thunderstorms comes from the meteorologists who staff the SPC 24 hours a day, 7 days a week, constantly scanning the latest satellite, radar, and other data on dozens of computer monitors. Even before they issue a watch or warning, SPC forecasters often anticipate severe weather outbreaks days in advance through their Convective Outlooks, updated several times daily and available at no charge on NOAA's web site.[2] (I confess to addictive checking of the Convective Outlooks web page, a habit I developed while researching this book.) A forecaster's job at the SPC is highly coveted and does not come open very often. Like much public service, it has its unglamorous side, including the long hours of boredom during quiet periods of the meteorological year. But on days when NOAA's NEXRAD radar network lights up with dangerous storms, the vigilance of the SPC's meteorologists has been lifesaving.

FIGURE C.2. NOAA's Storm Prediction Center in Norman, Oklahoma, which issues all severe weather watches and warnings for the nation.
Photograph by the author.

TORNADOES AND CHAOS

Howard Bluestein, whom his colleagues and students know as Howie, is an unassuming, bespectacled man with a wiry build and gray-white hair. Professorial yet outdoorsy, he spends every spring chasing tornadoes with his graduate students in mobile radar trucks. When I contacted him before my trip, he warned that if the day of our meeting happened to be stormy, he would be out in the field and would need to reschedule. The day turned out clear, so I met him in his fifth-floor office in the NWC. I commented on the bird's eye view of the surrounding landscape from his windows. "Yes, I wanted an office in the northwest corner, so it's a 270-degree view," he said. But, he added, laughing, "when interesting things are happening, I tend not to be here."[3]

Bluestein was a five-year-old in Boston when the 1953 tornado killed 94 people in Worcester, 40 miles to the west. He was playing in the street that afternoon when his mother called him inside because of the reports from Worcester. "Tornadoes take little boys and suck them up," he recalls her saying. "And I didn't believe that. But I remember the day and it made an impression on me." Later, as an undergraduate at MIT, he studied electrical engineering before completing his doctorate there in

FIGURE C.3. Howard B. Bluestein, the George Lynn Cross Research Professor at OU. Photograph by K. E. Welch.

tropical meteorology. The first tornadoes he saw were waterspouts that occurred while he was working at the National Hurricane Research Laboratory in Florida. He laid eyes on an Oklahoma twister for the first time in the spring of 1977, just months after he had moved to Norman. He estimated that in the four decades since, he had seen several hundred tornadoes. "Some years you have a good year and you see 10 or 20, and other years you have a bad year and you don't see very many, maybe just a couple," he said. Bluestein's appreciation of tornadoes is not only scientific but aesthetic. A skilled photographer, he took many of the storm photos that grace the hallways of the NWC. Opportune photographic moments seem to follow him. During my stay in Norman, he won a prize at a photography exhibit for a fortuitous shot he took from inside the Denver International Airport as a tornado descended from a cloud there in June 2013. That twister triggered a warning that sent thousands of passengers to safe rooms in the terminal. Though the storm briefly touched down, it caused no injuries or damage.[4]

We got down to business when I asked Bluestein about his observation in *Tornado Alley* (1999), his book for laypeople, that tornadoes are "one of the last frontiers of atmospheric science."[5] Might scientists eventually cross this frontier, or would certain things about tornadoes always remain beyond their grasp? Here the conversation turned to mathematics, which, for all the excitement and adrenaline of

FIGURE C.4. Howard Bluestein photographing tornadoes near Dodge City, Kansas, May 24, 2016. Photograph by Dylan Reif.

storm-chasing, is the inescapable foundation of meteorological research. (My NWC tour guide commented that among students in the OU School of Meteorology, "our big retention killers are calculus and physics.") "There's an inherent unpredictability" about tornadoes, Bluestein said. "You'll never be able to really predict that a thunderstorm will form in this exact location and then an hour and 20 minutes later will go on to produce a tornado." The reasons are mathematical. "If you look at the equations, you'll see that they're highly nonlinear. They're variables times variables, so that means that if you make a small error or are unable to observe a particular variable beyond a certain precision, . . . what goes into the equation is not just an error, it's a product, and once you start to get a product, you start to create tremendous unknowns."

Unlike linear systems, which can be graphed with a straight line, the nonlinear equations used to describe meteorological behavior are quite difficult to solve and in many instances have no exact solutions. Another word for nonlinearity is chaos, and the first to theorize it was one of Bluestein's mentors at MIT, the meteorologist and mathematician Edward Lorenz (1917–2008). In a famous 1963 article, Lorenz reported his discovery that one of the characteristics of chaotic systems is *sensitive dependence on initial conditions.* That is, a small alteration in one of the variables (in his modeling, a tiny fraction of one percent), could have large and unpredictable consequences for the evolution of the system.[6] For weather, this meant that a minute change in wind speed, temperature, or any other variable could eventually produce very different results than if the change had not occurred. This came to be known as the Butterfly Effect. The term is associated with Lorenz's 1972 conference presentation, "Predictability: Does the Flap of a Butterfly's Wings in Brazil Set Off a Tornado in Texas?" Lorenz cited Ray Bradbury's 1952 short story, "A Sound of Thunder," in which the death of a prehistoric butterfly changes the outcome of a present-day presidential election.[7]

Lorenz's discovery was a "game changer," according to meteorological historian James Rodger Fleming, in that he identified "a fundamental chaotic limit to our ability to forecast the future." This "brick wall blocking prevision" is not because weather systems are random. While they often *appear* random, they are in fact deterministic, but scientists' ability to predict their behavior with perfect accuracy, especially over the long term, will always be thwarted by incomplete or imperfect measurements and by limitations in the power of computers.[8] Journalist James Gleick aptly summarized the problem in his bestseller *Chaos* (1987): "Suppose the earth could be covered with sensors spaced one foot apart, rising at one-foot intervals all the way to the top of the atmosphere. Suppose every sensor gives perfectly accurate readings of temperature, pressure, humidity, and any other quantity a meteorologist would want." The computer would still be unable to predict whether a certain town would have sun or rain on a day one month away because the spaces between the sensors would still hide small fluctuations capable of producing unpredictable consequences down the line. In fact, the earth could never be covered with enough sensors to ensure perfect forecasting accuracy.[9]

This is not to say that meteorologists are not trying to gain better measurements and develop more sophisticated computer modeling techniques. Bluestein explained that some of his colleagues are modeling tornadoes with heretofore unattainable resolution, which will only get finer as computers are able to handle more data. Yet to predict whether a particular thunderstorm will spawn a tornado still depends on a mind-boggling set of factors. Consider air temperature. "It's like Goldilocks," Bluestein said. "You need to have some cold air but not too much cold air. And how much cold is the optimum amount depends on the vertical shear in the lower part of the storm. . . . To make a prediction, you need to predict the strength of the cold pool. To do that, you really need to understand how the rain is evaporating. But to do that, you need to start modeling raindrops." The complexity, in other words, is exponential. "And this is above and beyond the issue of chaos—the nonlinear equations," Bluestein added. "No matter how fine you make your measurements, you need to be making them in a finer scale. So that's something that needs to be dealt with. That's a philosophical issue."[10]

It is also a theological issue. In the past several decades, theologians have begun to reckon with the implications of chaos theory for the doctrine of providence, just as William Pollard wrestled with quantum theory in the 1950s. One significant effort was a conference sponsored by the Center for Theology and the Natural Sciences in Berkeley, California, in 1993. Its participants included the two British scientists-turned-theologians Arthur Peacocke and John Polkinghorne, as well as the University of Chicago's Langdon Gilkey. The papers were erudite and wide-ranging, but the conference was at best inconclusive on how to reconcile divine action with the workings of a quantum and chaotic world.[11] Nine years later, the British physicist-theologian Nicholas Saunders offered a sobering assessment in his book on modern science and SDA, or Special Divine Action—the contemporary buzzword for God's interventionist providence. Saunders concluded that the prospects for supporting anything like a traditional understanding of divine activity in the world were "extremely bleak." "In fact," he added, "it is no real exaggeration to state that contemporary theology is in crisis."[12] A more hopeful note came from the American evangelical theologian John Jefferson Davis, who argued that science and theology did not threaten each other, but rather should be thought of as complementary languages, a notion Saunders faulted as abandoning the quest for a unified understanding of reality.[13] Davis acknowledged the unsettling implications of chaos theory, which dealt the final blow to the predictable universe envisioned by Pierre-Simon Laplace in the eighteenth century. Yet in Davis's view, chaotic uncertainties simply highlighted the need for multiple ways of knowing. "Scientific reductionism has become less tenable in the wake of chaos theory," he wrote. It gives us "further reason to adopt a stance of epistemic humility in the face of a complex and unpredictable world."[14]

In *Tornado Alley*, Bluestein likewise stressed the need for multiple languages, urging the necessity of cultivating an aesthetic sensibility: "I am a firm believer that in order to study a meteorological phenomenon properly, you must actually experience it and appreciate it aesthetically."[15] When I asked him about this, he spoke of the special feelings that tornadoes evoked in him. "I still have the same excitement and awe that I did when I first saw one. Because the power is just so overwhelming.

There's nothing you can do about it. Absolutely nothing you can do about it." Ancient humans, he said, were similarly awestruck by the whirlwind's uncontrollable power. "Two thousand years ago, people had absolutely no idea what [a tornado] was, and so it was religious," he said. "But we can still look at it and say that, yes, we have religious awe for it, even though we know that the tornado should follow Newton's Second Law." Chaos theory has simply added a layer of awe-inspiring complexity—the element of unpredictability—to Newtonian physics. "You can say that the conditions are right for a storm to produce a tornado. But you can't actually say that a storm will go on to produce a tornado at this time and in this location," Bluestein explained. "To that extent, they'll always be a mystery."

The sense of awe described by Bluestein is the intoxicating elixir that keeps storm chasers coming back to Tornado Alley, season after season. Stefan Bechtel, who once teamed up with the legendary Tim Samaras, describes the experience of seeing an EF4 tornado near Quinter, Kansas, in 2008: "It is now so black it looks satanic. Yet there is something about this furiously spinning whirlwind that is so mortifyingly sublime, something that so transcends this particular day, and this particular place— something that is so utterly *other*—that any comment at all seems ridiculous."[16] A tornado's otherness—its unconquerable mystery—is ultimately the reason that it arouses wonder in scientists even when its basic meteorological causes are known. Environmental ethicist Lisa Sideris calls this "compatibilist wonder," or "wonder at an experience of a phenomenon that continues even after a causal explanation is found." Compatibilist wonder engages us not at the level of rationality or logic, but at the level of experience and the senses. It is acutely, even unnervingly, aware of the indomitability of its object. "We are all intimately related to a natural world that remains other and even alien," notes Sideris, "a world that operates independently of us, autonomously expressing recalcitrance and unpredictability, and behaving in ways both fascinating and inconvenient to us."[17]

CULTURALLY PECULIAR YET RELIGIOUSLY PRIMAL

The alien quality of tornadoes does not negate their peculiarly American character. As we have seen, no storm so epitomizes the fascination and perils of the nation's frontier. Americans have been trying to subdue the frontier since colonial contact, believing that civilization would neutralize many of nature's threats. The apogee of such optimism was the late nineteenth century, when John Park Finley and others anticipated that tornado forecasting would so improve that fear of the whirlwind would be no more. Although storm prediction has indeed made tremendous strides, these advances have revealed the inherent limitations in all weather forecasting.

Similarly, the march of civilization, rather than taming the frontier, is actually making it wilder and more unpredictable as human activities have altered the climate and weather. Americans today are haunted by the distinct possibility that they have sown the wind and shall reap the whirlwind, to recall the words of Hosea 8:7.

Tornadoes are culturally peculiar to the United States in another way in that they fit perfectly with the dominant biblicism of American religion, the raging of the Old Testament God, and the inscrutability of his ways. These motifs, heavily inflected by American Protestantism, also draw from the cultural traits of ancient Near Eastern religion, with its monarchial, gendered notion of God as an all-powerful king.[18] So ingrained is this image that many Americans cannot help but think of tornadoes and other violent weather as acts of God, or as the theologian B. A. Gerrish has put it, the "periodic divine incursions" of an omnipotent monarch on high. More than two centuries ago, Friedrich Schleiermacher faulted this view for rendering God (to quote Gerrish's summary) "one personal agent among others in space and time, making ad hoc decisions, doing this and doing that as the occasion demands."[19] Schleiermacher's liberal alternative edged toward pantheism (identification of God with the universe), or at least the idea that God and the world cannot be sharply separated.[20] Pantheism found its own American adherents, emerging full-blown in Transcendentalism and later in nature spirituality. The contemporary Christian theologian Sallie McFague's notion of the world as God's body has unmistakable pantheistic overtones. In her book on theology and climate change, she writes: "I am not even afraid of pantheism; the line between God and the world is fuzzy."[21]

Yet monarchists, pantheists, and other theists are still left with profound logical conundrums, including the perennial problem of evil. Whether the world is controlled by or identical with God, how does a theist explain the natural evil of a tornado that violently snuffs out human lives? Scarcely more explicable is the moral evil of humans' negligence toward each other and the planet. "This then is the real mystery of evil; that it presupposes itself," Reinhold Niebuhr once observed.[22] Evil acts invariably seem to assume some prior temptation, or some incomprehensible surd in an otherwise law-governed universe.[23] The problem of evil exposes the limits of humans' explanatory power, not because explanations are lacking, but because they inevitably fail to convince.

This sense of intractable mystery is finally why the tornado is more than an American phenomenon. While culturally peculiar, it is also religiously primal, for it evokes the pre-rational and intensely human experience of standing in the presence of an unpredictable, uncontrollable, and unfathomable power. This is the reason the Storm God persists—why meteorological metaphors for divine mystery are still compelling, despite the prediction of Harvard president Charles Eliot (quoted in the epigraph) that such personifications would pass away in an enlightened, scientific age.[24] The meteorological imagery of the Hebrew Bible is time-bound yet timeless, occurring repeatedly in scripture precisely because it so sublimely depicts the divine mystery. It is no coincidence that when Yahweh gives the law on Sinai, he is shrouded in cloud and storm. And it is no coincidence that when he later returns to interrogate Job, he appears in the whirlwind. Rudolf Otto was right that the words of Job chapter 38 "may well rank among the most remarkable in the history of religion."[25] The mouth-stopping force of this text comes not from any explanation of the evils that have befallen Job but from the fact that God offers no explanation at all. "In the last resort," Otto wrote, "it relies on something quite different from anything that can be exhaustively rendered in rational concepts, namely, on the sheer absolute wondrousness that transcends thought, on the *mysterium*, presented in its pure, non-rational form."[26]

Americans often resist mystery. They gravitate toward black-and-white explanations and unambiguous conclusions. Many people believe that science and religion offer such certainties, rendering the world predictable according to law or doctrine. But the tornado has continually frustrated the quest for predictability. The German physicist Hermann von Helmholtz (1821–1894) seemed to foresee the limits on predicting storms when he spoke of how the winds and rain are the "most fugitive" elements of nature, escaping "every attempt of ours to catch them in the enclosure of law."[27] In religion, the tornado is an emblem of everything that humans cannot capture. Even the most confident believers in providence sooner or later fall back on mystery when pressed to explain why one person lived and another died.

The mystery is nowhere more palpable than among survivors. Academic theologians can spin out complicated doctrines of providence or attempt to reconcile quantum mechanics with Special Divine Action. But the tornado silences these voices, leaving in its wake stupefied and awestruck witnesses, for whom pre-rational personifications may make as much sense as any scientific or doctrinal logic. Journalist Robert King interviewed survivors of a fearsome EF4 tornado that barreled through southern Indiana in March 2012 with top winds of 175 miles an hour. "Some described what was about to upset their lives as if it were a living animal," King wrote. "It roared like a beast, they said, and ate the objects in its path. To others, it seemed to stalk them like a predator or pursue them as they fled." The most dreadful mystery was that which haunted the bereaved relatives of the 11 people who died. King put it succinctly: "Was this wrath from above part of a divine order or merely the number they had drawn in a meteorological lottery?"[28]

I cannot presume to answer this question for grieving victims, whose coping strategies must remain deeply personal. My own conclusion after working on this book for nearly a decade is that neither theology nor science can fully explain life's death-dealing storms. A theologian who claims to know the ways of providence is to me no better than a meteorologist who claims infallible knowledge of next week's weather. That the tornado still bedevils theologians and meteorologists alike points to something permanently elusive in nature.

Is that elusive thing evil? So it would seem from the never-ending arguments over theodicy. But the sheer wondrousness of a tornado—to say nothing of cosmic whirlpools like black holes—suggests that what appears evil from our perspective is neutral from nature's. That is what Reinhold Niebuhr meant in his sermon on Matthew 5:45 when he said that "a nonmoral nature is made into the symbol of [God's] transmoral mercy."[29] The sun shines on the evil and the good. The rain falls on the just and the unjust. The tornado descends impartially, like other life-altering events beyond our control. Yet the fact that there is life at all sustains my hope that nature conceals a greater glory.

The tornado is a veil, like the cloud on Sinai, that shrouds the secrets of life and death. To pursue the tornado is to join the enduring quest at the heart of religion: the primal search for meaning that survives, and even thrives, on the mystery of the Whirlwind.

INTRODUCTION

1. Weather forecast from *Boston Daily Globe*, June 9, 1953; biography of Father Devincq from the obituary in the *Worcester (Mass.) Evening Gazette*, June 11, 1953.

2. "Enormous, revolving cylinder" from Thomas P. Grazulis, *The Tornado: Nature's Ultimate Windstorm* (Norman: University of Oklahoma Press, 2001), xiii.

3. No one really knows the maximum strength of tornadoes and hurricanes. The Enhanced Fujita (EF) Scale, adopted by the US government in 2007, classifies the strongest (EF5) tornadoes as having winds exceeding 200 miles per hour, whereas the Saffir-Simpson Hurricane Scale rates the strongest (Category 5) hurricanes as having winds of 157 miles per hour or higher. In 1999, University of Oklahoma researchers, using Doppler on Wheels technology, measured the highest tornado winds ever recorded, 301 miles per hour, in a monster tornado that devastated part of metro Oklahoma City. By contrast, the possibly record-strength typhoon (hurricane) that hit the Philippines on November 8, 2013, had wind gusts of up to 235 miles per hour. Nancy Mathis, *Storm Warning: The Story of a Killer Tornado* (New York: Touchstone, 2007), 134; Floyd Whaley, "A Powerful Typhoon Speeds across the Philippines," *New York Times*, November 9, 2013.

4. Md. Shahadat Hosen and Abu Jubayer, "Chronological History and Destruction Pattern of Tornados in Bangladesh," *American Journal of Environmental Protection* 5, no. 4 (2016): 71–81; Dan Bikos, Jonathan Finch, and Jonathan L. Case, "The Environment Associated with Significant Tornadoes in Bangladesh," *Atmospheric Research* 167 (2016): 183–95. Outside of Bangladesh, tornado outbreaks have occurred in, among other places, Europe, where they are typically less severe. See, e.g., M. W. Rowe and G. T. Meaden, "Britain's Greatest Tornado Outbreak," *Weather* 40, no. 8 (1985): 230–35.

5. For a succinct description of the ingredients necessary for tornado formation, see Brantley Hargrove, *The Man Who Caught the Storm: The Life of Legendary Tornado Chaser Tim Samaras* (New York: Simon & Schuster, 2018), 49–51.

6. Tornadoes outside of the Great Plains seem to be increasing, likely because of climate change; see Chapter 5.

7. "Stained-Glass Windows from Former Assumption Campus Unveiled," Assumption College news release accessed November 1, 2013, http://www.assumption.edu/news/stained-glass-windows-former-assumption-campus-unveiled. The account of Father Devincq's death is from John M. O'Toole, *Tornado! 84 Minutes, 94 Lives* (Worcester, Mass.: Chandler House Press, 1993), 62–63.

8. Ian Menzies, "Tornado Kills 100," *Boston Daily Globe*, June 10, 1953.

9. Anthony F. C. Wallace, *Tornado in Worcester: An Exploratory Study of Individual and Community Behavior in an Extreme Situation* (Washington, D.C.: National Academy of Sciences, National Research Council, 1956), 36–38; "Tornadoes Kill 106 in Michigan and Ohio," *Boston Daily Globe*, June 9, 1953.

10. "Tornado Fiercer than Hurricane, but Not as Large," *Boston Daily Globe*, June 10, 1953; "Radar System to Spot Twisters Urged by Expert," *Boston Daily Globe*, June 11, 1953; data on 1953 tornado season from Grazulis, *Tornado*, xiv.

11. Representative Edith Nourse Rogers, speaking in the US House of Representatives on June 15, 1953, about the Worcester disaster, 83rd Cong., 1st sess., *Congressional Record* 99, pt. 5:6565.

12. Snowden D. Flora, *Tornadoes of the United States*, rev. ed. (Norman: University of Oklahoma Press, 1954); on the significance of Flora's book, Grazulis, *Tornado*, xv. Regarding the ban on the word *tornado*, see Marlene Bradford, *Scanning the Skies: A History of Tornado Forecasting* (Norman: University of Oklahoma Press, 2001), 19, 42–43, and Chapter 3 in this volume.

13. Such was the case with the April 25–28, 2011, Super Outbreak, which killed 324 people, and the March 2–3, 2012, outbreak, which killed 41. In both instances, the SPC issued Convective Outlook weather maps well in advance that showed a high probability of tornadoes in the areas that were ultimately hit. The SPC has archived the outlooks since 2003; searchable database at http://www.spc.noaa.gov/products/outlook/.

14. Howard B. Bluestein, *Tornado Alley: Monster Storms of the Great Plains* (New York: Oxford University Press, 1999), 2. On Bluestein, see the Conclusion in this volume.

15. Wallace, *Tornado in Worcester*.

16. Anthony F. C. Wallace, *Religion: An Anthropological View* (New York: Random House, 1966), 255–67.

17. As Freud put it: "Man gives the forces of nature the character of a father; he turns them into gods." Sigmund Freud, *The Future of an Illusion*, trans. James Strachey (New York: W. W. Norton, 1961), 21. Cf. Friedrich Engels in *Anti-Dühring* (1878): "All religion . . . is nothing but the fantastic reflection in men's minds of those external forces which control their daily life." In Karl Marx and Friedrich Engels, *On Religion* (New York: Schocken Books, 1964), 147.

18. Bernard le Bovier de Fontenelle, *De l'Origine des Fables* (1724), trans. Leonard M. and Ann Marsak, in *The Achievement of Bernard le Bovier de Fontenelle*, ed. Leonard M. Marsak (New York: Johnson Reprint, 1970), 36. On Fontenelle, see also Frank E. Manuel, *The Eighteenth Century Confronts the Gods* (1959; reprint, New York: Atheneum, 1967), 41–46; and J. Samuel Preus, *Explaining Religion: Criticism and Theory from Bodin to Freud* (New Haven, Conn.: Yale University Press, 1987), 40–55.

19. David Hume, *The Natural History of Religion*, ed. Tom L. Beauchamp (Oxford: Clarendon Press, 2007), 52.

20. Eastern Orthodox theologian David Bentley Hart has noted the irony that Enlightenment thinkers' moral expectation of a loving God owed much to the Christian teachings that the most radical Enlightenment philosophers claimed to reject. David Bentley Hart, *The Doors of the Sea: Where Was God in the Tsunami?* (Grand Rapids, Mich.: Eerdmans, 2005), 24–25. On theodicy as a particularly modern problem, see Susan Neiman, *Evil in Modern Thought: An Alternative History of Philosophy*, rev. ed. (Princeton, N.J.: Princeton University Press, 2015). See also the more theological reflections by William C. Placher, *The Domestication of Transcendence: How Modern Thinking about God Went Wrong* (Louisville, Ky.: Westminster John Knox Press, 1996), 202–13.

21. A classic in comparative religion is the chapter on "The Sky and Sky Gods" in Mircea Eliade, *Patterns in Comparative Religion*, trans. Rosemary Sheed (1958; reprint, New York: World, 1963), 38–123. Important cultural histories of weather that touch on religion in various ways include, for the British context, Jan Golinski, *British Weather and the Climate of Enlightenment* (Chicago: University of Chicago Press, 2007); and Vladimir Janković, *Reading the Skies: A Cultural History of English Weather, 1650–1820* (Chicago: University of Chicago Press, 2000). For the American context, see David Laskin, *Braving the Elements: The Stormy History of American Weather* (New York: Anchor Books, 1996); Bernard Mergen, *Weather Matters: An American Cultural History since 1900* (Lawrence: University Press of Kansas, 2008); and William B. Meyer, *Americans and Their Weather* (New York: Oxford University Press, 2000).

22. The phrase "Nature's nation" is from Perry Miller, *Nature's Nation* (Cambridge, Mass.: Belknap Press, Harvard University Press, 1967).

23. Paglia's comments from her commentary on Norman H. Russell's poem "The Tornado" in Camille Paglia, *Break, Blow, Burn* (New York: Pantheon Books, 2005), 204. Mergen (*Weather Matters*, 4, 112) also notes the sublime nature of violent weather in the United States.

24. Judith Kerman, "In Tornado Weather," in *Poetry 180: A Turning Back to Poetry*, ed. Billy Collins (New York: Random House, 2003), 126.

25. On early hopes to subdue the climate, see Anya Zilberstein, *A Temperate Empire: Making Climate Change in Early America* (New York: Oxford University Press, 2016).

26. Bonar Menninger, *And Hell Followed with It: Life and Death in a Kansas Tornado* (Austin, Tex.: Emerald Book, 2011), 61–63, 72–74, 302–4.

27. On the persistent logic that everything happens for a reason, see Kate Bowler, *Everything Happens for a Reason: And Other Lies I've Loved* (New York: Random House, 2018).

28. Edmund Burke, *A Philosophical Enquiry into the Origin of Our Ideas of the Sublime and Beautiful*, ed. Paul Guyer (Oxford: Oxford University Press, 2015), 47–48, 57.

29. Immanuel Kant, *Critique of Judgment*, trans. James Creed Meredith and ed. Nicholas Walker (Oxford: Oxford University Press, 2007), 90–94. On Burke's influence on Kant, see Paul Guyer's introduction to Burke, *Philosophical Enquiry*, xxix, xxxi–xxxiii. See also the discussion of the category of the sublime in Burke and Kant in Charles Taylor, *A Secular Age* (Cambridge, Mass.: Harvard University Press, 2007), 334–44.

30. Friedrich Schleiermacher, *On Religion: Addresses in Response to Its Cultured Critics*, trans. Terrence N. Tice (Richmond, Va.: John Knox Press, 1969), 62. On the similarity between Otto and Schleiermacher in privileging experience over ethics as the heart of genuine religion, see Jacqueline Mariña, "Friedrich Schleiermacher and Rudolf Otto," in *The Oxford Handbook of Religion and Emotion*, ed. John Corrigan (New York: Oxford University Press, 2008), 457–58.

31. Rudolf Otto, *The Idea of the Holy: An Inquiry into the Non-rational Factor in the Idea of the Divine and Its Relation to the Rational*, trans. John W. Harvey, 2nd ed. (Oxford: Oxford University Press, 1950), 5–7; for Otto's use of "sublime," 63 (*das Erhabene*; see Rudolf Otto, *Das Heilige: Über das Irrationale in der Idee des Göttlichen und sein Verhältnis zum Rationalen* [1917; reprint, Munich: Verlag C. H. Beck, 2014], 82). On the original Latin meaning of *numen*, see Richard A. Muller, *Dictionary of Latin and Greek Theological Terms: Drawn Principally from Protestant Scholastic Theology*, 2nd ed. (Grand Rapids, Mich.: Baker Academic, 2017), 236. On Otto and the sublime, see Lynn Poland, "The Idea of the Holy and the History of the Sublime," *Journal of Religion* 72 (1992): 175–97.

32. On differentiation from Kant in distinguishing the holy from the good, see Todd Gooch, "Rudolf Otto and 'The Irrational in the Idea of the Divine,'" in *Religion und Irrationalität: Historisch-systematische Perspektiven*, ed. Jochen Schmidt and Heiko Schulz (Tübingen: Mohr Siebeck, 2013), 91–92.

33. Otto, *Idea of the Holy*, 12–15, 31, 35. On the *mysterium tremendum* and the *mysterium fascinans*, see also Mircea Eliade, *The Sacred and the Profane: The Nature of Religion*, trans. Willard R. Trask (New York: Harcourt, 1959), 9.

34. Otto, *Idea of the Holy*, 18–19, 77–80. The ostrich and Behemoth appear in Job 39:13–18 and 40:15–24; cf. the comment on Otto's treatment of them in Timothy K. Beal, *Religion and Its Monsters* (New York: Routledge, 2002), 53–55; and in Mark Larrimore, *The Book of Job: A Biography* (Princeton, N.J.: Princeton University Press, 2013), 177–81.

35. Otto, *Idea of the Holy*, 7–8, 60–61, 79, 81; "Wirbelsturm" in Otto, *Das Heilige*, 101.

36. Robert A. Orsi, "The Problem of the Holy," in *The Cambridge Companion to Religious Studies*, ed. Robert A. Orsi (Cambridge: Cambridge University Press, 2012), 103.

37. Otto, *Idea of the Holy*, 7, 124.

38. Orsi, "Problem of the Holy," 85, 90. For more general critiques of the *sui generis* perspective, see Russell T. McCutcheon, *Manufacturing Religion: The Discourse on Sui Generis Religion and the Politics of Nostalgia* (New York: Oxford University Press, 1997), esp. 17–18, 28; Ann Taves, *Religious Experience Reconsidered: A Building-Block Approach to the Study of Religion and Other Special Things* (Princeton, N.J.: Princeton University Press, 2009), 3–22; and Thomas A. Tweed, *Crossing and Dwelling: A Theory of Religion* (Cambridge, Mass.: Harvard University Press, 2006), 60. Other scholars have faulted Otto's numinous for especially privileging dramatic or supernatural experiences as religious; see Omar M. McRoberts, "Beyond *Mysterium Tremendum*: Thoughts toward an Aesthetic Study of Religious Experience," *Annals of the American Academy of Political and Social Science* 595 (September 2004): 190–203, esp. 199. Scholars have also noted the Christian (and Protestant) bias of Otto, a point acknowledged by Orsi ("The Problem of the Holy," 85) and, in reference to Otto's forebear Schleiermacher, by Richard R. Niebuhr, *Schleiermacher on Christ and Religion: A New Introduction* (New York: Scribner's, 1964), 176.

39. Brent Nongbri, *Before Religion: A History of a Modern Concept* (New Haven, Conn.: Yale University Press, 2013), 7.

40. Orsi, "Problem of the Holy," 99. Cf. the comments on this issue by Melissa Raphael, *Rudolf Otto and the Concept of Holiness* (Oxford: Clarendon Press, 1997), 149–50. Elsewhere, Orsi faults the reductionistic tendency of modern religious studies: "Whatever it is, religion is not about itself." See Robert A. Orsi, *History and Presence* (Cambridge, Mass.: Belknap Press, Harvard University Press, 2016).

41. William G. Pollard, *Transcendence and Providence: Reflections of a Physicist and Priest* (Edinburgh: Scottish Academic Press, 1987), 205, 207.

42. Rudolf Otto, "How Schleiermacher Re-discovered the Sensus Numinis," in *Religious Essays: A Supplement to* The Idea of the Holy, trans. Brian Lunn (London: Oxford University Press, 1931), 71.

43. Mark Levine, *F5: Devastation, Survival, and the Most Violent Tornado Outbreak of the Twentieth Century* (New York: Miramax Books, 2007), 65. To borrow another metaphor from the philosopher Charles Taylor, tornadoes break through the "immanent frame" of secular culture, visiting persons with a transcendent, otherworldly presence. On the "immanent frame," see Taylor, *A Secular Age*, 539–93.

44. On the enduring popularity of the King James Bible after four centuries, see Philip Goff, Arthur E. Farnsley II, and Peter J. Thuesen, eds., *The Bible in American Life* (New York: Oxford University Press, 2017), 9–11.

45. Though I use a few published diaries as sources, I have chosen not to scour the country for references to the weather in ordinary people's unpublished diaries. Given the ubiquity of the weather as an American concern—Mark Twain once quipped that everybody talks about the weather but nobody does anything about it—it would make for an interesting project to trace mentions of storms in manuscript diaries and letters. But that would be a different kind of study than the intellectual history I have written. Mark Twain quoted in Robert Underwood Johnson, *Remembered Yesterdays* (Boston: Little, Brown, 1923), 322.

CHAPTER I

1. On *theoxeny*, see Bruce Louden, *Homer's* Odyssey *and the Near East* (Cambridge: Cambridge University Press, 2011), 31–32.

2. On the Shawnee legend, see Joanne Huist Smith, "Devil Winds: City's Curse or Tall Tale?" *Dayton (Ohio) Daily News*, September 16, 2001. At least one other Midwestern locale claims a similar legend. When Kokomo, Indiana, was hit by an F4 tornado during the Palm Sunday tornado outbreak of 1965, the local newspaper reported that the area south of Wildcat Creek, which runs through the city, was known to the Miami Indians as the "land of the devil winds." See "No Tornado Immunity," *Kokomo (Ind.) Tribune*, April 15, 1965.

3. Helen Hooven Santmyer, *Ohio Town* (1962; reprint, New York: Harper and Row, 1984), 11.

4. Polk Laffoon IV, *Tornado* (New York: Harper and Row, 1975), 42.

5. Michael Coogan, *The Ten Commandments: A Short History of an Ancient Text* (New Haven, Conn.: Yale University Press, 2014), 1–8.

6. Mircea Eliade, *Patterns in Comparative Religion*, trans. Rosemary Sheed (1958; reprint, New York: World, 1963), 109.

7. Peter C. Chemery, "Meteorological Beings," in *Encyclopedia of Religion*, ed. Lindsay Jones, 2nd ed., 15 vols. (Detroit: Macmillan Reference, 2005), 9:5992.

8. Mircea Eliade, *The Sacred and the Profane: The Nature of Religion*, trans. Willard R. Trask (New York: Harcourt, 1959), 121–22.

9. Michael York, "Dyaus Pitr," in *Encyclopedia of Hinduism*, ed. Denise Cush, Catherine Robinson, and Michael York (London: Routledge, 2010), 218; Walter Burkert, *Greek Religion*, trans. John Raffan (Cambridge, Mass.: Harvard University Press, 1985), 125–26.

10. Rig Veda 1.32.15, 2.12.13, in *The Rig Veda: An Anthology*, trans. Wendy Doniger (London: Penguin Books, 1981), 151, 162.

11. Bhagavata Purana, 10.24.9 ("seminal discharge"), 10.24.13–15, 10.25.15 ("tremendously heavy showers"), 10.25.19; in *The Bhagavata Purana*, Part 4, trans. Ganesh Vasudeo Tagare, in *Ancient Indian Tradition and Mythology*, vol. 10, ed. J. L. Shastri (Delhi: Motilal Banarsidass, 1976), 1411, 1412, 1418. The Govardhan hill, in Uttar Pradesh, India, is still a popular pilgrimage site. I thank my Indiana University colleague David Haberman for alerting me to this tradition.

12. Burkert, *Greek Religion*, 126; E. O. James, *The Worship of the Sky-God: A Comparative Study in Semitic and Indo-European Religion* (London: University of London, Athlone Press, 1963), 114–15.

13. Chemery, "Meteorological Beings," 5993.

14. Derek M. Elsom, *Lightning: Nature and Culture* (London: Reaktion Books, 2015), 25; on Mjölnir and the cross, Anders Winroth, *The Age of the Vikings* (Princeton, N.J.: Princeton University Press, 2014), 199. On Thor in more recent culture, see Donald Dewey, "Thor-oughly Mythological," *Scandinavian Review* 102, no. 3 (2015): 54–63.

15. Albert J. Raboteau, *Slave Religion: The "Invisible Institution" in the Antebellum South* (New York: Oxford University Press, 1978), 19–21, 23, 81.

16. Geraldine Pinch, *Egyptian Mythology: A Guide to the Gods, Goddesses, and Traditions of Ancient Egypt* (New York: Oxford University Press, 2002), 100.

17. Michio Araki, "Kami," in Jones, ed., *Encyclopedia of Religion*, 8:5071–74; Joseph M. Kitagawa, *Religion in Japanese History* (New York: Columbia University Press, 1990), 93; Serinity Young, "Religion and Weather," in *Encyclopedia of Climate and Weather*, ed. Stephen H. Schneider, Terry L. Root, and Michael D. Mastrandrea, 2nd ed., 3 vols. (New York: Oxford University Press, 2011), 3:7.

18. James H. Howard, *Shawnee! The Ceremonialism of a Native Indian Tribe and Its Cultural Background* (Athens: Ohio University Press, 1981), 173–74.

19. Michael D. Coogan and Mark S. Smith, eds. and trans., *Stories from Ancient Canaan* (Louisville, Ky.: Westminster John Knox Press, 2012), 15; James L. Kugel, *The God of Old: Inside the Lost World of the Bible* (New York: Free Press, 2003), 96; Neal H. Walls, "Baal" and "El," in Jones, ed., *Encyclopedia of Religion*, 2:723–25, 4:2742–43.

20. Mark S. Smith, *The Early History of God: Yahweh and the Other Deities in Ancient Israel*, 2nd ed. (Grand Rapids, Mich.: Eerdmans, 2002), 7.

21. Psalm 18:13–14 (NRSV); Smith, *Early History of God*, 55–56.

22. See the discussion of key passages in Alberto R. W. Green, *The Storm-God in the Ancient Near East* (Winona Lake, Ind.: Eisenbrauns, 2003), 258–75.

23. Psalm 29:9 (NRSV); "causes the oaks to whirl" appears as "causes the deer to calve" in an alternate reading. On Psalm 29, see E. Theodore Mullen, Jr., *The Divine Council in Canaanite and Early Hebrew Literature* (Chico, Calif.: Scholars Press, 1980), 199–200; and Coogan and Smith, eds., *Stories from Ancient Canaan*, 15. For analysis of the meteorological imagery in Psalm 29, see Steve A. Wiggins, *Weathering the Psalms: A Meteorotheological* Survey (Eugene, Ore.: Cascade Books, 2014), 57–61.

24. Frank Moore Cross, *Canaanite Myth and Hebrew Epic: Essays in the History of the Religion of Israel* (Cambridge, Mass.: Harvard University Press, 1973), 193–94.

25. The most comprehensive study is Wiggins, *Weathering the Psalms*. See also R. B. Y. Scott, "Meteorological Phenomena and Terminology in the Old Testament," *Zeitschrift für die*

Alttestamentliche Wissenshaft 64 (1952): 11–25. On the sirocco, see Aloysius Fitzgerald, *The Lord of the East Wind*, Catholic Biblical Quarterly Monograph Series 34 (Washington, D.C.: Catholic Biblical Association of America, 2002). See also Robert M. Grant, "God and Storms in Early Christian Thought," in *God in Early Christian Thought: Essays in Memory of Lloyd G. Patterson*, ed. Andrew B. McGowan, Brian E. Daley, and Timothy J. Gaden (Leiden: Brill, 2009), 351–60.

26. Quran 13:12–13, 30:48, in *The Study Quran: A New Translation and Commentary*, ed. Seyyed Hossein Nasr et al. (New York: HarperOne, 2015), 618, 996.

27. *Gleanings from the Writings of Bahá'u'lláh* 161.2, trans. Shoghi Effendi (Wilmette, Ill.: Bahá'í, 2005), 385.

28. Coogan makes this point in *The Ten Commandments*, 119–22. So also James L. Crenshaw, *Defending God: Biblical Responses to the Problem of Evil* (New York: Oxford University Press, 2005), 54.

29. Alphonse de Lamartine (1790–1869), French writer and politician, quoted in James L. Crenshaw, "Job," in *The Oxford Bible Commentary*, ed. John Barton and John Muddiman (New York: Oxford University Press, 2001), 331.

30. On the significance of the whirlwind, see Mark S. Smith, *The Origins of Biblical Monotheism: Israel's Polytheistic Background and the Ugaritic Texts* (New York: Oxford University Press, 2001), 38–39.

31. Job 38:3–4, 25, 35 (NRSV).

32. Job 40:9, 42:2–3 (NRSV).

33. See the summary of this perspective in Kathryn Schifferdecker, *Out of the Whirlwind: Creation Theology in the Book of Job*, Harvard Theological Studies 61 (Cambridge, Mass.: Harvard Divinity School, Harvard University Press, 2008), 8, 8n29, and for her own similar view, 126–27. See also J. Gerald Janzen, *At the Scent of Water: The Ground of Hope in the Book of Job* (Grand Rapids, Mich.: Eerdmans, 2009), 95–110.

34. Carol A. Newsom, *The Book of Job: A Contest of Moral Imaginations* (New York: Oxford University Press, 2003), 252–58.

35. Job: 1:21; cf. Newsom's comment on this in *The Book of Job*, 257.

36. On apocalypticism as one biblical answer to the problem of theodicy, see the popular treatment in Bart D. Ehrman, *God's Problem: How the Bible Fails to Answer Our Most Important Question—Why We Suffer* (New York: HarperOne, 2008), 197–260.

37. For summaries of the apocalyptic worldview, see Frederick J. Murphy, *Apocalypticism in the Bible and Its World: A Comprehensive Introduction* (Grand Rapids, Mich.: Baker Academic, 2012), 8–14; and Ehrman, *God's Problem*, 215–19.

38. Literal translation of Daniel 7:13; cf. the more inclusive NRSV: "one like a human being." On the parallels to Genesis 1:2 (in Daniel 7:2) and to Baal (in Daniel 7:13), see John J. Collins, *The Apocalyptic Imagination: An Introduction to Jewish Apocalyptic Literature*, 3rd ed. (Grand Rapids, Mich.: Eerdmans, 2016), 125–27.

39. On the apocalyptic dimension of Jesus' message, see Bart D. Ehrman, *Jesus: Apocalyptic Prophet of the New Millennium* (New York: Oxford University Press, 1999), 141–62.

40. John F. Walvoord and John E. Walvoord, *Armageddon, Oil, and the Middle East Crisis: What the Bible Says about the Future of the Middle East and the End of Western Civilization* (Grand Rapids, Mich.: Zondervan, 1974); Walter K. Price, *The Coming Antichrist* (Chicago: Moody Press, 1974), 48–49; and Thomas S. McCall and Zola Levitt, *The Coming Russian Invasion of Israel* (Chicago: Moody Press, 1974), 54; all cited or quoted in Paul Boyer, *When Time Shall*

Be No More: Prophecy Belief in Modern American Culture (Cambridge, Mass.: Belknap Press, Harvard University Press, 1992), 134–35, 163–64, 242.

41. Statistics from Lee R. Hoxit and Charles F. Chappell, *Tornado Outbreak of April 3–4, 1974; Synoptic Analysis* (Washington, D.C.: U.S. Department of Commerce, 1975), 1, 44; Thomas P. Grazulis, *The Tornado: Nature's Ultimate Windstorm* (Norman: University of Oklahoma Press, 2001), 243; "F5 and EF5 Tornadoes of the United States," Storm Prediction Center, National Oceanic and Atmospheric Administration, http://www.spc.noaa.gov/faq/tornado/f5torns.html; and Dean Narciso, "Xenia Residents Struggle with Tornado Memories," *Columbus Dispatch*, April 3, 2014.

42. "Storm Moving In," *Xenia Daily Gazette*, April 3, 1974; other details from Laffoon, *Tornado*, 2, 7, 14, 16–17, 26. See the old Fujita scale at the web site of the Storm Prediction Center, NOAA, http://www.spc.noaa.gov/faq/tornado/f-scale.html.

43. Laffoon, *Tornado*, 38–39. Accounts differ on the identity of the resident who made the recording, which is available at Homer G. Ramby's web site, http://www.xeniatornado.com/audio.htm.

44. Narciso, "Xenia Residents."

45. Laffoon, *Tornado*, 29, 49.

46. Rich Heiland, "Gazette Staffer Saw It All: 'We Should All Be Dead,'" *Xenia Daily Gazette*, April 4, 1974; Hupman quoted in Laffoon, *Tornado*, 43; LaVersa Motes, "'My God, My God,' Was All We Could Say," *Xenia Daily Gazette*, April 4, 1974.

47. Des Ruisseaux quoted in Robert E. Deitz, *April 3, 1974: Tornado!* (Louisville, Ky.: Courier-Journal and Louisville Times, 1974), 85; Dunnavant in "I Laid in a Shallow Ditch," *Huntsville Times*, April 5, 1974, and quoted in Mark Levine, *F5: Devastation, Survival, and the Most Violent Tornado Outbreak of the Twentieth Century* (New York: Miramax Books, 2007), 165.

48. Levine, *F5*, 65–66.

49. Laffoon, *Tornado*, 65–66, 78–80.

50. Delores Fisher, "Devastation Roared into Xenia at 4:40," *Xenia Daily Gazette*, April 4, 1974.

51. Jack Jordan and Randy Blackeby, "Xenia Digging Out from Day of Horror," *Xenia Daily Gazette*, April 4, 1974; "Gazette's Little Late," *Xenia Daily Gazette*, April 4, 1974.

52. Details from Jack Jordan, "Shock Is Slow in Wearing Off," *Xenia Daily Gazette*, April 4, 1974; "Tornado-Hit Town Has Rites for 30" (Associated Press), *New York Times*, April 8, 1974; and Laffoon, *Tornado*, 41. On the destruction of Xenia's churches, see also Barbara Lynn Riedel and Peter Wayne Kyryl II, *Tornado at Xenia: April 3, 1974* (Cleveland: Carpenter Printing, 1974), 54–56.

53. Murphy, *Apocalypticism*, 38, 40–41; Richard H. Hiers, "Day of the Lord," and K. J. Cathcart, "Day of Yahweh," in *The Anchor Bible Dictionary*, ed. David Noel Freedman et al., 6 vols. (New York: Doubleday, 1992), 2:82–85.

54. Isaiah 2:12, 15, 19; 13:9 (NRSV).

55. Joel 2:11, Zephaniah 1:14–15 (NRSV).

56. Revelation 5:6–12; cf. John 1:29.

57. Revelation 6:16–17 (NRSV); "Fall on us" quoting Hosea 10:8, which Jesus also quotes on his way to the Crucifixion (Luke 23:30). See Anthony Tyrrell Hanson, *The Wrath of the Lamb* (London: S.P.C.K., 1957), 124. On the paradox of the "wrath of the Lamb," see Stephen H. Travis, *Christ and the Judgement of God: The Limits of Divine Retribution in New Testament Thought* (Peabody, Mass.: Hendrickson, 2008), 295–97.

58. Peter K. Klein, "Introduction: The Apocalypse in Medieval Art," in *The Apocalypse in the Middle Ages*, ed. Richard K. Emmerson and Bernard McGinn (Ithaca, N.Y.: Cornell University Press, 1992), 167, 193, 194; cf. Yves Christe, "The Apocalypse in Monumental Art of the Eleventh through Thirteenth Centuries," ibid., 238.

59. On the origin of the term "Little Ice Age," see Emmanuel Le Roy Ladurie, *Times of Feast, Times of Famine: A History of Climate since the Year 1000* (Garden City, N.Y.: Doubleday, 1971), 221–23. The main period of the Little Ice Age was 1600–1850; see Geoffrey Parker, *Global Crisis: War, Climate Change and Catastrophe in the Seventeenth Century* (New Haven, Conn.: Yale University Press, 2013).

60. John Aberth, *From the Brink of the Apocalypse: Confronting Famine, War, Plague, and Death in the Later Middle Ages*, 2nd ed. (New York: Routledge), 8–17.

61. John Shinners, ed., *Medieval Popular Religion, 1000–1500: A Reader*, 2nd ed. (Toronto: University of Toronto Press, 2009), 292.

62. A. H. Pearson, ed., *The Sarum Missal in English* (1868; reprint, Eugene, Ore.: Wipf and Stock, 2004), 542.

63. *Malleus Maleficarum* excerpted in Shinners, *Medieval Popular Religion*, 274.

64. Keith Thomas, *Religion and the Decline of Magic: Studies in Popular Beliefs in Sixteenth and Seventeenth Century England* (New York: Oxford University Press, 1971), 30–31, 41.

65. David Hugh Farmer, *The Oxford Dictionary of Saints*, 5th rev. ed. (Oxford: Oxford University Press, 2011), 35 (on Barbara), 89–90 (on Christopher), 147 (on Erasmus), and 171 (on the Fourteen Holy Helpers). Christopher was also immensely popular, even up to modern times. See the novena invoking his help against "harmful elementary forces, such as earthquake, lightning, fire, and flood" in *Mary, Help of Christians, and the Fourteen Saints Invoked as Holy Helpers*, ed. Bonaventure Hammer (New York: Benziger Brothers, 1909), 226.

66. Johan Huizinga, *The Waning of the Middle Ages: A Study of the Forms of Life, Thought and Art in France and the Netherlands in the XIVth and XVth Centuries*, trans. Frederik Hopman (London: Edward Arnold, 1924), 155.

67. H. Maynard Smith, *Pre-Reformation England* (London: Palgrave Macmillan, 1963), 167; *The Catechism of the Council of Trent, Published by Command of Pope Pius the Fifth*, trans. Jeremiah Donovan (New York: Christian Press Association, 1905), 327.

68. See the doubts expressed by Scott H. Hendrix, *Martin Luther: Visionary Reformer* (New Haven, Conn.: Yale University Press, 2015), 33; cf. the more favorable assessment in Heiko A. Oberman, *Luther: Man between God and the Devil*, trans. Eileen Walliser-Schwarzbart (New York: Image Books, Doubleday, 1992), 92–94.

69. See Luther's own discussion of this in Preface to Johannes Lichtenberger, *The Prophecy of Johannes Lichtenberger in German, Carefully Edited* (1527), trans. Marion Salzmann, in *Luther's Works*, Vol. 59, *Prefaces*, ed. Christopher Boyd Brown (St. Louis: Concordia, 2012), 182, 184, cited by Hendrix, *Martin Luther*, 12–13.

70. Lyndal Roper, *Martin Luther: Renegade and Prophet* (New York: Random House, 2017), 35.

71. Quoted in Carol Piper Heming, *Protestants and the Cult of the Saints in German-Speaking Europe, 1517–1531* (Kirksville, Mo.: Truman State University Press, 2003), 61. On Anne, see Farmer, *Oxford Dictionary of Saints*, 20–21.

72. Martin Luther, "The Sacrament of the Body and Blood of Christ—Against the Fanatics" (1526), in *Luther's Works*, Vol. 36, *Word and Sacrament II*, ed. Abdel Ross Wentz (Philadelphia: Fortress Press, 1959), 344.

73. Benjamin Wirt Farley, *The Providence of God* (Grand Rapids, Mich.: Baker Book House, 1988), 138.

74. John Calvin, *Institutes of the Christian Religion* (1536 ed.), ed. and trans. Ford Lewis Battles (London: Collins, 1975), 49; cf. Charles Partee, *The Theology of John Calvin* (Louisville, Ky.: Westminster John Knox Press, 2008), 107.

75. John Calvin, *Institutes of the Christian Religion* (1559 ed.), ed. John T. McNeill and trans. Ford Lewis Battles (Philadelphia: Westminster Press, 1960), 197–228 (I.16–I.17). See the discussion in François Wendel, *Calvin: Origins and Development of His Religious Thought*, trans. Philip Mairet (Grand Rapids, Mich.: Baker Books, 1963), 177–84.

76. On the Genevan context, see Bruce Gordon, *Calvin* (New Haven, Conn.: Yale University Press, 2009), 305.

77. Calvin, *Institutes* (1559 ed.), 878–80 (III.20.20–22).

78. Susan E. Schreiner, *The Theater of His Glory: Nature and the Natural Order in the Thought of John Calvin* (Grand Rapids, Mich.: Baker Books, 1991), 16–21.

79. Ibid., 13, 22, 22, 24–25, 28, 30, 31.

80. Calvin, *Institutes* (1559 ed.), 203–4, 206 (I.16.5, I.16.7). Amos 4:9 cited from the Vulgate.

81. Ibid., 199, 205, 207 (I.16.2, I.16.6, I.16.8).

82. Ibid., 209 (I.16.9).

83. Calvin, commentary on Psalm 7, quoted in Schreiner, *Theater of His Glory*, 33.

84. Calvin, *Institutes* (1599 ed.), 225–27 (I.17.12–13); Schreiner, *Theater of His Glory*, 35.

85. Calvin, *Institutes* (1559 ed.), 223 (I.17.10).

86. Schreiner, *Theater of His Glory*, 35.

87. Ibid., 36.

88. Richard Lenzi (quoting Job 1:21), "Dependent on Creator," letter to the editor, *Xenia Daily Gazette*, April 20, 1974.

89. Laffoon, *Tornado*, 146.

90. David Graham, quoted in Laffoon, 143. The notion that Satan is the prince of the power of the air comes from Ephesians 2:2.

91. Jack Jordan, "Editor's Note," *Xenia Daily Gazette*, April 20, 1974.

92. Clergy quoted in Rich Heiland, "Easter Theme One of Hope," *Xenia Daily Gazette*, April 13, 1974; Jordan, "Editor's Note."

93. Laffoon, *Tornado*, 54–55, 135–38.

94. Levine, *F5*, 270–72. On theodicy, Job, and a later Alabama tornado (Tuscaloosa in 2011), see the poignant reflections by Thomas Albert Howard, "Clouds of Unknowing: Making Sense of the Tornadoes," *Commonweal* 138, no. 12 (June 17, 2011): 8–9.

95. On the different senses of the sublime in Otto and Kant, see the Introduction to this volume.

96. Jack Jordan, "Whole Story Will Never Be Told," *Xenia Daily Gazette*, April 10, 1974; Kevin G. Cook, "Xenia Does Exist" (letter to the editor), *Xenia Daily Gazette*, April 15, 1974.

97. Martha Wolfenstein, *Disaster: A Psychological Essay* (Glencoe, Ill.: Free Press, 1957), 189, 191; cited in James B. Taylor, Louis A. Zurcher, and William H. Key, *Tornado: A Community Responds to Disaster* (Seattle: University of Washington Press, 1970), 68.

98. "Brandenburg, Ky.: A Day of Mourning" (Associated Press), *Xenia Daily Gazette*, April 8, 1974; Keith Runyon, "Crescent Hill Churches Form Joint Ministry," *Courier-Journal* (Louisville, Ky.), November 28, 1974.

99. Laffoon, *Tornado*, 172–73. On the MDS today, see http://www.mds.mennonite.net.

100. Paul Delaney, "Swindlers Preying on Victims of Tornado in Ohio Community," *New York Times*, April 14, 1974.

101. Paul Delaney, "Nixon Pledges Aid in Tour of Tornado Area in Ohio," *New York Times*, April 10, 1974; Paul Delaney, "Storm Proves Aid to Black Schools," *New York Times*, April 20, 1974.

102. Victor K. McElheny, "Tornado Danger Spurs Funds Bid," *New York Times*, July 10, 1974.

103. Victor K. McElheny, "How Killer Tornadoes Were Formed: Cold Front Plus the Gulf's Warm Air," *New York Times*, April 5, 1974; "Violent Mystery of the Tornado," *New York Times*, April 7, 1974.

104. Sarah Iles Johnston, ed., *Religions of the Ancient World: A Guide* (Cambridge, Mass.: Belknap Press, Harvard University Press, 2004), 270; and F. Graf, "Zeus," in *The Oxford Companion to Classical Civilization*, ed. Simon Hornblower and Antony Spawforth, 2nd ed. (Oxford: Oxford University Press, 2014), 856.

105. Calvin, *Institutes* (1559 ed.), 223 (I.17.10).

CHAPTER 2

1. On Mather's early life, see David Levin, *Cotton Mather: The Young Life of the Lord's Remembrancer, 1663–1703* (Cambridge, Mass.: Harvard University Press, 1978); Kenneth Silverman, *The Life and Times of Cotton Mather* (1984; reprint, New York: Welcome Rain, 2002), 13–49; and Robert Middlekauff, *The Mathers: Three Generations of Puritan Intellectuals, 1596–1728* (Berkeley: University of California Press, 1999), 191–208.

2. *Diary of Cotton Mather*, 2 vols. (Boston: Massachusetts Historical Society, 1911–12), 1:86–87. The angelic visitation has been fodder for the psychoanalysis of Mather; see the criticism in Jan Stievermann's introduction to *Cotton Mather and* Biblia Americana: *America's First Bible Commentary: Essays in Reappraisal*, ed. Reiner Smolinski and Jan Stievermann (Grand Rapids, Mich.: Baker Academic, 2011), 16–18.

3. [Cotton Mather], *Brontologia Sacra: The Voice of the Glorious God in the Thunder: Explained and Applyed In a Sermon uttered by a Minister of the Gospel in a Lecture unto an Assembly of Christians abroad, at the very same time when the Thunder was by the Permission and Providence of God falling upon his own House at home* (London, 1695), A3, 1–5. The lightning episode is also mentioned in Levin, *Cotton Mather*, 250–51.

4. Cotton Mather, *Magnalia Christi Americana: or, the Ecclesiastical History of New-England, from Its First Planting in the Year 1620. unto the Year of our Lord, 1698. In Seven Books* (London, 1702), 14–20.

5. Mather, *Brontologia Sacra*, 5, 6, 31.

6. Mather, *Magnalia Christi Americana*, 14.

7. On the term *providence* as well as the contributions of Stoicism, see Benjamin Wirt Farley, *The Providence of God* (Grand Rapids, Mich.: Baker Book House, 1988), 16–17, 61–70.

8. Alexandra Walsham, *Providence in Early Modern England* (Oxford: Oxford University Press, 1999), 225. On popular views of weather among the New England colonists and the new rhythms of Protestant ritualism, see David D. Hall, *Worlds of Wonder, Days of Judgment: Popular Religious Belief in Early New England* (Cambridge, Mass.: Harvard University Press, 1989), 71–72, 77–79, 166–67.

9. Details of the storm and vows in *The Diario of Christopher Columbus's First Voyage to America, 1492–1493*, abstracted by Bartolomé de las Casas and trans. Oliver Dunn and James E. Kelley, Jr. (Norman: University of Oklahoma Press, 1989), 362–77; quotations on 363, 369.

10. Claude Chauchetière, "Narration annuelle de la fondation de la Mission du Sault jusqu'à 1685," in *The Jesuit Relations and Allied Documents: Travels and Explorations of the Jesuit Missionaries in New France, 1610–1791*, vol. 63 (Cleveland: Burrows, 1900), 228–29.

11. Allan Greer, *Mohawk Saint: Catherine Tekakwitha and the Jesuits* (New York: Oxford University Press, 2005), 19–22, 193.

12. John Winthrop, *Winthrop's Journal: "History of New England," 1630–1649*, ed. James Kendall Hosmer, 2 vols. (New York: Scribner's, 1908), 2:126. The Newbury storm may have been a squall line rather than a tornado; see David M. Ludlum, *Early American Tornadoes, 1586–1870* (Boston: American Meteorological Society, 1970), 3.

13. Winthrop, *Journal*, 1:25 (April 2–3, 1630), 1:37–38 (May 1–2, 1630). Phillips, a Cambridge-trained minister, subsequently became the first pastor of the church at Watertown, Mass.

14. Ibid., 1:55, 98, 156, 166, 278; 2:272, 289.

15. Ibid., 1:291.

16. For a provocative argument on this point, see Baird Tipson, "Thomas Hooker, Martin Luther, and the Terror at the Edge of Protestant Faith," *Harvard Theological Review* 108 (2015): 530–51, esp. 250–551.

17. Verses paralleled in Luke 12:6–7. Calvin had cited Matthew 10:30 in his discussion of providence; see John Calvin, *Institutes of the Christian Religion* (1559 ed.), ed. John T. McNeill and trans. Ford Lewis Battles (Philadelphia: Westminster Press, 1960), 199 (I.16.2).

18. Richard Sibbes, "Of the Providence of God," in *The Complete Works of Richard Sibbes, D.D.*, ed. Alexander Balloch Grosart, vol. 5 (Edinburgh, 1863), 35.

19. Stephen Charnock, *A Discourse of Divine Providence. I. In General: That there is a Providence Exercised by God in the World. II. In Particular: How all Gods Providences in the World, are in order to the good of his People* (London, 1684), 30.

20. Increase Mather, *A Discourse Concerning the Uncertainty of the Times of Men, and The Necessity of being Prepared for Sudden Changes & Death. Delivered in a Sermon Preached at Cambridge in New England. Decemb. 6. 1969. On Occasion of the Sudden Death of Two Scholars belonging to Harvard Colledge* (Boston, 1697), 17.

21. Increase Mather, *A Brief Discourse Concerning the Prayse Due to God, for His Mercy, in Giving Snow like Wool. Delivered in a Sermon* (Boston, 1704), 77.

22. The sermon was posthumously published as part of Samuel Willard, *A Compleat Body of Divinity in Two Hundred and Fifty Expository Lectures on the Assembly's Shorter Catechism* (Boston, 1726), 133; cf. 147. Though Willard's *Compleat Body* is often credited as the first systematic theology published in America, it likely owed much to the unpublished *Whole Body of Divinity* by Hartford, Connecticut, cofounder Samuel Stone (1602–1663). Willard and others copied Stone's work in longhand as part of their theological studies. See Baird Tipson, *Hartford Puritanism: Thomas Hooker, Samuel Stone, and Their Terrifying God* (New York: Oxford University Press, 2015), 52–53 and 52n83.

23. John Flavel (here spelled "Flavell"), *Divine Conduct: or, The Mysterie of Providence. Wherein the Being and Efficacy of Providence is Asserted, and Vindicated: The Methods of Providence as it passes through the several Stages of our Lives opened; and the proper course of improving all Providences directed, in a Treatise upon Psalm 57. Ver. 2* (London, 1678), 160. On Calvin's reluctance to pry into providential secrets, see Ronald J. VanderMolen, "Providence as Mystery, Providence as Revelation: Puritan and Anglican Modifications of John Calvin's Doctrine of Providence," *Church History* 47 (1978): 27–47.

24. Flavel, *Divine Conduct*, 160. (Later editions of the work appeared in 1681, 1698, 1712, 1727, 1750, 1753, 1776, and 1791.)

25. Ibid., 104, 122–25, 128–29, 160. Flavel was one of several English Dissenters of his era who defended a thoroughgoing providentialism against its detractors; see Michael P. Winship, *Seers of God: Puritan Providentialism in the Restoration and Early Enlightenment* (Baltimore: Johns Hopkins University Press, 1996), 53–60.

26. Keith Thomas, *Religion and the Decline of Magic: Studies in Popular Beliefs in Sixteenth and Seventeenth Century England* (New York: Oxford University Press, 1971), 82. Cf. the similar observation by Barbara Donagan, "Providence Chance and Explanation: Some Paradoxical Aspects of Puritan Views of Causation," *Journal of Religious History* 11 (1981): 387.

27. Flavel, *Divine Conduct*, 137–38.

28. Charnock, *Discourse of Divine Providence*, 160–61. On the failure of Puritan exegetes to read Matthew 5:45 as evidence that weather events might be morally neutral, see Margo Todd, "Providence, Chance and the New Science in Early Stuart Cambridge," *Historical Journal* 29 (1986): 703.

29. Thomas Aquinas, *Summa Theologiae*, Blackfriars ed., vol. 5, *God's Will and Providence (Ia. 19–26)*, trans. Thomas Gilby (London: Eyre and Spottiswoode, 1967), Ia.22.2 (p. 97), Ia.22.3 (p. 101). As one scholar explains it, Aquinas was able to affirm both divine and human causing at the same time since "God is not to be reduced to the causes that we normally experience." Humans "really cause, as moved by God to act; God respects and deploys their causing, for God's ends." Joseph P. Wawrykow, *The Westminster Handbook to Thomas Aquinas* (Louisville, Ky.: Westminster John Knox Press, 2005), 120.

30. Aquinas, *Summa Theologiae*, Ia.22.2 (p. 95), Ia.22.4 (p. 103).

31. William Fulke, *A Goodly Gallerye with a Most Pleasaunt Prospect, into the garden of naturall contemplation, to behold the naturall causes of all kynde of Meteors* (London, 1563), fols. 44–46. Later editions of this work appeared in 1571, 1602, 1634, 1639, and 1640. On Fulke, see Todd, "Providence, Chance and the New Science," 703–4.

32. A "truism": Richard A. Muller, *Dictionary of Latin and Greek Theological Terms: Drawn Principally from Protestant Scholastic Theology*, 2nd ed. (Grand Rapids, Mich.: Baker Academic, 2017), s.v. "causae secundae," 60. On "second causes" as standard Puritan doctrine, cf. E. Brooks Holifield, *Theology in America: Christian Thought from the Age of the Puritans to the Civil War* (New Haven, Conn.: Yale University Press, 2003), 37, 74; and Perry Miller, *The New England Mind: The Seventeenth Century* (Cambridge, Mass.: Belknap Press, Harvard University Press, 1939), 487.

33. Westminster Confession of Faith, in *The Creeds of Christendom: With a History and Critical Notes*, ed. Philip Schaff and David S. Schaff, 6th ed., 3 vols. (Grand Rapids, Mich.: Baker Books, 1983), Ch. V ("Of Providence"), 3:612–13.

34. Blair Worden, *God's Instruments: Political Conduct in the England of Oliver Cromwell* (Oxford: Oxford University Press, 2012), 33–62, quotation on 45–46.

35. Winship, *Seers of God*, 29–52.

36. John Spencer, *A Discourse concerning Prodigies: Wherein the Vanity of Presages by them is reprehended, and their true and proper Ends asserted and vindicated. The Second Edition corrected and inlarged. To which is added a short Treatise concerning Vulgar Prophecies* (London, 1665), 236, 294–95; Thomas Sprat, *The History of the Royal-Society of London, For the Improving of Natural Knowledge* (London, 1667), 364. For further analysis of these texts, see William E. Burns, *An Age*

of Wonders: Prodigies, Politics and Providence in England, 1657–1727 (Manchester: Manchester University Press, 2002), 58–68 (on Spencer) and 69–70 (on Sprat).

37. Mark Valeri, *Heavenly Merchandize: How Religion Shaped Commerce in Puritan America* (Princeton, N.J.: Princeton University Press, 2010), 111–13, 209–11; Winship, *Seers of God*, 143. Winship observes that Cotton Mather "juggled two languages, one of human agency, reasonableness, and morality, the other of a complex and vital supernatural realm and a depraved, if occasionally supernaturally privileged, humanity" (91).

38. Charnock, *Discourse of Divine Providence*, 37.

39. Willard, *Compleat Body of Divinity*, 132, 134. Willard's *Compleat Body*, published posthumously in 1726, was a compilation of his catechetical lectures delivered between 1687 and 1706 (Holifield, *Theology in America*, 62).

40. Worden (*God's Instruments*, 39) makes the same point about Cromwellian England.

41. Increase Mather, *The Voice of God in Stormy Winds. Considered, in Two Sermons, Occasioned by the Dreadful and Unparallel'd Storm, in the European Nations. Novemb. 27th. 1703* (Boston, 1704), 42.

42. [Cotton Mather], *The Voice of God in a Tempest. A Sermon Preached in the Time of the Storm; Wherein many and heavy and unknown Losses were Suffered at Boston (and Parts Adjacent,) Febr. 24. 1722–3. By One of the Ministers in Boston* (Boston, 1723), 10–11, 14. Mather was bucking the more common practice among theologians of referring to God's *permitting* rather than actually creating or causing evil. Cf. the Lutheran Formula of Concord (1577), which states that "God does not create evil or produce it, and he does not aid or abet it"; Formula of Concord, Solid Declaration, Article XI: Election, in *The Book of Concord: The Confessions of the Evangelical Lutheran Church*, ed. Robert Kolb and Timothy J. Wengert, trans. Charles Arand et al. (Minneapolis: Fortress Press, 2000), 642.

43. Jonathan Edwards, "The State of Public Affairs" (1731 or 1732), in *The Works of Jonathan Edwards*, Vol. 17, *Sermons and Discourses, 1730–1733*, ed. Mark Valeri (New Haven, Conn.: Yale University Press, 1999), 359; "Fast Days in Dead Times" (1734), in *The Works of Jonathan Edwards*, Vol. 19, *Sermons and Discourses, 1734–1738*, ed. M. X. Lesser (New Haven, Conn.: Yale University Press, 2001), 77.

44. Sarah Osborn, diary entries for February 11, 1757, and December 7, 1761, in Catherine A. Brekus, ed., *Sarah Osborn's Collected Writings* (New Haven, Conn.: Yale University Press, 2017), 125, 225. On Osborn's fears that people were denying providence, see Catherine A. Brekus, *Sarah Osborn's World: The Rise of Evangelical Christianity in Early America* (New Haven, Conn.: Yale University Press, 2013), 59.

45. Esther Edwards Burr, diary entries for January 1, 1755, and June 15, 1755, in Carol F. Karlsen and Laurie Crumpacker, eds., *The Journal of Esther Edwards Burr, 1754–1757* (New Haven, Conn.: Yale University Press, 1984), 76, 124–25.

46. Jan Golinski, *British Weather and the Climate of Enlightenment* (Chicago: University of Chicago Press, 2007), 193, 195; Karen Ordahl Kupperman, "The Puzzle of American Climate in the Early Colonial Period," *American Historical Review* 87 (1982): 1272–74. On Aristotle and meteors, see H. Howard Frisinger, *The History of Meteorology to 1800* (New York: Science History Publications, American Meteorological Society, 1977), 15–23. Some early settlers believed that land cultivation would eventually moderate the harsh American climate; see Anya Zilberstein, *A Temperate Empire: Making Climate Change in Early America* (New York: Oxford University Press, 2016).

47. Fulke, *A Goodly Gallerye*, fol. 33; John Goad, *Astro-Meteorologica, or Aphorisms and Discourses of the Bodies Coelestial, their Natures and Influences* (London, 1686), 2.

48. Increase Mather, *An Essay for the Recording of Illustrious Providences: Wherein, An Account is given of many Remarkable and very Memorable Events, which have happened in this last Age; especially in New-England* (Boston, 1684), 313–16.

49. Increase Mather, *The Latter Sign Discoursed of, in a Sermon Preached at the Lecture of Boston in New-England; August, 31. 1682. Wherein is shewed, that the Voice of God in Signal Providences, especially when repeated and Iterated, ought to be Hearkned unto*, bound with *Heaven's Alarm to the World* (Boston, 1682), 19, 23, 27–28. Winship (*Seers of God*, 67) comments on the juxtaposition of this sermon with the comparatively dispassionate observation of the tornado in the *Essay*.

50. On the Great Storm and European interpretations of it, see Golinski, *British Weather*, 41–52; and Vladimir Janković, *Reading the Skies: A Cultural History of English Weather, 1650–1820* (Chicago: University of Chicago Press, 2000), 59–64.

51. Mather, *Voice of God in Stormy Winds*, 9, 11–12, 28–29, 31–32, 52, 57–58.

52. Eliphalet Adams, *A Discourse Occasioned By the late Distressing Storm Which began Feb. 20th. 1716,17. As it was Deliver'd March 3d. 1716.7* (New London, Conn., 1717), 3–5, 7–8. Jeremiah 30:23 is parallel to Jeremiah 23:19, cited by Increase Mather (noted earlier). Details on the so-called Great Snow of 1717 are from the New England Historical Society: http://www.newenglandhistoricalsociety.com/great-snow-of-1717.

53. Eliphalet Adams, *God sometimes Answers His People, by Terrible Things in Righteousness. A Discourse Occasioned by that Awful Thunder-clap Which Struck the Meeting-House in N. London, Aug. 31st. 1735. At what Time One was Killed outright and diverse Others much hurt and wounded, Yet graciously & remarkably Preserved, together with the rest of the Congregation, from Immediate Death. As it was Delivered (Sept. 7th) the Lord's Day Following* (New London, Conn., 1735), 1, 7.

54. *The Works of Jonathan Edwards*, Vol. 14, *Sermons and Discourses, 1723–1729*, ed. Kenneth P. Minkema (New Haven, Conn.: Yale University Press, 1997), 196; *The Works of Jonathan Edwards*, Vol. 11, *Typological Writings*, ed. Wallace E. Anderson, Mason I. Lowance, Jr., and David H. Watters (New Haven, Conn.: Yale University Press, 1993), 76; cf. 92; *The Works of Jonathan Edwards*, Vol. 13, *The "Miscellanies," a–500*, ed. Thomas A. Schafer (New Haven, Conn.: Yale University Press, 1994), 270.

55. Anthony's diary excerpted by her pastor, Samuel Hopkins (a disciple of Jonathan Edwards) in *The Life and Character of Miss Susanna Anthony* (Worcester, Mass., 1796), 91–92, 93, 96, 162–63.

56. Whitall's diary excerpted in *John M. Whitall: The Story of His Life* (Philadelphia, 1879), 15.

57. Anthony in Hopkins, *Life and Character*, 93; Adams, *Discourse*, 9; Burr, *Journal*, 210–11. Burr identified the location of the tornado as "the Mountains"—i.e., Newark Mountains, as the Oranges were once known. For details on this storm, see Thomas P. Grazulis, *Significant Tornadoes, 1680–1991* (St. Johnsbury, Vt.: Environmental Films, 1993), 552; and Ludlum, *Early American Tornadoes*, 39.

58. "An Account of the late Whirlwind at Wethersfield," *Connecticut Courant*, reprinted in *Worcester Magazine*, 3, no. 22 (August 1787): 283. Cf. the reprint in Ludlum, *Early American Tornadoes*, 13–15.

59. "Summary of Late Intelligence," *Worcester Magazine* 3, no. 22 (August 1787): 293.

60. *Connecticut Courant*, reprinted in *Worcester Magazine* 3, no. 22 (August 1787): 285; "Summary of Late Intelligence," *Worcester Magazine* 3, no. 22 (August 1787): 293.

61. "Summary of Late Intelligence," *Worcester Magazine* 3, no. 23 (September 1787): 305.

62. "Remark on Massachusetts," *Worcester Magazine* 3, no. 24 (September 1787): 318.

63. *A True and Particular Narrative of the late Tremendous Tornado, or Hurricane, At Philadelphia and New-York, on Sabbath-Day, July 1, 1792* (broadside) (Boston, 1792); the theory that the storm was a squall line comes from Ludlum, *Early American Tornadoes*, 204. *An Impartial Relation of the Hail-Storm on the Fifteenth of July and the Tornado on the Second of August 1799. Which Appeared in the Towns of Bozrah, Lebanon, and Franklin, in the State of Connecticut* (Norwich, Conn., 1799), 27–29; cf. the comment in Ludlum, *Early American Tornadoes*, 18.

64. See Introduction to this volume. Scholars of course will always argue over which comes first: that numinous feeling or the concepts used to describe it. We need not settle this debate in order to recognize the prevalence of weather in the stock phrases of colonial spirituality.

65. Portsmouth, Long Island, and Virginia accounts quoted in Thomas S. Kidd, *The Great Awakening: The Roots of Evangelical Christianity in Colonial America* (New Haven, Conn.: Yale University Press, 2007), 103, 243, 275–76, 282; David Brainerd diary entry for August 8, 1745, in Norman Pettit, ed., *The Works of Jonathan Edwards*, Vol. 7, *The Life of David Brainerd* (New Haven, Conn.: Yale University Press, 1985), 308. On the ubiquity of the Acts 2:2 imagery in periods of revival, see also Douglas L. Winiarski, *Darkness Falls on the Land of Light: Experiencing Religious Awakenings in Eighteenth-Century New England* (Chapel Hill: University of North Carolina Press, 2017), 215.

66. Increase Mather, "The Works of Divine Providence are Great and Wonderfull," in *The Doctrine of Divine Providence Opened and Applied: Also Sundry Sermons on Several other Subjects* (Boston, 1684), 55. On Mather's optimism in this sermon about New England's elect status, see Emory Elliott, *Power and the Pulpit in Puritan New England* (Princeton, N.J.: Princeton University Press, 1975), 128.

67. Jonathan Edwards, "Pressing into the Kingdom of God," in Lesser, ed., *Sermons and Discourses, 1734–1738*, 296–97; Jonathan Edwards, "God's Care in Time of Public Commotions" (1741), in *The Works of Jonathan Edwards*, Vol. 22, *Sermons and Discourses, 1739–1742*, ed. Harry S. Stout and Nathan O. Hatch, with Kyle P. Farley (New Haven, Conn.: Yale University Press, 2003), 358–59.

68. Jonathan Edwards, "Sinners in the Hands of an Angry God" (1741), in Stout, Hatch, and Farley, eds., *Sermons and Discourses, 1739–1742*, 410–12.

69. See the related discussion of a "pan-Protestant vernacular" in T. J. Tomlin, *A Divinity for All Persuasions: Almanacs and Early American Religious Life* (New York: Oxford University Press, 2014), 161–62.

70. Mather quoted in Winiarski, *Darkness Falls*, 55; on Haverhill, 54, 75.

71. On the high rates of literacy in colonial New England, see David D. Hall, "Readers and Writers in Early New England," in *A History of the Book in America*, Vol. 1, *The Colonial Book in the Atlantic World*, ed. Hugh Amory and David D. Hall (Cambridge: Cambridge University Press, 2000), 119–31. On the abundance of biblical quotations in lay conversion relations, see Winiarski, *Darkness Falls*, 51–52.

72. Mather, *Voice of God in Stormy Winds*, quoted verses from 9, 12, 13, 14, 25, 26, 32, 33, 45, 48, 60.

73. Stephen A. Marini, *Sacred Song in America: Religion, Music, and Public Culture* (Urbana: University of Illinois Press, 2003), 75–76.

74. Isaac Watts, *Horae Lyricae. Poems, Chiefly of the Lyric Kind, in Three Books*, 9th ed. corr. (Boston, 1748), 23–24. This hymn also appears with musical score in James Lyon, *Urania, or, A Choice Collection of Psalm-Tunes, Anthems, and Hymns* (Philadelphia, 1761), 196–98, which Marini identifies as the "first major compilation of sacred music edited and published in America" (*Sacred Song in America*, 78).

75. Isaac Watts, *Hymns and Spiritual Songs. In Three Books,* 16th ed. (Boston, 1742), 186; Isaac Watts, *The Psalms of David, Imitated in the Language of the New Testament, And apply'd to the Christian State and Worship*, 7th ed. (Philadelphia, 1729), 59, 283–84. Publication figures from Marini, *Sacred Song in America*, 76.

76. John Wesley and Charles Wesley, *Hymns and Sacred Poems* (London, 1740), 67. On this hymn as the second most popular, see Stephen A. Marini, "American Protestant Hymns Project: A Ranked List of Most Frequently Printed Hymns, 1737–1960," in *Wonderful Words of Life: Hymns in American Protestant History and Theology*, ed. Richard J. Mouw and Mark A. Noll (Grand Rapids, Mich.: Eerdmans, 2004), 253. John Wesley's criticism of the hymn quoted in Murray R. Adamthwaite, *Through the Christian Year with Charles Wesley: 101 Psalms and Hymns* (Eugene, Ore.: Wipf and Stock, 2016), 196.

77. Brekus, ed., *Sarah Osborn's Collected Writings*, 32–33. The phrase "all-wise providence" on 65, 83, 88, 149, 184, 187, 200, 223, 224, 235, 259. On Flavel, Osborn, and the cataloguing of providences, see Brekus, *Sarah Osborn's World*, 19, 53.

78. Diary entry for May 27, 1745, in Brekus, ed., *Sarah Osborn's Collected Writings*, 78, 80–81.

79. Jonathan Edwards, "Notes on Scripture," no. 389 (on Ezekiel 1), in *The Works of Jonathan Edwards*, Vol. 15, *Notes on Scripture*, ed. Stephen J. Stein (New Haven, Conn.: Yale University Press, 1998), 373–75; Matthew Henry, *An Exposition of All the Books of the Old and New Testament*, 3rd ed., 6 vols. (London, 1721–1725), 4:404. For Calvin's own remarks connecting Ezekiel's wheel with providence, see John Calvin, *Commentaries on the First Twenty Chapters of the Book of the Prophet Ezekiel*, trans. Thomas Myers, 2 vols. (Edinburgh: Calvin Translation Society, 1849–1850), 1:67–68.

80. Ezekiel 1:24 rendered in the NRSV as "the thunder of the Almighty"; cf. "the voice of the Almighty," KJV.

81. Edwards, "Notes on Scripture," no. 393 (Ezekiel 1:4), in Stein, ed., *Notes on Scripture*, 387.

82. Jonathan I. Israel and Geoffrey Parker, "Of Providence and Protestant Winds: The Spanish Armada of 1588 and the Dutch Armada of 1688," in *The Anglo-Dutch Moment: Essays on the Glorious Revolution and Its World Impact*, ed. Jonathan I. Israel (Cambridge: Cambridge University Press, 1991), 335–36, 359; Janković, *Reading the Skies*, 56, 58–59. Burnet quoted in Thomas Babington Macaulay, *The History of England from the Accession of James II*, 5 vols. (Chicago, 1884–86), 2:435. On Burnet's latitudinarian skepticism about absolute predestination, see Robert W. Prichard, *The Nature of Salvation: Theological Consensus in the Episcopal Church, 1801–73* (Urbana: University of Illinois Press, 1997), 45–47; and Peter J. Thuesen, *Predestination: The American Career of a Contentious Doctrine* (New York: Oxford University Press, 2009), 81–83.

83. A story told in Thomas S. Kidd, *The Protestant Interest: New England after Puritanism* (New Haven, Conn.: Yale University Press, 2004).

84. On Edwards and the Jacobite plots, see Peter J. Thuesen, *The Works of Jonathan Edwards*, Vol. 26, *Catalogues of Books* (New Haven, Conn.: Yale University Press, 2008), 87–89. [Elisha Williams], *The essential Rights and Liberties of Protestants. A seasonable Plea for The Liberty*

of Conscience, and the Right of private Judgement . . . By a Lover of Truth and Liberty (Boston, 1744), 43.

85. Jonathan Edwards to a Scottish correspondent, probably the Rev. John MacLaurin of Glasgow, November 1745, in *The Works of Jonathan Edwards*, Vol. 16, *Letters and Personal Writings*, ed. George S. Claghorn (New Haven, Conn.: Yale University Press, 1998), 195–96. On the context of the Louisbourg campaign, see George M. Marsden, *Jonathan Edwards: A Life* (New Haven, Conn.: Yale University Press, 2003), 310–14. On the details of Pepperrell's assault, see Paul David Nelson, "Sir William Pepperrell, First Baronet," *Oxford Dictionary of National Biography* (Oxford: Oxford University Press, 2004–), http://www.oxforddnb.com.

86. The story is recounted in, among other places, Catherine Drinker Bowen, *John Adams and the American Revolution* (Boston: Little, Brown, 1950), 10–12; and Benjamin B. Wisner, *History of the Old South Church in Boston, in Four Sermons* (Boston, 1830), 30. On D'Anville's ill-fated expedition, see James Pritchard, *Anatomy of a Naval Disaster: The 1746 French Naval Expedition to North America* (Montreal: McGill-Queen's University Press, 1995).

87. Henry Wadsworth Longfellow, "A Ballad of the French Fleet" (1877), in *The Complete Poetical Works of Henry Wadsworth Longfellow* (Boston: Houghton, Mifflin, 1900), 376–77. Prince himself mentions the October 16 fast day only briefly in Thomas Prince, *The Salvations of God in 1746: In Part Set Forth in a Sermon at the South Church in Boston, Nov. 27. 1746* (Boston, 1746), 31.

88. Thomas Foxcroft, *A seasonable Memento for New Year's Day. A Sermon Preached (summarily) at the Old Church Lecture in Boston, On Thursday January 1. 1746,–7* (Boston, 1747), 71; Samuel Haven, *Joy and Salvation by Christ; his Arm displayed in the Protestant Cause. A Sermon Preached in the South Parish in Portsmouth; Occasioned by the remarkable Success of His Majesty's Arms in the Late War, and by the happy Peace of 1763* (Portsmouth, N.H., 1763), 29; Jonathan French, *A Sermon, Delivered on the Anniversary Thanksgiving November 29, 1798* (Andover, Mass., 1799), 13–14.

89. Nicholas Guyatt has helpfully distinguished between "personal providentialism" (God's involvement in the lives of individuals) and "national providentialism" (in this case, God's favoring of the American cause). He contends that the latter proved more durable in American history, whereas personal providentialism suffered under the perennial suspicion that it was "superstitious and backward." Nicholas Guyatt, *Providence and the Invention of the United States, 1607–1876* (Cambridge: Cambridge University Press, 2007), 5–6, 60. While I do not dispute his conclusion in light of the evidence he examines (which deals mainly with national providentialism), I would argue that personal providentialism—at least insofar as the weather is concerned—has been more resilient throughout American history than scholarship has acknowledged. Conversely, national providentialism has appeared dubious to a few critics (see the following discussion of the *American Magazine and Historical Chronicle*).

90. The evidence for Gridley's editorship of the *American Magazine and Historical Chronicle* is laid out in John K. Reeves, "Jeremy Gridley, Editor," *New England Quarterly* 17 (1944): 265–81. Gridley later became a Freemason and held the title of Grand Master of the Masons in North America from 1754 until his death. As a Mason, he was committed to Enlightenment notions of the search for truth, the communication of knowledge, and the creation of a rational society. Details of his life from L. Kinvin Wroth, "Jeremiah Gridley," *American National Biography* (New York: Oxford University Press, 2000-), http://www.anb.org; and David G. Hackett, *That*

Religion in Which All Men Agree: Freemasonry in American Culture (Berkeley: University of California Press, 2014), 50–51.

91. "Of Superstitious Fears, and their Causes natural and accidental," *American Magazine and Historical Chronicle* (May 1744): 372–75. On Gridley's likely authorship of this piece, see Reeves, "Jeremy Gridley, Editor," 276–78.

92. "An Essay on Divine Judgments, shewing the Wickedness and Absurdity of applying them to Men and Events," *American Magazine and Historical Chronicle* (July 1744): 458–61. Though this article is signed "P. N.," the author was likely either Gridley or one of his followers, according to Reeves, "Jeremy Gridley, Editor," 279.

93. "Remarkable Deliverances the British Nation has had in the most imminent Dangers, with suitable Reflections," *American Magazine and Historical Chronicle* (August 1746): 340–44; cf. [James Burgh], *Britain's Remembrancer: or, The Danger not over* (London, 1746), 35. That *Britain's Remembrancer* was the source of the magazine's article is pointed out in Edward W. R. Pitcher, ed., *The American Magazine and Historical Chronicle (Boston 1743–1746): An Annotated Catalogue of the Prose* (Lewiston, Me.: Edwin Mellen Press, 2003), 65. On the popularity of Burgh's text in America, see Thuesen, ed., *Catalogues of Books*, 323.

94. Jonathan Edwards, "Catalogue," no. 295, in Thuesen, ed., *Catalogues of Books*, 178; "Things to be Considered an[d] Written fully about," unnumbered series, no. 26 (circa 1726), in *The Works of Jonathan Edwards*, Vol. 6, *Scientific and Philosophical Writings*, ed. Wallace E. Anderson (New Haven, Conn.: Yale University Press, 1980), 287–88. Alfred Owen Aldridge judges these reflections more original than the early observations on lightning published by Benjamin Franklin in the *Pennsylvania Gazette* in 1737. (Franklin's 1737 observations are to be distinguished from his more famous experiments published in 1751.) See Alfred Owen Aldridge, "Benjamin Franklin and Jonathan Edwards on Lightning and Earthquakes," in *Early American Science*, ed. Brooke Hindle (New York: Science History Publications, 1976), 34–36. On lightning and electricity as a focus of the Enlightenment, see James Delbourgo, *A Most Amazing Scene of Wonders: Electricity and Enlightenment in Early America* (Cambridge, Mass.: Harvard University Press 2006); and Patricia Fara, *An Entertainment for Angels: Electricity in the Enlightenment* (New York: Columbia University Press, 2002).

95. "God's artillery" from Edwards, "Notes on Scripture," no. 218 (Isaiah 30:27–31:9), in Stein, ed., *Notes on Scripture*, 152; Jonathan Edwards, "Personal Narrative," in Claghorn, ed., *Letters and Personal Writings*, 794; Jonathan Edwards, "Children Ought to Love the Lord Jesus Christ Above All" (1740), in Stout, Hatch, and Farley, eds., *Sermons and Discourses, 1739–1742*, 179.

96. Gilbert Tennent, *All Things come alike to All: A Sermon, On Eccles. IX. 1, 2 and 3 Verses. Occasioned by a Person's being struck by the Lightning of Thunder. Preached at Philadelphia, July the 28th, 1745* (Philadelphia, 1745), 3, 22, 29, 34, 36–37, 40; Milton J. Coalter, Jr., *Gilbert Tennent, Son of Thunder: A Case Study of Continental Pietism's Impact on the First Great Awakening in the Middle Colonies* (New York: Greenwood Press, Presbyterian Historical Society, 1986), 125–26.

97. Silverman, *Cotton Mather*, 350, 359–60; Thomas S. Kidd, *Benjamin Franklin: The Religious Life of a Founding Father* (New Haven, Conn.: Yale University Press, 2017), 21–22. On the inoculation controversy, see Thuesen, *Predestination*, 87–88. Franklin's reference to his son in *The Autobiography of Benjamin Franklin*, ed. Leonard W. Labaree, Ralph L. Ketcham, Helen C. Boatfield, and Helene H. Fineman, 2nd ed. (New Haven, Conn.: Yale University Press, 2003), 170.

98. "A Letter, giving an Account of the most dreadful Earthquake," printed as an appendix to Thomas Prince, *An Improvement of the Doctrine of Earthquakes, Being the Works of God, and Tokens of his just Displeasure* (Boston, 1755), 15–16.

99. Thomas Prince, *Earthquakes the Works of God, and Tokens of His just Displeasure* (Boston, 1755); John Winthrop, *A Lecture on Earthquakes; Read in the Chapel of Harvard-College in Cambridge, N.E., November 26th 1755* (Boston, 1755), 27–28, 36. On the Prince-Winthrop dispute, see also Philip Dray, *Stealing God's Thunder: Benjamin Franklin's Lightning Rod and the Invention of America* (New York: Random House, 2005), 102–11; and Andrew Dickson White, *A History of the Warfare of Science with Theology*, 2 vols. (New York: Appleton, 1896), 364–66.

100. James Cogswell, *The Danger of disregarding the Works of God: A Sermon, Delivered at Canterbury, November 23, 1755. Being the next Sabbath after the late surprizing Earthquake* (New Haven, Conn., 1755), 19; Thomas Foxcroft, *The Earthquake, a Divine Visitation: A Sermon Preached to the Old Church in Boston, January 8, 1756* (Boston, 1756), 5, 41, 44–46. The literature on the Lisbon earthquake is voluminous. Three recent accounts are Mark Molesky, *This Gulf of Fire: The Destruction of Lisbon, or Apocalypse in the Age of Science and Reason* (New York: Vintage, 2015); Edward Paice, *Wrath of God: The Great Lisbon Earthquake of 1755* (London: Quercus, 2008); and Nicholas Shrady, *The Last Day: Wrath, Ruin, and Reason in the Great Lisbon Earthquake of 1755* (New York: Viking, 2008). See also Theodore E. D. Braun and John B. Radner, eds., *The Lisbon Earthquake of 1755: Representations and Reactions* (Oxford: Voltaire Foundation, 2005).

101. John Winthrop to Ezra Stiles, April 17, 1756, Stiles manuscripts, Yale University, quoted in Winfred E. A. Bernhard, "John Winthrop," *American National Biography*. For an overview emphasizing the traditional aspects of Winthrop's providentialism, see Louis Graham, "The Scientific Piety of John Winthrop of Harvard," *New England Quarterly* 46 (1973): 112–18.

102. John Winthrop, "An Account of a Meteor seen in New England, and of a Whirlwind felt in that Country," *Philosophical Transactions* 52 (1761): 10–11, 14–16. Winthrop's article seems to indicate that the tornado happened in 1760, but independent evidence confirms the date of 1759, according to Ludlum, *Early American Tornadoes*, 6.

103. On the debate in the 1750s, see the excellent overview by Jonathan I. Israel, *Democratic Enlightenment: Philosophy, Revolution, and Human Rights, 1750–1790* (Oxford: Oxford University Press, 2011), 39–55. A key work arguing for the pivotal role of Lisbon is Susan Neiman, *Evil in Modern Thought: An Alternative History of Philosophy*, rev. ed. (Princeton, N.J.: Princeton University Press 2015). But see the opposing view of Ryan Nichols, "Re-evaluating the Effects of the 1755 Lisbon Earthquake on Eighteenth-Century Minds: How Cognitive Science of Religion Improves Intellectual History with Hypothesis Testing Methods," *Journal of the American Academy of Religion* 82 (2014): 970–1009; for the observation that Hume never discusses Lisbon, 981.

104. David Hume, *The Natural History of Religion*, ed. Tom L. Beauchamp (Oxford: Clarendon Press, 2007), 37–38, 40–41. Hume did not originate the anthropomorphic principle in his theory of religion, which can be found as far back as the Ionian philosopher Xenophanes, but he was the first to integrate it into a coherent epistemological analysis. See J. Samuel Preus, *Explaining Religion: Criticism and Theory from Bodin to Freud* (New Haven, Conn.: Yale University Press, 1987), 99. For additional helpful explication of Hume's argument, see Frank E. Manuel, *The Eighteenth Century Confronts the Gods* (1959; Reprint, New York: Atheneum, 1967), 172–77.

105. Hume, *Natural History*, 52–53.

106. David Hume, *Dialogues Concerning Natural Religion*, in *Principal Writings on Religion, including* Dialogues Concerning Natural Religion *and* The Natural History of Religion, ed. J. C.

A. Gaskin (Oxford: Oxford University Press, 1993), 112–13. While some passages in the *Natural History* make Hume sound like a supporter of the design argument, Philo in the *Dialogues* seems to express Hume's own empirical skepticism that anything coherent can be proven about God from nature. On Hume and the design argument, see Keith E. Yandell, *Hume's "Inexplicable Mystery": His Views on Religion* (Philadelphia: Temple University Press, 1990), 16–23, esp. 18; and Gaskin's introduction to Hume, *Principal Writings*, xxiii–xxvi.

107. On Hume's influence, see Preus, *Explaining Religion*, 99n44, 207.

108. On Hume and Franklin, see Kidd, *Benjamin Franklin*, 188, 191–92. Jonathan Edwards to the Rev. John Erskine, December 11, 1755, in Claghorn, ed., *Letters and Personal Writings*, 679. On Hume's paucity of American fans, see Henry F. May, *The Enlightenment in America* (New York: Oxford University Press, 1976), 119–21. For early American writings about Hume, see Mark G. Spencer, ed., *Hume's Reception in Early America*, rev. ed. (London: Bloomsbury Academic, 2017).

109. Timothy Dwight, *The Nature and Danger of Infidel Philosophy, Exhibited in Two Discourses, Addressed to the Candidates for the Baccalaureate, in Yale College* (New Haven, 1798), 13–16, 29–30, 38. On Dwight and Hume, see John R. Fitzmier, *New England's Moral Legislator: Timothy Dwight, 1752–1817* (Bloomington: Indiana University Press, 1998), 60, 83. On Dwight's biblicism, see Mark A. Noll, *America's God: From Jonathan Edwards to Abraham Lincoln* (New York: Oxford University Press, 2002), 234–35. On Hume and adultery, see Annette C. Baier, *The Pursuits of Philosophy: An Introduction to the Life and Thought of David Hume* (Cambridge, Mass.: Harvard University Press, 2011), 92.

110. Jonathan Israel argues that by 1750, there were three irreconcilable positions regarding natural disasters: (1) that they were always directed by providence, (2) that they were sometimes natural and sometimes divinely directed, and (3) that they were always due to natural causes. He adds that (2), which he terms the moderate mainstream, "certainly had to work the hardest to sound coherent." Israel, *Democratic Enlightenment*, 43–44.

111. Thomas Paine, *The Age of Reason, Being an Investigation of True and Fabulous Theology* (Paris, 1794), 81; modern edition in *The Complete Writings of Thomas Paine*, ed. Philip S. Foner, 2 vols. (New York: Citadel, 1969), 1:498.

112. Bryan A. Garner, ed., *Black's Law Dictionary*, 7th ed. (St. Paul, Minn.: West Group, 1999), s.v. "act of God," 34.

113. For an overview of the issues, see Denis Binder, "Act of God? or Act of Man?: A Reappraisal of the Act of God Defense in Tort Law," *Review of Litigation* 15, no. 1 (1996): 1–79. See also the reflections by Daniel Silliman, "This Is the Reason Your Insurance Company Calls Blizzards an 'Act of God,'" *Washington Post* (online), January 22, 2016, www.washingtonpost.com.

114. In recent times, the lack of religious meaning to the "act of God" defense has occasionally prompted satire. In 2010, when lightning incinerated a giant statue of Jesus (nicknamed "Touchdown Jesus") outside Cincinnati, the online humor site *The Spoof* reported that insurance investigators had refused to pay out damages because they ruled the incident an "Act of a Wrathful God." See "Fiery Destruction of 'Touchdown Jesus' Ruled an Act of God," *The Spoof*, June 15, 2010, https://www.thespoof.com/spoof-news/us/76858/fiery-destruction-of-touchdown-jesus-ruled-an-act-of-god. For the real facts of the incident, see "Six-Story Jesus Statue Struck by Lightning," *Wall Street Journal*, June 16, 2010.

115. Golinski, *British Weather*, 12.

116. Mather, *Voice of God in Stormy Winds*, 41, 43.

CHAPTER 3

1. Details on the Nauvoo Temple from Dean E. Garner, "Nauvoo's Temple," *Perspective* [Brigham Young University–Idaho] 2, no. 2 (Summer 2002): 79–91; and Matthew S. McBride, *A House for the Most High: The Story of the Original Nauvoo Temple* (Salt Lake City: Greg Kofford, 2006), 268, 360.

2. Emile Vallet, *Communism: History of the Experiment at Nauvoo of the Icarian Settlement* (1917; reprint, Springfield: Illinois State Historical Society, 1971), 22–23. Vallet's account is also quoted in McBride, *A House for the Most High*, 362, and in David M. Ludlum, *Early American Tornadoes, 1586–1870* (Boston: American Meteorological Society, 1970), 112. Bourg quoted in (among other newspapers) *Daily National Intelligencer* (Washington, D.C.), June 21, 1850; and *Daily Sanduskian* (Sandusky, Ohio), June 25, 1850.

3. "Dreadful Tornado—Destruction of the Temple Walls," *Hancock Patriot* (Hancock County, Ill.), reprinted in the Latter-day Saints' *Millennial Star* 21 (November 1, 1850), 334–35.

4. Étienne Cabet, *Le vrai Christianisme suivant Jésus-Christ*, 3rd ed. (Paris, 1848), 278.

5. Cabet quoted in Christopher H. Johnson, *Utopian Communism in France: Cabet and the Icarians, 1839–1851* (Ithaca, N.Y.: Cornell University Press, 1974), 233; cf. 93–95 on his religious views. For background, see also Robert P. Sutton, "An American Elysium: The Icarian Communities," in *America's Communal Utopias*, ed. Donald E. Pitzer (Chapel Hill: University of North Carolina Press, 1997), 279–96; Robert P. Sutton, introduction to Étienne Cabet, *Travels in Icaria*, trans. Leslie J. Roberts (Syracuse, N.Y.: Syracuse University Press, 2003), vii–xlix; and Robert P. Sutton, *Les Icariens: The Utopian Dream in Europe and America* (Urbana: University of Illinois Press, 1994).

6. Vallet, *Communism*, 31.

7. Doctrine and Covenants 63:6 (given at Kirtland, Ohio, in August 1831).

8. Joseph Smith, Jr., dedicatory prayer at Kirtland, March 27, 1836, in *History of the Church of Jesus Christ of Latter-day Saints*, 8 vols., 2nd ed. rev. (Salt Lake City: Deseret Book, 1948–70), 2:422; cf. Doctrine and Covenants 109:30.

9. Joseph Smith, Jr., "Remarks of the Prophet on the Death of Lorenzo D. Barnes—The Resurrection," April 15, 1843, in *History of the Church*, 5:362.

10. "Signs of the Times," *Times and Seasons* 2, no. 10 (March 15, 1841), 351–52, and reprinted in *Millennial Star* 2, no. 2 (June 1841), 28.

11. "The Nauvoo Temple Again Destroyed," *Detroit Free Press*, June 25, 1850. Among the Latter-day Saints, on the other hand, the legend arose that the tornado that finished off the temple was ordained by God to prevent the human desecration of the holy place; see Fawn M. Brodie, *No Man Knows My History: The Life of Joseph Smith, the Mormon Prophet*, 2nd ed. (New York: Knopf, 1971), 400.

12. "Address by President Brigham Young," *Millennial Star* 16, no. 16 (April 22, 1854), 241.

13. I borrow the phrase "intellectual weather of the nineteenth century" from James Turner, "Charles Hodge in the Intellectual Weather of the Nineteenth Century," in James Turner, *Language, Religion, Knowledge: Past and Present* (Notre Dame, Ind.: University of Notre Dame Press, 2003), 31–49.

14. "Signs of the Times" (quoting an anonymous writer for the *Liverpool Albion*), *Times and Seasons* 3, no. 12 (April 15, 1842), 758.

15. Indeed, if the Mississippi Valley is defined broadly as the region between the Allegheny Mountains and the Rocky Mountains (as the Mississippi Valley Historical Association [MVHA] delimited it in 1908), this area encompasses both the traditional Tornado Alley of the Great Plains and the Dixie Alley region, which is the other epicenter of violent tornadoes. On the MVHA definition, see Ian Tyrrell, "Public at the Creation: Place, Memory, and Historical Practice in the Mississippi Valley Historical Association, 1907–1950," *Journal of American History* 94 (2007): 25.

16. On these revolutions in transportation and communication, see Daniel Walker Howe, *What Hath God Wrought: The Transformation of America, 1815–1848* (New York: Oxford University Press, 2007), 211–35.

17. ProQuest's American Periodicals database, https://search.proquest.com/americanperiodicals, yielded the following hits for the search term "tornado" by decade: 79 (1800–1810), 158 (1810–1820), 455 (1820–1830), and 1,264 (1830–1840); accessed December 2, 2015.

18. "Dreadful Calamity at Charleston," *Charleston Courier*, September 11 and 12, 1811, reprinted in *Maryland Gazette* (Annapolis, Md.), September 26, 1811.

19. *Pennsylvania Gazette* (Philadelphia), June 22, 1814; "rideth upon the wings of the wind" invoking Psalm 104:3. Ludlum (*Early American Tornadoes*, 98) reprints the same account from the *Greensburgh (Pa.) Gazette*.

20. The soldier's account is that of George Robert Gleig, *The Campaigns of the British Army at Washington and New Orleans, in the Years 1814–1815*, 3rd ed. (London: John Murray, 1827), 142. For Cockburn's comment, see Anthony S. Pitch, *The Burning of Washington: The British Invasion of 1814* (Annapolis, Md.: Naval Institute Press, 1998), 142. For additional details of the storm, see Ludlum, *Early American Tornadoes*, 46.

21. "Tornado," *Christian Register* 1, no. 6 (September 21, 1821): 23.

22. "A Terrible Tornado," *Western Pioneer* (Springfield, Ohio), April 13, 1833; reprinted in *Hartford (Conn.) Courant*, April 30, 1833.

23. "Tornado in Virginia," *Friend; a Religious and Literary Journal* 7, no. 32 (May 17, 1834): 251. Similarly, an account from the *Poughkeepsie Journal*, reprinted in William Lloyd Garrison's abolitionist paper the *Liberator*, used the language of sublimity to recount an 1837 tornado in Dutchess County, New York: "The clouds mixed angrily together, which rendered the aspect sublime and beautiful." A new Baptist church was obliterated into a "heap of promiscuous rubbish," with even the wall of its foundation torn to pieces, while many barns were left "so that one stick lay not upon another." "These ruins are richly worth a visit," the article concluded; "they cannot but inculcate a striking proof of Almighty Power"; "Destructive Tornado," *Liberator* 7, no. 25 (June 16, 1837): 100.

24. James Rodger Fleming, *Meteorology in America, 1800–1870* (Baltimore: Johns Hopkins University Press, 1990), 31–35; Thomas P. Grazulis, *The Tornado: America's Ultimate Windstorm* (Norman: University of Oklahoma Press, 2001), 219; Lee Sandlin, *Storm Kings: The Untold History of America's First Tornado Chasers* (New York: Pantheon Books, 2013), 31–33.

25. *New Brunswick Times*, June 20, 1835, quoted in Ludlum, *Early American Tornadoes*, 58. The archaic meaning of the term "devoted," which often appears in nineteenth-century tornado accounts, is "formally or surely consigned to evil or destruction; doomed." *Oxford English Dictionary*, http://www.oed.com.

26. *Protestant Vindicator*, quoted in *New York Evangelist* 6, no. 26 (June 27, 1835): 103.

27. *Temple of Reason; Devoted to Free Inquiry, Moral Science, Universal Education, and Human Happiness* 1, no. 8 (June 27, 1835), 57–58. On this periodical, see J. William Frost, *A Perfect Freedom: Religious Liberty in Pennsylvania* (Cambridge: Cambridge University Press, 1990), 96. (*Temple of Reason* is not to be confused with the earlier deist periodical of the same name, published in New York, 1800–1803.)

28. Ranking from the Storm Prediction Center: http://www.spc.noaa.gov/faq/tornado/killers.html. Cf. Grazulis, *Tornado*, 220–21.

29. "Dreadful Visitation of Providence," *Natchez (Miss.) Free Trader*, May 8, 1840, reprinted in *Catholic Telegraph* 9, no. 21 (May 23, 1840): 164; *Christian Observer* 19, no. 22 (May 28, 1840): 87; *Albion* 2, no. 21 (May 23, 1840): 171; and others. See also the composite accounts in Grazulis, *Tornado*, 220–21; and Angus M. Gunn, *Encyclopedia of Disasters*, Vol. 1, *Environmental Catastrophes and Human Tragedies* (Westport, Conn.: Greenwood Press, 2008), 103–5.

30. Flint's account printed in "A Tornado," *New York Observer and Chronicle* 18, no. 37 (September 12, 1840): 148. His account also appeared in *Christian Register and Boston Observer* 19, no. 35 (August 29, 1840): 138, which noted that it was Flint's last published writing before his death on August 16 from largely unrelated causes.

31. "Dreadful Calamity at Natchez," *New Orleans Bulletin*, May 9, 1840, reprinted in *Liberator* 10, no. 22 (May 29, 1840): 88; "The Tornado at Natchez," *Christian Watchman* 21, no. 23 (June 5, 1840): 91.

32. "Horrible Storm—Natchez in Ruins," *Natchez (Miss.) Courier*, May 8, 1840, reprinted in *Catholic Telegraph* 9, no. 21 (May 23, 1840): 164; and in *New Yorker* 9, no. 10 (May 23, 1840): 158.

33. "Tornado at Natchez," *Christian Secretary* 3, no. 11 (May 29, 1840): 3; Mrs. V. E. Howard, "Tornado at Natchez," *Vicksburg (Miss.) Sentinel* (no date), reprinted in *Liberty (Miss.) Advocate* 5, no. 25 (June 18, 1840): 1.

34. *Episcopal Recorder* 18, no. 11 (June 6, 1840): 42. The Philadelphia-based paper did not specify the sins committed by the country. Prior to the Civil War, the paper was circumspect on slavery for fear of losing low-church allies in the South. But at the war's conclusion, the editor called for the hanging of ex-Confederate bishops along with other leading rebels. See Mark Mohler, "The Episcopal Church and National Reconciliation, 1865," *Political Science Quarterly* 41 (1926): 570–71.

35. *Times and Seasons* 1, no. 7 (May 1840), excerpts from *Natchez Free Trader*, 104–6, and editorial commentary, 106–8. On the history of this periodical, see Reed C. Durham, Jr., "Times and Seasons," in *Encyclopedia of Mormonism*, 4 vols., ed. Daniel H. Ludlow (New York: Macmillan, 1992), 4:1479–80.

36. Lewis Saum, in his painstaking study of the diaries of ordinary Americans, argued that the calamity of the war fundamentally shook earlier assumptions about an orderly providence. See Lewis O. Saum, *The Popular Mood of America, 1860–1890* (Lincoln: University of Nebraska Press, 1990), 13–39. More recently, Sean Scott has shown that providentialism was more durable than Saum acknowledged. See Sean A. Scott, *A Visitation of God: Northern Civilians Interpret the Civil War* (New York: Oxford University Press, 2011), 13. Scott's work builds on the work of Mark Noll, who concludes that after the war, American thinkers were increasingly divided between those who continued to trust in providence and those who embraced agnosticism about the world's ultimate meaning. See Mark A. Noll, *The Civil War as a Theological Crisis* (Chapel Hill: University of North Carolina Press, 2006), 94.

37. A story told in Jon H. Roberts, *Darwinism and the Divine in America: Protestant Intellectuals and Organic Evolution, 1859–1900* (Madison: University of Wisconsin Press, 1988).

See also Bradley J. Gundlach, *Process and Providence: The Evolution Question at Princeton, 1845–1929* (Grand Rapids, Mich.: Eerdmans, 2013).

38. Moses Stuart, *A Commentary on the Apocalypse*, 2 vols. (Andover, Mass., 1845), 2:168–69. On Stuart's significance, see Jerry Wayne Brown, *The Rise of Biblical Criticism in America, 1800–1870: The New England Scholars* (Middletown, Conn.: Wesleyan University Press, 1969), 45–59, 94–110.

39. John P. Finley, *Tornadoes: What They Are and How to Observe Them; with Practical Suggestions for the Protection of Life and Property* (New York, 1887). Regarding the rarity of tornadoes in Bible lands, an article published seven years after Stuart's death noted the prevalence of the sirocco, a desert windstorm that is different from a tornado; see Denison Olmsted, "Meteorology of Palestine," *New Englander and Yale Review* 17, no. 66 (May 1859): 450–69. More recently, cf. Phyllis A. Bird, "Wind," in *Harper's Bible Dictionary*, ed. Paul J. Achtemeier et al. (San Francisco: Harper and Row, 1985): 1134.

40. [Moncure Conway], "Memoir of Professor Espy," *The Dial: A Monthly Magazine for Literature, Philosophy, and Religion* 1, no. 4 (April 1860): 259. On Conway, see Leigh Eric Schmidt, *Restless Souls: The Making of American Spirituality*, 2nd ed. (Berkeley: University of California Press, 2012), 101–2.

41. Sandlin, *Storm Kings*, 36–37, 87. As Sandlin notes, though Espy's term for the release of latent heat, "latent caloric," is no longer used, the term used by meteorologists today, "convective available potential energy," or CAPE, means essentially the same thing.

42. James P. Espy, *The Philosophy of Storms* (Boston, 1841), 341–43, 345. On Tooley, see John G. Jones, *A Complete History of Methodism as Connected with the Mississippi Conference of the Methodist Episcopal Church, South*, 2 vols. (Nashville: Methodist Episcopal Church, South, 1908), 1:248–50. On Forshey, see Fleming, *Meteorology in America*, 27.

43. "The Tornado at Natchez," *Louisville (Ky.) Journal* (no date), reprinted in *Friend; a Religious and Literary Journal* 13, no. 44 (August 1, 1840): 351; cf. "Natchez Tornado," *Western Journal of Medicine and Surgery* 2, no. 7 (July 25, 1840), 74–78.

44. See the explanation in Grazulis, *Tornado*, 150–51.

45. On the Espy-Redfield dispute, see Fleming, *Meteorology in America*, 24–31; Grazulis, *Tornado*, 219–20; Ludlum, *Early American Tornadoes*, 192–94; and Sandlin, *Storm Kings*, 40–87.

46. James Rodger Fleming, *Fixing the Sky: The Checkered History of Weather and Climate Control* (New York: Columbia University Press, 2010), 4, 53–58. On Espy and weather control, see also William B. Meyer, *Americans and Their Weather* (New York: Oxford University Press, 2000), 85–89. For a countervailing example of one community's attempt to adapt to, rather than alter, the weather, see William B. Meyer, "The Perfectionists and the Weather: The Oneida Community's Quest for Meteorological Utopia, 1848–1879," *Environmental History* 7 (2002): 589–610. The history of American attempts to remake weather and climate goes back to colonial times. See Anya Zilberstein, *A Temperate Empire: Making Climate Change in Early America* (New York: Oxford University Press, 2016).

47. "Signs of the Times," *Times and Seasons* 4, no. 10 (April 1, 1843): 153.

48. James Pollard Espy, *The Human Will: A Series of Posthumous Essays on Moral Accountability, the Legitimate Object of Punishment, and the Powers of the Will* (Cincinnati: The Dial, 1860), 30, 40, 65; Espy, *Philosophy of Storms*, 283. Sandlin (*Storm Kings*, 86) describes the thesis of Espy's *Human Will* this way: "Any apparent evil in the world—even the destructive chaos of the tornado—was a surface illusion; behind it was a simple, lucid, and radiantly harmonious pattern in the mind of the Almighty."

49. Espy's will quoted in L. M. Morehead, *A Few Incidents in the Life of Professor James P. Espy, by His Niece* (Cincinnati, 1888), 19.

50. On doxological science, see Theodore Dwight Bozeman, *Protestants in an Age of Science: The Baconian Ideal and Antebellum Religious Thought* (Chapel Hill: University of North Carolina Press, 1977), 81–86. On the influence of Paley (and Hitchcock) see James Turner, *Without God, Without Creed: The Origins of Unbelief in America* (Baltimore: Johns Hopkins University Press, 1985), 96–97; and E. Brooks Holifield, *Theology in America: Christian Thought from the Age of the Puritans to the Civil War* (New Haven, Conn.: Yale University Press, 2003), 181–82.

51. Edward Hitchcock, "Special Divine Interpositions in Nature," *Bibliotheca Sacra* 11 (1854): 780–81, 794, 798.

52. Providence also came under attack during the mid-nineteenth century from such critics as Herbert Spencer and John Stuart Mill. See Charles D. Cashdollar, "The Social Implications of the Doctrine of Divine Providence: A Nineteenth-Century Debate in American Theology," *Harvard Theological Review* 71 (1978): 265–84.

53. Martha Mitchell, "George Ide Chace," *Encyclopedia Brunoniana*, Brown University Library, http://www.brown.edu/Administration/News_Bureau/Databases/Encyclopedia/search.php?serial=C0280.

54. George I. Chace, *The Relation of Divine Providence to Physical Laws: A Discourse Delivered Before the Porter Rhetorical Society, of Andover Theological Seminary, August 1, 1854* (Boston, 1854), 16–19, 22.

55. Ibid., 17, 20–21, 28–29. On the Puritan tendency to attribute lightning strikes either to God or Satan, Chace undoubtedly had in mind Increase Mather, *An Essay for the Recording of Illustrious Providences* (Boston, 1684), 124–28.

56. Chace, *Relation of Divine Providence to Physical Laws*, 28–29, 32–33, 38.

57. Ibid., 39, 43–44.

58. Ibid., 57–59.

59. "The Providence of God in Human Life," *Christian Watchman and Reflector* 35, no. 43 (October 26, 1854): 171.

60. George I. Chace, "Divine Providence," *Christian Watchman and Reflector* 35, no. 48 (November 30, 1854): 189–90.

61. "The Doctrine of Special Providence," *Christian Watchman and Reflector* 35, no. 48 (November 30, 1854): 190. Chace was not the only figure in the 1850s who expressed misgivings about the excesses of traditional providentialism. James McCosh, president of Princeton University, argued that the distinction between general providence (God's regular operation of world through natural laws) and special providence (God's intervention for or against particular individuals) should be discarded in favor of a single "universal providence." See Cashdollar, "Social Implications," 279–81; and Charles D. Cashdollar, *The Transformation of Theology, 1830–1890: Positivism and Protestant Thought in Britain and America* (Princeton, N.J.: Princeton University Press, 1989), 346–56.

62. "Editor's Collectanea," *Monthly Religious Magazine* 12, no. 5 (November 1854): 291–92; "Divine Providence," *Christian Review* 20, no. 79 (January 1, 1855): 119–20, 123; "Literary Notices," *Universalist Quarterly and General Review* 2 (1854): 431.

63. On Park, see Douglas A. Sweeney and Allen C. Guelzo, eds., *The New England Theology: From Jonathan Edwards to Edwards Amasa Park* (Grand Rapids, Mich.: Baker Academic, 2006), 245–46.

64. Edwards A. Park, "The Relation of Divine Providence to Physical Laws," *Bibliotheca Sacra* 12 (1855): 187–88, 190, 203–4.

65. Charles Hodge, "Free Agency," *Biblical Repertory and Princeton Review* 29 (1857): 101–35; quotations from 108, 127, 132. On Hodge's rivalry with Park, see Paul C. Gutjahr, *Charles Hodge: Guardian of American Orthodoxy* (New York: Oxford University Press, 2011), 267–72.

66. On Hodge's *Systematic Theology* as the largest up to that time, see Gutjahr, *Charles Hodge*, 349.

67. Charles Hodge, *Systematic Theology*, 3 vols. (New York: Scribner's, 1871–73), 1:173, 302–3 (on Schleiermacher); 1:582, 584, 586–87, 607–9. On Hodge's understanding of Schleiermacher as a pantheist, see B. A. Gerrish, "Charles Hodge and the Europeans," in *Charles Hodge Revisited: A Critical Appraisal of His Life and Work*, ed. John W. Stewart and James H. Moorhead (Grand Rapids, Mich.: Eerdmans, 2002), 129–58, esp. 149, 156–57.

68. John Calvin, *Institutes of the Christian Religion* [1559 edition], 2 vols., ed. John T. McNeill and trans. Ford Lewis Battles (Philadelphia: Westminster Press, 1960), 199 (I.16.2), 204 (I.16.5). On the sparrow and hairs passage (Matthew 10:29–30), see the discussion in the previous chapter.

69. Walter H. Conser, Jr., *God and the Natural World: Religion and Science in Antebellum America* (Columbia: University of South Carolina Press, 1993), 72.

70. Hodge, *Systematic Theology*, 1:10, 11, 15.

71. Turner, *Without God, Without Creed*, 226.

72. "Spiritual barbarism" from Henry Ward Beecher, "Theological Statement of Belief," in *Henry Ward Beecher: A Sketch of His Career*, ed. Lyman Abbott (New York, 1883), 482; "so gross and so undiscriminating" quoted in Peter J. Thuesen, *Predestination: The American Career of a Contentious Doctrine* (New York: Oxford University Press, 2009), 183. Harriet Beecher Stowe was also well-known for her critiques of Calvinism. In her novel *The Minister's Wooing* (1859), Mrs. Marvyn compares the predestinarian system of New England Calvinism to the inexorable and unforgiving laws of Nature: "Storms, earthquakes, volcanoes, sickness, death, go on without regarding us. Everywhere I see the most hopeless, unrelieved suffering,—and for aught I see, it may be eternal." Harriet Beecher Stowe, *The Minister's Wooing*, ed. Susan K. Harris (New York: Penguin Books, 1999), 206–7.

73. Marie Caskey, *Chariot of Fire: Religion and the Beecher Family* (New Haven, Conn.: Yale University Press, 1978), 229. On Beecher's emphasis on experience, see also Gary Dorrien, *The Making of American Liberal Theology: Imagining Progressive Religion, 1805–1900* (Louisville, Ky.: Westminster John Knox Press, 2001), 185. On Beecher's intellectual milieu, see William R. Hutchison, *The Modernist Impulse in American Protestantism* (Durham, N.C.: Duke University Press, 1992), 76–110.

74. Beecher, "Theological Statement of Belief," 494.

75. Henry Ward Beecher, "How to Learn about God" (March 17, 1872), in *The Sermons of Henry Ward Beecher, in Plymouth Church, Brooklyn*, 8th ser., ed. T. J. Ellinwood (New York, 1873), 64; Beecher, "Theological Statement of Belief," 497–98. On the prevalence of the notion that God uses natural law (his natural government) to influence human behavior (his moral government), see Cashdollar, *Transformation of Theology*, 347–48.

76. Henry Ward Beecher, "Divine Influence on the Human Soul" (November 29, 1868), in *The Sermons of Henry Ward Beecher, in Plymouth Church, Brooklyn*, first ser., ed. T. J. Ellinwood (New York, 1873), 182–83.

77. On Beecher's friendship with Grinnell, see Josiah Bushnell Grinnell, *Men and Events of Forty Years: Autobiographical Reminiscences of an Active Career from 1850 to 1890* (Boston, 1891), 227–35.

78. Joseph Frazier Wall, *Grinnell College in the Nineteenth Century: From Salvation to Service* (Ames: Iowa State University Press, 1997), xiii, 182.

79. Park quoted in Wall, *Grinnell College*, 183.

80. Edward Barstow, "The Bells of Grinnell," in S. H. Herrick, "The Grinnell Cyclone of June 17, 1882," *Annals of Iowa* 3 (1897): 81–96, quoted on 95. Details of the tornado come from Herrick (including "sulphurous fires of Tartarus," 85–86); Wall, *Grinnell College*, 182–86; and John Scholte Nollen, *Grinnell College* (Iowa City: State Historical Society of Iowa, 1953), 78–81. The number of fatalities appears variously as 39 (Herrick, 89), 38 (Wall, 185), and 32 (Nollen, 79).

81. Grinnell (quoting a proverb from Laurence Sterne's *A Sentimental Journey through France and Italy*), in Grinnell, *Men and Events*, 354. Details about Grinnell's commencement and baccalaureate from Wall, *Grinnell College*, 188–89.

82. Grinnell quoted in Wall, *Grinnell College*, 191. On Grinnell's appearances in Chicago and New York, see Grinnell, *Men and Events*, 361–62; and Wall, *Grinnell College*, 189.

83. See Paul A. Carter, *The Spiritual Crisis of the Gilded Age* (DeKalb: Northern Illinois University Press, 1971), 157–75.

84. Henry Ward Beecher, "Conceptions of God" (December 17, 1882), in *Plymouth Pulpit* 5, no. 12 (December 27, 1882): 248, 250–52; Henry Ward Beecher, "God in Christ" (December 24, 1882), in *Plymouth Pulpit* 5, no. 13 (January 3, 1883): 263–64.

85. "In Ruins! St. Cloud and Sauk Rapids Swept by a Tornado," *Minneapolis Tribune*, April 15, 1886; "Death! Scenes among the Ruins of St. Cloud and Sauk Rapids," *Minneapolis Tribune*, April 16, 1886.

86. "Tornado Lessons," *Minneapolis Tribune*, April 19, 1886. On Simmons's career, see Thomas E. Graham, "Henry Martyn Simmons," in *American National Biography* (New York: Oxford University Press, 2000–), http://www.anb.org.

87. Mark Svenvold, *Big Weather: Chasing Tornadoes in the Heart of America* (New York: Henry Holt, 2005), 40. On Finley's career, see the two-part article by Joseph G. Galway, "J. P. Finley: The First Severe Storms Forecaster," *Bulletin of the American Meteorological Society* 66 (1985): 1389–95, 1506–10. See also Sandlin, *Storm Kings*, 121–79.

88. Finley, *Tornadoes*, 7–9, 19, 35, 68–69.

89. William A. Eddy, "Progress in Tornado-Prediction," *Popular Science Monthly* 28 (January 1886): 314. On Eddy, see Marlene Bradford, *Scanning the Skies: A History of Tornado Forecasting* (Norman: University of Oklahoma Press, 2001), 42.

90. John P. Finley, *Tornadoes, What They Are, and How to Escape Them* (Washington, D.C.: J. H. Soulé, 1888), 30–31, 65.

91. *Annual Report of the Chief Signal Officer of the Army to the Secretary of War for the Year 1885* (Washington, D.C.: Government Printing Office, 1885), 52; Bradford, *Scanning the Skies*, 42–44; Sandlin, *Storm Kings*, 157–58, 171. See also F. C. Bates, "Severe Local Storm Forecasts and Warnings to the General Public," *Bulletin of the American Meteorological Society* 43 (1962): 288–91.

92. *Annual Report of the Chief Signal Officer of the Army to the Secretary of War for the Year 1887* (Washington, D.C.: Government Printing Office, 1887), 21–22.

93. Finley, *Tornadoes* (1888), 68. On Finley's later career, see Galway, "J. P. Finley," 1509.

94. "Prospect for Litigation," *Courier-Journal* (Louisville, Ky.), March 28, 1890. The estimated death toll of 76 in Louisville is from Thomas P. Grazulis, *Significant Tornadoes, 1680–1991* (St. Johnsbury, Vt.: Environmental Films, 1993), 651; cf. Grazulis, *Tornado*, 228.

95. On the deaths at Falls City Hall, "Hundreds of Lives Lost; Awful Work of the Southwestern Tornadoes," *New York Times*, March 29, 1890; "Rev. Barnwell's Death: Awful End of the Rector of

St. John's Church," *Courier-Journal*, March 28, 1890. For a more recent overview of the disaster, see Keven McQueen, *The Great Louisville Tornado of 1890* (Charleston, S.C.: History Press, 2010).

96. On the 1860 outbreak, see Grazulis, *Significant Tornadoes*, 566–68. On the 1884 event, later dubbed the "Enigma Outbreak" because of the uncertain death tolls in rural areas, see ibid., 624, and Kelly Kazek, *A History of Alabama's Deadliest Tornadoes: Disaster in Dixie* (Charleston, S.C.: History Press, 2010), 22.

97. Technically, according to the 1890 Census, St. Louis was still fifth largest, after New York, Chicago, Philadelphia, and Brooklyn, but after 1898 Brooklyn was absorbed by New York.

98. Julian Curzon [pseud.], ed., *The Great Cyclone at St. Louis and East St. Louis, May 27, 1896* (1896; reprint, Carbondale: Southern Illinois University Press, 1997), 18, 31.

99. Details from Mary K. Dains, "The St. Louis Tornado of 1896," *Missouri Historical Review* 66 (1972): 431–45; Rod Beemer, *The Deadliest Woman in the West: Mother Nature on the Prairies and the Plains, 1800–1900* (Caldwell, Idaho: Caxton Press, 2006), 94; Curzon, *Great Cyclone*, 57; Grazulis, *Significant Tornadoes*, 676–77.

100. "Sliced like a turbine" from Tim O'Neil, "The Great Cyclone of 1896," *St. Louis Post-Dispatch*, May 29, 2011.

101. "The Tornado," *Nature: A Weekly Illustrated Journal of Science* 54 (June 4, 1896): 105.

102. Details from Dains, "St. Louis Tornado," 437; O'Neil, "Great Cyclone"; Curzon, *Great Cyclone*, 117; and "History of the Blow," *New York Times*, May 29, 1896.

103. Death toll and injury estimates from Grazulis, *Tornado*, 229; and Grazulis, *Significant Tornadoes*, 676.

104. Curzon, *Great Cyclone*, 18, 128, 134, 205–6, 213.

105. On the destroyed churches, see Curzon, *Great Cyclone*, 166, 277; "Buildings Wrecked," *New York Times*, May 30, 1896; and "Churches in Ruins," *Marion County Herald* (Palmyra, Mo.), June 4, 1896. On the service at East St. Louis, "Scene at St. Patrick's," *St. Louis Post-Dispatch*, June 1, 1896.

106. Ted Steinberg, *Acts of God: The Unnatural History of Natural Disaster in America*, 2nd ed. (New York: Oxford University Press, 2000), 221n61. On the influx of tourists, see also Curzon, *Great Cyclone*, 259; "Crowds of Sightseers," *St. Louis Post-Dispatch*, May 30, 1896; "Throngs of Visitors," *St. Louis Post-Dispatch*, June 3, 1896.

107. On the role of changing technology, see Tim O'Neil, foreword to Curzon, *Great Cyclone*, xv, xxi; *Harper's Weekly* cover story on June 13, 1896. The three instant books were Curzon, *Great Cyclone*; *The Great Tornado at St. Louis, May 27th, 1896* (St. Louis: Graf Engraving, 1896); and *Der grosse Tornado, 27 Mai 1896: 80 Photographien von den durch den Sturm verursachten Ruinen* (St. Louis: Westliche Post, Graf Engraving, 1896). Advertisement for Kodaks in *St. Louis Post-Dispatch*, May 28, 1896.

108. "Bright Side of the Disaster," *St. Louis Post-Dispatch*, June 3, 1896; "One Week since the Big Storm," *St. Louis Post-Dispatch*, June 4, 1896; George Grantham Bain, "St. Louis—The Convention City," *Harper's Weekly*, June 20, 1896, p. 610.

109. "The Passing Show," *St. Louis Post-Dispatch*, May 31, 1896.

110. The philosopher Charles Taylor calls this "fragilization," or the mutual weakening of religious perspectives amid a genuine pluralism of religious options. See Charles Taylor, *A Secular Age* (Cambridge, Mass.: Belknap Press, Harvard University Press, 2007), 303–4, 437.

111. "Moral of St. Louis' Woe," *Chicago Daily Tribune*, June 1, 1896; H. W. Thomas, "Our Passing Years," in *Life and Sermons of Dr. H. W. Thomas*, ed. Austin Bierbower (Chicago: Smith

and Fobes, 1880), 241. On Thomas's career, see "Death Takes Dr. H. W. Thomas," *Chicago Daily Tribune*, August 14, 1909.

112. All quoted in "Moral of St. Louis' Woe," *Chicago Daily Tribune*.

113. "God's Hand in Calamities," *Christian Observer* 84, no. 24 (June 10, 1896): 2.

114. "Church News & Comment," *Lutheran Witness* 15, no. 1 (June 7, 1896): 5. The historic one-year lectionary, then common to Catholics, Lutherans, and Anglicans, can be found in, e.g., *Book of Worship, Published by the General Synod of the Evangelical Lutheran Church in the United States*, rev. ed. (Philadelphia: Lutheran Publication Society, 1870), xxxiv.

115. Marquis and Hicks quoted in "Did the Devil Send a Tornado?" *St. Louis Post-Dispatch*, November 9, 1896. On Marquis's connection to Billy Sunday, see Lyle W. Dorsett, *Billy Sunday and the Redemption of Urban America* (Grand Rapids, Mich.: Eerdmans, 1991), 38. Hicks's prediction appears in Irl R. Hicks, *Almanac*, in his *Quarterly Echoes* 2, no. 2 (1895; reprint, St. Louis: Word and Works, 1897), 26–27; see his biography in the same reprint, 161–64. On Hicks as a household name, see "Hicks' Great Works," *Great Bend (Kans.) Tribune*, January 17, 1896. Hicks is also mentioned in Dains, "St. Louis Tornado," and in Curzon, *Great Cyclone*, 56, 61–63.

116. Tipple quoted in "Tornadoes for a Text," *Kansas City Journal*, June 1, 1896; W. C. Miller in "Sermons on the Storm," *Daily Review* (Decatur, Ill.), June 2, 1896. On the Johnstown Flood and human negligence, see David McCullough, *The Johnstown Flood* (New York: Simon & Schuster, 1968).

117. "The Horror at St. Louis," *Philadelphia Inquirer*, May 29, 1896.

118. "Blasted by Winds: Rev. Dr. Talmage Points a Moral in the Cyclone," *Burlington (Vt.) Weekly Free Press*, June 11, 1896; "The Tornado: Affords the Rev. Dr. Talmage Thoughts for a Sermon," *Courier-Journal* (Louisville, Ky.), June 8, 1896; and in other newspapers. On the east wind as a common biblical image, see Steve A. Wiggins, *Weathering the Psalms: A Meteorotheological Survey* (Eugene, Ore.: Cascade Books, 2014), 67–68.

119. "To Blow Up Tornadoes: Professor Hazen's Scheme for Destroying Funnel Clouds," *Times* (Philadelphia), June 28, 1896; W. T. Foster, "That Rebuke to Prof. Hazen," *Pittsburgh Daily Post*, Sept. 6, 1896; Sandlin, *Storm Kings*, 185–86.

CHAPTER 4

1. "Awful Calamity to Befall Pine Bluff Says a Crazy Negro Woman," *Pine Bluff (Ark.) Daily Graphic*, May 18, 1903.

2. "Terror Reigns in Pine Bluff, Ark., Where a Negress Has Predicted an Awful Cyclone," *Cincinnati Enquirer*, May 27, 1903; "Negroes at Pine Bluff in a Panic," *Pittsburgh Daily Post*, May 22, 1903; "Prophecy Empties a Town of Negroes," *New York Times*, May 29, 1903. Other coverage included "Negroes Scared by a Tornado Prediction," *Reading (Pa.) Times*, May 23, 1903; "Prophecy Brings Frenzied Flight," *Santa Cruz (Calif.) Sentinel*, May 24, 1903; "Negroes Quitting Pine Bluff," *Daily Review* (Decatur, Ill.), May 27, 1903; "Woman Depopulates an Arkansas Town," *Saint Paul (Minn.) Globe*, May 29, 1903; "Exodus from Pine Bluff," *Indianapolis Journal*, May 29, 1903.

3. "Ellen Burnett the Pine Bluff 'Prohetess' [sic] in Pulaski Jail," *Arkansas Democrat*, May 29, 1903. Her affiliation with the Sanctified Church is noted in Robert Moody, "The Lord Selected Me," *Southern Exposure* 7, no. 4 (1979): 4.

4. Cheryl Townsend Gilkes, *If It Wasn't for the Women: Black Women's Experience and Womanist Culture in Church and Community* (Maryknoll, N.Y.: Orbis Books, 2001), 81–82.

5. "Ellen Burnett . . . in Pulaski Jail"; with an identical transcript of her narrative in "No Evidences Yet of Ellen Burnett's Cyclone Have Put in an Appearance," *Pine Bluff Daily Graphic*, May 29, 1903. The vision of the scale, reminiscent of the writing on the wall of Daniel 5:27, is an image that also famously appears in the autobiography of Richard Allen, the founder of the African Methodist Episcopal Church. See *The Life, Experience, and Gospel Labours of the Rt. Rev. Richard Allen* (Philadelphia, 1833), 7.

6. Elizabeth L. Wheeler, "Isaac Fisher: The Frustrations of a Negro Educator at Branch Normal College, 1902–1911," *Arkansas Historical Quarterly* 41, no. 1 (1982): 3–50; 17n50 on DuBois.

7. Isaac Fisher's letter printed in "Alarm Increasing on Part of Negroes over Prophecy of Ellen Burnett," *Pine Bluff Daily Graphic*, May 20, 1903.

8. Fisher's second statement printed in "Ellen Burnett in Jail," *Pine Bluff Daily Graphic*, May 21, 1903.

9. "Fulfillment of Prophecies," *Pine Bluff Daily Graphic*, May 20, 1903.

10. "Exodus On with a Rush," *Pine Bluff Daily Graphic*, May 27, 1903; "The Exodus about Over," *Pine Bluff Daily Graphic*, May 28, 1903; "Ellen Burnett . . . in Pulaski Jail"; "No Evidences Yet."

11. "Ellen Is Still Prophesying," *Daily Arkansas Gazette*, May 29, 1903; J. Harvie Hudson, "The Ellen Burnett Prophesy," *Jefferson County Historical Quarterly* 4 no. 2 (1973): 38.

12. "Pine Bluff Still on Map," *Pine Bluff Daily Graphic*, May 31, 1903; "Prophetess Goes to Pine Bluff," *Daily Arkansas Gazette*, May 30, 1903.

13. Untitled editorial comment, *Pine Bluff Daily Graphic*, May 31, 1903; "Not a Negro Is to Be Seen in Pine Bluff," *Arkansas Democrat*, May 30, 1903; W. P. Whaley, "An Extreme Case of Negro Superstition," *Current Literature* 35, no. 2 (August 1903): 227–28.

14. Robert Orsi makes a similar point about modern disdain for supernaturalism or the idea that god(s) are really present: "Practices of presence became—and to a great extent they remain—the province of people of color, women, the poor and marginalized, children and childish or child-like adults, the eccentric, the romantic, the insane, and those unhinged by life experiences that overwhelm their reason." See Robert A. Orsi, *History and Presence* (Cambridge, Mass.: Belknap Press, Harvard University Press, 2016), 41–42.

15. "Pine Bluff Still on Map."

16. Romans 11:33, which in the King James Version partly echoes Job 9:10.

17. Erik Larson, *Isaac's Storm* (New York: Vintage Books, 1999), 80.

18. One trade magazine was pleased to credit the accuracy of DeVoe's prediction: see *National Druggist* 30, no. 11 (November 1900): 405. Cf. "DeVoe Predicted the Storm," *New York Times*, September 13, 1900; and Larson, *Isaac's Storm*, 79.

19. Larson, *Isaac's Storm*, 167–68. See also the more recent account by Al Roker, *The Storm of the Century: Tragedy, Heroism, Survival, and the Epic Story of America's Deadliest Natural Disaster: The Great Gulf Hurricane of 1900* (New York: Morrow, 2015).

20. Larson, *Isaac's Storm*, 195–97, 204–5, 210, 255–57.

21. Accounts by Austin and Monagan in *Through a Night of Horrors: Voices from the 1900 Galveston Storm*, ed. Casey Edward Greene and Shelly Henley Kelly (College Station: Texas A&M University Press, 2000), 69–70, 103–4. On the burning of bodies, see also Larson, *Isaac's Storm*, 240–41.

22. "Satan Was Behind Galveston Flood," *Philadelphia Inquirer*, September 24, 1900; "Thinks the Devil Caused the Galveston Horror," *Atlanta Constitution*, September 17, 1900.

23. "Lessons Taught by Galveston Flood," *Democrat and Chronicle* (Rochester, N.Y.), September 17, 1900; "Galveston Their Theme," *New-York Tribune*, September 17, 1900.

24. "Talks on 'God at Galveston,'" *Daily Inter Ocean* (Chicago), September 17, 1900. The Canadian-born Youker was an outspoken social activist who frequently criticized the churches' alliance with the wealthy. See Heath W. Carter, *Union Made: Working People and the Rise of Social Christianity in Chicago* (New York: Oxford University Press, 2015), 162.

25. Sociologist Tony Walter has noted how faith in technology is its own kind of theodicy. See Tony Walter, "Disaster, Modernity, and the Media," in *Death and Religion in a Changing World*, ed. Kathleen Garces-Foley (New York: Routledge, 2006), 273–74.

26. "Miss Safford's Sunday Sermon: The Goodness of God and Great Natural Calamities," *Des Moines (Iowa) Register*, November 7, 1900.

27. Thomas P. Grazulis, *The Tornado: America's Ultimate Windstorm* (Norman: University of Oklahoma Press, 2001), 86.

28. "Nearly 100 Killed by a Tornado at Gainesville, Ga., Monday Afternoon," *Pine Bluff Daily Graphic*, June 2, 1903. Other details from Thomas P. Grazulis, *Significant Tornadoes, 1680–1991* (St. Johnsbury, Vt.: Environmental Films, 1993), 700.

29. "Nurses Badly Needed, Says Dr. Floyd M'Rae," *Atlanta Constitution*, June 3, 1903; "Commissioner Hawkins Figures 111 Are Dead," *Atlanta Constitution*, June 3, 1903.

30. "The Helping Heart and Hand," *Atlanta Constitution*, June 3, 1903.

31. "Moore Memorial," *Atlanta Constitution*, June 8, 1903.

32. Grazulis, *Tornado*, 230; graphs of annual fatalities, 1900–2011, in Kevin M. Simmons and Daniel Sutter, *Deadly Season: Analysis of the 2011 Tornado Outbreaks* (Boston: American Meteorological Society, 2012), 7, and in Kevin M. Simmons and Daniel Sutter, *Economic and Societal Impacts of Tornadoes* (Boston: American Meteorological Society, 2011), 47; and list by year in Harold Brooks, "U.S. Annual Tornado Death Tolls, 1875–Present," *NSSL News*, March 1, 2009, https://blog.nssl.noaa.gov/nsslnews/2009/03/us-annual-tornado-death-tolls-1875-present/.

33. Figures of dead and injured from Grazulis, *Tornado*, 230; and Grazulis, *Significant Tornadoes*, 713.

34. "Cyclone Kills 308, Injures 1091, in Southern States," *St. Louis Post-Dispatch*, April 25, 1908; "Over Two Hundred Killed," *Vicksburg (Miss.) Herald*, April 25, 1908.

35. "Storm Sweeps Amite," *Times-Democrat* (New Orleans), April 25, 1908. The version involving the Angelus bell appears in (among others) "Five Hundred Dead," *Omaha (Neb.) Daily Bee*, April 26, 1908; and "Ghoulish Hordes Raid the Stricken Districts," *Cincinnati Enquirer*, April 26, 1908. Biographical details from Subiaco Abbey, Arkansas, https://countrymonks.org/necrology, s.v. "Father Felix Rumpf"; and "Father Rumpf's Death," *Times-Democrat*, April 25, 1908.

36. "Presentment or Dream?" *Catholic Advance* (Wichita, Kans.), August 22, 1908; "A Prophetic Dream," *Assumption Pioneer* (Napoleonville, La.), May 23, 1908.

37. "Why Sermons So Seldom Count," *Times-Democrat*, April 26, 1908.

38. Tony Walter argues that in contemporary society, the media generally have taken over from the clergy the task of interpreting the meaning of death and suffering. The one exception is when "the tragedy is so huge or so evil that even television newscasters cannot cope and remained

composed, then churches and church leaders may return to fill the vacuum." Walter, "Disaster, Modernity, and the Media," 279.

39. "Tornado Rips Broad Road through Thickly Built Western Part of Omaha," *Omaha Daily Bee*, March 24, 1913; "Great Section of Omaha Is Devastated by the Most Destructive Storm in the State's History," *Omaha Daily Bee*, March 25, 1913. Fatality figures from Grazulis, *Significant Tornadoes*, 737–38. For an overview of the storm's effects, see Travis Sing, *Omaha's Easter Tornado of 1913* (Charleston, S.C.: Arcadia, 2003).

40. Among the Jewish residents were Ida and Samuel Lerner, whose second child, just one year old at the time, went on to become the famous writer and feminist Tillie Olsen. For the Lerners, as for most Omahans, the disaster meant that time was now reckoned "before the tornado" or after it. See Panthea Reid, *Tillie Olsen: One Woman, Many Riddles* (New Brunswick, N.J.: Rutgers University Press, 2010), 14–15.

41. "Disasters God's Warnings," *Nebraska State Journal* (Lincoln), March 27, 1913; "Storm a Visitation of God's Anger," *Lincoln (Neb.) Star*, March 27, 1913. On Scoville, see C. Roy Stauffer, "Evangelism, Evangelists: Twentieth Century, Christian Church (Disciples of Christ)," in *The Encyclopedia of the Stone-Campbell Movement*, ed. Douglas A. Foster, Paul M. Blowers, Anthony L. Dunnavant, and D. Newell Williams (Grand Rapids, Mich.: Eerdmans, 2004), 318; and H. H. Peters, *Charles Reign Scoville: The Man and His Message* (St. Louis: Bethany Press, 1924).

42. "Immense Crowd Attend Revival," *Daily Ardmoreite* (Ardmore, Okla.), March 28, 1913. On Norris, see David Edwin Harrell, Jr., "American Revivalism from Graham to Robertson," in *Modern Christian Revivals*, ed. Edith L. Blumhofer and Randall Balmer (Urbana: University of Illinois Press, 1993), 198–99; and Barry Hankins, *God's Rascal: J. Frank Norris and the Beginnings of Southern Fundamentalism* (Lexington: University Press of Kentucky, 1996). On the Dayton disaster, see Allan W. Eckert, *A Time of Terror: The Great Dayton Flood* (Boston: Little, Brown, 1965).

43. "Man's Limitations Lesson of Storms," *Des Moines Register*, March 31, 1913.

44. Ibid. (Gage quotation); "A Crushing Blow" (editorial), *Omaha Daily Bee*, March 25, 1913; "Jewish Relief Committee of Forty Will Assist," *Omaha Daily Bee*, March 27, 1913.

45. "Tornado Is Not the Wrath of God, Says Dr. Mackay in Pulpit," *Omaha Daily Bee*, April 8, 1913.

46. Anthony M. Easterling, "Was the Tornado God-Sent?" *Omaha Daily Bee*, April 10, 1913; anonymous, "Protest against Nonsense," *Omaha Daily Bee*, April 12, 1913; Adolph Hult, "Afraid to Think?" *Omaha Daily Bee*, April 14, 1913.

47. Jonathan H. Ebel, *Faith in the Fight: Religion and the American Soldier in the Great War* (Princeton, N.J.: Princeton University Press, 2010), 68–69. That Otto's *Idea of the Holy* (1917) appeared amid the Great War undoubtedly accounted for some of its immediate popularity. On Otto's complex relationship to what the theologian and historian Adolf von Harnack, in reviewing Otto's book, called the "mood of the times," see Todd A. Gooch, *The Numinous and Modernity: An Interpretation of Rudolf Otto's Philosophy of Religion* (Berlin: Walter de Gruyter, 2000), 132–59.

48. Ranlett and Hall quoted in Ebel, *Faith in the Fight*, 70–71.

49. Total outbreak fatalities from May 25 to June 1, 1917, as recorded in Grazulis, *Significant Tornadoes*, 751–54; Mattoon figure, 752.

50. "Tornado Strikes City Today . . . Path Half Mile Wide Is Cut Through City," *Journal Gazette* (Mattoon, Ill.), May 26, 1917; "Death Toll Exacted by Storm of Saturday Has Reached 52 . . . 496 Dwellings Are Totally Destroyed," *Journal Gazette*, May 28, 1917.

51. "Sunday Services at City Churches," *Journal Gazette*, June 2, 1917; "Church and the Minsters Extend Their Welcome," *Journal Gazette*, June 2, 1917.

52. "Sermon Delivered by Rev. A. H. Kennedy," *Ogden (Utah) Standard*, May 28, 1917; Aubrey Parker, "God in the Wind" (letter to editor), *Ogden Standard*, May 31, 1917.

53. Estimates of the total fatalities vary widely, from 153 (Grazulis, *Significant Tornadoes*, 38), to 163 ("The Thirteen Tornadoes of March 28, 1920," *Monthly Weather Review* 48 [1920]: 191–202), to 380 (Steven L. Horstmeyer, *The Weather Almanac: A Reference Guide to Weather, Climate, and Related Issues in the United States and Its Key Cities*, 12th ed. [Hoboken, N.J.: Wiley, 2011], 202).

54. "Tornado Reaches Chicago," *New York Times*, March 29, 1920; "7 Die in Elgin; Girls Crushed in Church Ruin," and "The Dead," in *Chicago Tribune*, March 29, 1920; "Pulverized Houses Mark Path of Illinois Tornado," *New-York Tribune*, March 30, 1920.

55. Fatality figure from Grazulis, *Significant Tornadoes*, 769–70.

56. "Tells How Tornadoes Come," *New York Times*, March 30, 1920; "Government Gives Warning of Tornadoes," *Pittsburgh Daily Post*, April 22, 1920.

57. "A Favored Section" (editorial), *Asheville (N.C.) Citizen-Times*, May 29, 1917; "Tornadoes," *Wichita (Kans.) Daily Eagle*, March 29, 1920. Though the chances of dying in a tornado are notoriously difficult to generalize (due to geographic variation, climate change, etc.), two researchers in 2009 estimated the odds of being killed by a tornado were actually greater (1 in 60,000) than the odds of being struck (if not killed) by lightning (1 in 84,000). See Stefan Bechtel with Tim Samaras, *Tornado Hunter: Getting Inside the Most Violent Storms on Earth* (Washington, D.C.: National Geographic, 2009), 250.

58. Frederic J. Haskin, "How Tornadoes Are Caused," *Akron (Ohio) Evening Times*, May 2, 1920; appearing also as "Deadly Power and Terror of Tornado," *News Journal* (Wilmington, Del.), May 7, 1920.

59. Biographical details from "Dr. Frank Crane, Noted Writer, Dies," *New York Times*, November 7, 1928; "Dr. Frank Crane, Newspaper Writer, Dies in Europe," *Hartford (Conn.) Courant*, November 7, 1928; "Dr. Frank Crane Dies in France," *Delaware County Daily Times* (Chester, Pa.), November 10, 1928. Mencken quoted in Paul Emory Putz, "From the Pulpit to the Press: Frank Crane's Omaha, 1892–1896," *Nebraska History* 96 (2015): 147.

60. Frank Crane, "Why Tornadoes?" *Akron Evening Times*, April 27, 1920.

61. William Jennings Bryan, "The Stilling of the Storm," *Evening News* (Harrisburg, Pa.), October 18, 1924. On Bryan's overlap with Crane in Omaha, see Putz, "From the Pulpit to the Press," 140, 147.

62. On the cultural influence of *Inherit the Wind* (1960), see Edward J. Larson, *Summer for the Gods: The Scopes Trial and America's Continuing Debate over Science and Religion*, rev. ed. (New York: Basic Books, 2006), 239–46.

63. Death and injury figures from Grazulis, *Significant Tornadoes*, 796.

64. The phrase "Nature's nation" is from Perry Miller; see Introduction to this volume.

65. Historical accounts include Wallace Akin, *The Forgotten Storm: The Great Tri-State Tornado of 1925* (Guilford, Conn.: Lyons Press, Rowman and Littlefield, 2002); Peter S. Felknor, *The Tri-State Tornado: The Story of America's Greatest Tornado Disaster* (New York: iUniverse, 2004); Angela Mason, *Death Rides the Sky: The Story of the 1925 Tri-State Tornado* (Rockford, Ill.: Black Oak Media, 2012); and Geoff Partlow, *America's Deadliest Twister: The Tri-State Tornado of 1925* (Carbondale: Southern Illinois University Press, 2014). See also Bernard Mergen,

Weather Matters: An American Cultural History since 1900 (Lawrence: University Press of Kansas, 2008), 272–74.

66. Akin, *Forgotten Storm*, xii; Grazulis, *Significant Tornadoes*, 796; weather forecast from *Daily Independent* (Murphysboro, Ill.), March 17, 1925.

67. "Wind-Driven Wall of Water Swept Gorham Where 90 Were Killed," *St. Louis Post-Dispatch*, March 20, 1925.

68. Grazulis, *Tornado*, 231.

69. Akin, *Forgotten Storm*, 58–59, 61; "Rebuild Murphysboro . . . West and North End Devastated," *Daily Independent*, March 20, 1925.

70. Felknor, *Tri-State Tornado*, 29, 36–37.

71. "'Eye-Witness' Story of Destruction Wrought by Storm at Murphysboro," *St. Louis Post-Dispatch*, March 19, 1925; Akin, *Forgotten Storm*, 67; Mason, *Death Rides the Sky*, 96.

72. "Tornado Likened to Specter of Death, Swinging a Scythe," Associated Press, *Indianapolis News*, March 20, 1925.

73. "Death List," *Daily Independent*, March 19, 1925.

74. "Disaster Shocks Italians; Pope Orders Prayers and Government Sends Sympathy," *New York Times*, March 21, 1925. Partlow (*America's Deadliest Twister*, 108) points out that Pius XI would become known for the principle of subsidiarity (articulated in *Quadragesimo Anno*, 1931), that the best institution to respond to a particular social need is the one closest or most proximate to it. Communities or families are therefore better able to respond than states. Partlow notes that this "thesis blended well with [US president Calvin] Coolidge's laissez-faire approach to disaster relief."

75. "Storm Relief Barely Pauses for Funerals," *Daily Free Press* (Carbondale, Ill.), March 23, 1925; "Memorial Services Held in Midst of Wreckage for Murphysboro's Dead," *St. Louis Post-Dispatch*, March 23, 1925; "Ministers Bid Suffering Put God into Their Plan of Building Greater City," *Daily Independent*, March 23, 1925.

76. "Tornado Result of Hatred, Says Robert F. Hall," *Des Moines (Iowa) Tribune*, March 30, 1925. See also comment on Hall in Partlow, *America's Deadliest Twister*, 71–72. On Unity teachings, see Catherine L. Albanese, *A Republic of Mind and Spirit: A Cultural History of American Metaphysical Religion* (New Haven, Conn.: Yale University Press, 2007), 327–29; Gail Hartley, "New Thought and the Harmonial Family," in *America's Alternative Religions*, ed. Timothy Miller (Albany: State University of New York Press, 1995), 327–28; and Dell deChant, "Unity School of Christianity," in *Dictionary of Christianity in America*, ed. Daniel G. Reid, Robert D. Linder, Bruce L. Shelley, and Harry S. Stout (Downers Grove, Ill.: InterVarsity Press, 1990), 1204–5.

77. "Sees Lesson in Tornado," *New York Times*, March 23, 1925; "That Twister" (editorial), *Dayton (Ohio) Daily News*, March 20, 1925.

78. Untitled editorial in *Alexandria (Ind.) Times-Tribune*, March 23, 1925; "God Not a Monster" (editorial), *Alexandria Times-Tribune*, March 25, 1925.

79. Reinhold Niebuhr, *Does Civilization Need Religion? A Study in the Social Resources and Limitations of Religion in Modern Life* (New York: Macmillan, 1927), 9, 24–25, 52, 54. For a discussion of this book in relation to the larger trajectory of Niebuhr's work, see Ronald H. Stone, *Professor Reinhold Niebuhr: A Mentor to the Twentieth Century* (Louisville, Ky.: Westminster John Knox Press, 1992), 40–46.

80. Reinhold Niebuhr, *Beyond Tragedy: Essays on the Christian Interpretation of History* (New York: Scribner's, 1937), 96–97. Details on the Niebuhr family's history from Richard Wightman Fox, *Reinhold Niebuhr: A Biography* (New York: Pantheon Books, 1985), 5, 8.

81. "Does Prayer Change the Weather?" *Christian Century* 47 (September 10, 1930): 1084–86. See also the analysis of the forum in Rick Ostrander, *The Life of Prayer in a World of Science: Protestants, Prayer, and American Culture, 1870–1930* (New York: Oxford University Press, 2000), 166–67. On Niebuhr's relationship with the *Christian Century*, see Fox, *Reinhold Niebuhr*, 72–75; and Elesha J. Coffman, The Christian Century *and the Rise of the Protestant Mainline* (New York: Oxford University Press, 2013), 70–71.

82. Ostrander, *Life of Prayer*, 168–69.

83. Reinhold Niebuhr, "Optimism, Pessimism and Religious Faith—I" (1934), in *Reinhold Niebuhr: Major Works on Religion and Politics*, ed. Elisabeth Sifton (New York: Library of America, 2015), 710–13; Niebuhr, *Beyond Tragedy*, 97–98.

84. "Did God Send the Tornado?" *Enterprise-Journal* (McComb, Miss.), April 20, 1936; fatality figure from Grazulis, *Significant Tornadoes*, 38. On Elvis Presley and the Tupelo tornado, see Bobbie Ann Mason, *Elvis Presley* (New York: Penguin, 2003), 15; and Elaine Dundy, *Elvis and Gladys* (1985; reprint, Jackson: University Press of Mississippi, 2004), 71–72.

85. Hubbard Keavy, "Youngster Sees 'Wizard of Oz' and Reviews It," distributed by the Associated Press to numerous outlets, including *Hartford (Conn.) Courant*, August 20, 1939. Production details from Jay Scarfone and William Stillman, *The Wizardry of Oz: The Artistry and Magic of the 1939 M-G-M Classic* (New York: Applause Theatre and Cinema Books, 2004), 152.

86. Reinhold Niebuhr, *The Nature and Destiny of Man: A Christian Interpretation*, 2 vols. (1941; reprint, Louisville, Ky.: Westminster John Knox Press, 1996), 1:219. For a summary of this work, see Fox, *Reinhold Niebuhr*, 201–5; and Jeremy L. Sabella, *An American Conscience: The Reinhold Niebuhr Story* (Grand Rapids, Mich.: Eerdmans, 2017), 51–56. On the distinction between natural and moral evils, see Nancey Murphy, "Natural Science," in *The Oxford Handbook of Systematic Theology*, ed. John Webster, Kathryn Tanner, and Iain Torrance (Oxford: Oxford University Press, 2007), 550–51.

87. Reinhold Niebuhr, "An End to Illusions" (1940), quoted in Sabella, *An American Conscience*, 56.

88. Cotton Mather is silent on Matthew 5:45 in his *Biblia Americana*, ed. Reiner Smolinski et al., 10 vols. (Tübingen: Mohr Siebeck, 2010–); correspondence with Douglas A. Sweeney (editor of the forthcoming volume containing Matthew), April 17, 2018. Similarly, Jonathan Edwards ignores the verse in both his "Blank Bible" and his "Notes on Scripture"; see Stephen J. Stein, ed., *The Works of Jonathan Edwards*, Vol. 15, *Notes on Scripture* (New Haven, Conn.: Yale University Press, 1998); and Stephen J. Stein, ed., *The Works of Jonathan Edwards*, Vol. 24, *The "Blank Bible"* (New Haven, Conn.: Yale University Press, 2006).

89. Reinhold Niebuhr, "The Providence of God" (1952), in *The Essential Reinhold Niebuhr: Selected Essays and Addresses*, ed. Robert McAfee Brown (New Haven, Conn.: Yale University Press, 1986), 33–40.

90. *United States Nuclear Tests: July 1945 through September 1992* (Las Vegas: United States Department of Energy, Nevada Operations Office, 2000), 4–5.

91. "Wild Weather and Atom Bombs," *Christian Century* 70 (May 27, 1953): 620. On the meteorological anomalies that spring, see "Weather Is Queer, Records Prove It," *New York Times*, May 10, 1953; and on public fears of a connection to the atomic testing, "Science in

Review: Massachusetts Tornado Repeats a History of Destruction Caused by Warring Winds," *New York Times*, June 14, 1953. Death toll of Waco outbreak from Horstmeyer, *Weather Almanac*, 204.

92. Marlene Bradford, *Scanning the Skies: A History of Tornado Forecasting* (Norman: University of Oklahoma Press, 2001), 144; Laura McEnaney, *Civil Defense Begins at Home: Militarization Meets Everyday Life in the Fifties* (Princeton, N.J.: Princeton University Press, 2000), 51–52; Christopher Mele, "Tornado Sirens, an Old Technology, Still Play a Vital Role," *New York Times* (online), May 23, 2016.

93. Snowden D. Flora, *Tornadoes of the United States*, rev. ed. (Norman: University of Oklahoma Press, 1954), 3. On Flora's career, see "Scientific News and Notes of Academy Interest," *Transactions of the Kansas Academy of Science* 60, no. 3 (1957): 246. On the sound of a tornado, see the comment by Howard B. Bluestein, *Tornado Alley: Monster Storms of the Great Plains* (New York: Oxford University Press, 1999), 112.

94. Robert Henson, *Weather on the Air: A History of Broadcast Meteorology* (Boston: American Meteorological Society, 2010), 9–11, 164–70; Gary A. England, *Weathering the Storm: Tornadoes, Television, and Turmoil* (Norman: University of Oklahoma Press, 1996), 17.

95. The postwar "age of anxiety" also turned some theologians back toward the doctrine of original sin. See Andrew S. Finstuen, *Original Sin and Everyday Protestants: The Theology of Reinhold Niebuhr, Billy Graham, and Paul Tillich in an Age of Anxiety* (Chapel Hill: University of North Carolina Press, 2009).

96. Roger Hazelton, *God's Way with Man: Variations on the Theme of Providence* (New York: Abingdon Press, 1956), 5–6, 50–51, 67–68, 146–47; Søren Kierkegaard, *Repetition: An Essay in Experimental Psychology*, trans. Walter Lowrie (Princeton, N.J.: Princeton University Press, 1941), 112–13. On Hazelton's career, see "Roger Hazelton, 78, Was Theology Professor," *Boston Globe*, April 24, 1988.

97. "Atomic Deacon," *Time*, June 18, 1951, p. 91; "Atomic Physicist Is Ordained," *Life*, May 10, 1954, p. 43. Other biographical details from Pam Bonee, "William G. Pollard," *Tennessee Encyclopedia of History and Culture*, ed. Carroll Van West (Knoxville: University of Tennessee Press, 1998–2018), http://tennesseeencyclopedia.net.

98. William G. Pollard, *Chance and Providence: God's Action in a World Governed by Scientific Law* (New York: Scribner's, 1958), 17–19, 45, 47, 50, 52–53, 54–55.

99. Ibid., 73–74, 80–81, 83, 93–94, 97. For a helpful discussion of the importance of chance and randomness in quantum mechanics, see Karl W. Giberson, "Chance, Divine Action, and the Natural Order of Things," in *Abraham's Dice: Chance and Providence in the Monotheistic Traditions*, ed. Karl W. Giberson (New York: Oxford University Press, 2016), 8–11. For a critical assessment of Pollard in light of later attempts to reconcile God's action with modern science, see Nicholas Saunders, *Divine Action and Modern Science* (Cambridge: Cambridge University Press, 2002), 105–110.

100. Pollard, *Chance and Providence*, 74, 106–110; Oscar Handlin, *Chance or Destiny: Turning Points in American History* (Boston: Little, Brown, 1955), 192. Though Pollard spoke of chance and accident as an impenetrable barrier, he clearly believed they concealed a divine reality. In a later work, he noted that "the contingency of nature implies that which is transcendent to nature— namely, the existence and reality of supernature." William G. Pollard, *Physicist and Christian: A Dialogue between the Communities* (Greenwich, Conn.: Seabury Press, 1961), 110.

101. Rosemary Skinner Keller, *Georgia Harkness: For Such a Time as This* (Nashville: Abingdon Press, 1992), 215–16, 323–24. Women had previously held positions in Christian education but not

in traditional theological disciplines such as systematic or applied theology. For a helpful overview of Harkness's theology, see also Gary Dorrien, *The Making of American Liberal Theology: Idealism, Realism, and Modernity, 1900–1950* (Louisville, Ky.: Westminster John Knox Press, 2003), 390–414.

102. Georgia Harkness, *The Providence of God* (New York: Abingdon Press, 1960), 88–90, 151–52. On Harkness's distinction between God's power and purpose, see Charles M. Wood, *The Question of Providence* (Louisville, Ky.: Westminster John Knox Press, 2008), 103–4.

103. Georgia Harkness, *The Recovery of Ideals* (New York: Scribner's, 1937), 176–81. This section is excerpted in the fine collection by Rebekah Miles, ed., *Georgia Harkness: The Remaking of a Liberal Theologian* (Louisville, Ky.: Westminster John Knox Press, 2010), 94–98.

104. Autobiographical details from Langdon Gilkey, *On Niebuhr: A Theological Study* (Chicago: University of Chicago Press, 2001), 10–11. On Gilkey's intellectual trajectory, especially in relation to the subfield of science and religion, see Ted Peters, "Langdon Gilkey: In Memoriam," *Dialog* 44, no. 1 (2005): 69–80.

105. Langdon B. Gilkey, "The Concept of Providence in Contemporary Theology," *Journal of Religion* 43, no. 3 (1963): 177–78.

106. On Arminianism, see Peter J. Thuesen, *Predestination: The American Career of a Contentious Doctrine* (New York: Oxford University Press, 2009), 37–39, 220.

107. Gilkey, "Concept of Providence," 179–81, 185–86. On Gilkey's call in relation to recent work on providence, see Charles M. Wood, "Providence," in Webster, Tanner, and Torrance, *Oxford Handbook of Systematic Theology*, 90–102, esp. 93–94.

108. Langdon Gilkey, *Naming the Whirlwind: The Renewal of God-Language* (Indianapolis: Bobbs-Merrill, 1969); Langdon Gilkey, *Reaping the Whirlwind: A Christian Interpretation of History* (New York: Seabury Press, 1976). The titles of these books are based, respectively, on Job 40:6–7 and Hosea 8:7. Interestingly, the use of the whirlwind image originated not with Gilkey but with a member of the Bobbs-Merrill editorial staff, who suggested it. See Jeff B. Pool, "Editor's Preface," in Langdon Gilkey, *Through the Tempest: Theological Voyages in a Pluralistic Culture*, ed. Jeff B. Pool (1991; reprint, Eugene, Ore.: Wipf and Stock, 2005), xiiin4.

109. Peters, "Langdon Gilkey," 75. On panentheism (which is different from pantheism, or the identification of God with the world), see Donald K. McKim, *The Westminster Dictionary of Theological Terms*, 2nd ed. (Louisville, Ky.: Westminster John Knox Press, 2014), 225.

110. Harkness also noted a debt to Whitehead; see *Recovery of Ideals*, 155, 167, 169n2.

111. C. T. McIntire, review of *Reaping the Whirlwind*, by Langdon Gilkey, *Catholic Historical Review* 68, no. 1 (1982): 55; Avery Dulles, review of *Reaping the Whirlwind*, by Langdon Gilkey, *Wilson Quarterly* 2, no. 1 (1978): 155.

112. The death toll is variously put at 256 (Grazulis, *Significant Tornadoes*, 38), 260 (Simmons and Sutter, *Economic and Societal Impacts of Tornadoes*, 61), and 271 ("April 11, 1965, Palm Sunday Tornado Outbreak," National Weather Service, Indianapolis Office, https://www.weather.gov/ind/palmsuntor).

113. Tetsuya T. Fujita, Dorothy L. Bradbury, and C. F. Van Thullenar, "Palm Sunday Tornadoes of April 11, 1965," *Monthly Weather Review* 98, no. 1 (1970): 31, 41, 44, 46, 68; Tetsuya Theodore Fujita, "Memoirs of an Effort to Unlock the Mystery of Severe Storms," Wind Research Laboratory, University of Chicago, 1992, p.27; Grazulis, *Tornado*, 34, 91.

114. Grazulis, *Significant Tornadoes*, 1066. Figures on numbers of tornadoes from "April 11th 1965 Palm Sunday Tornado Outbreak," National Weather Service, Northern Indiana Office, https://www.weather.gov/iwx/1965_palmsunday_50.

115. Boyd Gill and Don Wallis, Jr., "Russiaville Hit by Tornadoes," *Kokomo (Ind.) Morning Times*, June 23, 1965.

116. Fujita, Bradbury, and Thullenar, "Palm Sunday Tornadoes," 38, 43–44; and "April 11th 1965 Palm Sunday Tornado Outbreak" (NWS, Northern Indiana).

117. Martin Biemer, "County Storm Dead 52; Property Damage Will Reach $100 Milliion; Indiana Death Total at 110," *Elkhart (Ind.) Truth*, April 12, 1965; "Doctor Saw 'Doll' in Air," *Elkhart Truth*, April 13, 1965.

118. On Johnson, see David Wagler, *The Mighty Whirlwind* (Aylmer, Ont.: Pathway, 1966), 223; "Oh, Yes, It Could Have Been Worse" (editorial), in "Tornado 1965," *Kokomo Morning Times* special edition, April 19, 1965; Phillip Swihart, "An Old, Old Story" (letter to the editor), *Kokomo Morning Times*, May 11, 1965; Mrs. Ted Corbett, "No Repentance Today" (letter to the editor), *Kokomo Morning Times*, May 19, 1965; "The Passion, Was It Recreated" (editorial), *Newport (R.I.) Daily News*, April 16, 1965; "The Passion; Recreated?" *News* (Frederick, Md.), April 16, 1965; Glen Banner, " 'Spirit of Cross Indestructible,' Congregation in Russiaville Told during Easter Morning Services," *Kokomo (Ind.) Tribune*, April 19, 1965.

119. Wagler, *Mighty Whirlwind*, 252–53. On Wagler's publishing company and sales of his book, see John A. Hostetler, *Amish Society*, 4th ed. (Baltimore: Johns Hopkins University Press, 1993), 378; and Donald B. Kraybill, *Concise Encyclopedia of Amish, Brethren, Hutterites, and Mennonites* (Baltimore: Johns Hopkins University Press, 2010), 162–63.

120. Brenda Ford Elliott, remarks at fiftieth anniversary commemoration of the Palm Sunday Tornadoes, Dunlap, Indiana, April 11, 2015 (author's notes); Brenda Ford Elliott, "Tears Still Fall Every Spring," *Elkhart Truth*, March 29, 2015.

121. Roger Schneider, "Remembering Sunnyside Addition: The Second Blow," *Goshen (Ind.) News*, April 10, 2015; Julie Crothers, "50 Years Later: Family Members Share Stories on Anniversary of Tornadoes," *Goshen News*, April 11, 2015.

122. On Gettysburg and similar sacred places, see Edward Tabor Linenthal, *Sacred Ground: Americans and Their Battlefields*, 2nd ed. (Urbana: University of Illinois Press, 1993).

123. Robert Wuthnow, *The God Problem: Expressing Faith and Being Reasonable* (Berkeley: University of California Press, 2012), 124–25. The 17 percent figure is from Paul Froese and Christopher Bader, *America's Four Gods: What We Say about God—and What That Says about Us* (New York: Oxford University Press, 2010), 128, 167, 191–93.

124. "Town Pauses for Easter, Then Resumes Rebuilding," Associated Press, *Elkhart Truth*, April 19, 1965.

CHAPTER 5

1. Day 4–8 Severe Weather Outlook, issued May 15, 2013, 4:00 a.m. CDT, archived at https://www.spc.noaa.gov/products/outlook/; Dan Barry and John Schwartz, "Racing Both Clock and Storm: A Way of Life in Tornado Alley," *New York Times*, May 24, 2013. Day 2 Convective Outlook, issued May 19, 2013, 1:05 a.m. CDT; Public Severe Weather Outlook, issued May 19, 2013, 3:04 a.m. CDT; archived at https://www.spc.noaa.gov/products/outlook/.

2. David Von Drehle and Jeffrey Kluger, "16 Minutes," *Time*, June 3, 2013, p. 26; Randy Ellis, "'It Took It All': Twisters Kill at Least 1, Leave Paths of Destruction in Oklahoma," *Oklahoman* (Oklahoma City), May 20, 2013.

3. Holly Bailey, *The Mercy of the Sky: The Story of a Tornado* (New York: Viking, 2015), 115. Much of the narrative in the next few paragraphs relies on Bailey's riveting account.

4. Bailey, *Mercy of the Sky*, 114; Joe Wertz, "Which Oklahoma Schools Have Storm Shelters," State Impact Oklahoma, National Public Radio, September 27, 2013, https://stateimpact.npr.org/oklahoma/2013/09/27/mapped-which-oklahoma-schools-have-storm-shelters/; "Why Don't More Homes in Oklahoma Have Basements?" The Weather Channel, May 21, 2013, https://weather.com/storms/tornado/news/why-dont-oklahoma-homes-have-basements-20130521.

5. Bailey, *Mercy of the Sky*, 122–23.

6. Ibid., 142, 158.

7. Ibid., 159.

8. Ibid., 201–3, 230–31, 250–51, 254, 277; Zeke Campfield, "Victim's Family Recalls Bright, Ornery Lad Who Was Always Smiling," *Oklahoman*, May 25, 2013.

9. Bailey, *Mercy of the Sky*, 1–3, 296; "Top Ten Costliest Oklahoma Tornadoes (1950-present)," National Weather Service, Norman Office, https://www.weather.gov/oun/tornadodata-ok-costliest; Nancy Mathis, *Storm Warning: The Story of a Killer Tornado* (New York: Touchstone, 2007), 134.

10. Tony Walter, "Disaster, Modernity, and the Media," in *Death and Religion in a Changing World*, ed. Kathleen Garces-Foley (New York: Routledge, 2006), 270–71.

11. John Locke, *An Essay Concerning the True Original, Extent, and End of Civil Government*, in *Two Treatises of Government* (London, 1690), 268.

12. Mary Ann Blochowiak, "Sooner," *The Encyclopedia of Oklahoma History and Culture*, ed. Dianna Everett (Oklahoma City: Oklahoma Historical Society, 2009), http://www.okhistory.org.

13. "A Tornado's Work," *Weekly Standard* (Leavenworth, Kans.), April 2, 1897; story of Elmer's Saloon from Leo Kelley, "'Not An Upright Stick Remained': Oklahoma: Home of the Real Twisters," *Chronicles of Oklahoma* 74 (Winter 1996–1997): 427; death toll from Thomas P. Grazulis, *Significant Tornadoes, 1680–1991* (St. Johnsbury, Vt.: Environmental Films, 1993), 680.

14. Bailey, *Mercy of the Sky*, 17, 23–24, 177.

15. Kelly P. Kissel and Thomas Peipert, "Veteran Storm Chasers from Colorado Killed by Okla. Tornado," *Fort Collins Coloradoan*, June 3, 2013; Brantley Hargrove, *The Man Who Caught the Storm: The Life of Legendary Tornado Chaser Tim Samaras* (New York: Simon & Schuster, 2018), 169.

16. Bailey, *Mercy of the Sky*, 52.

17. Pew Research Center 2014 Religious Landscape Study, http://www.pewforum.org/religious-landscape-study/. For the identification of central Oklahoma as the hub of the traditional Tornado Alley, see, e.g., Howard B. Bluestein, *Tornado Alley: Monster Storms of the Great Plains* (New York: Oxford University Press, 1999), 7, fig. 1.1; and Peggy R. Concannon, Harold E. Brooks, and Charles A. Doswell III, "Climatological Risk of Strong and Violent Tornadoes in the United States," Second Conference on Environmental Applications, American Meteorological Society, Long Beach, California, January 8–12, 2000, https://www.nssl.noaa.gov/users/brooks/public_html/concannon/. On the debate over Dixie Alley, see P. Grady Dixon, Andrew E. Mercer, Jinmu Choi, and Jared S. Allen, "Tornado Risk Analysis: Is Dixie Alley an Extension of Tornado Alley?" *Bulletin of the American Meteorological Society* 92 (April 2011): 433–41; and Timothy A. Coleman and P. Grady Dixon, "An Objective Analysis of Tornado Risk in the United States," *Weather and Forecasting* 29 (April 2014): 366–76.

18. One frequently cited enumeration of evangelicalism's distinctives is historian David Bebbington's "evangelical quadrilateral" of biblicism, conversionism, crucicentrism, and activism. See D. W. Bebbington, *Evangelicalism in Modern Britain: A History from the 1730s to the 1980s* (1989; reprint, London: Routledge, 1993), 2–3. I will focus here on the first two (biblicism and conversionism) and add another: providentialism.

19. Nicole Neroulias, "Most Don't Blame God for Disasters," *Christian Century* 128, no. 8 (April 19, 2011): 14–15. The poll also found that in contrast to white evangelicals, 59 percent of whom identified disasters as signs from God, a comparable proportion of minority Christians (61 percent) said that disasters are God's way of testing their faith. On providentialism as a pervasive feature of contemporary evangelicalism, see Peter J. Thuesen, *Predestination: The American Career of a Contentious Doctrine* (New York: Oxford University Press, 2009), 209–18.

20. On Robertson and his critics, see Laurie Goodstein, "Even Pat Robertson's Friends Are Wondering . . . " *New York Times*, January 8, 2006; and Faye Fiore, "A Wholly Controversial Holy Man," *Los Angeles Times*, February 12, 2006. On Hagee and McCain, see Libby Quaid, "McCain Rejects Endorsements of Two Controversial Clerics," *Arizona Daily Star* (Tucson), May 23, 2008. The literature on Hurricane Katrina is extensive. For an overview, see Douglas Brinkley, *The Great Deluge: Hurricane Katrina, New Orleans, and the Mississippi Gulf Coast* (New York: William Morrow, 2006). A decade after the disaster, the exact death toll remained unclear. See Jim Mustian, "Katrina's Death Toll Unresolved: 1,833 Counted, But Factors Make Number Uncertain," *New Orleans Advocate*, August 28, 2015.

21. Bob Allen, "Twisters Not Random, Says Calvinist Preacher Piper," *Christian Century* 129, no. 7 (April 4, 2012): 18. For Piper's original blog post, see John Piper, "The Tornado, the Lutherans, and Homosexuality," August 20, 2009, https://www.desiringgod.org/articles/the-tornado-the-lutherans-and-homosexuality. A similar response came from the conservative Lutheran WordAlone Network: Jaynan L. Clark, "God Will Not Be Mocked—Especially When Steeples Fall," *Network News* 10, no. 5 (September–October 2009): 3–5. The 2009 vote ultimately led hundreds of congregations to withdraw from the ELCA, a mainline denomination (despite the "Evangelical" in its name).

22. President Barack Obama, address at Joplin Tornado Memorial Service, May 29, 2011, in Randy Turner and John Hacker, *5:41: Stories from the Joplin Tornado* (Lexington, Ky.: n.p., 2011), 148.

23. Death toll and other details from "A Town in Ruin," *Manhattan (Kans.) Mercury*, May 6, 2007; "Tornado Toll Rises in Splintered Remains of a Kansas Town," *New York Times*, May 8, 2007; and Keith Schneider, "After a Tornado, a Kansas Town Rebuilds Green," *New York Times*, September 23, 2009.

24. Eric Unruh and Fern Unruh, *Tornado! Up from the Debris to Thank God* (Newton, Kans.: Mennonite Press, 2007), vii–ix, 82, 84, 154. Though the tornado missed the Unruhs' own farm, they later moved to West Union, Iowa, to help with a congregation of their denomination, the Church of God in Christ, Mennonite (an Anabaptist body with nineteenth-century roots that today shares many of the characteristics of broader American evangelicalism). Information on the Unruhs from Matthew Wilde, "Hothouse Vegetable Business Warming Up," *Courier* (Waterloo, Iowa), December 15, 2012.

25. Death toll from Jeffry S. Evans, Corey M. Mead, and Steven J. Weiss, "Forecasting the Super Tuesday Outbreak at the SPC: Why Forecast Uncertainty Does Not Necessarily Decrease as You Get Closer to a High Impact Weather Event," 24th Conference on Severe Local Storms, October 27–31, 2008, Savannah, Ga., https://www.spc.noaa.gov/publications/evans/sup-tues.pdf.

26. David S. Dockery, "Union Thankful to All Who Helped," *Jackson (Tenn.) Sun*, February 13, 2008; Tim Ellsworth, *God in the Whirlwind: Stories of Grace from the Tornado at Union University* (Nashville: B&H, 2008), 3, 7.

27. On Garcia, see Carmen Forman, "Volunteers Begin Work on First Moore Rebuild," *Oklahoman*, July 20, 2013; and Bailey, *Mercy of the Sky*, 273–74. Connie Schultz, "She Thanked God; Debate Rages," *Altoona (Pa.) Mirror*, May 26, 2013.

28. *Where Was God? Stories of Hope after the Storm*, directed by Travis Palmer and produced by Steven Earp, Brian Cates, and Chris Forbes (Tulsa, Okla.: VCI Entertainment, 2015), DVD.

29. Steven Earp with Jennifer Spinola, *Storms of Life: Learning to Trust God Again* (Oklahoma City: ElevateFaith, 2015), 131, 135–36, 138, 140–41.

30. Ibid., 139; Sam Storms, "Tornadoes, Tsunamis, and the Mystery of Suffering and Sovereignty," May 20, 2013, https://www.samstorms.com/enjoying-god-blog/post/tornadoes--tsunamis--and-the-mystery-of-suffering-and-sovereignty. On Storms's Calvinism, see, e.g., his *Chosen for Life: The Case for Divine Election*, rev. ed. (Wheaton, Ill.: Crossway Books, 2007).

31. R. C. Sproul, *Chosen by God* (Wheaton, Ill.: Tyndale House, 1986), 26–27; R. C. Sproul, *The Invisible Hand: Do All Things Really Work for Good?* (1996; reprint, Phillipsburg, N.J.: P&R, 2003), 156; Erwin W. Lutzer, *An Act of God? Answers to Tough Questions about God's Role in Natural Disasters* (Carol Stream, Ill.: Tyndale House, 2011), 27.

32. Dale Clem, *Winds of Fury, Circles of Grace: Life after the Palm Sunday Tornadoes* (Nashville: Abingdon Press, 1997), 17, 51, 98–99.

33. Carla Hinton, "Clergy Respond to Difficult Question," *Oklahoman*, May 25, 2013.

34. Scholastic Protestants and Catholics alike called God's infallible foreknowledge of human free choices "middle knowledge" (*scientia media*). See Thuesen, *Predestination*, 39, 226; and Richard A. Muller, *Dictionary of Latin and Greek Theological Terms: Drawn Principally from Protestant Scholastic Theology*, 2nd ed. (Grand Rapids, Mich.: Baker Academic, 2017), s.v. "scientia Dei," 325–26.

35. Linwood Urban and Douglas N. Walton, eds., *The Power of God: Readings on Omnipotence and Evil* (New York: Oxford University Press, 1978), 8–9, 35–36, 44–45, 54–58.

36. Francis John McConnell, *Is God Limited?* (New York: Abingdon Press, 1924), 62. For helpful analysis, see Gary Dorrien, *The Making of American Liberal Theology: Idealism, Realism, and Modernity, 1900–1950* (Louisville, Ky.: Westminster John Knox Press, 2003), 317–18.

37. Edgar Sheffield Brightman, *The Problem of God* (New York: Abingdon Press, 1930), 125, 130–31, 137–38; Edgar Sheffield Brightman, *A Philosophy of Religion* (1940; reprint, New York: Greenwood Press, 1969), 205 and 243 (on tornadoes), 245–46, 318, 337; Horace M. Kallen, *Why Religion* (New York: Boni and Liveright, 1927), 300 ("A surd lurks under every law of nature, a flaw in every design of God"). For discussion of Brightman's views, see Dorrien, *Making of American Liberal Theology*, 313–26. Brightman's students at Boston University included Martin Luther King, Jr., who adopted a Personalist view of God; see "Edgar Sheffield Brightman (1884–1953)," in Clayborne Carson et al., *The Martin Luther King, Jr., Encyclopedia* (Westport, Conn.: Greenwood Press, 2008), 42–43. Another of Brightman's students was the evangelical theologian E. J. Carnell, who rejected his mentor's view of a finite God limited by the surd; see his critique in Edward John Carnell, *A Philosophy of the Christian Religion* (Grand Rapids, Mich.: Baker Book House, 1952), 299–323.

38. Georgia Harkness, *The Providence of God* (New York: Abingdon Press, 1960), 105; Dorrien, *Making of American Liberal Theology*, 401–2; Albert C. Outler, *Who Trusts in God: Musings on the Meaning of Providence* (New York: Oxford University Press, 1968), 90.

39. Terence E. Fretheim, *Creation Untamed: The Bible, God, and Natural Disasters* (Grand Rapids, Mich.: Baker Academic, 2010), 59.

40. Among these leading proponents, Richard Rice, a Seventh-day Adventist theologian, is often credited with coining the term Open Theism with his book *The Openness of God: The Relationship of Divine Foreknowledge and Human Free Will* (Nashville: Review and Herald, 1980). For overviews of the movement, see James Rissler, "Open Theism," in *Internet Encyclopedia of Philosophy*, ed. James Fieser and Bradley Dowden, https://www.iep.utm.edu/o-theism/; and Garrett J. DeWeese, "Open Theism," in *Dictionary of Christianity and Science*, ed. Paul Copan, Tremper Longman III, Christopher L. Reese, and Michael G. Strauss (Grand Rapids, Mich.: Zondervan, 2017), 493.

41. On God's changeless love and reliability, see Richard Rice, "Biblical Support for a New Perspective," and on God's delighting in a universe he does not fully control, see Clark H. Pinnock, "Systematic Theology," both in Clark Pinnock, Richard Rice, John Sanders, William Hasker, and David Basinger, *The Openness of God: A Biblical Challenge to the Traditional Understanding of God* (Downers Grove, Ill.: InterVarsity Press, 1994), 48, 117.

42. On differences between Open Theism and Brightman's view, see John Sanders, *The God Who Risks: A Theology of Providence* (Downers Grove, Ill.: InterVarsity Press, 1998), 242, 303n113. On Open Theism's differences with Process Theology, see William Hasker, "A Philosophical Perspective," in Pinnock et al., *Openness of God*, 138–40. Regarding the distinct logics used by Brightman and the Process theologians for rejecting divine omnipotence, see Gary Dorrien, *The Making of American Liberal Theology: Crisis, Irony, and Postmodernity, 1950–2005* (Louisville, Ky.: Westminster John Knox Press, 2006), 234–35; see also the comment by John Hick in *Encountering Evil: Live Options in Theodicy*, ed. Stephen T. Davis, rev. ed. (Louisville, Ky.: Westminster John Knox Press, 2001), 128–29.

43. Clark H. Pinnock, *Most Moved Mover: A Theology of God's Openness* (Carlisle, UK: Paternoster Press, 2001), 132; Sanders, *God Who Risks*, 85–86, 224–27, 272–73, 275–76; John Calvin, *Institutes of the Christian Religion* (1559 ed.), ed. John T. McNeill and trans. Ford Lewis Battles (Philadelphia: Westminster Press, 1960), 205–6 (I.16.7).

44. Gregory A. Boyd, *God of the Possible: A Biblical Introduction to the Open View of God* (Grand Rapids, Mich.: Baker Books, 2000), 109–10.

45. Fretheim, *Creation Untamed*, 21–22, 66, 73–74, 77, 82, 87. See also the discussion of Fretheim's view of natural disasters in Michael J. Chan and Brent A. Strawn, "Introducing Fretheim: His Theology and His God," in *What Kind of God? Collected Essays of Terence E. Fretheim*, ed. Michael J. Chan and Brent A. Strawn (Winona Lake, Ind.: Eisenbrauns, 2015), 14–17.

46. Eric Gorski, "'Open Theists' Say God Allows Give-and-Take," *Tennessean* (Nashville); Richard N. Ostling, "Eternal Debate: Theologians Dispute God's Knowledge," *Wisconsin State Journal* (Madison), February 3, 2002.

47. On the shared commitment to inerrancy, see Dennis W. Jowers, "Conclusion," in *Four Views on Divine Providence*, ed. Dennis W. Jowers (Grand Rapids, Mich.: Zondervan, 2011), 246. For an argument that Open Theism is compatible with inerrancy, see Jason A. Nicholls, "Openness and Inerrancy: Can They Be Compatible?" *Journal of the Evangelical Theological Society* 45 (2002): 629–49.

48. John Frame, *No Other God: A Response to Open Theism* (Phillipsburg, N.J.: P&R, 2001), 92–93. Other evangelical rejoinders to Open Theism include Bruce A. Ware, *God's Lesser*

Glory: The Diminished God of Open Theism (Wheaton, Ill.: Crossway Books, 2000); and John Piper, Justin Taylor, and Paul Kjoss Helseth, eds., *Beyond the Bounds: Open Theism and the Undermining of Biblical Christianity* (Wheaton, Ill.: Crossway Books, 2003).

49. R. Albert Mohler, Jr., "God and the Tsunami—Theology in the Headlines, Part One," January 2, 2005, and "God and the Tsunami—Theology in the Headlines, Part Two," January 3, 2005, blog posts archived at http://albertmohler.com.

50. David Bentley Hart, "Tremors of Doubt," *Wall Street Journal*, December 31, 2004; David Bentley Hart, *The Doors of the Sea: Where Was God in the Tsunami?* (Grand Rapids, Mich.: Eerdmans, 2005), 35, 51.

51. Gary Stern, *Can God Intervene? How Religion Explains Natural Disasters* (Westport, Conn.: Praeger, 2007), 176 (Narayanan), 192–93 (Kusala). On the complexities of karma in Hindu-derived theodicies, and for a denial that karma "solves" the problem of evil, see Wendy Doniger O'Flaherty, *The Origins of Evil in Hindu Mythology* (Berkeley: University of California Press, 1976), 14–20.

52. Kushner, interviewed in Stern, *Can God Intervene?* 47–48.

53. Harold S. Kushner, *When Bad Things Happen to Good People* (New York: Avon Books, 1981), 43, 51–53, 55; Mohler, "God and the Tsunami . . . Part Two." Kushner stressed that God's original act of creation imposed order where before there had been only randomness. "This is what it means to create: not to make something out of nothing, but to make order out of chaos. A creative scientist or historian does not make up facts but orders facts; he sees connections between them rather than seeing them as random data" (Kushner, *When Bad Things Happen*, 51).

54. Jaweed Kaleem, "Hurricane Sandy Presents Complex Questions about God for Clergy and the Faithful as Victims Cope," *Huffington Post*, October 29, 2012, http://www.huffingtonpost.com.

55. On the concept of the Anthropocene and debates about when the epoch began, see Erle C. Ellis, *Anthropocene: A Very Short Introduction* (New York: Oxford University Press, 2018).

56. Ted Steinberg, *Acts of God: The Unnatural History of Natural Disaster in America*, 2nd ed. (New York: Oxford University Press, 2006), 198, 201, 204. See also Stuart B. Schwartz, *Sea of Storms: A History of Hurricanes in the Greater Caribbean from Columbus to Katrina* (Princeton, N.J.: Princeton University Press, 2015), 331–32. On disaster inequalities, see Chester Hartman and Gregory D. Squires, eds., *There Is No Such Thing as a Natural Disaster: Race, Class, and Hurricane Katrina* (New York: Routledge, 2006). On the lack of restrictions on coastal development, see also Stephen M. Strader, "We Keep Moving to the Bull's Eye," *New York Times*, September 16, 2018.

57. James Hudnut-Beumler, *Strangers and Friends at the Welcome Table: Contemporary Christianities in the American South* (Chapel Hill: University of North Carolina Press, 2018), 134.

58. Martha Wolfenstein, *Disaster: A Psychological Essay* (1957; reprint, Abingdon, Oxford: Routledge, 1998), 189–90, 193. On Wolfenstein, see the obituary in the *New York Times*, December 1, 1976. Regarding the "post-disaster utopia," see also James B. Taylor, Louis A. Zurcher, and William H. Key, *Tornado: A Community Responds to Disaster* (Seattle: University of Washington Press, 1970), 68–75, 141–44.

59. Geoffrey Parker, *Global Crisis: War, Climate Change and Catastrophe in the Seventeenth Century* (New Haven, Conn.: Yale University Press, 2013), 689.

60. "2011 Killer Tornadoes: Updated 2011 Fatality Statistics," Storm Prediction Center, National Weather Service, https://www.spc.noaa.gov/climo/torn/STATIJ11.txt; and Kevin M. Simmons

and Daniel Sutter, *Deadly Season: Analysis of the 2011 Tornado Outbreaks* (Boston: American Meteorological Society, 2012), 8–9. The 2011 Super Outbreak is not to be confused with the Super Tuesday Outbreak of 2008.

61. Sharon Begley, "Are You Ready for More?" *Newsweek*, June 6, 2011, p. 42.

62. Bluestein and Wurman quoted in Laura Gottesdiener, "2011 Tornadoes: Is Climate Change to Blame for the Devastating Weather?" *Huffington Post*, June 29, 2011, www.huffingtonpost.com.

63. Nathaniel Rich, "Losing Earth: The Decade We Almost Stopped Climate Change. A Tragedy in Two Acts," *New York Times Magazine*, August 5, 2018, pp. 8, 9. And speculation about the problem began even earlier: The *New York Times* reported in 1953 that there was "abundant evidence" of rising global temperatures and that some scientists attributed this to "a small but definite increase in the past century in the percentage of carbon dioxide in the atmosphere." Leonard Engel, "The Weather Is Really Changing," *New York Times*, July 12, 1953. For an overview of the emergence of climate change as a scientific and public concern, see Spencer R. Weart, *The Discovery of Global Warming*, rev. ed. (Cambridge, Mass.: Harvard University Press, 2008).

64. Thomas F. Stocker and Dahe Qin, eds., *Climate Change 2013: The Physical Science Basis. Working Group I Contribution to the Fifth Assessment Report of the Intergovernmental Panel on Climate Change* (Cambridge: Cambridge University Press, 2013), 5. Already by 2007, the IPCC had reported that scientific modeling of climate change had ruled out natural variation as a likely explanation for the rapid warming in the second half of the twentieth century. See Susan Solomon, Dahe Qin, and Martin Manning, eds., *Climate Change 2007: The Physical Science Basis. Contribution of Working Group I to the Fourth Assessment Report of the Intergovernmental Panel on Climate Change* (Cambridge: Cambridge University Press, 2007), 702–3.

65. Justin Gillis, "Heat-Trapping Gas Passes Milestone, Raising Fears," *New York Times*, May 11, 2013.

66. *Global Warming of 1.5° C . . . Summary for Policymakers* (Geneva: Intergovernmental Panel on Climate Change, 2018), 6; Brad Plumer and Nadja Popovich, "Why Half a Degree of Warming Is a Big Deal," *New York Times*, October 9, 2018.

67. Somini Sengupta, "The Year Global Warming Turned Model into Menace," *New York Times*, August 10, 2018.

68. Kerry Emanuel, *Divine Wind: The History and Science of Hurricanes* (New York: Oxford University Press, 2005), 256–57; and on the critics, Robert Henson, *The Thinking Person's Guide to Climate Change* (Boston: American Meteorological Society, 2014), 183–85.

69. For scientific postmortems suggesting that climate change may have contributed to the high winds of recent hurricanes, see Christina M. Patricola and Michael F. Wehner, "Anthropogenic Influences on Major Tropical Cyclone Events," *Nature* 563 (2018): 339–46; and H. Murakami, E. Levin, T. L. Delworth, R. Gudgel, and P.-C. Hsu, "Dominant Effect of Relative Tropical Atlantic Warming on Major Hurricane Occurrence," *Science* 362 (2018): 794–99. On intense rainfall and storm surge, see Nicholas Kristof, "It's Not Too Late to Learn from Our Mistakes," *New York Times*, September 3, 2017; and Noah S. Diffenbaugh, "How We Know It Was Climate Change," *New York Times*, December 31, 2017.

70. Richard A. Muller, "The Truth about Tornadoes," *New York Times*, November 21, 2013. The rebuttal (by Paul Markowski, Harold Brooks, Yvette Richardson, Robert J. Trapp, John Allen, and Noah Diffenbaugh) is quoted in Andrew C. Revkin, "A Closer Look at Tornadoes in a Human-Heated Climate," Dot Earth (*New York Times* blog), December 9, 2013, https://dotearth.blogs.nytimes.com/2013/12/09/a-closer-look-at-tornadoes-and-global-warming/.

71. Vittorio (Victor) A. Gensini and Harold E. Brooks, "Spatial Trends in United States Tornado Frequency," *Climate and Atmospheric Science* 1, no. 38 (2018): 1–5, https://www.nature.com/npjclimatsci; and Seth Borenstein, "Tornadoes Spinning to East," *Star Tribune* (Minneapolis), October 21, 2018. On the shift in the dry line, see Richard Seager, Jamie Feldman, Nathan Lis, Mingfang Ting, Alton P. Williams, Jennifer Nakamura, Haibo Liu, and Naomi Henderson, "Whither the 100th Meridian? The Once and Future Physical Geography of America's Arid-Humid Divide. Part II: The Meridian Moves East," *Earth Interactions* 22, no. 5 (2018): 1–24. On the high rate of fatalities in the Deep South, see Walker S. Ashley, "Spatial and Temporal Analysis of Tornado Fatalities in the United States: 1880–2005," *Weather and Forecasting* 22 (2007): 1214–1228.

72. "Restoring Creation for Ecology and Justice: A Report Adopted by the 202nd General Assembly of the Presbyterian Church (U.S.A.)" (Louisville, Ky.: Office of the General Assembly, 1990), n.p.; "Environmental Justice for a Sustainable Future" (1992), in *The Book of Resolutions of the United Methodist Church* (Nashville: United Methodist, 1992), 63; "Caring for Creation: Vision, Hope, and Justice" (1993), Division for Church in Society (Chicago: Evangelical Lutheran Church in America, 1993), 4.

73. "The Science of Global Climate Change," sidebar in "Global Climate Change: A Plea for Dialogue, Prudence, and the Common Good" (Washington, D.C.: United States Conference of Catholic Bishops, 2001), 19; Pope Francis, *Laudato Si'*, encyclical letter (Vatican City: Vatican Press, 2015), 18.

74. On "Climate Change: An Evangelical Call to Action," see Katharine K. Wilkinson, *Between God and Green: How Evangelicals Are Cultivating a Middle Ground on Climate Change* (New York: Oxford University Press, 2012), 24–25, 44–50, and for the text of the statement, 152–56. The signatories are listed at http://www.christiansandclimate.org/statement. For background, see also Brian McCammack, "Hot Damned America: Evangelicalism and the Climate Change Policy Debate," *American Quarterly* 59 (2007): 645–68; and Laurie Goodstein, "Evangelical Leaders Join Global Warming Initiative," *New York Times*, February 8, 2006. Efforts such as the Evangelical Climate Initiative notwithstanding, evangelicals were less likely than other groups to be worried about climate change. When asked in a 2014 poll about the scientific consensus that the climate is changing and that humans are a significant cause, only 29 percent of evangelicals agreed, compared with 42 percent of mainline Protestants; 45 percent of Catholics; 48 percent of Jews; 57 percent of atheists, agnostics, and unaffiliated; and 63 percent of adherents of non-Western religions. Of all adults nationwide, 43% agreed. See Elaine Howard Ecklund and Christopher P. Scheitle, *Religion vs. Science: What Religious People Really Think* (New York: Oxford University Press, 2018), 104–6.

75. Antony Alumkal, *Paranoid Science: The Christian Right's War on Reality* (New York: New York University Press, 2017), 165–66.

76. Alumkal, *Paranoid Science*, 153, 156–58; Wilkinson, *Between God and Green*, 66–67, 69.

77. "The Cornwall Declaration on Environmental Stewardship," https://cornwallalliance.org/landmark-documents/the-cornwall-declaration-on-environmental-stewardship/, which includes a link to a separate page of the notable signatories.

78. "An Evangelical Declaration on Global Warming," https://cornwallalliance.org/2009/05/evangelical-declaration-on-global-warming/, which includes a link to a separate page of the notable signatories.

79. Kim Cross, *What Stands in a Storm: Three Days in the Worst Superstorm to Hit the South's Tornado Alley* (New York: Atria Books, 2015), 22. Spann's accusation is quoted in "The Spann Principle," unsigned editorial, *Anniston (Ala.) Star*, January 25, 2007. Frank's comment appears in Joel Achenbach, "The Tempest," *Washington Post Magazine*, May 28, 2006, in which another prominent meteorologist, Colorado State University hurricane expert William Gray, is quoted as calling global warming "one of the greatest hoaxes ever perpetrated on the American people." Gray later lent his name to the Cornwall Alliance when the organization issued a new statement criticizing Pope Francis's *Laudato Si'*. See "An Open Letter to Pope Francis on Climate Change" (2015), https://cornwallalliance.org/anopenlettertopopefrancisonclimatechange/.

80. Frank's "hoax" comment, for example, is invoked in Brian Sussman, *Climategate: A Veteran Meteorologist Exposes the Global Warming Scam* (Washington, D.C.: WND Books, 2010), 138–39. On the climate change debate among broadcast meteorologists, see Robert Henson, *Weather on the Air: A History of Broadcast Meteorology* (Boston: American Meteorological Society, 2010), 198–200.

81. See, for example, his speech from the Senate floor soon after he became chair of the Senate Committee on Environment and Public Works: James M. Inhofe, "The Science of Climate Change: Senate Floor Statement," in Bill McKibben, ed., *The Global Warming Reader: A Century of Writing about Climate Change* (New York: Penguin Books, 2012), 165–70.

82. Jim Myers, "Global Warming: Another Attack: Inhofe Calls Climate Warnings Hysteria Fed by Activist Media," *Tulsa World*, September 26, 2006; see also Chris Casteel, "Inhofe Challenges 'Hoax' of Global Warming," *Oklahoman*, October 2, 2006.

83. James Inhofe, "We Don't Need a Climate Tax on the Poor," *Wall Street Journal*, June 3, 2008.

84. On his early chafing at regulation, see James Inhofe, *The Greatest Hoax: How the Global Warming Conspiracy Threatens Your Future* (Washington, D.C.: WND Books, 2012), 3–5. On his church affiliation, see "Inhofe Speaks on the Senate Floor about President Trump's Accomplishments," September 5, 2018, https://www.inhofe.senate.gov/newsroom/press-releases/inhofe-speaks-on-the-senate-floor-about-president-trumps-accomplishments.

85. Inhofe, *Greatest Hoax*, 70–71, 175.

86. "Sen. Jim Inhofe Embarrasses the GOP and the U.S." (editorial), *Washington Post*, March 1, 2015; Stewart quoted in Matt Patterson, "'Personhood' Bill, Moore Tornado, SAE's Chant Part of Host's History," *Oklahoman*, August 6, 2015.

87. Jim Inhofe and Scott Pruitt, "Senate Bill 676 Protects Oklahoma Businesses, Families from EPA's Overreach," *Tulsa World*, April 1, 2015.

88. Barbara Hoberock, "Oklahoma Gov. Mary Fallin Vetoes Bill That Would Have Required State AG Approval of Carbon-Reduction Plan," *Tulsa World*, May 2, 2015.

89. According to the *Huffington Post*, Pruitt had sued the EPA 13 times by early 2017. Dominique Mosbergen, "Scott Pruitt Has Sued the Environmental Protection Agency 13 Times. Now He Wants to Lead It," *Huffington Post*, January 17, 2017, www.huffingtonpost.com.

90. "Open Letter Supporting Scott Pruitt for EPA Administrator," Cornwall Alliance, January 5, 2017, https://cornwallalliance.org/landmark-documents/open-letter-supporting-scott-pruitt-for-epa-administrator/; "Letter Calls Pruitt 'Well Qualified' for EPA," Baptist Press, December 16, 2016, http://www.bpnews.net/48067/letter-calls-pruitt-well-qualified-for-epa; "Evangelical Open Letter to President Elect Trump, Reconsider Pruitt for EPA," Evangelical Environmental

Network, December 15, 2016, https://www.creationcare.org/evangelical_open_letter_to_president_elect_trump_reconsider_pruitt_for_epa.

91. Coral Davenport, "New Administrator Stacks E.P.A. with Climate Change Skeptics," *New York Times*, March 8, 2017; Michael Biesecker and Matthew Daly, "Climate Change Is No Hoax, Says EPA Nominee," *Chicago Tribune*, January 19, 2017; Matthew Daly, "EPA Administrator: CO2 Isn't a Main Warming Contributor," *Chicago Tribune*, March 10, 2017.

92. Coral Davenport, "E.P.A. Head Erases Obama-Era Rules in Blazing Start," *New York Times*, July 2, 2017.

93. On the Paris accord, see Coral Davenport, "Nations Approve Landmark Climate Deal," *New York Times*, December 13, 2015. On Trump's Rose Garden ceremony announcing the US withdrawal, see Michael D. Shear, "Trump Will Withdraw U.S. from Paris Climate Agreement," *New York Times*, June 1, 2017.

94. Coral Davenport, Lisa Friedman, and Maggie Haberman, "Mired in Scandal, Pruitt Is Pushed to Exit E.P.A. Post," *New York Times*, July 6, 2018; Brady Dennis and Juliet Eilperin, "Watchdog: Pruitt's $43,000 Soundproof Phone Booth Violated Spending Laws," *Washington Post*, April 17, 2018; Juliet Eilperin and Brady Dennis, "Trump Cabinet Members Are Accused of Living Large at Taxpayer Expense," *Washington Post*, March 15, 2018.

95. "The Full Text of EPA Administrator Scott Pruitt's Resignation Letter to President Trump," *USA Today* (online), July 5, 2018, https://www.usatoday.com/story/news/politics/onpolitics/2018/07/05/scott-pruitt-resignation-letter/761174002/.

96. Mark Landler and Coral Davenport, "Climate Warning Hits Silent Wall on Trump's Desk," *New York Times*, October 9, 2018; Tarpley Hitt, "EPA on U.N. Climate-Change Report: 'What Report? Haven't Heard of It,'" *Daily Beast*, October 19, 2018, https://www.thedailybeast.com/epa-on-un-climate-change-report-what-report-havent-heard-of-it.

97. Lisa Friedman, "Trump Says Ex-Lobbyist Is His Pick for E.P.A.," *New York Times*, November 17, 2018.

98. Michael Lewis, *The Fifth Risk* (New York: W. W. Norton, 2018), 170–72.

99. Ibid., 175. See the advertisement at https://corporate.accuweather.com/stories/moore-oklahoma-tornado (accessed November 21, 2018).

100. Robert O'Harrow, Jr., "NOAA Nominee's Financial Conflicts Draw Rare Criticism from Past Chiefs," *Washington Post*, December 13, 2017; Jason Samenow, "Trump Taps AccuWeather CEO to Head NOAA, Breaking with Precedent of Nominating Scientists," Capital Weather Gang (*Washington Post* blog), October 12, 2017, https://www.washingtonpost.com/news/capital-weather-gang/wp/2017/10/12/trump-taps-barry-myers-accuweather-ceo-to-head-noaa-choice-seen-as-controversial.

101. Meyers's testimony in *Restoring U.S. Leadership in Weather Forecasting, Part I: Hearing Before the Subcommittee on Environment, Committee on Science, Space, and Technology, House of Representatives, One Hundred Thirteenth Congress, First Session, Thursday, May 23, 2013* (Washington, D.C.: U.S. Government Printing Office, 2013), 52.

102. A point made by Lewis, *Fifth Risk*, 63–64.

103. Bernard DeVoto, introduction to Wallace Stegner, *Beyond the Hundredth Meridian: John Wesley Powell and the Second Opening of the West* (1953; reprint, New York: Penguin Books, 1992), xx. DeVoto is quoted in David Laskin, *Braving the Elements: The Stormy History of American Weather* (New York: Anchor Books, 1996), 121.

104. Clip of Ferrell's skit posted at https://www.youtube.com/watch?v=01gC8qWh2Hs (accessed November 19, 2018).

105. Peter Baker, "16 Years Later, Bush's Climate Pact Exit Holds Lessons for Trump," *New York Times*, June 4, 2017.

106. Trump quotations and Meyer's analysis from Robinson Meyer, "Trump Slightly Revises His Views on Climate Change. Again," *Atlantic* (online), October 16, 2018, https://www.theatlantic.com/science/archive/2018/10/trumps-always-shifting-views-on-climate-change/573037/.

107. Nadja Popovich and Blacki Migliozzi, "Dangerous Days: Your Hometown Is Getting Hotter," *New York Times*, September 25, 2018.

108. David G. Victor, Keigo Akimoto, Yoichi Kaya, Mitsutsune Yamaguchi, Danny Cullenward, and Cameron Hepburn, "Prove Paris Was More than Paper Promises," *Nature* 548 (2017): 25–27; Somini Sengupta, "Coal Endangers a Planet Unable to Stop Using It," *New York Times*, November 25, 2018.

109. Coral Davenport and Kendra Pierre-Louis, "U.S. Climate Study Has Grim Warning of Economic Risks," *New York Times*, November 24, 2018; *Fourth National Climate Assessment*, Vol. 2, *Impacts, Risks, and Adaptation in the United States* (Washington, D.C.: U.S. Global Change Research Program, 2018), 35; Coral Davenport, "White House Mutes Alarm on Warming," *New York Times*, November 26, 2018.

110. Willis Jenkins, *The Future of Ethics: Sustainability, Social Justice, and Religious Creativity* (Washington, D.C.: Georgetown University Press, 2013), 20, 29–31. The term "wicked problem" comes originally from the design theorists and urban planners Horst Rittel and Melvin Webber. See Kevin J. O'Brien, *The Violence of Climate Change: Lessons of Resistance from Nonviolent Activists* (Washington, D.C.: Georgetown University Press, 2017), 17–19.

111. Miranda Leitsinger, "'Not Going to Die in Vain': Grieving Oklahoma Parents Crusade for Storm Shelters," NBC News, August 13, 2013, https://www.nbcnews.com/news/us-news/not-going-die-vain-grieving-oklahoma-parents-crusade-storm-shelters-flna6C10901794; Mark Schlachtenhaufen, "Tornado Victim's Mom Visits Edmond, Touts School Shelters," *Edmond (Okla.) Sun*, August 12, 2013; Juliana Keeping, "Tornado Victims' Families Call for School Shelters," *Oklahoman*, August 21, 2013.

112. Tim Willert, "School Shelter Supporters Challenge Title Revision," *Oklahoman*, October 18, 2013; Randy Ellis, "School Shelter Supporters Want Pruitt Off Case," *Oklahoman*, November 7, 2013; Graham Lee Brewer, "School Storm Shelter Appeal Nears Deadline for Signatures," *Oklahoman*, December 14, 2013; Tim Willert, "School Shelter Group's Attorney Criticizes State AG," *Oklahoman*, December 19, 2013; Matt Dinger, "State Supreme Court to Hear Arguments on Wording in School Shelter Bond Ballot," *Oklahoman*, January 18, 2014.

113. Barbara Hoberock, "Lawmaker Files Measure for Vote on School Storm Shelter Bond," *Oklahoman*, January 16, 2014; Rick Green, "Shelter Backers Get More Time for Signatures," *Oklahoman*, April 2, 2014; Randy Ellis, "Group's School Shelter Petition on Hold until May," *Oklahoman*, April 22, 2014; Randy Ellis, "House OKs School Shelter Bill," *Oklahoman*, May 23, 2014; Rick M. Green, "Drama-Filled Session Ends: Last Day of Legislature's Year Is Marked by Senate's Defeat of School Shelter Bill," *Oklahoman*, May 24, 2014; Kyle Fredrickson, "Jackson Joins Push for Shelters," *Oklahoman*, June 5, 2014; "Storm Shelter Efforts Are Inherently Political" (editorial), *Oklahoman*, June 6, 2014; Randy Ellis, "Supporters Launch School Shelter Petition Drive," *Oklahoman*, July 3, 2014.

114. Rick M. Green, "Storm Shelter, Marijuana Petitions Fall Short," *Oklahoman*, October 22, 2014.

115. Ben Felder and Darla Slipke, "The Moore Effect: Dozens of Schools Built Safe Rooms after Tornado," *Oklahoman*, May 20, 2018.

116. Jane Glenn Cannon, "Moore City Council Takes Historic Step in Bolstering Homes," *Oklahoman*, March 18, 2014; William Crum, "For Moore Students, A Homecoming," *Oklahoman*, August 20, 2014.

117. Sarah Lobban, "Memorial Honors Tornado's 7 Victims," *Oklahoman*, November 18, 2014.

118. "May 20, 2013: Another Storm, Another Prayer" (editorial), *Oklahoman*, May 21, 2013, echoing a similar editorial published after the 1999 Moore tornado: "The Storm—and a Prayer," *Daily Oklahoman*, May 5, 1999. (The *Daily Oklahoman* changed its name to the *Oklahoman* in 2003.)

119. Carla Hinton, "The Many Faces of Oklahoma Atheism," *Oklahoman*, July 6, 2013. The Vitsmun interview has been likened to a "coming out" for secularists; see Melanie E. Brewster, "The Other Closet: An Introduction to Atheism and Coming Out Processes," in *Atheists in America*, ed. Melanie E. Brewster (New York: Columbia University Press, 2014), 16–17. For background on atheism and secularism in America, see Leigh Eric Schmidt, *Village Atheists: How America's Unbelievers Made Their Way in a Godly Nation* (Princeton, N.J.: Princeton University Press, 2016); and Christopher Grasso, *Skepticism and American Faith: From the Revolution to the Civil War* (New York: Oxford University Press, 2018).

120. Vitsmun described herself as a "Tornado Atheist" on the Twitter handle (@ ActuallyAtheist) she established after the CNN interview (Twitter page accessed December 10, 2018).

CONCLUSION

1. For Bluestein's firsthand account of TOTO, see Howard B. Bluestein, *Tornado Alley: Monster Storms of the Great Plains* (New York: Oxford University Press, 1999), 93–104.

2. https://www.spc.noaa.gov/products/outlook/.

3. Howard Bluestein, the George Lynn Cross Research Professor of Meteorology, University of Oklahoma, interview with author, April 20, 2015.

4. On the tornado at DIA, see Kevin Vaughan and Burt Hubbard, "Living at the Edge of Tornado Alley," *Fort Collins Coloradoan*, June 22, 2013.

5. Bluestein, *Tornado Alley*, 2. See also his comment on the knowledge frontier in Howard B. Bluestein, *Severe Convective Storms and Tornadoes: Observations and Dynamics* (Berlin: Springer Verlag, 2013), xi.

6. Edward N. Lorenz, "Deterministic Nonperiodic Flow," *Journal of the Atmospheric Sciences* 20 (1963): 130–41; Edward N. Lorenz, "The Evolution of Dynamic Meteorology," in *Historical Essays on Meteorology, 1919–1995: The Diamond Anniversary History Volume of the American Meteorological Society*, ed. James Rodger Fleming (Boston: American Meteorological Society, 1996), 15–16.

7. Edward N. Lorenz, *The Essence of Chaos* (Seattle: University of Washington Press, 1993), 14–15; and, for a reprint of the 1972 essay, 181–84. Bradbury's story first appeared in *Collier's* magazine in 1952 and was included the following year in Ray Bradbury, *The Golden Apples of the Sun* (Garden City, N.Y.: Doubleday, 1953), 135–50.

8. James Rodger Fleming, *Inventing Atmospheric Science: Bjerknes, Rossby, Wexler, and the Foundations of Modern Meteorology* (Cambridge, Mass.: MIT Press, 2016), 11.

9. James Gleick, *Chaos: Making a New Science*, rev. ed. (New York: Penguin Books, 2008), 21.

10. Bluestein, interview. On the challenge of modeling raindrops while reckoning with nonlinearity, compare his observation in Bluestein, *Severe Convective Storms and Tornadoes*, 406: "Tornadogenesis . . . is highly nonlinear and involves precipitation microphysics, which also contributes to the nonlinearity."

11. The papers from the 1993 Berkeley conference appear in Robert John Russell, Nancey Murphy, and Arthur R. Peacocke, *Chaos and Complexity: Scientific Perspectives on Divine Action*, 2nd ed. (Vatican City: Vatican Observatory, 1997).

12. Nicholas Saunders, *Divine Action and Modern Science* (Cambridge: Cambridge University Press, 2002), 215. Of course, part of the difficulty is that few theologians have the scientific background to navigate the forbidding complexities of quantum and chaos theory. Saunders called on theologians to become more scientifically aware, a task pursued by Oxford University's Ian Ramsey Centre for Science and Religion (of which Saunders was a onetime fellow) when it received in 2014 a $2.4 million grant from the John Templeton Foundation for an interdisciplinary project on SDA. Two American institutions, Western Michigan University and the Texas Center for Applied Technology at Texas A&M, were collaborators on the grant. See the project site at http://sda.bodleian.ox.ac.uk.

13. John Jefferson Davis, *The Frontiers of Science and Faith: Examining Questions from the Big Bang to the End of the Universe* (Downers Grove, Ill.: InterVarsity Press, 2002), 7, 172–73; Saunders, *Divine Action and Modern Science*, 32–34.

14. Davis, *The Frontiers of Science and Faith*, 82–83. On a different front, Davis later weighed in on global warming, urging his fellow evangelicals to accept the reality of climate change and calling the election of Donald Trump a disaster. Ryan Spencer, "Gordon-Conwell Prof. Analyzes How Trump Campaign Appealed to Evangelicals," *Brandeis Hoot* (Waltham, Mass.), January 27, 2017, http://brandeishoot.com. (On the evangelical debate over global warming, see Chapter 5.)

15. Bluestein, *Tornado Alley*, vii.

16. Stefan Bechtel with Tim Samaras, *Tornado Hunter: Getting Inside the Most Violent Storms on Earth* (Washington, D.C.: National Geographic, 2009), 84.

17. Lisa H. Sideris, *Consecrating Science: Wonder, Knowledge, and the Natural World* (Oakland: University of California Press, 2017), 173–75, 202, 251. The British philosopher R. W. Hepburn made a related point: "Wonder does not see its objects possessively: they remain 'other' and unmastered." R. W. Hepburn, *"Wonder" and Other Essays: Eight Studies in Aesthetics and Neighbouring Fields* (Edinburgh: Edinburgh University Press, 1984), 134.

18. On the monarchial model of God, see Sallie McFague, *A New Climate for Theology: God, the World, and Global Warming* (Minneapolis: Fortress Press, 2008), 69–70.

19. B. A. Gerrish, *A Prince of the Church: Schleiermacher and the Beginnings of Modern Theology* (1984; reprint, Eugene, Ore.: Wipf and Stock, 2001), 64, 67. Schleiermacher himself wrote: "It is not necessary . . . to regard the deity as an object, individual and isolated. If one does, it is very difficult to avoid causing the impression that the deity is capable of passivity after the manner of other objects." Friedrich Schleiermacher, *On Religion: Addresses in Response to Its Cultured Critics*, trans. Terrence N. Tice (Richmond, Va.: John Knox Press, 1969), 94. This resistance to seeing God as one agent among others has considerable precedent in academic theology. See Kathryn Tanner, "Is God in Charge? Creation and Providence," in *Essentials of Christian Theology*, ed. William C. Placher (Louisville, Ky.: Westminster John Knox, 2003), 123. Cf. the similar point in Denys Turner, *Thomas Aquinas: A Portrait* (New Haven, Conn.: Yale University Press, 2013), 120.

20. Gerrish, *Prince of the Church*, 59–60. On Schleiermacher, pantheism, and providence, see Dawn DeVries and B. A. Gerrish, "Providence and Grace: Schleiermacher on Justification and Election," in *The Cambridge Companion to Friedrich Schleiermacher*, ed. Jacqueline Mariña (Cambridge: Cambridge University Press, 2005), 190–92.

21. McFague, *A New Climate for Theology*, 120. For her earlier explication of the world as God's body, see Sallie McFague, *Models of God: Theology for an Ecological, Nuclear Age* (Philadelphia: Fortress Press, 1987), 69–78.

22. Reinhold Niebuhr, "Mystery and Meaning," in *Discerning the Signs of the Times: Sermons for Today and Tomorrow* (New York: Scribner's, 1946), 166.

23. On the surd in theology, see Chapter 5.

24. The quotation appears in Charles W. Eliot, *The Religion of the Future* (Boston: John W. Luce, 1909), 9.

25. Rudolf Otto, *The Idea of the Holy: An Inquiry into the Non-rational Factor in the Idea of the Divine and Its Relation to the Rational*, trans. John W. Harvey, 2nd ed. (Oxford: Oxford University Press, 1950), 77. Compare the striking observation of Jack Miles: "Few speeches in all of literature can more properly be called overpowering than the Lord's speeches to Job from the whirlwind (Job 38–41). Were they to be set to music, nothing but Igor Stravinsky's *Rite of Spring* would come close to their surging, crashing power." Jack Miles, *God: A Biography* (New York: Knopf, 1995), 314.

26. Otto, *Idea of the Holy*, 79.

27. Helmholtz's comment, which originally appeared in "Wirbelstürme und Gewitter," *Deutsche Rundschau* 6 (1876): 363, was quoted by the Norwegian meteorologist Vilhelm Bjerknes in a lecture series delivered at the California Institute of Technology in Pasadena in 1924. Vilhelm Bjerknes, "A Course of Twenty-nine Lectures on Physical Hydrodynamics," Lecture 13, quoted in Fleming, *Inventing Atmospheric Science*, 61–62.

28. Robert King, "49 Miles, 49 Minutes: Part I," *Indianapolis Star*, May 13, 2012; Robert King, "49 Miles, 49 Minutes: Part III," *Indianapolis Star*, May 27, 2012.

29. Reinhold Niebuhr, "The Providence of God" (1952), in *The Essential Reinhold Niebuhr: Selected Essays and Addresses*, ed. Robert McAfee Brown (New Haven, Conn.: Yale University Press, 1986), 34. See the discussion of this sermon in Chapter 4.

BIBLIOGRAPHY OF WORKS CITED

SECULAR NEWSPAPERS

Akron (Ohio) Evening Times
Alexandria (Ind.) Times-Tribune
Altoona (Pa.) Mirror
Anniston (Ala.) Star
Arizona Daily Star (Tucson)
Arkansas Democrat (Little Rock)
Asheville (N.C.) Citizen-Times
Assumption Pioneer (Napoleonville, La.)
Atlanta Constitution
Boston Globe
Brandeis Hoot (Waltham, Mass.)
Burlington (Vt.) Weekly Free Press
Charleston (S.C.) Courier
Chicago Tribune
Cincinnati Enquirer
Columbus (Ohio) Dispatch
Connecticut Courant (Hartford, Conn.)
Courier (Waterloo, Iowa)
Courier-Journal (Louisville, Ky.)
Daily Ardmoreite (Ardmore, Okla.)
Daily Arkansas Gazette (Little Rock)
Daily Free Press (Carbondale, Ill.)

Daily Independent (Murphysboro, Ill.)
Daily Inter Ocean (Chicago)
Daily National Intelligencer (Washington, D.C.)
Daily Review (Decatur, Ill.)
Daily Sanduskian (Sandusky, Ohio)
Dayton (Ohio) Daily News
Delaware County Daily Times (Chester, Pa.)
Democrat and Chronicle (Rochester, N.Y.)
Des Moines (Iowa) Register
Des Moines (Iowa) Tribune
Detroit Free Press
Edmond (Okla.) Sun
Elkhart (Ind.) Truth
Enterprise-Journal (McComb, Miss.)
Evening News (Harrisburg, Pa.)
Fort Collins Coloradan
Goshen (Ind.) News
Great Bend (Kans.) Tribune
Greensburgh (Pa.) Gazette
Hancock Patriot (Hancock Co., Ill.)
Hartford (Conn.) Courant
Huntsville (Ala.) Times
Indianapolis Journal
Indianapolis News
Indianapolis Star
Jackson (Tenn.) Sun
Journal Gazette (Mattoon, Ill.)
Kansas City Journal
Kokomo (Ind.) Morning Times
Kokomo (Ind.) Tribune
Liberty (Miss.) Advocate
Lincoln (Neb.) Star
Los Angeles Times
Louisville (Ky.) Journal
Manhattan (Kans.) Mercury
Marion County Herald (Palmyra, Mo.)
Maryland Gazette (Annapolis, Md.)
Natchez (Miss.) Courier
Natchez (Miss.) Free Trader
Nebraska State Journal (Lincoln)
New Brunswick (N.J.) Times
New Orleans Advocate
New Orleans Bulletin
Newport (R.I.) Daily News
News (Frederick, Md.)

New York Times
New-York Tribune
News Journal (Wilmington, Del.)
Ogden (Utah) Standard
Oklahoman (Oklahoma City)
Omaha (Neb.) Daily Bee
Pennsylvania Gazette (Philadelphia)
Philadelphia Inquirer
Pine Bluff (Ark.) Daily Graphic
Pittsburgh Daily Post
Poughkeepsie (N.Y.) Journal
Reading (Pa.) Times
St. Louis Post-Dispatch
Saint Paul (Minn.) Globe
Santa Cruz (Calif.) Sentinel
Star Tribune (Minneapolis)
Tennessean (Nashville)
Times (Philadelphia)
Times-Democrat (New Orleans)
Tulsa (Okla.) World
USA Today
Vicksburg (Miss.) Sentinel
Vicksburg (Miss.) Herald
Wall Street Journal
Washington Post
Weekly Standard (Leavenworth, Kans.)
Western Pioneer (Springfield, Ohio)
Wichita (Kans.) Daily Eagle
Wisconsin State Journal (Madison)
Worcester (Mass.) Evening Gazette
Xenia (Ohio) Daily Gazette

OTHER PERIODICALS

Albion
American Magazine and Historical Chronicle
Atlantic
Catholic Advance
Catholic Telegraph
Christian Century
Christian Observer
Christian Register
Christian Register and Boston Observer
Christian Review
Christian Secretary

Christian Watchman
Christian Watchman and Reflector
Congressional Record
Current Literature
Dial
Episcopal Recorder
Friend
Harper's Weekly
Liberator
Life
Lutheran Witness
Millennial Star
Monthly Religious Magazine
Monthly Weather Review
National Druggist
Nature
Network News (WordAlone Ministries)
New Yorker
New York Evangelist
New York Observer and Chronicle
Newsweek
Protestant Vindicator
Quarterly Echoes
Temple of Reason
Time
Times and Seasons
Transactions of the Kansas Academy of Science
Universalist Quarterly and General Review
Western Journal of Medicine and Surgery
Worcester Magazine

BLOGS AND OTHER WEB SITES

AccuWeather: http://www.accuweather.com
American National Biography: http://www.anb.org
Assumption College (Worcester, Mass.): http://www.assumption.edu
Baptist Press (Southern Baptist Convention): http://www.bpnews.net
Capital Weather Gang (*Washington Post* blog): http://www.washingtonpost.com/news/capital-weather-gang
Cornwall Alliance: http://cornwallalliance.org
Daily Beast: http://www.thedailybeast.com
Dot Earth (*New York Times* blog): http://dotearth.blogs.nytimes.com
Encyclopedia Brunoniana (Brown University): http://www.brown.edu/Administration/News_Bureau/Databases/Encyclopedia

Evangelical Climate Initiative: http://www.christiansandclimate.org

Evangelical Environmental Network: http://www.creationcare.org

Huffington Post: http://www.huffingtonpost.com

Inhofe, James (US Senate): http://www.inhofe.senate.gov

Mennonite Disaster Service: http://www.mds.mennonite.net

Mohler, R. Albert, Jr.: http://www.albertmohler.com

National Weather Service, Indianapolis Office: http://www.weather.gov/ind

National Weather Service, Norman, Okla., Office: http://www.weather.gov/oun

National Weather Service, Northern Indiana Office: http://www.weather.gov/iwx

NBC News: http://www.nbcnews.com

New England Historical Society: http://www.newenglandhistoricalsociety.com

Newspapers.com: http://www.newspapers.com

NSSL News (National Severe Storms Laboratory): http://blog.nssl.noaa.gov/nsslnews

Oxford Dictionary of National Biography: http://www.oxforddnb.com

Oxford English Dictionary: http://www.oed.com

Pew Research Center: http://www.pewforum.org

Piper, John: http://www.desiringgod.org

Ramby, Homer G.: http://www.xeniatornado.com

Special Divine Action (SDA) Project, Oxford University: http://sda.bodleian.ox.ac.uk

The Spoof: http://www.thespoof.com

State Impact Oklahoma: https://stateimpact.npr.org/oklahoma

Storm Prediction Center, National Weather Service: http://www.spc.noaa.gov

Storms, Sam: http://www.samstorms.com

Subiaco Abbey (Subiaco, Ark.): http://www.countrymonks.org

Weather Channel: http://www.weather.com

YouTube: http://www.youtube.com

BOOKS AND ARTICLES (PRIMARY AND SECONDARY)

Aberth, John. *From the Brink of the Apocalypse: Confronting Famine, War, Plague, and Death in the Later Middle Ages*. 2nd ed. New York: Routledge, 2010.

Adams, Eliphalet. *A Discourse Occasioned By the late Distressing Storm Which began Feb. 20th. 1716,17. As it was Deliver'd March 3d. 1716.7*. New London, Conn., 1717.

Adams, Eliphalet. *God sometimes Answers His People, by Terrible Things in Righteousness. A Discourse Occasioned by that Awful Thunder-clap Which Struck the Meeting-House in N. London, Aug. 31st. 1735. At what Time One was Killed outright and diverse Others much hurt and wounded, Yet graciously & remarkably Preserved, together with the rest of the Congregation, from Immediate Death. As it was Delivered (Sept. 7th) the Lord's Day Following*. New London, Conn., 1735.

Adamthwaite, Murray R. *Through the Christian Year with Charles Wesley: 101 Psalms and Hymns*. Eugene, Ore.: Wipf and Stock, 2016.

Akin, Wallace. *The Forgotten Storm: The Great Tri-State Tornado of 1925*. Guilford, Conn.: Lyons Press, Rowman and Littlefield, 2002.

Albanese, Catherine L. *A Republic of Mind and Spirit: A Cultural History of American Metaphysical Religion*. New Haven, Conn.: Yale University Press, 2007.

Aldridge, Alfred Owen. "Benjamin Franklin and Jonathan Edwards on Lightning and Earthquakes." In *Early American Science*, edited by Brooke Hindle. New York: Science History Publications, 1976.

Allen, Richard. *The Life, Experience, and Gospel Labours of the Rt. Rev. Richard Allen*. Philadelphia, 1833.

Alumkal, Antony. *Paranoid Science: The Christian Right's War on Reality*. New York: New York University Press, 2017.

Annual Report of the Chief Signal Officer of the Army to the Secretary of War for the Year 1885. Washington, D.C.: Government Printing Office, 1885.

Annual Report of the Chief Signal Officer of the Army to the Secretary of War for the Year 1887. Washington, D.C.: Government Printing Office, 1887.

Anthony, Susanna. *The Life and Character of Miss Susanna Anthony*. Edited by Samuel Hopkins. Worcester, Mass., 1796.

Aquinas, Thomas. *Summa Theologiae*. Blackfriars ed. Vol. 5. *God's Will and Providence (Ia. 19–26)*. Translated by Thomas Gilby. London: Eyre and Spottiswoode, 1967.

Araki, Michio. "Kami." In *Encyclopedia of Religion*, edited by Lindsay Jones. 2nd ed. Vol. 8. Detroit: Macmillan Reference, 2005.

Ashley, Walker S. "Spatial and Temporal Analysis of Tornado Fatalities in the United States: 1880–2005." *Weather and Forecasting* 22 (2007): 1214–1228.

Bahá'u'lláh. *Gleanings from the Writings of Bahá'u'lláh*. Translated by Shoghi Effendi. Wilmette, Ill.: Bahá'í, 2005.

Baier, Annette C. *The Pursuits of Philosophy: An Introduction to the Life and Thought of David Hume*. Cambridge, Mass.: Harvard University Press, 2011.

Bailey, Holly. *The Mercy of the Sky: The Story of a Tornado*. New York: Viking, 2015.

Bates, F. C. "Severe Local Storm Forecasts and Warnings to the General Public." *Bulletin of the American Meteorological Society* 43 (1962): 288–91.

Beal, Timothy K. *Religion and Its Monsters*. New York: Routledge, 2002.

Bebbington, D. W. *Evangelicalism in Modern Britain: A History from the 1730s to the 1980s*. 1989. Reprint, London: Routledge, 1993.

Bechtel, Stefan, with Tim Samaras. *Tornado Hunter: Getting Inside the Most Violent Storms on Earth*. Washington, D.C.: National Geographic, 2009.

Beecher, Henry Ward. "Conceptions of God." *Plymouth Pulpit* 5, no. 12 (December 27, 1882): 243–57.

Beecher, Henry Ward. "God in Christ." *Plymouth Pulpit* 5, no. 13 (January 3, 1883): 263–77.

Beecher, Henry Ward. *The Sermons of Henry Ward Beecher, in Plymouth Church, Brooklyn*. Edited by T. J. Ellinwood. New York, 1873.

Beecher, Henry Ward. "Theological Statement of Belief." In *Henry Ward Beecher: A Sketch of His Career*, edited by Lyman Abbott. New York, 1883.

Beemer, Rod. *The Deadliest Woman in the West: Mother Nature on the Prairies and the Plains, 1800–1900*. Caldwell, Idaho: Caxton Press, 2006.

The Bhagavata Purana. Part 4. Translated by Ganesh Vasudeo Tagare. In *Ancient Indian Tradition and Mythology*, edited by J. L. Shastri. Vol. 10. Delhi: Motilal Banarsidass, 1976.

Bikos, Dan, Jonathan Finch, and Jonathan L. Case. "The Environment Associated with Significant Tornadoes in Bangladesh." *Atmospheric Research* 167 (2016): 183–95.

Binder, Denis. "Act of God? or Act of Man?: A Reappraisal of the Act of God Defense in Tort Law." *Review of Litigation* 15, no. 1 (1996): 1–79.

Bird, Phyllis A. "Wind." In *Harper's Bible Dictionary*, edited by Paul J. Achtemeier et al. San Francisco: Harper and Row, 1985.

Blochowiak, Mary Ann. "Sooner." In *The Encyclopedia of Oklahoma History and Culture*, edited by Dianna Everett. Oklahoma City: Oklahoma Historical Society, 2009. http://www.okhistory.org.

Bluestein, Howard B. *Severe Convective Storms and Tornadoes: Observations and Dynamics*. Berlin: Springer Verlag, 2013.

Bluestein, Howard B. *Tornado Alley: Monster Storms of the Great Plains*. New York: Oxford University Press, 1999.

Bonee, Pam. "William G. Pollard." In *Tennessee Encyclopedia of History and Culture*, edited by Carroll Van West. Knoxville: University of Tennessee Press, 1998–2018. http://tennesseeencyclopedia.net.

The Book of Concord: The Confessions of the Evangelical Lutheran Church. Edited by Robert Kolb and Timothy J. Wengert and translated by Charles Arand et al. Minneapolis: Fortress Press, 2000.

Book of Worship, Published by the General Synod of the Evangelical Lutheran Church in the United States. Rev. ed. Philadelphia: Lutheran Publication Society, 1870.

Bowen, Catherine Drinker. *John Adams and the American Revolution*. Boston: Little, Brown, 1950.

Bowler, Kate. *Everything Happens for a Reason: And Other Lies I've Loved*. New York: Random House, 2018.

Boyd, Gregory A. *God of the Possible: A Biblical Introduction to the Open View of God*. Grand Rapids, Mich.: Baker Books, 2000.

Boyer, Paul. *When Time Shall Be No More: Prophecy Belief in Modern American Culture*. Cambridge, Mass.: Belknap Press, Harvard University Press, 1992.

Bozeman, Theodore Dwight. *Protestants in an Age of Science: The Baconian Ideal and Antebellum Religious Thought*. Chapel Hill: University of North Carolina Press, 1977.

Bradbury, Ray. *The Golden Apples of the Sun*. Garden City, N.Y.: Doubleday, 1953.

Bradford, Marlene. *Scanning the Skies: A History of Tornado Forecasting*. Norman: University of Oklahoma Press, 2001.

Braun, Theodore E. D., and John B. Radner, eds. *The Lisbon Earthquake of 1755: Representations and Reactions*. Oxford: Voltaire Foundation, 2005.

Brekus, Catherine A. *Sarah Osborn's World: The Rise of Evangelical Christianity in Early America*. New Haven, Conn.: Yale University Press, 2013.

Brewster, Melanie E. "The Other Closet: An Introduction to Atheism and Coming Out Processes." In *Atheists in America*, edited by Melanie E. Brewster. New York: Columbia University Press, 2014.

Brightman, Edgar Sheffield. *A Philosophy of Religion*. 1940. Reprint, New York: Greenwood Press, 1969.

Brightman, Edgar Sheffield. *The Problem of God*. New York: Abingdon Press, 1930.

Brinkley, Douglas. *The Great Deluge: Hurricane Katrina, New Orleans, and the Mississippi Gulf Coast*. New York: William Morrow, 2006.

Brodie, Fawn M. *No Man Knows My History: The Life of Joseph Smith, the Mormon Prophet*. 2nd ed. New York: Knopf, 1971.

Brown, Jerry Wayne. *The Rise of Biblical Criticism in America, 1800–1870: The New England Scholars*. Middletown, Conn.: Wesleyan University Press, 1969.

Burgh, James. *Britain's Remembrancer: or, The Danger not over.* London, 1746.

Burke, Edmund. *A Philosophical Enquiry into the Origin of Our Ideas of the Sublime and Beautiful.* Edited by Paul Guyer. Oxford: Oxford University Press, 2015.

Burkert, Walter. *Greek Religion.* Translated by John Raffan. Cambridge, Mass.: Harvard University Press, 1985.

Burns, William E. *An Age of Wonders: Prodigies, Politics and Providence in England, 1657–1727.* Manchester: Manchester University Press, 2002.

Burr, Esther Edwards. *The Journal of Esther Edwards Burr, 1754–1757.* Edited by Carol F. Karlsen and Laurie Crumpacker. New Haven, Conn.: Yale University Press, 1984.

Cabet, Étienne. *Travels in Icaria.* Translated by Leslie J. Roberts. Syracuse, N.Y.: Syracuse University Press, 2003.

Cabet, Étienne. *Le vrai Christianisme suivant Jésus-Christ.* 3rd ed. Paris, 1848.

Calvin, John. *Commentaries on the First Twenty Chapters of the Book of the Prophet Ezekiel.* Translated by Thomas Myers. 2 vols. Edinburgh: Calvin Translation Society, 1849–1850.

Calvin, John. *Institutes of the Christian Religion.* 1536 ed. Edited and translated by Ford Lewis Battles. London: Collins, 1975.

Calvin, John. *Institutes of the Christian Religion.* 1559 ed. Edited by John T. McNeill and translated by Ford Lewis Battles. 2 vols. Philadelphia: Westminster Press, 1960.

"Caring for Creation: Vision, Hope, and Justice." Chicago: Evangelical Lutheran Church in America, 1993.

Carnell, Edward John. *A Philosophy of the Christian Religion.* Grand Rapids, Mich.: Baker Book House, 1952.

Carson, Clayborne, et al. *The Martin Luther King, Jr., Encyclopedia.* Westport, Conn.: Greenwood Press, 2008.

Carter, Paul A. *The Spiritual Crisis of the Gilded Age.* DeKalb: Northern Illinois University Press, 1971.

Carter, Heath W. *Union Made: Working People and the Rise of Social Christianity in Chicago.* New York: Oxford University Press, 2015.

Cashdollar, Charles D. "The Social Implications of the Doctrine of Divine Providence: A Nineteenth-Century Debate in American Theology," *Harvard Theological Review* 71 (1978): 265–84.

Cashdollar, Charles D. *The Transformation of Theology, 1830–1890: Positivism and Protestant Thought in Britain and America.* Princeton, N.J.: Princeton University Press, 1989.

Caskey, Marie. *Chariot of Fire: Religion and the Beecher Family.* New Haven, Conn.: Yale University Press, 1978.

The Catechism of the Council of Trent, Published by Command of Pope Pius the Fifth. Translated by Jeremiah Donovan. New York: Christian Press Association, 1905.

Chace, George I. *The Relation of Divine Providence to Physical Laws: A Discourse Delivered Before the Porter Rhetorical Society, of Andover Theological Seminary, August 1, 1854.* Boston, 1854.

Chan, Michael J., and Brent A. Strawn, eds. *What Kind of God? Collected Essays of Terence E. Fretheim.* Winona Lake, Ind.: Eisenbrauns, 2015.

Charnock, Stephen. *A Discourse of Divine Providence. I. In General: That there is a Providence Exercised by God in the World. II. In Particular: How all Gods Providences in the World, are in order to the good of his People.* London, 1684.

Chauchetière, Claude. "Narration annuelle de la fondation de la Mission du Sault jusqu'à 1685." In *The Jesuit Relations and Allied Documents: Travels and Explorations of the Jesuit Missionaries in New France, 1610–1791*. Vol. 63. Cleveland: Burrows, 1900.

Chemery, Peter C. "Meteorological Beings." In *Encyclopedia of Religion*, edited by Lindsay Jones. 2nd ed. Vol. 9. Detroit: Macmillan Reference, 2005.

Clem, Dale. *Winds of Fury, Circles of Grace: Life after the Palm Sunday Tornadoes*. Nashville: Abingdon Press, 1997.

Coalter, Milton J., Jr. *Gilbert Tennent, Son of Thunder: A Case Study of Continental Pietism's Impact on the First Great Awakening in the Middle Colonies*. New York: Greenwood Press, Presbyterian Historical Society, 1986.

Coffman, Elesha J. *The Christian Century and the Rise of the Protestant Mainline*. New York: Oxford University Press, 2013.

Cogswell, James. *The Danger of disregarding the Works of God: A Sermon, Delivered at Canterbury, November 23, 1755. Being the next Sabbath after the late surprizing Earthquake*. New Haven, Conn., 1755.

Coleman, Timothy A., and P. Grady Dixon. "An Objective Analysis of Tornado Risk in the United States." *Weather and Forecasting* 29 (April 2014): 366–76.

Collins, Billy, ed. *Poetry 180: A Turning Back to Poetry*. New York: Random House, 2003.

Collins, John J. *The Apocalyptic Imagination: An Introduction to Jewish Apocalyptic Literature*. 3rd ed. Grand Rapids, Mich.: Eerdmans, 2016.

Columbus, Christopher. *The Diario of Christopher Columbus's First Voyage to America, 1492–1493*. Abstracted by Bartolomé de las Casas and translated by Oliver Dunn and James E. Kelley, Jr. Norman: University of Oklahoma Press, 1989.

Concannon, Peggy R., Harold E. Brooks, and Charles A. Doswell III. "Climatological Risk of Strong and Violent Tornadoes in the United States." Second Conference on Environmental Applications, American Meteorological Society, Long Beach, California, January 8–12, 2000. https://www.nssl.noaa.gov/users/brooks/public_html/concannon/.

Conser, Walter H., Jr. *God and the Natural World: Religion and Science in Antebellum America*. Columbia: University of South Carolina Press, 1993.

Coogan, Michael. *The Ten Commandments: A Short History of an Ancient Text*. New Haven, Conn.: Yale University Press, 2014.

Coogan, Michael D., and Mark S. Smith, eds. and trans. *Stories from Ancient Canaan*. Louisville, Ky.: Westminster John Knox Press, 2012.

Crenshaw, James L. *Defending God: Biblical Responses to the Problem of Evil*. New York: Oxford University Press, 2005.

Crenshaw, James. L. "Job." In *The Oxford Bible Commentary*, edited by John Barton and John Muddiman. New York: Oxford University Press, 2001.

Cross, Frank Moore. *Canaanite Myth and Hebrew Epic: Essays in the History of the Religion of Israel*. Cambridge, Mass.: Harvard University Press, 1973.

Cross, Kim. *What Stands in a Storm: Three Days in the Worst Superstorm to Hit the South's Tornado Alley*. New York: Atria Books, 2015.

Curzon, Julian [pseud.], ed. *The Great Cyclone at St. Louis and East St. Louis, May 27, 1896*. 1896. Reprint, Carbondale: Southern Illinois University Press, 1997.

Dains, Mary K. "The St. Louis Tornado of 1896." *Missouri Historical Review* 66 (1972): 431–45.

Davis, John Jefferson. *The Frontiers of Science and Faith: Examining Questions from the Big Bang to the End of the Universe.* Downers Grove, Ill.: InterVarsity Press, 2002.

Davis, Stephen T., ed. *Encountering Evil: Live Options in Theodicy.* Rev. ed. Louisville, Ky.: Westminster John Knox Press, 2001.

Deitz, Robert E. *April 3, 1974: Tornado!* Louisville, Ky.: Courier-Journal and Louisville Times, 1974.

Delbourgo, James. *A Most Amazing Scene of Wonders: Electricity and Enlightenment in Early America.* Cambridge, Mass.: Harvard University Press, 2006.

DeVoto, Bernard. Introduction to *Beyond the Hundredth Meridian: John Wesley Powell and the Second Opening of the West* by Wallace Stegner. 1953. Reprint, New York: Penguin Books, 1992.

DeVries, Dawn, and B. A. Gerrish. "Providence and Grace: Schleiermacher on Justification and Election." In *The Cambridge Companion to Friedrich Schleiermacher*, edited by Jacqueline Mariña. Cambridge: Cambridge University Press, 2005.

DeWeese, Garrett J. "Open Theism." In *Dictionary of Christianity and Science*, edited by Paul Copan, Tremper Longman III, Christopher L. Reese, and Michael G. Strauss. Grand Rapids, Mich.: Zondervan, 2017.

Dewey, Donald. "Thor-oughly Mythological." *Scandinavian Review* 102, no. 3 (2015): 54–63.

Dixon, P. Grady, Andrew E. Mercer, Jinmu Choi, and Jared S. Allen. "Tornado Risk Analysis: Is Dixie Alley an Extension of Tornado Alley?" *Bulletin of the American Meteorological Society* 92 (April 2011): 433–41.

Donagan, Barbara. "Providence Chance and Explanation: Some Paradoxical Aspects of Puritan Views of Causation." *Journal of Religious History* 11 (1981): 385–403.

Dorrien, Gary. *The Making of American Liberal Theology: Crisis, Irony, and Postmodernity, 1950–2005.* Louisville, Ky.: Westminster John Knox Press, 2006.

Dorrien, Gary. *The Making of American Liberal Theology: Idealism, Realism, and Modernity, 1900–1950.* Louisville, Ky.: Westminster John Knox Press, 2003.

Dorrien, Gary. *The Making of American Liberal Theology: Imagining Progressive Religion, 1805–1900.* Louisville, Ky.: Westminster John Knox Press, 2001.

Dorsett, Lyle W. *Billy Sunday and the Redemption of Urban America.* Grand Rapids, Mich.: Eerdmans, 1991.

Dray, Philip. *Stealing God's Thunder: Benjamin Franklin's Lightning Rod and the Invention of America.* New York: Random House, 2005.

Dulles, Avery. Review of *Reaping the Whirlwind*, by Langdon Gilkey. *Wilson Quarterly* 2, no. 1 (1978): 155.

Dundy, Elaine. *Elvis and Gladys.* 1985. Reprint, Jackson: University Press of Mississippi, 2004.

Dwight, Timothy. *The Nature and Danger of Infidel Philosophy, Exhibited in Two Discourses, Addressed to the Candidates for the Baccalaureate, in Yale College.* New Haven, Conn., 1798.

Earp, Steven, with Jennifer Spinola. *Storms of Life: Learning to Trust God Again.* Oklahoma City: ElevateFaith, 2015.

Ebel, Jonathan H. *Faith in the Fight: Religion and the American Soldier in the Great War.* Princeton, N.J.: Princeton University Press, 2010.

Eckert, Allan W. *A Time of Terror: The Great Dayton Flood.* Boston: Little, Brown, 1965.

Ecklund, Elaine Howard, and Christopher P. Scheitle. *Religion vs. Science: What Religious People Really Think.* New York: Oxford University Press, 2018.

Eddy, William A. "Progress in Tornado-Prediction." *Popular Science Monthly* 28 (January 1886): 307–14.

Edwards, Jonathan. *The Works of Jonathan Edwards*, Vol. 6, *Scientific and Philosophical Writings*. Edited by Wallace E. Anderson. New Haven, Conn.: Yale University Press, 1980.

Edwards, Jonathan. *The Works of Jonathan Edwards*, Vol. 7, *The Life of David Brainerd*. Edited by Norman Pettit. New Haven, Conn.: Yale University Press, 1985.

Edwards, Jonathan. *The Works of Jonathan Edwards*, Vol. 11, *Typological Writings*. Edited by Wallace E. Anderson, Mason I. Lowance, Jr., and David H. Watters. New Haven, Conn.: Yale University Press, 1993.

Edwards, Jonathan. *The Works of Jonathan Edwards*, Vol. 13, *The "Miscellanies," a–500*. Edited by Thomas A. Schafer. New Haven, Conn.: Yale University Press, 1994.

Edwards, Jonathan. *The Works of Jonathan Edwards*, Vol. 14, *Sermons and Discourses, 1723–1729*. Edited by Kenneth P. Minkema. New Haven, Conn.: Yale University Press, 1997.

Edwards, Jonathan. *The Works of Jonathan Edwards*, Vol. 15, *Notes on Scripture*. Edited by Stephen J. Stein. New Haven, Conn.: Yale University Press, 1998.

Edwards, Jonathan. *The Works of Jonathan Edwards*, Vol. 16, *Letters and Personal Writings*. Edited by George S. Claghorn. New Haven, Conn.: Yale University Press, 1998.

Edwards, Jonathan. *The Works of Jonathan Edwards*, Vol. 17, *Sermons and Discourses, 1730–1733*. Edited by Mark Valeri. New Haven, Conn.: Yale University Press, 1999.

Edwards, Jonathan. *The Works of Jonathan Edwards*, Vol. 19, *Sermons and Discourses, 1734–1738*. Edited by M. X. Lesser. New Haven, Conn.: Yale University Press, 2001.

Edwards, Jonathan. *The Works of Jonathan Edwards*, Vol. 22, *Sermons and Discourses, 1739–1742*. Edited by Harry S. Stout and Nathan O. Hatch, with Kyle P. Farley. New Haven, Conn.: Yale University Press, 2003.

Edwards, Jonathan. *The Works of Jonathan Edwards*, Vol. 24, *The "Blank Bible."* Edited by Stephen J. Stein. New Haven, Conn.: Yale University Press, 2006.

Edwards, Jonathan. *The Works of Jonathan Edwards*, Vol. 26, *Catalogues of Books*. Edited by Peter J. Thuesen. New Haven, Conn.: Yale University Press, 2008.

Ehrman, Bart D. *God's Problem: How the Bible Fails to Answer Our Most Important Question—Why We Suffer*. New York: HarperOne, 2008.

Ehrman, Bart D. *Jesus: Apocalyptic Prophet of the New Millennium*. New York: Oxford University Press, 1999.

Eliade, Mircea. *Patterns in Comparative Religion*. Translated by Rosemary Sheed. 1958. Reprint, New York: World, 1963.

Eliade, Mircea. *The Sacred and the Profane: The Nature of Religion*. Translated by Willard R. Trask. New York: Harcourt, 1959.

Eliot, Charles W. *The Religion of the Future*. Boston: John W. Luce, 1909.

Elliott, Emory. *Power and the Pulpit in Puritan New England*. Princeton, N.J.: Princeton University Press, 1975.

Ellis, Erle C. *Anthropocene: A Very Short Introduction*. New York: Oxford University Press, 2018.

Ellsworth, Tim. *God in the Whirlwind: Stories of Grace from the Tornado at Union University*. Nashville: B&H, 2008.

Elsom, Derek M. *Lightning: Nature and Culture*. London: Reaktion Books, 2015.

Emanuel, Kerry. *Divine Wind: The History and Science of Hurricanes*. New York: Oxford University Press, 2005.

Emmerson, Richard K., and Bernard McGinn, eds. *The Apocalypse in the Middle Ages*. Ithaca, N.Y.: Cornell University Press, 1992.

England, Gary A. *Weathering the Storm: Tornadoes, Television, and Turmoil*. Norman: University of Oklahoma Press, 1996.

"Environmental Justice for a Sustainable Future." In *The Book of Resolutions of the United Methodist Church*. Nashville: United Methodist, 1992.

Espy, James P. *The Human Will: A Series of Posthumous Essays on Moral Accountability, the Legitimate Object of Punishment, and the Powers of the Will*. Cincinnati, 1860.

Espy, James P. *The Philosophy of Storms*. Boston, 1841.

Evans, Jeffry S., Corey M. Mead, and Steven J. Weiss. "Forecasting the Super Tuesday Outbreak at the SPC: Why Forecast Uncertainty Does Not Necessarily Decrease as You Get Closer to a High Impact Weather Event." 24th Conference on Severe Local Storms, October 27–31, 2008, Savannah, Ga. https://www.spc.noaa.gov/publications/evans/sup-tues.pdf.

Fara, Patricia. *An Entertainment for Angels: Electricity in the Enlightenment*. New York: Columbia University Press, 2002.

Farley, Benjamin Wirt. *The Providence of God*. Grand Rapids, Mich.: Baker Book House, 1988.

Farmer, David Hugh. *The Oxford Dictionary of Saints*. 5th rev. ed. Oxford: Oxford University Press, 2011.

Felknor, Peter S. *The Tri-State Tornado: The Story of America's Greatest Tornado Disaster*. New York: iUniverse, 2004.

Finley. John P. *Tornadoes, What They Are, and How to Escape Them*. Washington, D.C., 1888.

Finley. John P. *Tornadoes: What They Are and How to Observe Them; with Practical Suggestions for the Protection of Life and Property*. New York, 1887.

Finstuen, Andrew S. *Original Sin and Everyday Protestants: The Theology of Reinhold Niebuhr, Billy Graham, and Paul Tillich in an Age of Anxiety*. Chapel Hill: University of North Carolina Press, 2009.

Fitzmier, John R. *New England's Moral Legislator: Timothy Dwight, 1752–1817*. Bloomington: Indiana University Press, 1998.

Flavel, John. *Divine Conduct: or, The Mysterie of Providence. Wherein the Being and Efficacy of Providence is Asserted, and Vindicated: The Methods of Providence as it passes through the several Stages of our Lives opened; and the proper course of improving all Providences directed, in a Treatise upon Psalm 57. Ver. 2*. London, 1678.

Fleming, James Rodger. *Fixing the Sky: The Checkered History of Weather and Climate Control*. New York: Columbia University Press, 2010.

Fleming, James Rodger. *Inventing Atmospheric Science: Bjerknes, Rossby, Wexler, and the Foundations of Modern Meteorology*. Cambridge, Mass.: MIT Press, 2016.

Fleming, James Rodger. *Meteorology in America, 1800–1870*. Baltimore: Johns Hopkins University Press, 1990.

Flora, Snowden D. *Tornadoes of the United States*. Rev. ed. Norman: University of Oklahoma Press, 1954.

Fontenelle, Bernard le Bovier de. *De l'Origine des Fables*. In *The Achievement of Bernard le Bovier de Fontenelle*, edited by Leonard M. Marsak. New York: Johnson Reprint, 1970.

Foster, Douglas A., Paul M. Blowers, Anthony L. Dunnavant, and D. Newell Williams, eds. *The Encyclopedia of the Stone-Campbell Movement*. Grand Rapids, Mich.: Eerdmans, 2004.

Fourth National Climate Assessment, Vol. 2, *Impacts, Risks, and Adaptation in the United States*. Washington, D.C.: U.S. Global Change Research Program, 2018.

Fox, Richard Wightman. *Reinhold Niebuhr: A Biography*. New York: Pantheon Books, 1985.

Foxcroft, Thomas. *The Earthquake, a Divine Visitation: A Sermon Preached to the Old Church in Boston, January 8, 1756*. Boston, 1756.

Foxcroft, Thomas. *A seasonable Memento for New Year's Day. A Sermon Preached (summarily) at the Old Church Lecture in Boston, On Thursday January 1. 1746–7*. Boston, 1747.

Frame, John. *No Other God: A Response to Open Theism*. Phillipsburg, N.J.: P&R, 2001.

Franklin, Benjamin. *The Autobiography of Benjamin Franklin*. Edited by Leonard W. Labaree, Ralph L. Ketcham, Helen C. Boatfield, and Helene H. Fineman. 2nd ed. New Haven, Conn.: Yale University Press, 2003.

Freedman, David Noel, et al., eds. *The Anchor Bible Dictionary*. 6 vols. New York: Doubleday, 1992.

French, Jonathan. *A Sermon, Delivered on the Anniversary Thanksgiving November 29, 1798*. Andover, Mass., 1799.

Fretheim, Terence E. *Creation Untamed: The Bible, God, and Natural Disasters*. Grand Rapids, Mich.: Baker Academic, 2010.

Freud, Sigmund. *The Future of an Illusion*. Translated by James Strachey. New York: W. W. Norton, 1961.

Frisinger, H. Howard. *The History of Meteorology to 1800*. New York: Science History Publications, American Meteorological Society, 1977.

Froese, Paul, and Christopher Bader. *America's Four Gods: What We Say about God—and What That Says about Us*. New York: Oxford University Press, 2010.

Frost, William J. *A Perfect Freedom: Religious Liberty in Pennsylvania*. Cambridge: Cambridge University Press, 1990.

Fujita, Tetsuya Theodore. "Memoirs of an Effort to Unlock the Mystery of Severe Storms." Wind Research Laboratory, University of Chicago, 1992.

Fujita, Tetsuya T., Dorothy L. Bradbury, and C. F. Van Thullenar. "Palm Sunday Tornadoes of April 11, 1965." *Monthly Weather Review* 98, no. 1 (1970): 29–69.

Fulke, William. *A Goodly Gallerye with a Most Pleasaunt Prospect, into the garden of naturall contemplation, to behold the naturall causes of all kynde of Meteors*. London, 1563.

Galway, Joseph G. "J. P. Finley: The First Severe Storms Forecaster." *Bulletin of the American Meteorological Society* 66 (1985): 1389–95, 1506–10.

Garner, Bryan A., ed. *Black's Law Dictionary*, 7th ed. St. Paul, Minn.: West Group, 1999.

Garner, Dean E. "Nauvoo's Temple." *Perspective* [Brigham Young University-Idaho] 2, no. 2 (Summer 2002): 79–91.

Gensini, Vittorio A., and Harold E. Brooks. "Spatial Trends in United States Tornado Frequency." *Climate and Atmospheric Science* 1, no. 38 (2018): 1–5. https://www.nature.com/npjclimatsci/.

Gerrish, B. A. "Charles Hodge and the Europeans." In *Charles Hodge Revisited: A Critical Appraisal of His Life and Work*, edited by John W. Stewart and James H. Moorhead. Grand Rapids, Mich.: Eerdmans, 2002.

Gerrish, B. A. *A Prince of the Church: Schleiermacher and the Beginnings of Modern Theology*. 1984. Reprint, Eugene, Ore.: Wipf and Stock, 2001.

Giberson, Karl W. "Chance, Divine Action, and the Natural Order of Things." In *Abraham's Dice: Chance and Providence in the Monotheistic Traditions*, ed. Karl W. Giberson. New York: Oxford University Press, 2016.

Gilkes, Cheryl Townsend. *If It Wasn't for the Women: Black Women's Experience and Womanist Culture in Church and Community*. Maryknoll, N.Y.: Orbis Books, 2001.

Gilkey, Langdon B. "The Concept of Providence in Contemporary Theology." *Journal of Religion* 43, no. 3 (1963): 171–92.

Gilkey, Langdon B. *Naming the Whirlwind: The Renewal of God-Language*. Indianapolis: Bobbs-Merrill, 1969.

Gilkey, Langdon B. *On Niebuhr: A Theological Study*. Chicago: University of Chicago Press, 2001.

Gilkey, Langdon B. *Reaping the Whirlwind: A Christian Interpretation of History*. New York: Seabury Press, 1976.

Gilkey, Langdon B. *Through the Tempest: Theological Voyages in a Pluralistic Culture*. Edited by Jeff B. Pool. 1991. Reprint, Eugene, Ore.: Wipf and Stock, 2005.

Gleick, James. *Chaos: Making a New Science*. Rev. ed. New York: Penguin Books, 2008.

Gleig, George Robert. *The Campaigns of the British Army at Washington and New Orleans, in the Years 1814–1815*. 3rd ed. London: John Murray, 1827.

"Global Climate Change: A Plea for Dialogue, Prudence, and the Common Good." Washington, D.C.: United States Conference of Catholic Bishops, 2001.

Global Warming of 1.5° C . . . Summary for Policymakers. Geneva: Intergovernmental Panel on Climate Change, 2018.

Goad, John. *Astro-Meteorologica, or Aphorisms and Discourses of the Bodies Coelestial, their Natures and Influences*. London, 1686.

Goff, Philip, Arthur E. Farnsley II, and Peter J. Thuesen, eds. *The Bible in American Life*. New York: Oxford University Press, 2017.

Golinski, Jan. *British Weather and the Climate of Enlightenment*. Chicago: University of Chicago Press, 2007.

Gooch, Todd A. "Rudolf Otto and 'The Irrational in the Idea of the Divine.'" In *Religion und Irrationalität: Historisch-systematische Perspektiven*, edited by Jochen Schmidt and Heiko Schulz. Tübingen: Mohr Siebeck, 2013.

Gooch, Todd A. *The Numinous and Modernity: An Interpretation of Rudolf Otto's Philosophy of Religion*. Berlin: Walter de Gruyter, 2000.

Gordon, Bruce. *Calvin*. New Haven, Conn.: Yale University Press, 2009.

Graham, Louis. "The Scientific Piety of John Winthrop of Harvard." *New England Quarterly* 46 (1973): 112–18.

Grant, Robert M. "God and Storms in Early Christian Thought." In *God in Early Christian Thought: Essays in Memory of Lloyd G. Patterson*, edited by Andrew B. McGowan, Brian E. Daley, and Timothy J. Gaden. Leiden: Brill, 2009.

Grasso, Christopher. *Skepticism and American Faith: From the Revolution to the Civil War*. New York: Oxford University Press, 2018.

Grazulis, Thomas P. *Significant Tornadoes, 1680–1991*. St. Johnsbury, Vt.: Environmental Films, 1993.

Grazulis, Thomas P. *The Tornado: America's Ultimate Windstorm*. Norman: University of Oklahoma Press, 2001.

The Great Tornado at St. Louis, May 27th, 1896. St. Louis: Graf Engraving, 1896.

Green, Alberto R. W. *The Storm-God in the Ancient Near East*. Winona Lake, Ind.: Eisenbrauns, 2003.

Greene, Casey Edward, and Shelly Henley Kelly, eds. *Through a Night of Horrors: Voices from the 1900 Galveston Storm*. College Station: Texas A&M University Press, 2000.

Greer, Allan. *Mohawk Saint: Catherine Tekakwitha and the Jesuits*. New York: Oxford University Press, 2005.

Grinnell, Josiah Bushnell. *Men and Events of Forty Years: Autobiographical Reminiscences of an Active Career from 1850 to 1890*. Boston, 1891.

Der grosse Tornado, 27 Mai 1896: 80 Photographien von den durch den Sturm verursachten Ruinen. St. Louis, Westliche Post, Graf Engraving, 1896.

Gundlach, Bradley J. *Process and Providence: The Evolution Question at Princeton, 1845–1929*. Grand Rapids, Mich.: Eerdmans, 2013.

Gunn, Angus M. *Encyclopedia of Disasters*, Vol. 1, *Environmental Catastrophes and Human Tragedies*. Westport, Conn.: Greenwood Press, 2008.

Gutjahr, Paul C. *Charles Hodge: Guardian of American Orthodoxy*. New York: Oxford University Press, 2011.

Guyatt, Nicholas. *Providence and the Invention of the United States, 1607–1876*. Cambridge: Cambridge University Press, 2007.

Hackett, David G. *That Religion in Which All Men Agree: Freemasonry in American Culture*. Berkeley: University of California Press, 2014.

Hall, David D. "Readers and Writers in Early New England." In *A History of the Book in America*, Vol. 1, *The Colonial Book in the Atlantic World*, edited by Hugh Amory and David D. Hall. Cambridge: Cambridge University Press, 2000.

Hall, David D. *Worlds of Wonder, Days of Judgment: Popular Religious Belief in Early New England*. Cambridge, Mass.: Harvard University Press, 1989.

Hammer, Bonaventure, ed. *Mary, Help of Christians, and the Fourteen Saints Invoked as Holy Helpers*. New York: Benziger Brothers, 1909.

Handlin, Oscar. *Chance or Destiny: Turning Points in American History*. Boston: Little, Brown, 1955.

Hankins, Barry. *God's Rascal: J. Frank Norris and the Beginnings of Southern Fundamentalism*. Lexington: University Press of Kentucky, 1996.

Hanson, Anthony Tyrrell. *The Wrath of the Lamb*. London: S.P.C.K., 1957.

Hargrove, Brantley. *The Man Who Caught the Storm: The Life of Legendary Tornado Chaser Tim Samaras*. New York: Simon and Schuster, 2018.

Harkness, Georgia. *Georgia Harkness: The Remaking of a Liberal Theologian*. Edited by Rebekah Miles. Louisville, Ky.: Westminster John Knox Press, 2010.

Harkness, Georgia. *The Providence of God*. New York: Abingdon Press, 1960.

Harkness, Georgia. *The Recovery of Ideals*. New York: Scribner's, 1937.

Harrell, David Edwin, Jr. "American Revivalism from Graham to Robertson." In *Modern Christian Revivals*, ed. Edith L. Blumhofer and Randall Balmer. Urbana: University of Illinois Press, 1993.

Hart, David Bentley. *The Doors of the Sea: Where Was God in the Tsunami?* Grand Rapids, Mich.: Eerdmans, 2005.

Hartley, Gail. "New Thought and the Harmonial Family." In *America's Alternative Religions*, edited by Timothy Miller. Albany: State University of New York Press, 1995.

Hartman, Chester, and Gregory D. Squires, eds. *There Is No Such Thing as a Natural Disaster: Race, Class, and Hurricane Katrina*. New York: Routledge, 2006.

Haven, Samuel. *Joy and Salvation by Christ; his Arm displayed in the Protestant Cause. A Sermon Preached in the South Parish in Portsmouth; Occasioned by the remarkable Success of His Majesty's Arms in the Late War, and by the happy Peace of 1763*. Portsmouth, N.H., 1763.

Hazelton, Roger. *God's Way with Man: Variations on the Theme of Providence*. New York: Abingdon Press, 1956.

Helmholtz, Hermann von. "Wirbelstürme und Gewitter." *Deutsche Rundschau* 6 (1876): 363–80.

Heming, Carol Piper. *Protestants and the Cult of the Saints in German-Speaking Europe, 1517–1531*. Kirksville, Mo.: Truman State University Press, 2003.

Hendrix, Scott H. *Martin Luther: Visionary Reformer*. New Haven, Conn.: Yale University Press, 2015.

Henry, Matthew. *An Exposition of All the Books of the Old and New Testament*. 3rd. ed. 6 vols. London, 1721–1725.

Henson, Robert. *The Thinking Person's Guide to Climate Change*. Boston: American Meteorological Society, 2014.

Henson, Robert. *Weather on the Air: A History of Broadcast Meteorology*. Boston: American Meteorological Society, 2010.

Hepburn, R. W. *"Wonder" and Other Essays: Eight Studies in Aesthetics and Neighbouring Fields*. Edinburgh: Edinburgh University Press, 1984.

Herrick, S. H. "The Grinnell Cyclone of June 17, 1882." *Annals of Iowa* 3 (1897): 81–96.

History of the Church of Jesus Christ of Latter-day Saints. 8 vols. 2nd ed. rev. Salt Lake City: Deseret Book, 1948–70.

Hitchcock, Edward. "Special Divine Interpositions in Nature." *Bibliotheca Sacra* 11 (1854): 776–800.

Hodge, Charles. "Free Agency." *Biblical Repertory and Princeton Review* 29 (1857): 101–35.

Hodge, Charles. *Systematic Theology*. 3 vols. New York: Scribner's, 1871–73.

Holifield, E. Brooks. *Theology in America: Christian Thought from the Age of the Puritans to the Civil War*. New Haven, Conn.: Yale University Press, 2003.

Hornblower, Simon, and Antony Spawforth., eds. *The Oxford Companion to Classical Civilization*. 2nd ed. Oxford: Oxford University Press, 2014.

Horstmeyer, Steven L. *The Weather Almanac: A Reference Guide to Weather, Climate, and Related Issues in the United States and Its Key Cities*. 12th ed. Hoboken, N.J.: Wiley, 2011.

Hosen, Md. Shahadat, and Abu Jubayer. "Chronological History and Destruction Pattern of Tornados in Bangladesh." *American Journal of Environmental Protection* 5, no. 4 (2016): 71–81.

Hostetler, John A. *Amish Society*. 4th ed. Baltimore: Johns Hopkins University Press, 1993.

Howard, James H. *Shawnee! The Ceremonialism of a Native Indian Tribe and Its Cultural Background*. Athens: Ohio University Press, 1981.

Howard, Thomas Albert. "Clouds of Unknowing: Making Sense of the Tornadoes." *Commonweal* 138, no. 12 (June 17, 2011): 8–9.

Howe, Daniel Walker. *What Hath God Wrought: The Transformation of America, 1815–1848*. New York: Oxford University Press, 2007.

Hoxit, Lee R., and Charles F. Chappell. *Tornado Outbreak of April 3–4, 1974; Synoptic Analysis*. Washington, D.C.: U.S. Department of Commerce, 1975.

Hudnut-Beumler, James. *Strangers and Friends at the Welcome Table: Contemporary Christianities in the American South*. Chapel Hill: University of North Carolina Press, 2018.

Hudson, J. Harvie. "The Ellen Burnett Prophesy." *Jefferson County Historical Quarterly* 4, no. 2 (1973): 36–38.

Huizinga, Johan. *The Waning of the Middle Ages: A Study of the Forms of Life, Thought and Art in France and the Netherlands in the XIVth and XVth Centuries*. Translated by Frederik Hopman. London: Edward Arnold, 1924.

Hume, David. *Dialogues Concerning Natural Religion*. In *Principal Writings on Religion, including Dialogues Concerning Natural Religion and* The Natural History of Religion. Edited by J. C. A. Gaskin. Oxford: Oxford University Press, 1993.

Hume, David. *The Natural History of Religion*. Edited by Tom L. Beauchamp. Oxford: Clarendon Press, 2007.

Hutchison, William R. *The Modernist Impulse in American Protestantism*. Durham, N.C.: Duke University Press, 1992.

An Impartial Relation of the Hail-Storm on the Fifteenth of July and the Tornado on the Second of August 1799. Which Appeared in the Towns of Bozrah, Lebanon, and Franklin, in the State of Connecticut. Norwich, Conn., 1799.

Inhofe, James. *The Greatest Hoax: How the Global Warming Conspiracy Threatens Your Future*. Washington, D.C.: WND Books, 2012.

Israel, Jonathan. *Democratic Enlightenment: Philosophy, Revolution, and Human Rights, 1750–1790*. Oxford: Oxford University Press, 2011.

Israel, Jonathan I., and Geoffrey Parker. "Of Providence and Protestant Winds: The Spanish Armada of 1588 and the Dutch Armada of 1688." In *The Anglo-Dutch Moment: Essays on the Glorious Revolution and Its World Impact*, edited by Jonathan I. Israel. Cambridge: Cambridge University Press, 1991.

James, E. O. *The Worship of the Sky-God: A Comparative Study in Semitic and Indo-European Religion*. London: University of London, Athlone Press, 1963.

Janković, Vladimir. *Reading the Skies: A Cultural History of English Weather, 1650–1820*. Chicago: University of Chicago Press, 2000.

Janzen, J. Gerald. *At the Scent of Water: The Ground of Hope in the Book of Job*. Grand Rapids, Mich.: Eerdmans, 2009.

Jenkins, Willis. *The Future of Ethics: Sustainability, Social Justice, and Religious Creativity*. Washington, D.C.: Georgetown University Press, 2013.

Johnson, Christopher H. *Utopian Communism in France: Cabet and the Icarians, 1839–1851*. Ithaca, N.Y.: Cornell University Press, 1974.

Johnson, Robert Underwood. *Remembered Yesterdays*. Boston: Little, Brown, 1923.

Johnston, Sarah Iles, ed. *Religions of the Ancient World: A Guide*. Cambridge, Mass.: Belknap Press, Harvard University Press, 2004.

Jones, John G. *A Complete History of Methodism as Connected with the Mississippi Conference of the Methodist Episcopal Church, South*. 2 vols. Nashville: Methodist Episcopal Church, South, 1908.

Jowers, Dennis W., ed. *Four Views on Divine Providence*. Grand Rapids, Mich.: Zondervan, 2011.

Kallen, Horace M. *Why Religion*. New York: Boni and Liveright, 1927.

Kant, Immanuel. *Critique of Judgment*. Translated by James Creed Meredith and edited by Nicholas Walker. Oxford: Oxford University Press, 2007.

Kazek, Kelly. *A History of Alabama's Deadliest Tornadoes: Disaster in Dixie*. Charleston, S.C.: History Press, 2010.

Keller, Rosemary Skinner. *Georgia Harkness: For Such a Time as This*. Nashville: Abingdon Press, 1992.

Kelley, Leo. "'Not An Upright Stick Remained': Oklahoma: Home of the Real Twisters." *Chronicles of Oklahoma* 74 (Winter 1996–1997): 426–35.

Kidd, Thomas S. *Benjamin Franklin: The Religious Life of a Founding Father*. New Haven, Conn.: Yale University Press, 2017.

Kidd, Thomas S. *The Great Awakening: The Roots of Evangelical Christianity in Colonial America*. New Haven, Conn.: Yale University Press, 2007.

Kidd, Thomas S. *The Protestant Interest: New England after Puritanism*. New Haven, Conn.: Yale University Press, 2004.

Kierkegaard, Søren. *Repetition: An Essay in Experimental Psychology*. Translated by Walter Lowrie. Princeton, N.J.: Princeton University Press, 1941.

Kitagawa, Joseph M. *Religion in Japanese History*. New York: Columbia University Press, 1990.

Kraybill, Donald B. *Concise Encyclopedia of Amish, Brethren, Hutterites, and Mennonites*. Baltimore: Johns Hopkins University Press, 2010.

Kugel, James L. *The God of Old: Inside the Lost World of the Bible*. New York: Free Press, 2003.

Kupperman, Karen Ordahl. "The Puzzle of American Climate in the Early Colonial Period." *American Historical Review* 87 (1982): 1262–89.

Kushner, Harold S. *When Bad Things Happen to Good People*. New York: Avon Books, 1981.

Ladurie, Emmanuel Le Roy. *Times of Feast, Times of Famine: A History of Climate since the Year 1000*. Garden City, N.Y.: Doubleday, 1971.

Laffoon, Polk, IV. *Tornado*. New York: Harper and Row, 1975.

Larrimore, Mark. *The Book of Job: A Biography*. Princeton, N.J.: Princeton University Press, 2013.

Larson, Edward J. *Summer for the Gods: The Scopes Trial and America's Continuing Debate over Science and Religion*. Rev. ed. New York: Basic Books, 2006.

Larson, Erik. *Isaac's Storm*. New York: Vintage Books, 1999.

Laskin, David. *Braving the Elements: The Stormy History of American Weather*. New York: Anchor Books, 1996.

Levin, David. *Cotton Mather: The Young Life of the Lord's Remembrancer, 1663–1703*. Cambridge, Mass.: Harvard University Press, 1978.

Levine, Mark. *F5: Devastation, Survival, and the Most Violent Tornado Outbreak of the Twentieth Century*. New York: Miramax Books, 2007.

Lewis, Michael. *The Fifth Risk*. New York: W. W. Norton, 2018.

Linenthal, Edward Tabor. *Sacred Ground: Americans and Their Battlefields*. 2nd ed. Urbana: University of Illinois Press, 1993.

Locke, John. *An Essay Concerning the True Original, Extent, and End of Civil Government*, in *Two Treatises of Government*. London, 1690.

Longfellow, Henry Wadsworth. *The Complete Poetical Works of Henry Wadsworth Longfellow*. Boston: Houghton, Mifflin, 1900.

Lorenz, Edward N. "Deterministic Nonperiodic Flow." *Journal of the Atmospheric Sciences* 20 (1963): 130–41.

Lorenz, Edward N. *The Essence of Chaos*. Seattle: University of Washington Press, 1993.

Lorenz, Edward N. "The Evolution of Dynamic Meteorology." In *Historical Essays on Meteorology, 1919–1995: The Diamond Anniversary History Volume of the American Meteorological Society*, edited by James Rodger Fleming. Boston: American Meteorological Society, 1996.

Louden, Bruce. *Homer's* Odyssey *and the Near East*. Cambridge: Cambridge University Press, 2011.

Ludlow, Daniel H., ed. *Encyclopedia of Mormonism*. 4 vols. New York: Macmillan, 1992

Ludlum, David M. *Early American Tornadoes, 1586–1870*. Boston: American Meteorological Society, 1970.

Luther, Martin. Preface to Johannes Lichtenberger, *The Prophecy of Johannes Lichtenberger in German, Carefully Edited*. Translated by Marion Salzmann. In *Luther's Works*, Vol. 59, *Prefaces*, edited by Christopher Boyd Brown. St. Louis: Concordia, 2012.

Luther, Martin. "The Sacrament of the Body and Blood of Christ—Against the Fanatics." In *Luther's Works*, Vol. 36, *Word and Sacrament II*, edited by Abdel Ross Wentz. Philadelphia: Fortress Press, 1959.

Lutzer, Erwin W. *An Act of God? Answers to Tough Questions about God's Role in Natural Disasters.* Carol Stream, Ill.: Tyndale House, 2011.

Lyon, James. *Urania, or, A Choice Collection of Psalm-Tunes, Anthems, and Hymns.* Philadelphia, 1761.

Macaulay, Thomas Babington. *The History of England from the Accession of James II.* 5 vols. Chicago, 1884–86.

Manuel, Frank E. *The Eighteenth Century Confronts the Gods.* 1959. Reprint, New York: Atheneum, 1967.

Mariña, Jacqueline. "Friedrich Schleiermacher and Rudolf Otto." In *The Oxford Handbook of Religion and Emotion*, edited by John Corrigan. New York: Oxford University Press, 2008.

Marini, Stephen A. "American Protestant Hymns Project: A Ranked List of Most Frequently Printed Hymns, 1737–1960." In *Wonderful Words of Life: Hymns in American Protestant History and Theology*, edited by Richard J. Mouw and Mark A. Noll. Grand Rapids, Mich.: Eerdmans, 2004.

Marini, Stephen A. *Sacred Song in America: Religion, Music, and Public Culture.* Urbana: University of Illinois Press, 2003.

Marsden, George M. *Jonathan Edwards: A Life.* New Haven, Conn.: Yale University Press, 2003.

Marx, Karl, and Friedrich Engels. *On Religion.* New York: Schocken Books, 1964.

Mason, Angela. *Death Rides the Sky: The Story of the 1925 Tri-State Tornado.* Rockford, Ill.: Black Oak Media, 2012.

Mason, Bobbie Ann. *Elvis Presley.* New York: Penguin, 2003.

Mather, Cotton. *Biblia Americana.* Edited by Reiner Smolinski et al. 10 vols. Tübingen: Mohr Siebeck, 2010-.

Mather, Cotton. *Brontologia Sacra: The Voice of the Glorious God in the Thunder: Explained and Applyed In a Sermon uttered by a Minister of the Gospel in a Lecture unto an Assembly of Christians abroad, at the very same time when the Thunder was by the Permission and Providence of God falling upon his own House at home.* London, 1695.

Mather, Cotton. *Diary of Cotton Mather.* 2 vols. Boston: Massachusetts Historical Society, 1911–12.

Mather, Cotton. *Magnalia Christi Americana: or, the Ecclesiastical History of New-England, from Its First Planting in the Year 1620. unto the Year of our Lord, 1698. In Seven Books.* London, 1702.

Mather, Cotton. *The Voice of God in a Tempest. A Sermon Preached in the Time of the Storm; Wherein many and heavy and unknown Losses were Suffered at Boston (and Parts Adjacent,) Febr. 24. 1722-3. By One of the Ministers in Boston.* Boston, 1723.

Mather, Increase. *A Brief Discourse Concerning the Prayse Due to God, for His Mercy, in Giving Snow like Wool. Delivered in a Sermon.* Boston, 1704.

Mather, Increase. *A Discourse Concerning the Uncertainty of the Times of Men, and The Necessity of being Prepared for Sudden Changes & Death. Delivered in a Sermon Preached at Cambridge in New England. Decemb. 6. 1969. On Occasion of the Sudden Death of Two Scholars belonging to Harvard Colledge.* Boston, 1697.

Mather, Increase. *The Doctrine of Divine Providence Opened and Applied: Also Sundry Sermons on Several other Subjects*. Boston, 1684.

Mather, Increase. *An Essay for the Recording of Illustrious Providences: Wherein, An Account is given of many Remarkable and very Memorable Events, which have happened in this last Age; especially in New-England*. Boston, 1684.

Mather, Increase. *The Latter Sign Discoursed of, in a Sermon Preached at the Lecture of Boston in New-England; August, 31. 1682. Wherein is shewed, that the Voice of God in Signal Providences, especially when repeated and Iterated, ought to be Hearkned unto*. Boston, 1682.

Mather, Increase. *The Voice of God in Stormy Winds. Considered, in Two Sermons, Occasioned by the Dreadful and Unparallel'd Storm, in the European Nations. Novemb. 27th. 1703*. Boston, 1704.

Mathis, Nancy. *Storm Warning: The Story of a Killer Tornado*. New York: Touchstone, 2007.

May, Henry F. *The Enlightenment in America*. New York: Oxford University Press, 1976.

McBride, Matthew S. *A House for the Most High: The Story of the Original Nauvoo Temple*. Salt Lake City: Greg Kofford, 2006.

McCall, Thomas S., and Zola Levitt. *The Coming Russian Invasion of Israel*. Chicago: Moody Press, 1974.

McCammack, Brian. "Hot Damned America: Evangelicalism and the Climate Change Policy Debate." *American Quarterly* 59 (2007): 645–68.

McConnell, Francis John. *Is God Limited?* New York: Abingdon Press, 1924.

McCullough, David. *The Johnstown Flood*. New York: Simon & Schuster, 1968.

McCutcheon, Russell T. *Manufacturing Religion: The Discourse on Sui Generis Religion and the Politics of Nostalgia*. New York: Oxford University Press, 1997.

McEnaney, Laura. *Civil Defense Begins at Home: Militarization Meets Everyday Life in the Fifties*. Princeton, N.J.: Princeton University Press, 2000.

McFague, Sallie. *Models of God: Theology for an Ecological, Nuclear Age*. Philadelphia: Fortress Press, 1987.

McFague, Sallie. *A New Climate for Theology: God, the World, and Global Warming*. Minneapolis: Fortress Press, 2008.

McIntire, C. T. Review of *Reaping the Whirlwind*, by Langdon Gilkey. *Catholic Historical Review* 68, no. 1 (1982): 55–56.

McKibben, Bill, ed. *The Global Warming Reader: A Century of Writing about Climate Change*. New York: Penguin Books, 2012.

McKim, Donald K. *The Westminster Dictionary of Theological Terms*. 2nd ed. Louisville, Ky.: Westminster John Knox Press, 2014.

McQueen, Keven. *The Great Louisville Tornado of 1890*. Charleston, S.C.: History Press, 2010.

McRoberts, Omar M. "Beyond *Mysterium Tremendum:* Thoughts toward an Aesthetic Study of Religious Experience." *Annals of the American Academy of Political and Social Science* 595 (September 2004): 190–203.

Menninger, Bonar. *And Hell Followed With It: Life and Death in a Kansas Tornado*. Austin, Tex.: Emerald Book, 2011.

Mergen, Bernard. *Weather Matters: An American Cultural History since 1900*. Lawrence: University Press of Kansas, 2008.

Meyer, William B. *Americans and Their Weather*. New York: Oxford University Press, 2000.

Meyer, William B. "The Perfectionists and the Weather: The Oneida Community's Quest for Meteorological Utopia, 1848–1879." *Environmental History* 7 (2002): 589–610.

Middlekauff, Robert. *The Mathers: Three Generations of Puritan Intellectuals, 1596–1728.* Berkeley: University of California Press, 1999.

Miles, Jack. *God: A Biography.* New York: Knopf, 1995.

Miller, Perry. *The New England Mind: The Seventeenth Century.* Cambridge, Mass.: Belknap Press, Harvard University Press, 1939.

Miller, Perry. *Nature's Nation.* Cambridge, Mass.: Belknap Press, Harvard University Press, 1967.

Mohler, Mark. "The Episcopal Church and National Reconciliation, 1865." *Political Science Quarterly* 41 (1926): 567–95.

Molesky, Mark. *This Gulf of Fire: The Destruction of Lisbon, or Apocalypse in the Age of Science and Reason.* New York: Vintage, 2015.

Moody, Robert. "The Lord Selected Me." *Southern Exposure* 7, no. 4 (1979): 4–10.

Morehead, L. M. *A Few Incidents in the Life of Professor James P. Espy, by His Niece.* Cincinnati, 1888.

Mullen, E. Theodore, Jr., *The Divine Council in Canaanite and Early Hebrew Literature.* Chico, Calif.: Scholars Press, 1980.

Muller, Richard A. *Dictionary of Latin and Greek Theological Terms: Drawn Principally from Protestant Scholastic Theology.* 2nd ed. Grand Rapids, Mich.: Baker Academic, 2017.

Murakami, H., E. Levin, T. L. Delworth, R. Gudgel, and P.-C. Hsu. "Dominant Effect of Relative Tropical Atlantic Warming on Major Hurricane Occurrence." *Science* 362 (2018): 794–99.

Murphy, Frederick J. *Apocalypticism in the Bible and Its World: A Comprehensive Introduction.* Grand Rapids, Mich.: Baker Academic, 2012.

Murphy, Nancey. "Natural Science." In *The Oxford Handbook of Systematic Theology*, ed. John Webster, Kathryn Tanner, and Iain Torrance. Oxford: Oxford University Press, 2007.

Neiman, Susan. *Evil in Modern Thought: An Alternative History of Philosophy.* Rev. ed. Princeton, N.J.: Princeton University Press 2015.

Newsom, Carol A. *The Book of Job: A Contest of Moral Imaginations.* New York: Oxford University Press, 2003.

Nichols, Ryan. "Re-evaluating the Effects of the 1755 Lisbon Earthquake on Eighteenth-Century Minds: How Cognitive Science of Religion Improves Intellectual History with Hypothesis Testing Methods." *Journal of the American Academy of Religion* 82 (2014): 970–1009.

Nicholls, Jason A. "Openness and Inerrancy: Can They Be Compatible?" *Journal of the Evangelical Theological Society* 45 (2002): 629–49.

Niebuhr, Reinhold. *Beyond Tragedy: Essays on the Christian Interpretation of History.* New York: Scribner's, 1937.

Niebuhr, Reinhold. *Discerning the Signs of the Times: Sermons for Today and Tomorrow.* New York: Scribner's, 1946.

Niebuhr, Reinhold. *Does Civilization Need Religion? A Study in the Social Resources and Limitations of Religion in Modern Life.* New York: Macmillan, 1927.

Niebuhr, Reinhold. *Justice and Mercy.* Edited by Ursula M. Niebuhr. Louisville, Ky.: Westminster John Knox Press, 1974.

Niebuhr, Reinhold. *The Nature and Destiny of Man: A Christian Interpretation.* 2 vols. 1941. Reprint, Louisville, Ky.: Westminster John Knox Press, 1996.

Niebuhr, Reinhold. "Optimism, Pessimism and Religious Faith—I." In *Reinhold Niebuhr: Major Works on Religion and Politics*, ed. Elisabeth Sifton. New York: Library of America, 2015.

Niebuhr, Reinhold. "The Providence of God." In *The Essential Reinhold Niebuhr: Selected Essays and Addresses*, ed. Robert McAfee Brown. New Haven, Conn.: Yale University Press, 1986.

Niebuhr, Richard R. *Schleiermacher on Christ and Religion: A New Introduction*. New York: Scribner's, 1964.

Noll, Mark A. *America's God: From Jonathan Edwards to Abraham Lincoln*. New York: Oxford University Press, 2002.

Noll, Mark A. *The Civil War as a Theological Crisis*. Chapel Hill: University of North Carolina Press, 2006.

Nollen, John Scholte. *Grinnell College*. Iowa City: State Historical Society of Iowa, 1953.

Nongbri, Brent. *Before Religion: A History of a Modern Concept*. New Haven, Conn.: Yale University Press, 2013.

Oberman, Heiko A. *Luther: Man between God and the Devil*. Translated by Eileen Walliser-Schwarzbart. New York: Image Books, Doubleday, 1992.

O'Brien, Kevin J. *The Violence of Climate Change: Lessons of Resistance from Nonviolent Activists*. Washington, D.C.: Georgetown University Press, 2017.

O'Flaherty, Wendy Doniger. *The Origins of Evil in Hindu Mythology*. Berkeley: University of California Press, 1976.

Olmsted, Denison. "Meteorology of Palestine." *New Englander and Yale Review* 17, no. 66 (May 1859): 450–69.

Orsi, Robert A. *History and Presence*. Cambridge, Mass.: Belknap Press, Harvard University Press, 2016.

Orsi, Robert A. "The Problem of the Holy." In *The Cambridge Companion to Religious Studies*, edited by Robert A. Orsi. Cambridge: Cambridge University Press, 2012.

Osborn, Sarah. *Sarah Osborn's Collected Writings*. Edited by Catherine A. Brekus. New Haven, Conn.: Yale University Press, 2017.

Ostrander, Rick. *The Life of Prayer in a World of Science: Protestants, Prayer, and American Culture, 1870–1930*. New York: Oxford University Press, 2000.

O'Toole, John M. *Tornado! 84 Minutes, 94 Lives*. Worcester, Mass.: Chandler House Press, 1993.

Otto, Rudolf. *Das Heilige: Über das Irrationale in der Idee des Göttlichen und sein Verhältnis zum Rationalen*. 1917. Reprint, Munich: Verlag C. H. Beck, 2014.

Otto, Rudolf. "How Schleiermacher Re-discovered the Sensus Numinis." In *Religious Essays: A Supplement to* The Idea of the Holy, translated by Brian Lunn. London: Oxford University Press, 1931.

Otto, Rudolf. *The Idea of the Holy: An Inquiry into the Non-rational Factor in the Idea of the Divine and Its Relation to the Rational*. Translated by John W. Harvey. 2nd ed. Oxford: Oxford University Press, 1950.

Outler, Albert C. *Who Trusts in God: Musings on the Meaning of Providence*. New York: Oxford University Press, 1968.

Paglia, Camille. *Break, Blow, Burn*. New York: Pantheon Books, 2005.

Paice, Edward. *Wrath of God: The Great Lisbon Earthquake of 1755*. London: Quercus, 2008.

Paine, Thomas. *The Age of Reason, Being an Investigation of True and Fabulous Theology*. Paris, 1794.

Paine, Thomas. *The Complete Writings of Thomas Paine*. Edited by Philip S. Foner. 2 vols. New York: Citadel, 1969.

Park, Edwards A. "The Relation of Divine Providence to Physical Laws." *Bibliotheca Sacra* 12 (1855): 179–205.

Parker, Geoffrey. *Global Crisis: War, Climate Change and Catastrophe in the Seventeenth Century*. New Haven, Conn.: Yale University Press, 2013.

Partee, Charles. *The Theology of John Calvin*. Louisville, Ky.: Westminster John Knox Press, 2008.

Partlow, Geoff. *America's Deadliest Twister: The Tri-State Tornado of 1925*. Carbondale: Southern Illinois University Press, 2014.

Patricola, Christina M., and Michael F. Wehner. "Anthropogenic Influences on Major Tropical Cyclone Events." *Nature* 563 (2018): 339–46.

Peters, H. H. *Charles Reign Scoville: The Man and His Message*. St. Louis: Bethany Press, 1924.

Peters, Ted. "Langdon Gilkey: In Memoriam." *Dialog* 44, no. 1 (2005): 69–80.

Pinch, Geraldine. *Egyptian Mythology: A Guide to the Gods, Goddesses, and Traditions of Ancient Egypt*. New York: Oxford University Press, 2002.

Pinnock, Clark H. *Most Moved Mover: A Theology of God's Openness*. Carlisle, UK: Paternoster Press, 2001.

Pinnock, Clark, Richard Rice, John Sanders, William Hasker, and David Basinger. *The Openness of God: A Biblical Challenge to the Traditional Understanding of God*. Downers Grove, Ill.: InterVarsity Press, 1994.

Piper, John, Justin Taylor, and Paul Kjoss Helseth, eds. *Beyond the Bounds: Open Theism and the Undermining of Biblical Christianity*. Wheaton, Ill.: Crossway Books, 2003.

Pitch, Anthony S. *The Burning of Washington: The British Invasion of 1814*. Annapolis, Md.: Naval Institute Press, 1998.

Pitcher, Edward W. R., ed. *The American Magazine and Historical Chronicle (Boston 1743–1746): An Annotated Catalogue of the Prose*. Lewiston, Me.: Edwin Mellen Press, 2003.

Placher, William C. *The Domestication of Transcendence: How Modern Thinking about God Went Wrong*. Louisville, Ky.: Westminster John Knox Press, 1996.

Poland, Lynn. "The Idea of the Holy and the History of the Sublime." *Journal of Religion* 72 (1992): 175–97.

Pollard, William G. *Chance and Providence: God's Action in a World Governed by Scientific Law*. New York: Scribner's, 1958.

Pollard, William G. *Physicist and Christian: A Dialogue between the Communities*. Greenwich, Conn.: Seabury Press, 1961.

Pollard, William G. *Transcendence and Providence: Reflections of a Physicist and Priest*. Edinburgh: Scottish Academic Press, 1987.

Pope Francis. *Laudato Si'* (encyclical letter). Vatican City: Vatican Press, 2015.

Preus, J. Samuel. *Explaining Religion: Criticism and Theory from Bodin to Freud*. New Haven, Conn.: Yale University Press, 1987.

Price, Walter K. *The Coming Antichrist*. Chicago: Moody Press, 1974.

Prichard, Robert W. *The Nature of Salvation: Theological Consensus in the Episcopal Church, 1801–73*. Urbana: University of Illinois Press, 1997.

Prince, Thomas. *Earthquakes the Works of God, and Tokens of His just Displeasure*. Boston, 1755.

Prince, Thomas. *An Improvement of the Doctrine of Earthquakes, Being the Works of God, and Tokens of his just Displeasure*. Boston, 1755.

Prince, Thomas. *The Salvations of God in 1746: In Part Set Forth in a Sermon at the South Church in Boston, Nov. 27. 1746*. Boston, 1746.

Pritchard, James. *Anatomy of a Naval Disaster: The 1746 French Naval Expedition to North America*. Montreal: McGill-Queen's University Press, 1995.

Putz, Paul Emory. "From the Pulpit to the Press: Frank Crane's Omaha, 1892–1896." *Nebraska History* 96 (2015): 136–52.

Raboteau, Albert J. *Slave Religion: The "Invisible Institution" in the Antebellum South*. New York: Oxford University Press, 1978.

Raphael, Melissa. *Rudolf Otto and the Concept of Holiness*. Oxford: Clarendon Press, 1997.

Reeves, John K. "Jeremy Gridley, Editor." *New England Quarterly* 17 (1944): 265–81.

Reid, Daniel G., Robert D. Linder, Bruce L. Shelley, and Harry S. Stout, eds. *Dictionary of Christianity in America*. Downers Grove, Ill.: InterVarsity Press, 1990.

Reid, Panthea. *Tillie Olsen: One Woman, Many Riddles*. New Brunswick, N.J.: Rutgers University Press, 2010.

"Restoring Creation for Ecology and Justice: A Report Adopted by the 202nd General Assembly of the Presbyterian Church (U.S.A.)." Louisville, Ky.: Office of the General Assembly, 1990.

Restoring U.S. Leadership in Weather Forecasting, Part I: Hearing Before the Subcommittee on Environment, Committee on Science, Space, and Technology, House of Representatives, One Hundred Thirteenth Congress, First Session, Thursday, May 23, 2013. Washington, D.C.: U.S. Government Printing Office, 2013.

Rice, Richard. *The Openness of God: The Relationship of Divine Foreknowledge and Human Free Will*. Nashville: Review and Herald, 1980.

Riedel, Barbara Lynn, and Peter Wayne Kyryl II. *Tornado at Xenia: April 3, 1974*. Cleveland: Carpenter Printing, 1974.

The Rig Veda: An Anthology. Translated by Wendy Doniger. London: Penguin Books, 1981.

Rissler, James. "Open Theism." In *Internet Encyclopedia of Philosophy*, edited by James Fieser and Bradley Dowden. https://www.iep.utm.edu/o-theism/.

Roberts, Jon H. *Darwinism and the Divine in America: Protestant Intellectuals and Organic Evolution, 1859–1900*. Madison: University of Wisconsin Press, 1988.

Roker, Al. *The Storm of the Century: Tragedy, Heroism, Survival, and the Epic Story of America's Deadliest Natural Disaster: The Great Gulf Hurricane of 1900*. New York: Morrow, 2015.

Roper, Lyndal. *Martin Luther: Renegade and Prophet*. New York: Random House, 2017.

Rowe, M. W., and G. T. Meaden. "Britain's Greatest Tornado Outbreak." *Weather* 40, no. 8 (1985): 230–35.

Russell, Robert John, Nancey Murphy, and Arthur R. Peacocke. *Chaos and Complexity: Scientific Perspectives on Divine Action*. 2nd ed. Vatican City: Vatican Observatory, 1997.

Sabella, Jeremy L. *An American Conscience: The Reinhold Niebuhr Story*. Grand Rapids, Mich.: Eerdmans, 2017.

Sanders, John. *The God Who Risks: A Theology of Providence*. Downers Grove, Ill.: InterVarsity Press, 1998.

Sandlin, Lee. *Storm Kings: The Untold History of America's First Tornado Chasers*. New York: Pantheon Books, 2013.

Santmyer, Helen Hooven. *Ohio Town*. 1962. Reprint, New York: Harper and Row, 1984.

The Sarum Missal in English. Edited by A. H. Pearson. 1868. Reprint, Eugene, Ore.: Wipf and Stock, 2004.

Saum, Lewis O. *The Popular Mood of America, 1860–1890*. Lincoln: University of Nebraska Press, 1990.

Saunders, Nicholas. *Divine Action and Modern Science*. Cambridge: Cambridge University Press, 2002.

Scarfone, Jay, and William Stillman. *The Wizardry of Oz: The Artistry and Magic of the 1939 M-G-M Classic*. New York: Applause Theatre and Cinema Books, 2004.

Schaff, Philip, and David S. Schaff, eds. *The Creeds of Christendom: With a History and Critical Notes*. 6th ed. 3 vols. Grand Rapids, Mich.: Baker Books, 1983.

Schifferdecker, Kathryn. *Out of the Whirlwind: Creation Theology in the Book of Job*. Harvard Theological Studies 61. Cambridge, Mass.: Harvard Divinity School, Harvard University Press, 2008.

Schleiermacher, Friedrich. *On Religion: Addresses in Response to Its Cultured Critics*. Translated by Terrence N. Tice. Richmond, Va.: John Knox Press, 1969.

Schmidt, Leigh Eric. *Restless Souls: The Making of American Spirituality*. 2nd ed. Berkeley: University of California Press, 2012.

Schmidt, Leigh Eric. *Village Atheists: How America's Unbelievers Made Their Way in a Godly Nation*. Princeton, N.J.: Princeton University Press, 2016.

Schreiner, Susan E. *The Theater of His Glory: Nature and the Natural Order in the Thought of John Calvin*. Grand Rapids, Mich.: Baker Books, 1991.

Schwartz, Stuart B. *Sea of Storms: A History of Hurricanes in the Greater Caribbean from Columbus to Katrina*. Princeton, N.J.: Princeton University Press, 2015.

"Scientific News and Notes of Academy Interest." *Transactions of the Kansas Academy of Science* 60, no. 3 (1957): 244–46.

Scott, R. B. Y. "Meteorological Phenomena and Terminology in the Old Testament." *Zeitschrift für die Alttestamentliche Wissenshaft* 64 (1952): 11–25.

Scott, Sean A. *A Visitation of God: Northern Civilians Interpret the Civil War*. New York: Oxford University Press, 2011.

Seager, Richard, Jamie Feldman, Nathan Lis, Mingfang Ting, Alton P. Williams, Jennifer Nakamura, Haibo Liu, and Naomi Henderson. "Whither the 100th Meridian? The Once and Future Physical Geography of America's Arid-Humid Divide. Part II: The Meridian Moves East." *Earth Interactions* 22, no. 5 (2018): 1–24.

Shinners, John., ed. *Medieval Popular Religion, 1000–1500: A Reader*. 2nd ed. Toronto: University of Toronto Press, 2009.

Shrady, Nicholas. *The Last Day: Wrath, Ruin, and Reason in the Great Lisbon Earthquake of 1755*. New York: Viking, 2008.

Sibbes, Richard. "Of the Providence of God." In *The Complete Works of Richard Sibbes, D.D.*, edited by Alexander Balloch Grosart. Vol. 5. Edinburgh, 1863.

Sideris, Lisa H. *Consecrating Science: Wonder, Knowledge, and the Natural World*. Oakland: University of California Press, 2017.

Silverman, Kenneth. *The Life and Times of Cotton Mather*. 1984. Reprint, New York: Welcome Rain, 2002.

Simmons, Kevin M., and Daniel Sutter. *Deadly Season: Analysis of the 2011 Tornado Outbreaks*. Boston: American Meteorological Society, 2012.

Simmons, Kevin M., and Daniel Sutter. *Economic and Societal Impacts of Tornadoes*. Boston: American Meteorological Society, 2011.

Sing, Travis. *Omaha's Easter Tornado of 1913*. Charleston, S.C.: Arcadia, 2003.

Smith, H. Maynard. *Pre-Reformation England*. London: Palgrave Macmillan, 1963.

Smith, Mark S. *The Early History of God: Yahweh and the Other Deities in Ancient Israel*. 2nd ed. Grand Rapids, Mich.: Eerdmans, 2002.

Smith, Mark S. *The Origins of Biblical Monotheism: Israel's Polytheistic Background and the Ugaritic Texts*. New York: Oxford University Press, 2001.

Smolinski, Reiner, and Jan Stievermann, eds. *Cotton Mather and* Biblia Americana: *America's First Bible Commentary: Essays in Reappraisal*. Grand Rapids, Mich.: Baker Academic, 2011.

Solomon, Susan, Dahe Qin, and Martin Manning, eds. *Climate Change 2007: The Physical Science Basis. Contribution of Working Group I to the Fourth Assessment Report of the Intergovernmental Panel on Climate Change*. Cambridge: Cambridge University Press, 2007.

Spencer, John. *A Discourse concerning Prodigies: Wherein the Vanity of Presages by them is reprehended, and their true and proper Ends asserted and vindicated. The Second Edition corrected and inlarged. To which is added a short Treatise concerning Vulgar Prophecies*. London, 1665.

Spencer, Mark G., ed. *Hume's Reception in Early America*. Rev. ed. London: Bloomsbury Academic, 2017.

Sprat, Thomas. *The History of the Royal-Society of London, For the Improving of Natural Knowledge*. London, 1667.

Sproul, R. C. *Chosen by God*. Wheaton, Ill.: Tyndale House, 1986.

Sproul, R. C. *The Invisible Hand: Do All Things Really Work for Good?* 1996. Reprint, Phillipsburg, N.J.: P&R, 2003.

Steinberg, Ted. *Acts of God: The Unnatural History of Natural Disaster in America*. 2nd ed. New York: Oxford University Press, 2000.

Stern, Gary. *Can God Intervene? How Religion Explains Natural Disasters*. Westport, Conn.: Praeger, 2007.

Stocker, Thomas F., and Dahe Qin, eds. *Climate Change 2013: The Physical Science Basis. Working Group I Contribution to the Fifth Assessment Report of the Intergovernmental Panel on Climate Change*. Cambridge: Cambridge University Press, 2013.

Stone, Ronald H. *Professor Reinhold Niebuhr: A Mentor to the Twentieth Century*. Louisville, Ky.: Westminster John Knox Press, 1992.

Storms, Sam. *Chosen for Life: The Case for Divine Election*. Rev. ed. Wheaton, Ill.: Crossway Books, 2007.

Stowe, Harriet Beecher. *The Minister's Wooing*. Edited by Susan K. Harris. New York: Penguin Books, 1999.

Stuart, Moses. *A Commentary on the Apocalypse*. 2 vols. Andover, Mass., 1845.

The Study Quran: A New Translation and Commentary. Edited by Seyyed Hossein Nasr et al. New York: HarperOne, 2015.

Sussman, Brian. *Climategate: A Veteran Meteorologist Exposes the Global Warming Scam*. Washington, D.C.: WND Books, 2010.

Sutton, Robert P. "An American Elysium: The Icarian Communities." In *America's Communal Utopias*, edited by Donald E. Pitzer. Chapel Hill: University of North Carolina Press, 1997.

Sutton, Robert P. *Les Icariens: The Utopian Dream in Europe and America*. Urbana: University of Illinois Press, 1994.

Svenvold, Mark. *Big Weather: Chasing Tornadoes in the Heart of America.* New York: Henry Holt, 2005.

Sweeney, Douglas A., and Allen C. Guelzo, eds. *The New England Theology: From Jonathan Edwards to Edwards Amasa Park.* Grand Rapids, Mich.: Baker Academic, 2006.

Tanner, Kathryn. "Is God in Charge? Creation and Providence." In *Essentials of Christian Theology,* edited by William C. Placher. Louisville, Ky.: Westminster John Knox, 2003.

Taves, Ann. *Religious Experience Reconsidered: A Building-Block Approach to the Study of Religion and Other Special Things.* Princeton, N.J.: Princeton University Press, 2009.

Taylor, Charles. *A Secular Age.* Cambridge, Mass.: Belknap Press, Harvard University Press, 2007.

Taylor, James B., Louis A. Zurcher, and William H. Key. *Tornado: A Community Responds to Disaster.* Seattle: University of Washington Press, 1970.

Tennent, Gilbert. *All Things come alike to All: A Sermon, On Eccles. IX. 1, 2 and 3 Verses. Occasioned by a Person's being struck by the Lightning of Thunder. Preached at Philadelphia, July the 28th, 1745.* Philadelphia, 1745.

Thomas, Hiram W. *Life and Sermons of Dr. H. W. Thomas.* Edited by Austin Bierbower. Chicago, 1880.

Thomas, Keith. *Religion and the Decline of Magic: Studies in Popular Beliefs in Sixteenth and Seventeenth Century England.* New York: Oxford University Press, 1971.

Thuesen, Peter J. *Predestination: The American Career of a Contentious Doctrine.* New York: Oxford University Press, 2009.

Tipson, Baird. *Hartford Puritanism: Thomas Hooker, Samuel Stone, and Their Terrifying God.* New York: Oxford University Press, 2015.

Tipson, Baird. "Thomas Hooker, Martin Luther, and the Terror at the Edge of Protestant Faith." *Harvard Theological Review* 108 (2015): 530–51.

Todd, Margo. "Providence, Chance and the New Science in Early Stuart Cambridge." *Historical Journal* 29 (1986): 697–711.

Tomlin, T. J. *A Divinity for All Persuasions: Almanacs and Early American Religious Life.* New York: Oxford University Press, 2014.

Travis, Stephen H. *Christ and the Judgement of God: The Limits of Divine Retribution in New Testament Thought.* Peabody, Mass.: Hendrickson, 2008.

A True and Particular Narrative of the late Tremendous Tornado, or Hurricane, At Philadelphia and New-York, on Sabbath-Day, July 1, 1792. Boston, 1792.

Turner, Denys. *Thomas Aquinas: A Portrait.* New Haven, Conn.: Yale University Press, 2013.

Turner, James. "Charles Hodge in the Intellectual Weather of the Nineteenth Century." Chap. 2 in *Language, Religion, Knowledge: Past and Present.* Notre Dame, Ind.: University of Notre Dame Press, 2003.

Turner, James. *Without God, Without Creed: The Origins of Unbelief in America.* Baltimore: Johns Hopkins University Press, 1985.

Turner, Randy, and John Hacker. *5:41: Stories from the Joplin Tornado.* Lexington, Ky.: n.p., 2011.

Tweed, Thomas A. *Crossing and Dwelling: A Theory of Religion.* Cambridge, Mass.: Harvard University Press, 2006.

Tyrrell, Ian. "Public at the Creation: Place, Memory, and Historical Practice in the Mississippi Valley Historical Association, 1907–1950." *Journal of American History* 94 (2007): 19–46.

United States Nuclear Tests: July 1945 through September 1992. Las Vegas: United States Department of Energy, Nevada Operations Office, 2000.

Unruh, Eric, and Fern Unruh. *Tornado! Up from the Debris to Thank God.* Newton, Kans.: Mennonite Press, 2007.

Urban, Linwood, and Douglas N. Walton, eds. *The Power of God: Readings on Omnipotence and Evil.* New York: Oxford University Press, 1978.

Valeri, Mark. *Heavenly Merchandize: How Religion Shaped Commerce in Puritan America.* Princeton, N.J.: Princeton University Press, 2010.

Vallet, Emile. *Communism: History of the Experiment at Nauvoo of the Icarian Settlement.* 1917. Reprint, Springfield: Illinois State Historical Society, 1971.

VanderMolen, Ronald J. "Providence as Mystery, Providence as Revelation: Puritan and Anglican Modifications of John Calvin's Doctrine of Providence." *Church History* 47 (1978): 27–47.

Victor, David G., Keigo Akimoto, Yoichi Kaya, Mitsutsune Yamaguchi, Danny Cullenward, and Cameron Hepburn. "Prove Paris Was More than Paper Promises." *Nature* 548 (2017): 25–27.

Wagler, David. *The Mighty Whirlwind.* Aylmer, Ont.: Pathway, 1966.

Wall, Joseph Frazier. *Grinnell College in the Nineteenth Century: From Salvation to Service.* Ames: Iowa State University Press, 1997.

Wallace, Anthony F. C. *Religion: An Anthropological View.* New York: Random House, 1966.

Wallace, Anthony F. C. *Tornado in Worcester: An Exploratory Study of Individual and Community Behavior in an Extreme Situation.* Washington, D.C.: National Academy of Sciences, National Research Council, 1956.

Walls, Neal H. "Baal." In *Encyclopedia of Religion*, edited by Lindsay Jones. 2nd ed. Vol. 2. Detroit: Macmillan Reference, 2005.

Walls, Neal H. "El." In *Encyclopedia of Religion*, edited by Lindsay Jones. 2nd ed. Vol. 4. Detroit: Macmillan Reference, 2005.

Walsham, Alexandra. *Providence in Early Modern England.* Oxford: Oxford University Press, 1999.

Walter, Tony. "Disaster, Modernity, and the Media." In *Death and Religion in a Changing World*, edited by Kathleen Garces-Foley. New York: Routledge, 2006.

Walvoord, John F., and John E. Walvoord. *Armageddon, Oil, and the Middle East Crisis: What the Bible Says about the Future of the Middle East and the End of Western Civilization.* Grand Rapids, Mich.: Zondervan, 1974.

Ware, Bruce A. *God's Lesser Glory: The Diminished God of Open Theism.* Wheaton, Ill.: Crossway Books, 2000.

Watts, Isaac. *Horae Lyricae. Poems, Chiefly of the Lyric Kind, in Three Books.* 9th ed. corr. Boston, 1748.

Watts, Isaac. *Hymns and Spiritual Songs. In Three Books.* 16th ed. Boston, 1742.

Watts, Isaac. *The Psalms of David, Imitated in the Language of the New Testament, And apply'd to the Christian State and Worship.* 7th ed. Philadelphia, 1729.

Wawrykow, Joseph P. *The Westminster Handbook to Thomas Aquinas.* Louisville, Ky.: Westminster John Knox Press, 2005.

Weart, Spencer R. *The Discovery of Global Warming* Rev. ed. Cambridge, Mass.: Harvard University Press, 2008.

Wendel, François. *Calvin: Origins and Development of His Religious Thought*. Translated by Philip Mairet. Grand Rapids, Mich.: Baker Books, 1963.

Wesley, John, and Charles Wesley. *Hymns and Sacred Poems*. London, 1740.

Whaley, W. P. "An Extreme Case of Negro Superstition." *Current Literature* 35, no. 2 (August 1903): 227–29.

Wheeler, Elizabeth L. "Isaac Fisher: The Frustrations of a Negro Educator at Branch Normal College, 1902–1911." *Arkansas Historical Quarterly* 41, no. 1 (1982): 3–50.

Where Was God? Stories of Hope after the Storm. Directed by Travis Palmer and produced by Steven Earp, Brian Cates, and Chris Forbes. Tulsa, Okla.: VCI Entertainment, 2015. DVD.

Whitall, Ann Cooper. *Diary*. Excerpted in *John M. Whitall: The Story of His Life*. Philadelphia, 1879.

White, Andrew Dickson. *A History of the Warfare of Science with Theology*. 2 vols. New York: Appleton, 1896.

Wiggins, Steve A. *Weathering the Psalms: A Meteorotheological Survey*. Eugene, Ore.: Cascade Books, 2014.

Wilkinson, Katharine K. *Between God and Green: How Evangelicals Are Cultivating a Middle Ground on Climate Change*. New York: Oxford University Press, 2012.

Willard, Samuel. *A Compleat Body of Divinity in Two Hundred and Fifty Expository Lectures on the Assembly's Shorter Catechism*. Boston, 1726.

Williams, Elisha. *The essential Rights and Liberties of Protestants. A seasonable Plea for The Liberty of Conscience, and the Right of private Judgement . . . By a Lover of Truth and Liberty*. Boston, 1744.

Winiarski, Douglas L. *Darkness Falls on the Land of Light: Experiencing Religious Awakenings in Eighteenth-Century New England*. Chapel Hill: University of North Carolina Press, 2017.

Winroth, Anders. *The Age of the Vikings*. Princeton, N.J.: Princeton University Press, 2014.

Winship, Michael P. *Seers of God: Puritan Providentialism in the Restoration and Early Enlightenment*. Baltimore: Johns Hopkins University Press, 1996.

Winthrop, John. "An Account of a Meteor seen in New England, and of a Whirlwind felt in that Country." *Philosophical Transactions* 52 (1761): 6–16.

Winthrop, John. *A Lecture on Earthquakes; Read in the Chapel of Harvard-College in Cambridge, N.E., November 26th 1755*. Boston, 1755.

Winthrop, John. *Winthrop's Journal: "History of New England," 1630–1649*. Edited by James Kendall Hosmer. 2 vols. New York: Scribner's, 1908.

Wisner, Benjamin B. *History of the Old South Church in Boston, in Four Sermons*. Boston, 1830.

Wolfenstein, Martha. *Disaster: A Psychological Essay*. 1957. Reprint, Abingdon, Oxford: Routledge, 1998.

Wood, Charles M. "Providence." In *The Oxford Handbook of Systematic Theology*, edited by John Webster, Kathryn Tanner, and Iain Torrance. Oxford: Oxford University Press, 2007.

Wood, Charles M. *The Question of Providence*. Louisville, Ky.: Westminster John Knox Press, 2008.

Worden, Blair. *God's Instruments: Political Conduct in the England of Oliver Cromwell*. Oxford: Oxford University Press, 2012.

Wuthnow, Robert. *The God Problem: Expressing Faith and Being Reasonable*. Berkeley: University of California Press, 2012.

Yandell, Keith E. *Hume's "Inexplicable Mystery": His Views on Religion*. Philadelphia: Temple University Press, 1990.

York, Michael. "Dyaus Pitr." In *Encyclopedia of Hinduism*, edited by Denise Cush, Catherine Robinson, and Michael York. London: Routledge, 2010.

Young, Serinity. "Religion and Weather." In *Encyclopedia of Climate and Weather*, edited by Stephen H. Schneider, Terry L. Root, and Michael D. Mastrandrea. 2nd ed. 3 vols. New York: Oxford University Press, 2011.

Zilberstein, Anya. *A Temperate Empire: Making Climate Change in Early America*. New York: Oxford University Press, 2016.

INDEX

Figures are indicated by *f* following the page number.

For the benefit of digital users, indexed terms that span two pages (e.g., 52–53) may, on occasion, appear on only one of those pages.

SCRIPTURAL INDEX

For the benefit of digital users, indexed terms that span two pages (e.g., 52–53) may, on occasion, appear on only one of those pages.